AFRICAN EARTHKEEPERS
Wholistic Interfaith Mission

Marthinus L. Daneel

ORBIS BOOKS

Maryknoll, New York 10545

Founded in 1979, Orbis Books endeavors to publish works that enlighten the mind, nourish the spirit, and challenge the conscience. The publishing arm of Maryknoll Fathers and Brothers, Orbis seeks to explore the global dimensions of the Christian faith and mission, to invite dialogue with diverse cultures and religious traditions, and to serve the cause of reconciliation and peace. The books published reflect the views of their authors and do not represent the official position of the Society. To learn more about Maryknoll and Orbis Books, please visit our website at www.maryknoll.com.

The Pew Charitable Trusts, based in Philadelphia, Pennsylvania, the main sponsor of the African Initiatives in Christianity Project, is a national and international philanthropy. Through their grant making, the Trusts seek to encourage individual development and personal achievement, cross-disciplinary problem solving, and innovative, practical approaches to meeting the changing needs of a global community. The opinions expressed in this publication are those of the author and do not necessarily reflect the views of the Pew Charitable Trusts.

Library of Congress Cataloging in Publication Data

Daneel, M. L.
  African earthkeepers / Martinus L. Daneel.
    p. cm
  Includes bibliographical references and index.
  ISBN 1-57075-329-6 (pbk.)
    1. Shona (African people)—Religion. 2. Human ecology—Religious aspects—Christianity. I. Title.

BL2480.M3   D27 2001
299'.683975—dc21   2001036579

CONTENTS

PART II

**AFRICAN INITIATED CHURCHES: ENVIRONMENTAL MISSION AND
LIBERATION IN CHRISTIAN PERSPECTIVE**

PREFACE TO THE 'AFRICAN INITIATIVES IN CHRISTIAN MISSION' EDITION

Literature on Christian mission in Africa has been biased toward the activity of Western-oriented mission. White missionaries, Western mission policies, and the relationship of mission to European imperialism have dominated the discussion of African missions. Little or no attention has been paid by scholars to African initiatives in Christian mission, nor have missiological studies been made from the perspective of the so-called 'recipients.' Yet the phenomenal growth of Christianity in Africa has occurred in the twentieth century, much of it after the independence of the continent from outside control. The series 'African Initiatives in Christian Mission' represents an attempt to address the reality that the spread of Christianity in Africa, its shape and character, has been the product of African Christians, both in the 'Mission Churches' and the 'African Initiated/Independent Churches' (AICs).[1]

Mission churches and AICs are the two primary ecclesial contexts in which African initiative has occurred. Mission churches are those that have evolved directly from the outreach of Western denominations, and still represent the collegial traditions concerned. African Initiated Churches are churches begun by Africans in Africa primarily for Africans. AICs have consistently asserted their own leadership autonomy and religio-cultural contextuality free from the immediate control of influence of Western-oriented church leaders. These classificatory terms are somewhat misleading in that AICs are missionary churches par excellence, and the Mission Churches, by virtue of the missionary contributions of their members from the beginnings of their history, could be characterized as African Initiated Churches. Nevertheless the distinction between the two families of churches remains important for historical and sociological reasons.

This series seeks to overcome some of the limitations in previous studies of missions in Africa. Mission Churches have been analyzed primarily as denominational institutions with a focus on educational work, or else as participants in political processes such as nation building. Less attention has been paid to Mission Churches as social movements, as products of indigenous culture and leadership, or as creators of African theologies. In short, the indigenous mission dimension has been weak in many of these studies. Works on Mission Churches today tend to be generalized rather than based on reliable, representative information gleaned from empirical enquiries. Thus the uniqueness and witness of these churches remain obscure. A predominantly male image of church history, moreover, has resulted in a paucity of literature on the contribution of women to church life and church expansion. The roles of black women pioneers in African churches are of particular interest to the editors of the series.

As regards the African Initiated Churches, the tendency in most of the earlier studies has been to assess AICs in terms of reaction to Western missions, sepa-

ratism, or protest against oppressive colonialism. As a result the missionary genius, missionary methods, and missiological significance of AICs have not been
studied in depth. However, the contribution of the AICs to the growth and reli-
gion-cultural rootedness of Christianity in Africa is of vital importance for the development of a relevant mission theology in Africa. It is increasingly evident that
in terms of growth rates, indigenized evangelization, missionary campaigns, and
ecclesiastic contextualization, the AICs are not peripheral but belong to the main-
stream of African Christianity. Their contribution therefore should be evaluated as
such, alongside that of the Mission Churches. Critical, yet open and fair-minded
field studies should overcome the bias that has frequently distorted AIC studies in
the past.

The ideas behind African Initiatives in Christian Mission originated in an interdisciplinary research project conceived by Professor Marthinus L. Daneel.
With thirty years of empirical research on AICs in Zimbabwe, Daneel gathered a
team of researchers from South Africa, Zimbabwe, and Malawi and received a
grant in 1994 from The Pew Charitable Trusts. Assisted by field workers, researchers set out to gather data on different facets of African initiative within various churches in southern Africa. Meeting periodically at the Department of Missiology at the University of South Africa, the researchers reported on the work in
progress and received feedback from other team members. The cooperative nature of the project was essential to its success, for the original team included
members of Mission Churches and AICs, academics and practitioners, blacks and
whites. The Research Institute for Theology and Religion at Unisa provided administrative support; and Professor Dana Robert participated as the representative
of Boston University, the official host institution for the project.

Out of the project meeting emerged a decision to hold an international conference in 1997 on 'African Initiatives in Christian Mission in Southern Africa.' As
well as the conference, the group decided to launch a publication series that
would make the results of the project available to scholars and church people in
Africa. Given the lack of research and its limitations as outlined above, the project participants decided to broaden the focus of the series beyond southern Africa
and, by implication, beyond the core group of scholars. The widest possible definition of 'mission' underlies the series. The participant scholars agreed to deal essentially with Christian mission: the outreach of Christian faith and life in the extension of Christ's good news beyond the boundaries of ignorance, cultures,
poverty, suffering, or whatever obstacles obscure a clear Christian witness in the
world. Nevertheless, not all contributors are missiologists and their research
methodologies include phenomenological, socio-anthropoliogical, historical, and
distinctly non-theological approaches, or a combination of these. Yet the team
feels that even if the joint venture, against the background of diverse disciplines,
runs the risk of controversy over diversity within the series, the overall outcome
will be both challenging and enriching. The qualification 'African initiative,' too,
is not subject to narrow definition. Black and white African theologians, for instance, are contributors in this series. And despite the predominant concern with
black African initiatives, a number of studies on white missionary endeavour will
be included, particularly the attempts of black African scholars to interpret the

legacy of white-controlled missions, their impact on African society, and the attitudes and response of African communities to such endeavour. In many respects white and black participation in mission in Africa are two sides of the same coin, the implication being that study of one enhances understanding of the other.

On behalf of all participants in this joint research and publishing venture, we express our appreciation to our sponsors, the staff of Unisa's Research Institute for Theology and Religion, and Unisa Press; their support remains crucial in the realisation of the envisaged goals.

ABOUT THIS BOOK

African Earthkeepers recounts an extraordinary story of African initiative in mission—that of Shona Traditionalists in Masvingo Province, Zimbabwe, who fight 'the war of the trees' against ecological degradation. Working in ecumenical partnership with indigenous Christians, the Traditionalist tree planters, led by chiefs and spirit mediums, have revitalized ancestral rights to protect the natural world. The second half of this volume deals with the second prong of this multi-faith movement in recounting its Christian dimension.

This fascinating volume fits into our series on 'African Initiatives in Christian Mission' for several reasons. As partners of the AICs, the Traditionalist African earthkeepers demonstrate interreligious dialogue and ecumenical cooperation at the grassroots—interaction so unique its story simply must be told.

The environmental movement among Shona Traditionalists shows a missionary dynamism and potential for development within African Traditional Religion that will astonish observers who have predicted its demise. Readers of this volume will wish to reflect on the missiological significance of Christian influence on the revitalisation of Shona Traditional Religion.

The author, Marthinus L. Daneel—more usually known as 'Inus,' or 'M. L. Daneel,' but also by his Shona name 'Muchakata' (the wild cork tree) and his AIC office and name 'Bishop Moses'—is founder of both the Traditional and Christian wings of the tree-planting movement. Inus exemplifies the missionary tension between firm Christian commitment and cooperation with non-Christians for the sake of God's Kingdom. His decision to engage in a common mission with Traditionalists acknowledges the seriousness of today's environmental crisis and the need for all people of good will to join in protecting God's sacred creation. Supporters of Christian mission will be challenged by the ramifications of *African Earthkeepers* for mission in peasant societies, and intrigued by the way in which African traditions have been reformulated to meet the needs of the present. Honest, thought-provoking and inspiring, this book raises vital issues for Christian mission in southern Africa.

Dana L. Robert
Series Editor

PREFACE TO THE ORBIS EDITION

Since the beginning of my involvement with the Zimbabwean Institute for Religious Research and Ecological Conservation (ZIRRCON) and the two groups affiliated with it, the Association of Zimbabwean Traditional Ecologists (AZTREC) and the Association of African Earthkeeping Churches (AAEC), I have had a lively sense of how three organizations embody the dynamism and creativity of the growing world church. It has been a matter of great pride and humility for me—a white African of Afrikaner descent—to have been adopted by the Zimbabweans among whom I have lived and worked for so many years.

I hope this abridged Orbis Books edition of my two-volume work *African Earthkeepers* will help many in the rest of the world understand better and join in solidarity with my Zimbabwean brothers and sisters in the struggle to achieve the goals they have set for themselves in the Earthkeeping Movement.

Those who know me realize that my vocation as activist invariably interferes with the writing program in which I should engage as sequel to empirical research. At ZIRRCON headquarters in Masvingo and elsewhere, there are many meters of shelves on which lie research material that I have gathered over the years, most of it my own work, as well as the information brought in by my research assistants over the past two decades. When Orbis Books and I began talking in 1991 about revising my 1987 book *Quest for Belonging: Introduction to a Study of African Independent Churches*, we began a conversation that culminated in their proposal for an abridgment of *African Earthkeepers* for an audience of persons interested in ecology, African Christianity, and African Initiated Churches. Such a study would be a worthwhile introduction to African Initiated Churches and would shed light on the remarkable effort of African Traditionalists and Christians in practical mission partnership.

The book you are now reading is that book and is about half the length of the original two-volume book. Approving the cuts has been in many ways a painful process, even though I understand the need to introduce the Earthkeeping Movement and Zimbabwean Independent Churches to a broader audience than will read my longer, more detail-filled and expansive books. The two-volume work is available from the University of South Africa Press at the address given on the copyright page. I commend that edition to those who want to go deeper into the questions, activities, and issues that are discussed below.

There can be no more urgent task in the contemporary world than creating both bonds of understanding and solidarity between the peoples of Africa and the rest of the world as together we face the challenge of living in ecologically sustainable communities. May this edition of *African Earthkeepers* advance that cause.

Inus Daneel—Muchakata
22 January 2001

ACKNOWLEDGMENTS

Financial support from various institutions enabled me to launch and actively engage in the African earthkeeping movement described in this publication. It also enabled me, during the 1980s and 1990s, to conduct extensive research into the movement's religio-ecological motivation and endeavor. For their assistance I wish to thank several organizations.

They include: the Human Sciences Research Council in South Africa for financial assistance that allowed me to employ a regular team of fieldworkers; the University of South Africa, Pretoria, for granting me the paid leave required for environmental involvement and research in Zimbabwe; the ecological Faith and Earthkeeping project at Unisa (funded by the mining house Goldfields) for supporting me as co-founder, senior researcher and senior consultant; the Research Institute for Theology and Religion at Unisa and Boston University for financial and other administration of the Pew research program; The Pew Charitable Trusts for a three-year grant to launch the research project African Initiatives in Christian Mission; the African Studies Center and the School of Theology at Boston University for providing me with office and library facilities during periods of academic work in the United States; the Center for the Study of World Religions, Harvard University for a fellowship (1995–1996) which enabled me to relate to scholars of religion from countries all over the world; the Evangelische Zentralstelle für Entwicklungshilfe (EZE), Bonn, Germany, without whose generous financial and moral support the entire earthkeeping venture of the Zimbabwean Institute of Religious Research and Ecological Conservation (ZIRRCON) and its two sister organizations, the Association of Zimbabwean Traditional Ecologists (AZTREC) and the Association of African Earthkeeping Churches (AAEC), would not have been possible.

Over the years representatives of all these institutions have given me loyal support. I am especially indebted to Ms. Asa Maree, senior representative of the Human Sciences Research Council, for her efficient handling of funding issues and research reports. The late Professor David Bosch, former head of the Department of Missiology at the University of South Africa (Unisa), generously enabled me to proceed with project work among the Shona in Zimbabwe despite pressing academic duties in our department. I salute the memory of one of South Africa's great missiologists. The brunt of my frequent absences from Unisa, however, was borne by my colleagues, Professors Willem Saayman and Klippies Kritzinger. Without their friendship, consistent backup, and altruistic consideration of my work in Zimbabwe I would not have been able to meet the demands of a near nomadic existence of endless commuting—between the academic world in Pretoria and a religio-environmental ministry in Masvingo.

Ms. Jansie Kilian, of the Research Institute for Theology and Religion at Unisa, has efficiently taken care of the finances and the arrangements for several workshops and a highly successful international conference of the Pew research program. The entire research team accords her high praise. Her counterpart at Boston University, Delores Markey, has also provided our research team with prompt and reliable financial service. Dr. Rolf Assman, the EZE representative for Zimbabwe, has been stalwart in his support of ZIRRCON's environmental programmes. His insight into African religiosity and readiness to take risks in the sponsorship of ecological innovation in African grassroots society have enhanced project implementation.

In Boston and Cambridge, my wife and companion, Professor Dana Lee Robert of the Boston University School of Theology, helped me settle into a new mold of academic endeavor and to plan meaningful interaction between Boston University and Unisa in the implementation of the Pew research project African Initiatives in Christian Mission. Dr. James McCann, director of Boston University's African Studies Center, and Dr. Larry Sullivan, director of the Center for the Study of World Religions at Harvard, helped to publicize my religio-environmental work by way of seminars. To all these friends and colleagues, my sincere thanks.

With admiration and respect I mention some of the key figures who have played a major role in our earthkeeping movement and who were always prepared to participate in research interviews: Chief Justice Simbi Mubako, patron of ZIRRCON; Chief Murinye, patron of AZTREC and Chiefs Gutu, Chitsa, Munyikwa, Cingombe, and Chiwara from the Gutu district; Chiefs Murinye, Shumba, Mugabe, Zimuto, Nhema, Mabika, Mukangangwi, Muzungunye, Ndanga, Negovano, and Ziki from the Bikita, Ndanga, and Masvingo districts; Chiefs Chivi, Makonese, and Maranda from Chivi, Chiredzi, and Mwenezi districts. I thank several spirit mediums who featured prominentntly in AZTREC: Zarira Marambatemwa (note I have omitted a b), Lydia Chabata, MuDende, Tovera Chaminuka, and the late Pfupajena. I thank also Bishop Dhliwayo Musariri, patron of the AAEC, and a few core leaders of the AAEC, which currently has 150 member churches; Bishops Rabson Machokoto (first president), Eriah Hore, Reuben Marinda, Kindiam Wapendama, Farao Murambiwa, Chimhangwa, Makuku, Marima, Dube, Job Kamudzi, Zacheo Chamutsa, Saul Kuudzerema, J. Chabanga, Gondo Chivire, Ndamba, David Masuka, and Ms. Miria Forridge, representing the late Bishop Matteo Forridge. With most of these bishops and their wives I have had close bonds of friendship for more than thirty years. We have shared dreams of a better future, the hardships of implementing joint projects in rural society, and the celebration of accomplishments in the ecumenical fellowship of Independent Churches. My deepest gratitude for an adventure shared and for a lasting investment in relationships of mutual trust.

The dedication and accountability of the senior staff of ZIRRCON, who guided our earthkeeping movement through previously uncharted territory and the ups and downs of unpredictable funding and human conflicts, have given a profound sense of meaning and accomplishment to my life. The excellent leadership of Rev. Solomon Zvanaka, my successor as director, has enabled me to withdraw from the Institute's day-to-day administration with a sense of relief and confidence in its future. The Rev. Zvanaka is ably assisted by Bishop Reuben Marinda, then senior officer of the training department, Raviro Mutonga, coordinator of the Women's Desk, Edwin Machokoto, coordinator of the ecological department, Abraham Mupuwi, senior bookkeeper and secretary, and a team of liaison officers, research workers, and salaried nursery keepers.

ZIRRCON, together with its sister organisations, AZTREC and AAEC, has provided me with a place of belonging, a family, in Zimbabwe. This has enriched my life and allowed me the privilege of participating at the very heart of African society. It is with humility and pride that I thank my African family. Throughout the research period I could rely on ZIRRCON's team of loyal and competent field assistants. Operating from our base in Masvingo town, they diligently and faithfully probed areas in which information was required.

I thank Tarisai Zvokuomba and Andison Chagweda for loyal and reliable service at all times; Farai Mafanyana and Taverengwa Chiwara for diligent and inventive teamwork; and Claver Gwizhu, my mentor on domestic and related affairs and trusted guardian of our Masvingo research base.

For the preparation of the original manuscript and typesetting, I wish to thank Michelle Ducci, Marietjie Willemse, and Maddie Goodwin for their excellent typing; Andre Goetz for expert care in the basic layout of the book; and Helga Nordhoff for her professional comments on my photography and the clear prints she made of the pictures reproduced in this study. My thanks also go to Unisa Press, especially Phoebe van der Walt, Erica De Beer, and Liz Stewart, for the final preparation of the manuscript prior to printing. Marcelle Manley not only gave me the benefit of her outstanding linguistic talents in editing this work, but also provided pertinent comments on the contents which stimulated critical reflection on research findings.

Dr. Bill Burrows, Managing Editor of Orbis Books, was the driving force behind the production of this abridged version of my two-volume work, *African Earthkeepers*. Without his enthusiasm for the content matter of this publication, the many hours he spent in shortening the original and crafting the new text, and his patience in working with me towards the final preparation of the manuscript, this edition would not have become a reality. To work alongside Bill was an experience of privilege and inspiration. To him and his staff at Orbis a special word of thanks. It is with deep gratitude that I mention the warm and unswerving support of my family. My late parents and sister, Nyasa, have left a rich legacy of missionary service in Malawi and Zimbabwe. Even though my ministry among the AICs has led me along a less conventional route in mission, our Protestant roots have remained essentially the same. My sons and daughters—Alec, Lidia, Talita, and Inus—have always filled my life with laughter and joy, despite my nomadic pursuits. Dana Lee, gracious companion, and my two stepsons, Samuel and John, are gifts from God.

As fellow editor of the series 'African Initiatives' Dana Lee has been an invaluable support to me and the entire team of contributors. Her understanding of my African roots has given me wholeness of purpose and being. In my Africa names are indicators of relationship. I thank AZTREC for calling me Muchakata and the AAEC for insisting generously on 'Bishop Moses.'

ABBREVIATIONS OF ORGANISATION NAMES

AACC   All African Church Conference
AACJM   African Apostolic Church of Johane Maranke
AAEC   Association of African Earthkeeping Churches
AEU   African Earthkeepers' Union
AIC   African Initiated (can also mean African "Independent" churches
            or "Instituted" churches) Churches
ASM   American Society of Missiology
AZTREC   Association of Zimbabwean Traditional Ecologists
EATWOT   Ecumenical Association of Third World Theologians
EEASA   Environmental Education Association of South Africa
F AND E   Faith and Earthkeeping (project at University of South Africa)
GDS   German Development Society
HSRC   Human Science Research Council
IAMS   International Association of Mission Studies
JPIC   Justice, Peace, and the Integrity of Creation
NGO   Nongovernment Organisation
RCZ   Reformed Church of Zimbabwe
TEE   Theological Education by Extension
WCC   World Council of Churches
WCRP   World Conference on Religion and Peace
WD   Women's Desk
WWF   World-Wide Fund
YD   Youth Desk
ZCC   Zion Christian Church
ZIRRCON   Zimbabwean Institute of Religious Research and Ecological
            Conservation
ZRP   Zimbabwe Republic Police

Southern Africa

Zimbabwean Insitute of Religious Research
and Conservation (ZIRRCON)
Spheres of Influence

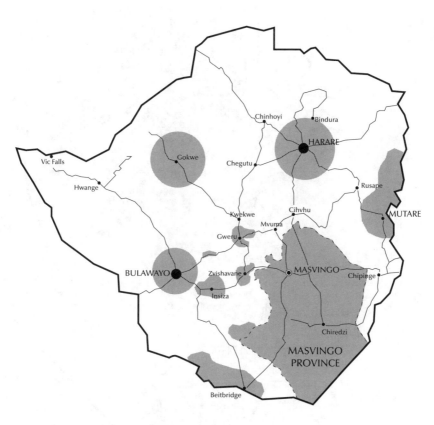

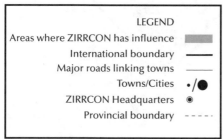

LEGEND

Areas where ZIRRCON has influence	
International boundary	—
Major roads linking towns	—
Towns/Cities	•/●
ZIRRCON Headquarters	◉
Provincial boundary	-----

ZIRRCON-Affiliated Earthkeepers
in Masvingo Province, Zimbabwe

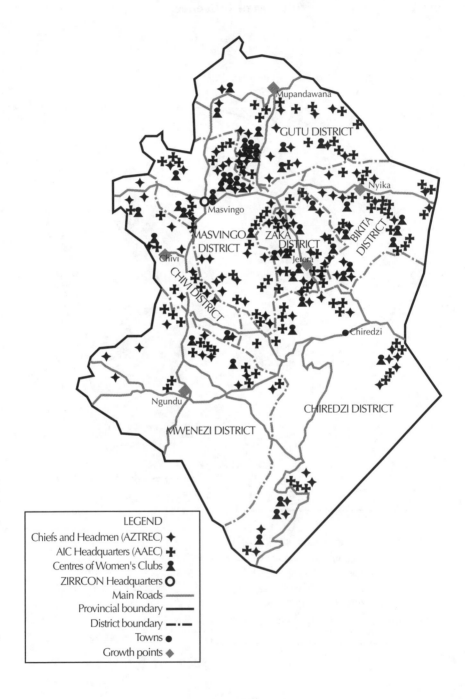

ZIRRCON Woodlots, Nurseries and Affiliated schools
in Masvingo Province, Zimbabwe

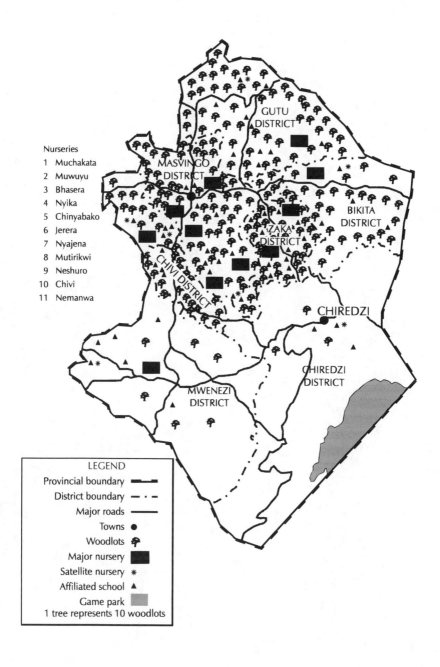

Nurseries
1 Muchakata
2 Muwuyu
3 Bhasera
4 Nyika
5 Chinyabako
6 Jerera
7 Nyajena
8 Mutirikwi
9 Neshuro
10 Chivi
11 Nemanwa

LEGEND
Provincial boundary
District boundary
Major roads
Towns ●
Woodlots
Major nursery
Satellite nursery *
Affiliated school ▲
Game park
1 tree represents 10 woodlots

INTRODUCTION

The Zimbabwean 'War of the Trees' and This Book

This book is about depicting and probing the religious motivation behind the liberation movement of both Traditionalist and Independent Christian Shona earth-keepers in Zimbabwe.

For many years, I have studied the origins, growth, and life of Shona Independent Churches. I turned next to the spirituality—both Traditional and Christian—of Zimbabwe's War for Independence, the *Chimurenga*. This latter phase of research culminated in the publication of a religio-historical novel called *Guerilla Snuff*, which I published under the name of Mafuranhunzi Gumbo.

From this period of research and writing grew a commitment to save our war-ravaged environment entered into by myself, my research team, and a large number of religious figures and ex-combatants in *chimurenga*. Many of them had played key roles in the struggle for Zimbabwean independence. Interviews with them in the communal lands of Masvingo Province led to intensive discussions about the state of the 'lost lands,' which—although politically freed from colonial rule—were becoming ecologically more lost than ever as a result of deforestation, overpopulation, and exploitive lands use. We survivors of *chimurenga* felt that, whereas the military and political liberation struggle was over, the environmental war had just begun. Thus we launched into a new phase of struggle, one aimed at delivering the 'lost lands' ecologically, and we declared what has become popularly known as the 'War of the Trees.'

Our earthkeeping movement is administered by the Zimbabwean Institute of Religious Research and Ecological Conservation (which I shall mercifully abbreviate as ZIRRCON) from offices in Masvingo town. This institute developed as an extension of my original research unit. ZIRRCON's 'green army' consists of two sister organizations:

- *The Association of Zimbabwean Traditional Ecologists* (AZTREC)—the 'Traditionalist' wing, composed mainly of chiefs, spirit mediums, headmen, ex-combatants, and (religiously) Traditionalist-oriented villagers; and
- *The Association of African Earthkeeping Churches* (AAEC)—the African Independent Christian wing, comprised of some 150 African Independent Churches, led in the field by the bishops, prophets, and women's associations of these geographically widespread movements.

The major thrust of the war of the trees has been in developing nurseries, cultivating (predominantly) indigenous tree seedlings, and annually planting close to a million trees in woodlots and orchards throughout Masvingo Province and adjacent regions. Field training includes lectures aimed at conscientizing local peoples and planting grass species to help reclaim gullies. Constitutionally, the aims of our green struggle go beyond the introduction of afforestation (reforestation) programs. Conserving wildlife and protecting water resources will gain prominence as our financial resources permit and our work force expands.

The purpose of this book is not to analyze all the environmental ramifications of ZIRRCON's work. Rather, I attempt to describe the religio-ecological worldviews and rituals at the core of our endeavor and the innovations that have evolved in our earthkeeping ministry. I try to assess some of the main trends of an emerging eco-theology in both its Traditionalist and Christian aspects, as both spontaneously and intuitively manifest themselves in ecological action. The paucity of literature on eco-theology in Africa in itself suggests a need for such an attempt.

Because our movement has its roots in *chimurenga*, I also try to highlight some of the liberationist motives in our concern for the ecologically lost lands of Zimbabwe. This focus does not override other considerations in religious development. I am not professing to have produced an African liberation theology. At most I identify liberationist trends that could serve as pointers to theologians or social scientists who wish to explore this dimension more fully.

The research method standing behind this book is that of *participant observation*. It involves the use of questionnaires to gauge the religio-ecological views and motives of Shona environmentalists and their response to innovative, contextualized earthkeeping strategies. We analyze speeches and sermons that were tape-recorded and observed at tree-planting rituals.

As founder and architect of the movement—a role emanating from and affirmed within African society, not imposed on it by me—I have been existentially too close to the inner world of ZIRRCON, too driven by the need to achieve in the face of at times impossible odds, to make any pretense of academic objectivity in assessing our environmental endeavor (if objectivity is a possible ideal in any case). Partly because ZIRRCON's story is also my own story, I may have written more success into it than outside observers will concede.

Nevertheless, there are saving graces that lend balance to my evaluation. First, my fellow earthkeepers' remarkable ability to contextualize and improvise in ritual and belief has helped them integrate some of my suggestions with such creativity that in most cases there is little left that I could call 'my contribution.' Hence I have, on the whole, not put too heavy a personal interpretational stamp on the policies and field strategies of our ecological war. Besides, the war of the trees has all along been a Shona people's movement and does not belong to any particular individual.

Second, I had the support of a team of ZIRRCON fieldworkers who conducted interviews, tape-recorded them, and then transcribed tapes of the proceedings. Consequently, I had access to a wide range of information, the critical interpretation of which was a team effort. This in itself counteracted tendencies to imposing my subjective views on what follows.

Third, I have had the opportunity to present some of the data of this study to academic audiences and to discuss them with ZIRRCON team members. In the process, errors were detected and corrected. Nevertheless, this study is a product of qualitative, not merely quantitative field research, and some of the characteristics singled out in relation to religious activity remain impressionistic as opposed to statistically quantified data.

Overall, I believe that what commends this book to various academic guilds—African studies, anthropology, missiology, ecology, theology, and religious studies—is the manner in which the African earthkeeping movement transcends conventional academic boundaries. I hope this book shows the way in which both Traditional and Christian religious motivations come together in the face of a potentially catastrophic ecological situation. In telling this story in the contemporary Zimbabwean context of social, ecological, and political instability, I hope I will have served well the many hundreds and thousands of Zimbabweans I have been privileged to work with in telling their story.

PART I

Rise of an African Traditionalist
Earthkeeping Movement

CHAPTER 1

Waiting for the Rain

THE BOUNTIFUL EARTH

January 1992. Fleeces of white cloud in shimmering pale blue skies—that is all we have. Halfway into the so-called rainy season there is nothing else. Here in Masvingo those white rainless clouds, barren omens of death, shroud from a distance the mud puddle of Lake Kyle, all that remains of the jewel of our province. Have even the symbols switched in the lament of a dying land? Does the whiteness of cloud now evoke thoughts of death, not purity, and the blackness of rain cloud signify life? Or do black and white, the colours of African spirit mediums, still symbolise ancestral protection—a protection apparently lost as grass and leaves shrivel in the heat?

For ten years we in Masvingo Province have been waiting for a really good season to break the chronic drought. Not just scattered showers, as we have had, to fill a few farm dams and nurture only some of the maize crops in outlying districts. We need torrential rains last seen in the mid-seventies; rains that swell the rivers countrywide, fill the lakes, blot out the sun for two weeks on end, until the damp produces a green sheen on the shoes under your bed. Rains as we saw regularly as youngsters, when it was impossible to travel the red quagmire of the mountain road leading to Morgenster mission. When, coming from Fort Victoria, we had to walk for miles across the granite rocks of Mount Mugabe—vehicles left far behind at Wayside Farm—to reach home.

Rains in those years brought abundance: gushing fountains, mountain streams which spoke to giant ferns for months at a time in their secret valleys; trees laden with swelling yellow wild loquats, wild figs, plums, and berries; trees hiding the delicious orange *mafirifiti* mushrooms under rotting leaves and logs, while the bulbuls, sunbirds, red-winged louries, birds of paradise, and a host of the feathered flock played hide and seek among the branches. To our young minds it was a mountain world of fantasy where fairies and trolls lived among the moss and ferns, drank from the clear dew beside rustling streams, and danced at night on black granite slopes, cleansed and polished by the eternal seepage of crystal water released by healthy sponge.

Mount Mugabe was a world of magic beauty. The rain was as regular as the sun. Between them they ripened the fruit; and we, the black and white children, the animals and the birds, harvested at leisure what was given to us so liberally. We also hunted birds, rock rabbits, and small antelopes. But we knew that the mountain imposed restraints on us, that there was no honour in disrupting the balance of life around us. It was the mountain of God! Did our fathers, the white missionaries, not tell us that the granite needle jutting high into the sky was the Fin-

7

ger Rock pointing towards God in heaven? That it was the symbol of the good news which our pioneer, *sekuru* Louw, had carried here many years ago? And were we not told to respect the graves of black elders who lay buried in granite crevices along the mountain slopes, not to disturb the beads, pots, and spears hugging the skeletal secrets of ancients behind piled rocks?

We regarded our holy mountain with awe. It was a natural *marambatemwa*, a holy grove of mile upon mile of dense forest protected against tree felling by time-honoured beliefs: those of my fellow Africans who heeded the timeless ecological laws of the ancestral guardians of the land, and those of my white friends who looked upon the wealth of trees as a kind of Christian paradise which evoked afresh God's primordial laws of human stewardship of all nature.

As children we took it all for granted: rain, trees, animals, birds. That idyllic setting in which a large community of industrious people—teachers, scholars, medics, carpenters, builders, farmers, administrators, and a host of ordinary folk, old and young—lived their lives. The holy mountain had a serene strength of its own. It would remain the same . . . always. No drought could destroy its rich vegetation. No Zimbabwean would dare desecrate the holy grove, risk the wrath of the spirit world. At least, so we, the young ones of Morgenster, thought. So we cherished our birthplace when we moved on to lead our lives elsewhere—saw it as a spiritual anchorage, a haven in the bosom of God's own country. Some of us travelled across the oceans. But our roots were firmly embedded at the centre of the universe, in ancient Africa, at the place of protection right next door to the citadel of Great Zimbabwe, the place which seldom if ever waited for the rain.

THE WOUNDED EARTH

Things change. Over many years of research in the communal lands I grew used to the sight of overgrazing, soil erosion, and deforestation around African villages. Europeans tended to believe that these land problems could be solved through proper land husbandry, control of population growth, and industrial development which would take the pressure off the land. Besides, the lush growth on commercial farms created the impression that overall the ecological situation in our country was reasonably good—at least not as critical as in some of the Sahel countries. One anticipated that after Zimbabwean Independence there would be a redistribution of land and that, if properly implemented, this would contribute towards greater equity and ecological balance. One assumed that there would be control and conservation in what had traditionally been regarded as sanctuaries. Surely the wonderful forested slopes of the Nyuni mountains at Glenlivet, the *marambatemwa* on Mount Mugabe and the catchment area of Lake Kyle would remain unscathed!

It was not to be. Soon after *chimurenga* a large number of squatters were allowed to settle in the catchment area of Lake Kyle near Great Zimbabwe. In no time large sections of the *msasa* and *mutondo* forests were gone, and the sandy soil lay bare in the sun, ready to be carried away by the ton to the watery depths of the lake where it would add to the problems of siltation and, as a side effect, bedevil the sugar cane industry in the lowveld. Where I used to hunt in dense forest as a child, the open veld now lay forlorn, lifeless tree stumps jutting hopelessly from the soil like beckoning fingers imploring someone to cover the wounded earth.

Lake Kyle's catchment area was threatened from all sides. Further up, on the portion of Morgenster Farm given back to Chief Mugabe for village settlement, the Bingura forest was fast disappearing, making way for row upon row of homesteads and cultivated fields. Callous profiteers had purchased sites in Glenlivet township and stripped the steep Nyuni slopes of their protective mountain acacias to earn a quick buck from firewood, leaving the soil exposed to inevitable erosion and adding to the siltation of the lake. Along the upper reaches of the Popoteke and Mtirikwi rivers in Gutu district poorly controlled resettlement schemes led to river bank cultivation which, in times of flooding, could only further compound the problems of Lake Kyle.

Worst of all was the invasion of Mount Mugabe. Some mindless exploiters went in there with fifteen-ton trucks and started mowing down the *muchakata*, *mushuku* and other wild fruit trees in order to market fuelwood. Impervious to the laws of *marambatemwa*, which prohibits the felling of *muchakata* (the tree of rain rituals, symbolising ancestral protection) and *mushuku* (the wild loquat, which God has given to both the guardian ancestors and their living descendants to augment their food supplies), these greedy exploiters desecrated the holy grove. To make matters worse, squatters, ignoring threats of eviction, tore open the mountain side. They cleared the bush and started planting their maize and millet crops in places totally unsuitable for cultivation, triggering a process of erosion such as the mountain had never known before.

Soon the mountain was dying. Everybody knew that it was madness to chop down ancestral trees in the holy groves, the epitome of human hubris in the face of the ultimate forces of life. Even the gods must go crazy at such mindless assault. I felt deep hurt and growing anger as I observed the slow destruction of the green mountain fortress. It was also an invasion of the inner soul of those of us who had grown up on the mountain, whose perception of privacy was moulded by the endless murmur of mountain streams among mosses and ferns. Gone were the streams, the abundance of fruit, the mushrooms, and the wingflap of birds. Even though I understand the plight of landless peasants, the voices and laughter of the squatter-invaders could not compensate for all that lost beauty and peace, now replaced by the rutted surfaces of erosion gulleys, rough tear streaks on the old mountain's distorted features.

Perhaps my anger related to the knowledge that destruction of the mountain's vegetation and ecosystem violated the feeling of ecological strength and indestructibility it had always radiated in the past. Now it was reduced to the same climatic vulnerability as the surrounding areas; it had lost its ability to 'draw rain'— its capacity for abundance, which it was known for even during distant seasons of drought. I knew that I might be overreacting, that had Mount Mugabe remained undisturbed it might still have battled to cope with the protracted drought in our country. Yet the remaining *mushuku* trees standing beside the mountain road—

listless and grey, year after year not bearing fruit—seemed to be an indictment of the unasked invasion and misuse of their territory. And the drying up of the mission dam reminded me that the drought had taxed the springs and underground sponge to the limit, irrespective of the mountain invaders' contribution to the general malaise. At last I had to concede that our mountain was as fallible and vulnerable as everything else in creation, that we human beings only make it more so.

One salutary thing that grew out of my regular pilgrimages to Morgenster, the emotional drain, the anger and emptiness I experienced each time I saw those ravaged, fruitless slopes, was a kind of ecological conversion. I recognised myself as one of the invaders who had helped deplete the mountain's bird and rock rabbit population. Did I not notice that not a single rock rabbit was to be seen on the granite kopjes around World's View where I used to hunt them?

The recognition of my own ecological guilt did not diminish my opposition to the squatters on the mountain. It did, however, sharpen my interest in ecological concerns, made me more alert to the land problems of my country—of which Morgenster's were but a symptom—and of our continent. My identification with the plight of the peasants and of nature itself in the communal lands grew. The Reformed missiologist could no longer focus his empirical research purely on religious beliefs and ceremonies. Neither could he maintain the Western dualism of spiritual as opposed to physical reality.

African holism became the hermeneutic for theological reorientation. Saving souls was important, I thought. But never at the expense of the salvation of all creation. In my situation conversion had little significance if it did not translate into full environmental stewardship. For the first time I really experienced myself as part of an abusing and abused creation which was reaching out for liberation, salvation. The biblical concept of a new heaven and a new earth no longer seemed merely a new dispensation to be ushered in by God, but a challenge to be realised in this existence. The myth of my childhood mountain fortress had to turn into a new myth. A myth born of vulnerability, but emerging from the unknown recesses of our common African unconscious. A myth which recognises Mwari in his African guise as the true *muridzi venyika* (guardian of the land), calling all of us to heal the wounded land.

At that time, in the mid-eighties, I came to know a Danish couple, Christian and Vibeke Rasmussen. Their friendship and interest in Zimbabwe further stimulated my growing interest in ecology. Christian was supervising the sinking of boreholes in Chivi district on behalf of the Lutheran World Federation. Together we observed the plight of peasant communities in Chivi in the grip of drought. Together we studied and discussed Lloyd Timberlake's (1985) *Africa in Crisis: The Causes, the Cures of Environmental Bankruptcy*.

What we were observing in Chivi, I realised, were the symptoms of desertification. Timberlake (1985:60) states: 'Desertification is not about spreading deserts. It is a rash which breaks out in patches wherever the planet's skin is mistreated.' Indeed, desertification concerns the wounding of the earth, human mismanagement through overcultivation, overgrazing, or deforestation, as a result of which productive dryland turns into wasteland. The rash had broken out all over Zimbabwe. To this the overcultivated and deforested areas in the Gutu and Chivi districts bear witness. Part of the cause of the malady, of course, is the land-apportionment practices of the colonial era. Yet one must ask whether enough is being done to rehabilitate the devastated communal lands. Harold Dregne, speaking on behalf of the United Nations Environment Programme (UNEP), for instance, writes (in Timberlake 1985:61):

> Governments [in Africa] do not see desertification as a high priority item. Rangeland deterioration, accelerated soil erosion, and salinisation and waterlogging do not command attention until they become crisis items. Lipservice is paid to combating desertification but the political will is directed elsewhere. There seems to be little appreciation that a major goal of many developing nations, that of food self-sufficiency, cannot be attained if soil and plant resources are allowed to deteriorate.

It takes little imagination to realise that we are fast reaching a point where tree planting as a major earthkeeping activity must become the concern of all people of all the nations of the world. In postcolonial Africa the redistribution of land has not curbed ecological destruction. With due respect to national tree-planting days, which are at least a symbolic gesture of ecological awareness, billions of trees need to be planted annually and taken care of if deforestation is to be checked and controlled. Much stricter measures for forest conservation are required, as well as universal conscientisation through ecological education programmes. Sustained production of firewood should be made a condition for the use of this commodity in all rural areas.

DISCUSSION AND RESOLVE

My ecological awareness and convictions grew from the Morgenster experience, from discussions with my Danish friends, and from reading *Earthscan* and similar publications. But the factor that eventually impelled me to ecological commitment was sharing my concern about our environment with rural people—traditionalists, ex-combatants, and African Initiated Church (AIC) members— amongst whom I was conducting research on the role of religion during the *chimurenga* struggle. The mounting crisis in which black peasants in Masvingo Province found themselves from the mid-eighties onwards is summed up by a research fellow, Cousins (1987:18):

> The land question that fuelled the liberation struggle has not been resolved by means of a land redistribution. Within the Communal Lands pressure on natural resources has continued to mount as a result of population growth, the declining availability of formal sector employment, and the recurrence of drought seasons. Peasant households have responded in various ways: one strategy is to intensify production using purchased inputs, another is to

increase the area under cash crops such as cotton [resulting in increased deforestation and pressure on grazing areas], and a third is the attempt to gain
access to new land resources. The latter has taken various forms: squatting,
'poaching' of the grazing of both commercial farms and resettlement
schemes . . . and migration to 'frontier' areas such as Gokwe, Kanyati, and
Dande.

The situation of the peasants on the land was further complicated by the introduction of Village Development Committees (VIDCOs) and Ward Development Committees (WADCOs) in 1984. These measures coincided with the curtailment of the judicial and land allocation powers of the chiefs—and, by
implication, also some loss of status for senior spirit mediums. As these traditional leaders still enjoyed widespread popular support, government restrictions
led to confusion and some disillusionment in their ranks (Cousins 1987:19; *The
Herald*, 17/12/85).

It was in these circumstances that I did my research into the *chimurenga*
struggle. Wherever I conducted interviews in the communal lands of Masvingo
Province the ravages of overcultivation, deforestation, and recurrent drought
were in evidence. You could not touch on any aspect of the struggle without the
subject of the land cropping up. Sitting with ex-combatants and spirit mediums
in the guerrilla *poshitos* up in the mountains discussing their war strategies and
convoy attacks, visiting the Musukutwa caves where a fierce battle was fought
during the war, or sitting under the trees talking to AIC prophets, we were forever looking out over dry fields, arid stretches of land, erosion gullies, and un-
dernourished cattle. Out there we were mere specks of creation, feeling the heat,
yearning like all of life around us for the coolness and promise of rain. Together
we waited . . .

The mood was often ambivalent: although key figures of the struggle took pride
in the political achievement of independence, they were despondent about the deterioration of the land they lived on and about the 'promised land' (the commercial
farms) not being returned to them as they had expected once victory was secured.
Women complained about the long distances they had to walk to collect fuelwood
and the peasants generally felt bitter about crop failures which left them unable to
pay for their children's schooling and to contend with the rising cost of living.

And the cause of the ongoing drought, or rural destitution? Was it human action or an act of God? Towards the mid-eighties a common belief in peasant society was that the numerous *chimurenga* deaths had caused a great upheaval in the
spirit world. Far too many spirits of deceased people roamed the 'wilderness' in
perpetual dissatisfaction because they had never been ritually elevated to the status of ancestorhood. The equilibrium between the living and the living dead had
been disturbed to the extent that even the seasons were disrupted. The bones of
some of the deceased lay about in the veld desecrated. Spirit dissatisfaction about
such blasphemy blocked the rain. But then the wrong was gradually redressed by
heroes' reburial ceremonies throughout Zimbabwe. The bones of the fighters
were respectfully placed in the soil they had fought for. These ceremonies functioned as improvised *kugadzira* rituals (Daneel 1971:101f), a form of 'home

bringing' of the deceased to the soil and nation of Zimbabwe (Daneel 1995, chapter 3), thus correcting the mystical imbalance and climatic disturbances.

More seriously, a second viewpoint gained currency as the drought persisted and the expected land distribution was delayed. It held that the government of the day provoked mystical retaliation both from the national ancestors and the Supreme Being, Mwari. The drought would persist, it was believed, particularly by the traditional elders (chiefs and spirit mediums), until such time as the top politicians in Harare made their pilgrimage to Great Zimbabwe and to the Matopo hills in official recognition of the recovery of the lost lands through the mystical intervention during the war of the senior ancestral guardians of the land (*varidzi venyika*) and of Mwari, the creator God of Zimbabwe. The president of Zimbabwe, it was expected, should go and 'show the recaptured lands' to the mystical forces of Africa which made victory possible in the first place. Such recognition would also entail restoring the land-allocation and related politico-religious powers of the chiefs and the spirit mediums. Only then would there be abundant rains.

Year after year this theme has persisted in traditionalist circles. It surfaces during *mukwerere* rain rituals in our province, in the dream life of the tribal elders, and in the oracular sessions of Mwari, the rain-giver, at the cultic shrines in the Matopo hills. As a participant observer at many of these rain-requesting rituals, I was in a position to follow the hardening line of interpretation closely. The drought was indeed a punitive act of God and of the ancestors. Yet it was in no way an arbitrary intervention. God and the ancestors were simply responding to the way the country was being governed, the neglect of the guardian ancestors, the disregard of customary principles governing societal order and land distribution. While the persistent drought kept rousing the conscience of the nation, local and Matopo rain rituals became forums where grievances about land issues could be aired, as well as occasions for reconciliation between a wayward yet suffering humanity and the neglected powers of the spirit world.

It would be misleading, however, to suggest that the blame was put only on the government of the day. In our discussions there was also a pervasive sense of common guilt, references to all of humanity as *vatadzi* (sinners), a perverted people who have abused the environment. As we watched the cloudless skies and the withering maize stalks the mood was one of sadness and dejection. Resignedly someone would say: '*Mwari hwatirasha!* God has thrown us away!' It reminded me of the lament in the cultic song to the Supreme Being sung in the Matopo hills after the 1896 rebellions had failed:

> Ay, the unburnt pot [the white man] has spoilt the world . . .
> Yelele, the unburnt pot just handles the world, twisting it,
> Yelele, we are troubled . . .
> Yelele, the God who is in heaven has given us his back;
> The God who is at the roof has thrown us away like dogs,
> Yelele, the Muali in heaven has given us his back.
> > (Ranger 1967:378; cultic song
> > collected by R. Werbner in 1960)

Except that in this instance there was a growing realisation that, much as the 'unburnt pot' may have spoilt the world, the ever-increasing destruction was the responsibility of all Zimbabweans. We started sharing our sense of loss in observing the wounded earth. I spoke about the invaded mountain fortress at Mount Mugabe. My peasant friends in turn sighed about the lost woodlands and the spoilt fountains from which the *njuzu* water spirits had fled. And so we came to talk about our brothers and sisters, the trees. We acknowledged that maybe the denuded earth had something to do with God's anger and the persistent drought. Maybe we had to start remedying the situation on a massive scale, in the same way that the nation was mobilised during *chimurenga* to win back the lost lands. It was no longer good enough simply to sit around waiting for the rain, to propitiate the ancestors, to send delegations to the Matopo hills, or to fast and confess our sins to God on mountain tops as the Zionists and Apostles were doing.

It was in 1988 that our shared convictions hardened into resolve, and our resolve into action. We decided to become earthkeepers, tree planters, healers of the wounded land. So we declared another *chimurenga*! This time it would be the war of the trees—later to be extended to the protection of wildlife and water resources. The old *chimurenga* of the lost lands, which had been won militarily and politically, was now to become the liberation struggle of the ecologically still lost, still enslaved land.

We were to form associations which would empower the spirit mediums and tribal elders once again to mobilise entire communities into united action on behalf of Mwari and the guardian ancestors, new movements of AIC solidarity which would enable prophets of the Holy Spirit to guide entire churches into the new warfare of ecological revolution. We resolved, too, that this would be a war based on racial reconciliation, extending as far as possible the spirit of mutuality and understanding which had characterised our initial discussions. Whereas this war was to draw its inspiration and impetus from diverse religious convictions, it was to be waged in a spirit of interreligious respect, tolerance, and dialogue.

To the chiefs this was an opportunity to develop new land initiatives which would earn them national acclaim. To the spirit mediums it offered the prospect of creating a new myth, a new mission in the public eye, as opposed to the obscurity and inaction which had threatened to envelop them in the Marxist-socialist state after the excitement and heroics of *chimurenga*. To the Independent Churches it later gave an added dimension of altruism to their healing ministry, whereby they could blaze an ecological trail in practice, a trail which theologians had only talked and written about.

As for myself, I had no illusions about the complications involved in founding, funding, and to some extent guiding such a diversified grassroots movement. I had been in the battlefield before, motivated by a vision of AIC ecumenism (see the *Fambidzano* story; Daneel 1989). One vision, I decided, was enough for a lifetime. But then, once you're engaged in constitution drafting, meetings, fund raising, and project implementation, the war around you gathers a momentum of its own. And you salute with raised fist at the battle cry: Forward the war of the trees!

The following newspaper account gives the flavor of the drama that began to unfold.

15 January 1992. The lead article in *The Herald* reads:

About 400,000 hungry people in the drought stricken Masvingo Province are now receiving food handouts at a cost of $1.5 million a month . . . The provincial administrator, Cde. Alphonse Chikurira, said yesterday that more than a quarter of the province's 1.5 million people were eligible for food handouts this month as the area goes into its worst drought in living memory.

17 January. Concern deepens. The spirit mediums of AZTREC (Association of Zimbabwean Traditional Ecologists), having received ancestral dream directives to visit the oracular shrines of Mwari in the Matopo hills, come into town with a delegation of chiefs. Together we set off for the distant shrines. That evening, 300 kilometers from Masvingo, in the granite world of the Matopos, our delegation sits listening to the voice of Mwari—an ancient female murmur in old chiRozvi addressing us from the mysterious cult cave: 'The world is spoilt. I shall give you only sparse rains . . . Persevere with the planting of trees! I shall keep my hand over you . . .'

There is consolation in the ancient words of African wisdom. There is lightness in the play of moonlight on black granite. The hardships ahead have become bearable . . . Mwari has spoken.

'Mbedzi! Dziva! Shoko!' The praise-names of Mwari ring out as we shuffle away from the oracle.

19 January. An hour before the commencement of the ecumenical prayer session for rain at Masvingo's civic centre, there is a slight drizzle. Out in the rural areas the tribal elders are shouting 'Tovera!' in acknowledgement of the oracular Mwari. They are saying that Mwari vaMatonjeni has sent the rain to blot out the footprints of the delegation that has been to the caves, a sign that the request has been granted. My Christian friends at the civic centre are thanking Mwari of the Bible for responding to prayer.

Perhaps Mwari, creator of us all, chuckles in the patter of raindrops.

The drought, however, is still with us as we near the month's end. Many of the trees we have planted are dying. People do not tend trees when they have hardly any drinking water left. We are still waiting for the rain. Only now there is a difference. Our waiting breathes hope. Some day our forests will once again draw rainclouds.

CHAPTER 2

Liberation of the Lost Lands

Mwari, the oracular high-God of the Shona, has traditionally been conceived of as an ecological deity, provider of life-giving rain and fertility in creation. Cult messengers (*vanyai*) made regular annual pilgrimages on behalf of their districts throughout central and south-eastern Zimbabwe. They would present their gifts and pleas for rain at the shrines in the Matopo hills—commonly known as Matonjeni or Mabweadziva ('rocks of the pool')—where the oracle gave them messages about seasonal, agricultural, and tribal-political issues, such as chieftaincy successions, to carry back home to their people. Individuals with ailments, especially barren women, were also allowed to confer with Mwari at the shrines. Thus an image emerged of a deity concerned with maintenance of both ecological and human wellbeing. A conservative deity, Mwari moreover became the mainstay of African religious and cultural values in the face of invasive and corroding Western influence.

During times of national crisis, however, Mwari emerged, albeit secretly, in the role of liberator of the oppressed. This was noticeable, for instance, during the 1896 rebellions and the recent liberation struggle that led to Independence. Upheavals of this nature triggered intensified collaboration between oracular deity and senior tribal ancestors of outlying chiefdoms. This belief manifested at the time in cooperation between Mwari cultists and regional spirit mediums in mobilising wide-spread resistance against a common enemy.

Such religious management of sociopolitical problems is convincing evidence of the capacity of African religion to deal with political and land issues of national import. This is the key to an understanding of the religious motivation and drive of the traditionalist earthkeepers who joined forces in recent years to combat environmental deterioration.

When one sits in the deep of night listening to Mwari's voice speaking in ancient Rozvi dialect from the cave shrine, one cannot but sense the significance of the cult in the history of the Zimbabwean people's struggle for liberation. I know that this experience was shared by my fellow earthkeepers, particularly those who had direct knowledge of the cult's influence during the liberation war. Inasmuch as they were interpreting their earthkeeping endeavours as an extension of the political struggle (*chimurenga*), they were bound to seek the blessing of the oracular deity at Matonjeni and in the process give ritual expression to the mystical interaction between Mwari and their regional 'guardians of the land' (*varidzi venyika*) in the interest of an afflicted earth.

In order to clarify the historic picture that underlies our entire earthkeeping movement, I shall outline the role of religion in the patterns of resistance to oppressive rule prior to and during the second *chimurenga*. This will reveal trends of both liberation, in the sense of expelling unwanted powers or influences, and healing, in the sense of restoring wellbeing, as they relate to the colonial era in Zimbabwe. A focal topic here is the (politically and ecologically) 'lost land,' as they were and remain the primary existential reality of peasant communities.

This outline includes the healing and liberationist activities of the AICs. Unlike Western-oriented mission churches, who could rely on foreign financial support and whose leadership was therefore largely independent of prevailing agro-economic conditions in rural areas, the AIC leaders—like those of traditionalist cults—were part of peasant society. As a result both of these groups suffered the same hardships as their fellow peasants, hardships caused by restrictive land apportionment, limited political power, dwindling forests and wildlife, and poor crops as a result of drought—hence their attempts to remedy these ills reflect a more characteristic grassroots African response, in both the traditionalist and the Christian context, than those of missions under foreign leadership.[1]

TRADITIONAL MANAGEMENT OF ENVIRONMENTAL AND SOCIOPOLITICAL ILLS (1890–1965)

In the healing of physical illness, the traditional diviner and/or *nganga* plays a major role. However, since our primary concern is with communal rather than individual ills, we concentrate on the Mwari cult as the territorially most wide-reaching religious institution, and on the senior spirit mediums at the top level of tribal politics in their respective districts.

THE MWARI CULT IN *CHIMURENGA* II

The origin of the Mwari cult has been a subject of debate and speculation.[2] Although difficult to verify, oral tradition has it that Chief NeMbire, along with several subordinate Karanga clans, immigrated from the Tanzanian lake regions in the fourteenth century, where the African high-God is known as Muali (Abraham 1966:33; Daneel 1970:22). Linguistic and archaeological evidence seems to confirm early contact with Central and West African tribes. Apparently the Mwari cult of the Mbire priests was adopted by the Rozvi monarchs who, from their headquarters at Great Zimbabwe (the ruins of which are a popular tourist attraction near Masvingo town), tried to unite some of the Shona tribes. Several sources indicate that the cult was an important centralising religious force at Zimbabwe, and later in the Matopo hills, before the Nguni broke up the Rozvi confederacy in the 1830s.

At Zimbabwe the Mwari cult to some extent absorbed the *mhondoro* cult of senior lineage ancestors which had developed more fully in the northern territories of the Mwenemutapa dynasty (Abraham 1959; 1966:32). In the north, tribal spirits were venerated through an officially recognised spirit medium (*svikiro*) who represented the guardians of their descendants' chiefdoms, demarcated by rivers into 'spirit provinces.' At one stage the principal *mhondoro* at Zimbabwe is said to have been Chaminuka. Although originally unconnected with Mwari, this hero-spirit was eventually seen as the spiritual 'son,' or at least as a direct emanation, of Mwari (Von Sicard 1994:162).

Whatever the connection, spirit mediums featured prominently in both the Mwari and the *mhondoro* cults. The development of Mwari as an oracular deity, which was completed only after the main shrines had shifted to the Matopo hills, may in fact have been stimulated by the partial integration of the two cults. But this syncretisation never completely identified Mwari with Chaminuka or other tribal spirits. Mwari remained the creator of the earth on whom Chaminuka, the entire spirit world, and all creation depended. Among the Southern Shona, especially the Karanga, the *mhondoro*-type cult never acquired the prestige that it had among nothern tribes.

When the Rozvi dynasty was at its zenith, the Mwari cult, then operating several major shrines in the Matopo hills, consolidated its wide influence. Its political significance, too, grew as it became increasingly important for affiliated Shona chiefs to demonstrate their loyalty to the Rozvi kings. One method was to regularly send messengers (*vanyai*) to Matonjeni with pleas for rain, to consult Mwari on chieftaincy successions and to dedicate *mbonga* women and praise-singers from remote chiefdoms to Mwari's service. Thus Mwari became the oracular deity of the chiefs and cultic priests.

After invading Rozvi territory in the 1830s, the Ndebele kings themselves honoured Mwari, whom they called Mlimo, with annual gifts and requests for rain. Under its new political masters the Mwari priesthood adopted a seemingly conciliatory attitude. The cult's political function was modified considerably during the Ndebele reign. In a highly centralised monarchic state the cult did not have to be a mechanism for political coordination, as it had been in the militarily weaker and more loosely federated state system of the varozvi. Only after the Ndebele monarchy had been defeated by European forces was the cult 'able to manifest its old vigour and its emissaries able to travel through the whole area of its influence' (Ranger 1966:104–105).

Yet it was under Ndebele rule that the oracular deity revealed him/herself as a liberator God who resists oppression. Shona resentment of Ndebele harassment surfaced in Mwari's oracular pronouncements.

When the pioneer settlers of the British South Africa Company started moving across the Limpopo in 1890, the Voice of Mwari reportedly said to Lobengula: 'You who are so busy killing people, you are a little man. Climb on top of a high hill and see these people who are coming up. See their dust rising in the south. My white sons whose ears are shining in the sun are coming up here' (Ranger 1967:144). To the Shona the arrival of Mwari's 'white sons' meant a radical curb on the oppressive power of the Ndebele invaders, and at first they welcomed the white settlers' arrival.

The picture soon changed, however. Mwari's 'white sons,' initially regarded as liberators, turned out to be land-usurping rulers who posed a far more serious threat to Shona tradition than the Ndebele did. They became the common enemy, to be resisted by Shona and Ndebele alike. In the process the Mwari cult functioned as a central source of information and a means of coordinating resistance over a wide area. The rebellion of 1896–1897—later known among Zimbab-

weans as the first *chimurenga*—illustrates this point. Within a relatively short period more than 400 whites (some 10 per cent of the white population of erstwhile
Rhodesia) were wiped out (Martin & Johnson 1981:49).

The Mwari cult played a significant role in ritually approving, supporting, and
coordinating a large-scale liberation struggle. Ranger (1966:96) rightly points out
that the cult officials '*set the seal of ritual approval on the decision of the community as a whole*. Their general involvement in the risings was in itself an indication of the total commitment of most of the traditional society to them' [my ital-
ics]. The cult blamed the white settlers for both the drought and the rinderpest
then afflicting peasant society (Ranger). The importance of the Mwari cult in providing religious sanction for the revolt and advice to the rebels in outlying districts is clearly illustrated by the roles played by some cult officials. Thus Mab-
wani, the most influential priest at Matonjeni at the time, was directly involved in
the attempts of the Shona rebels in the district to drive white farmers off the land.

In western Mashonaland the messengers of Mwari played an active role in organising the risings after they had visited the caves in May 1896. The Native
Commissioner at Hartley was warned about these visits but attached little importance to them. Two weeks later the Native Commissioner was killed near Mashiangombi's kraal in the first out-break of rebellion in Mashonaland. In the ensuing
struggle the Mwari messengers and the remarkably courageous spirit medium of
Kaguwi coordinated their activities to organise the resistance of Mashiangombi's
people. This was the last desperate attempt at concerted action, at a stage when
many Shona chiefs were already considering peace talks. During these last-
minute negotiations the bitter-enders invoked the Voice of Mwari as the final uncompromising authority, the African God of justice and liberation.

As regards the development of traditional concepts of Mwari, it appears as if
there were historical mutations, reflecting crises and changing circumstances. The
predominantly creator God of rain, crops, and human fertility captured the imagination of his/her people during the rebellion as a militant deity: *the God of war
and peace and the God of justice opposing oppressive rule*. Christian influence, as
reflected in the fatherhood of Mwari and the absorption of the Christ figure as the
white people's *mhondoro* spirit, is also apparent. The image of the liberator God
may have receded into the background at times, but it persisted in the minds of the
people until it re-emerged forcefully during *chimurenga* II. The failure of the first
rebellion, while causing despondency among cult officials and the indigenous
population generally, was rationalised: it was attributed to the black people's in-
ability to unite against the whites rather than to any lack of power on the part of
Mwari. After the rebellion the deity continued providing oracular support for
black resistance to colonial rule. Veiled in secrecy, the oracle continued to propagate resistance and the liberation of the lost lands.

How was this achieved? Though driven underground for a time after the rebellion, the wide-spread cult organisation was kept intact (Daneel 1970:36f) if increasingly secret.[3] Mwari's rejection of white rule took the form of criticism of
breaches of customary law, for instance when laws of inheritance were ignored or
misapplied by white district commissioners in the appointment of new chiefs.
Droughts and the concomitant suffering of peasant communities were attributed

to the oppressor's discriminatory land legislation, specific incidents of maladministration in outlying districts, and also to the prophetic rain-making activities of opposing religious groups such as the Zion Christian Church of Bishop Mutendi.

But Mwari did not merely sanction black reaction against conquest. He/she also insisted on reciprocity as a condition for social and ecological wellbeing. For the rains to fall regularly, Mwari required a show of right-mindedness, demonstrated annually by the gifts sent from each district to the Matonjeni shrines, along with requests for rain. In addition the traditional rest day of the ancestors (*chisi*), ancestral rituals and a host of customary marital and other laws had to be observed. Essentially, therefore, Mwari featured as a conservative force, preserving African values in the face of change and maintaining a close link between just rule, agro-economic progress, and the wellbeing of the environment.

THE SENIOR DISTRICT SPIRIT MEDIUMS

At district level in the south the senior spirit medium represents the dominant tribe's founding ancestor or a related ancestor at the apex of the local spirit hierarchy. In peacetime the medium's link with the high-God may not be consistently apparent. Yet in those areas where the influence of the Mwari cult is strong, it is the senior *svikiro* who, with the local chief and the district's cult messenger, displays the high-God's gifts to the ancestors at the chief's court prior to the messenger's visit to the cult caves in the Matopo hills. By placing the seal of ritual approval on the community's plea for rain, the *svikiro* confirms the interaction of the local tribal spirit(s) with Mwari of Matonjeni. The same spirit interaction is reaffirmed in local *mukwerere* rain rituals, when the senior tribal ancestors are requested to approach Mwari/Dzivaguru directly for rain.

As a traditional ecologist the *svikiro* has important conservationist duties. On behalf of the local *varidzi venyika* (ancestral guardians of the land), who receive their mandate for environmental protection directly from Mwari, the *svikiro* is empowered to prohibit the cutting of certain trees; to take polluters of springs who disturb the water spirits (*njuzu*) to the chief's court; to enforce the boundaries of *marambatemwa* (holy groves where the ancestors dwell) by bringing treefellers to court; and to guard over certain species of game. The *svikiro*'s ecological duties are believed to be divinely inspired. It is not uncommon to hear *masvikiro* appealing to the creator God, in addition to the guardian ancestors, as the source of their authority for environmental protection. In this sense the *masvikiro* can be described as traditional 'healers of the earth' who, prior to and in some respects also under white rule, maintained an equilibrium between human exploitation of nature and its conservation or recovery. The *masvikiro* exert great influence on tribal affairs: they are the historians of the tribe who have to recount ancestral history during seances; in a sense they are 'elder statesmen' at the chief's court; and they are tribal politicians par excellence, responsible for the mystical sanction and official approval of a new chief at a time of succession. Less compromised than the chief, who was salaried by the white administration and therefore suspected of having divided loyalties, and professionally steeped in the customary laws of the ancestors, the *svikiro* was pre-eminently the person to verbalise opposition and lobby against unpopular measures introduced by local government, as when district commissioners opposed or ignored ancestral directives concerning the installation of new chiefs, or in boundary disputes.

Although not always effective, the psychological release of expressing communal frustration and criticism against the oppressor in the name of the mystical guardians of the land should not be underrated. In their defiance of white rule the *masvikiro* were reinforcing the bonds between the living and the living dead, thereby encouraging peasant communities to bear oppression with dignity and to keep up the resolve to seek liberation. In this respect the *svikiro* was a key mobiliser of resistance, a mainstay of customary law and traditional culture, and a healer of the mental malady of subservience and serfdom inflicted by white political domination.

After the suppression of African nationalist parties in 1964, spirit mediums remained on the whole unmolested, partly because they enjoyed the respect of black employees in government administration and in the police force, and partly because government policy respected the more traditional elements of Shona culture. Those mediums who took an interest in politics thus became the only force for national sentiments (Bourdillon 1982:265).

As black nationalism gained momentum in the rural areas and people started reaching back to their roots, spirit mediums increasingly promoted a grassroots re-evaluation and appreciation of a proud ancestral past. Obscure as it may have been at the time to the white administration, whose representatives invariably underestimated the political significance of traditional religion (Daneel 1970:34, 87; Ranger 1966:118), the combined influence of the senior *svikiro* and the messenger of the Mwari cult at the chief's court and elsewhere in their chiefdoms served to prepare the rural population for war. Mwari's oracular opposition to the injustice perpetrated by his *vazukuru* (sister's sons, that is the whites) against his black offspring (Daneel 1970:71f), combined with the opposition of the ancestral guardians to white exploitation of the lost lands, provided an unassailable sanction for revolt.

HEALING AND LIBERATION IN AICs

The AICs are not generally credited with having a liberation theology. Yet it is quite evident that ever since their inception in erstwhile Rhodesia early in the twentieth century, they spontaneously developed what one could call their own unique brand of *religio-cultural liberation*.

Their exodus from the religious white house of slavery was evidence of their emancipation from imperialist structures which the mission churches had maintained by means of funding and staffing. By ridding themselves of the trusteeship of Western churches, the Independents managed to shed austere, rational, and dogmatically 'correct' forms of worship and find their own religious identity in dramatic, emotionally uninhibited religious practices. Organisational emancipation led to liturgical innovation and transformation.

At the core of this process was a re-evaluation of indigenous culture and religion, as a result of which numerous rites became informed by the traditional worldview. This entailed either straightforward accommodation (for example the integration of ancestor veneration in the Ethiopian-type churches; cf Daneel 1973:64f) or confrontation and Christianising transformation in the Spirit-type churches. In the latter case the gospel message was introduced at an existential level in order to cater for African needs in a new way, just as the high-God cult, ancestor veneration, and magical rites had done in the traditional context. Prime examples of such transformation were the replacement of the high-God cult's rainmaking and related ecological functions with Zionist seed conferences (*ungano yembeu*) at the onset of the rainy season (Daneel 1974:104–109); the replacement of the key ancestral ritual of *kugadzira* (accommodating the deceased's spirit) by Spirit-type consolation (*runyaradzo*) ceremonies (Daneel 1974:116f); and prophetic concern for a Christianised and reconciliatory version of wizard eradication (Daneel 1974:278f).

Faith-healing practices, which featured so prominently as a recruitment factor during the period of rapid AIC growth from the 1930s to the 1960s, clearly reflect that religio-cultural liberation was not just a reaction against Western missionary control[4] and medical science, accompanied by uncritical affirmation of indigenous customs. It also brought liberation from the besetting fear of evil powers and life-threatening wizardry inculcated by traditional religion. The creativity and originality of Zionist and Apostolic prophetic healers lay in the genuine pastoral and psychological liberation they offered to patients afflicted by destructive forces. Their diagnoses were couched in intelligible terms, being solidly based on the traditional worldview and understanding of physical affliction (Daneel 1974:214f; 1989b:59–62). Prophetic therapy, in turn, demonstrated the protective and healing power of Christ and the Holy Spirit in vividly enacted purificatory or exorcist rites. Thus the Christian God was convincingly and visibly incarnated as one directly involved in the joys and woes of African society.

The notion of a personal God, a caring God with a black face, hands, and feet, was reinforced in the numerous prophetic healing colonies. Here the prophetic healers maintained close contact with their patients, giving them a sense of security and a new identity through regular laying on of hands, intercession, and counselling. Healing in the holy cities (popularly called Zion City, Moriah—after the biblical Mount Moriah—or Jerusalem) was holistic, encompassing all of life. Salvation unfolded not as a remote, future state of wellbeing, but as concrete healing here and now: psychosomatic healing of human beings, stewardship of nature, and even prophetic therapy for the stresses and strains of the conflict-laden interaction between tribal politics and white rule. In a very real way, therefore, the wide scope of prophetic activities at healing colonies implied healing of the earth, the *salvation of all creation* (Daneel 1991 passim).

The seeds of a Zionist theology of the environment were present all along in Mutendi's holy city. As founding leader of the Zion Christian Church (ZCC) in Zimbabwe, the 'man of God' took a keen interest in agricultural progress. Himself a master farmer and conservationist, he taught his followers the benefits of proper farming methods, combating soil erosion through the upkeep of contour ridges and the protection of water resources. His earthkeeping measures, moreover, perpetuated—in a Christianised form—the agro-religious cycle of the traditional Mwari cult. ZCC delegations from the surrounding districts were required to bring gifts when they came to request rain at Moriah, as the traditional *vanyai* did at the Matonjeni shrines. Then, if it did not rain, the 'man of God' would travel to drought-stricken areas to intercede for rain. Through his mutual aid scheme of maize distribution from church headquarters to outlying congregations he could, moreover, act as benefactor to the unfed. Even though Bishop Mutendi's agricultural and environmental policies suggest pragmatic motives of fostering improved farming methods, economic progress, and church growth through aid, Zionist steps towards more altruistic forms of nature conservation were taken even at that early stage; for instance through small-scale tree-planting projects.

Mutendi demonstrated that his church was not only concerned with religio-cultural liberation, was not just a prophetic 'hospital' for the physically afflicted; it also represented a formidable power for the healing of sociopolitical ills. At an early stage he entered the political arena by opposing the colonial administration's policy on education, land allocation, and religious issues. For this he was detained by the police several times. To his followers he became a Spirit-led Moses figure, champion of the oppressed. Like Shembe of the Zulu Nazarites in South Africa, Mutendi drew many chiefs and headmen into his church. Through numerous discussions about local district government at Zion City's supreme court and the appointment of Zionist prophets as advisors to the courts of affiliated chiefs, the Zionist bishop managed to secure considerable influence in tribal political affairs. Zion City became an information centre, a kind of religiopolitical governing and broadcasting house with a geographically widespread network of interaction, similar to that of the Mwari cult. During the 1950s and 1960s many Zionist chiefs openly stated that the power of the Holy Spirit, represented by supportive Zionist prophets, enabled them to cope—that is, to maintain some form of just rule and balance amid the complex and conflicting demands of white rule and black nationalism.

Just as Christ failed to introduce a messianic order which would satisfy Jewish nationalist aspirations, Mutendi did not promise another Rozvi confederation or a Zionist empire which would overthrow white rule. But throughout his life he set an example to the chiefs of how one could realistically cooperate with the rulers of the day without loss of dignity and how one could fearlessly resist unjust legislation and action even if this did not always bring about the desired results. In a sense his Zion City became to the chiefs a halfway house between white local government and African nationalist factions, a refuge from where they could subtly resist foreign influence without entirely jeopardising their position in relation to the white administration on which they depended financially. Like Isaiah Shembe did for his 'Israelites' in South Africa, Bishop Mutendi did for his Zionist followers, presenting them not with an indifferent, remote deity, but with 'a God who walks on feet and who heals with hands, and who can be known by men, as a God who loves and has compassion' (Sundkler 1961:278).

In the late sixties, the Apostles of Maranke (popularly known as the *vaPostori*, the largest AIC in Zimbabwe) voiced the mood of black nationalism in even more aggressive anti-white statements than the Zionist. Here the interjections during sermons were not 'Peace in Zion' or 'Joy be with you all' but, challengingly and stridently, 'Peace to us Africans!' and even, in some cases, 'Peace to Africans only!' Feelings of naked resentment surfaced in repeated accusations that the white race had killed Jesus and that the whites, in their oppression of the blacks, had deliberately repressed the message and benefits of the Holy Spirit.

The following excerpt from a sermon preached at the Pentecostal festivities of the *vaPostori* near Mutare in April 1966 illustrates Apostolic sentiments at the time:

> The true witnesses of Mwari were buried by the Europeans, until God gave them the task of witnessing to us, the Apostles of Africa. They killed Jesus and the early Apostles because they wanted to eliminate the church of the Holy Spirit. So God decided to send the church of the Holy Spirit to our race in Africa. Peace to Africa!

Racial bias and desire for a unique supernatural mandate for the church, free from white interference, were evident at the time in Apostolic sermons. They were delivered on the eve of *chimurenga*, when anxiety and uncertainty were rife and intimidation and detentions were becoming more frequent. Basically the Apostolic preachers aimed at reassuring their people. They were using the church as a place to vent their frustrations at white rule and were virtually claiming the work of the Holy Spirit exclusively for their liberationist cause.

It should be noted that the Zionist and Apostolic movements during the 1960s officially maintained a certain aloofness from politically organised violence and subversion. Bishop Mutendi even explicitly dissociated the ZCC from the then banned political parties, ZANU and ZAPU. Nevertheless, these churches gave full expression to African nationalist sentiments. They became propagators of equality between the races, the dignity of black Africans, and their ability to rule themselves. In doing so they sharpened the concept of a just God who sided with the oppressed and who, through his Spirit, could be counted upon to inspire the poor and the dispossessed in their struggle for the lost lands. At this stage, therefore, the prophetic contribution to political liberation, particularly in the rural context, lay in providing what was considered to be a sound, scripturally based legitimation and justification of the struggle.

THE ROLE OF RELIGION DURING THE LIBERATION STRUGGLE
(1965–1980)

TRADITIONAL RELIGION

The escalating crisis of *chimurenga* from the mid-sixties onwards fanned the resurgence of traditional religion which had been triggered by the rise of African nationalism. As Shamuyarira (quoted in Ranger 1968:635; also Huizer 1991:25) puts it:

The past heritage was revived through prayers and traditional singing, ancestral spirits were invoked to guide and lead the new nation. Christianity and civilisation took a back seat and new forms of worship and new attitudes were thrust forward dramatically . . . the spirit pervading the meetings was African and the desire was to put the twentieth century in an African context.

As resistance and political agitation turned into a full-scale liberation struggle, traditional religion inspired the guerrilla fighters, often informed and even directed strategic operations at the front, and did much to secure close cooperation between rural communities and fighters.

The Mwari Cult

In 1965 armed conflict broke out in rural areas. Joshua Nkomo, then leader of the banned ZAPU (Zimbabwe African People's Union), was confined to a camp for political prisoners at Gonakudzingwa. Mrs. Nkomo then sought counsel at the shrine of Wirirani. Having presented Mlimo with a sacrificial black ox and beer, she was told by the voice: 'Do not fear for your husband. I will look after him. Things will be settled very soon. But go and speak to the white man peacefully' (Kazembe, in *Drum*, October 1965; Daneel 1970:72). Like Mrs. Nkomo, many others travelled to Matonjeni at that time to attend cult ceremonies. The increasing popularity of the cult was demonstrated by the mass attendance of Africans at the October rain ceremony in 1967, on which occasion several black oxen were ritually slaughtered (*The Chronicle*, October 1967).

Mwari's propagation of peaceful negotiations in 1965 could have reflected the initial will of African nationalists to secure more rights for their people through political negotiation. The mood at Matonjeni, however, was changing. In 1967, when I personally attended a cult ceremony at the Wirirani shrine, Mwari launched into a scathing attack on Westernisation at the expense of customary law and beliefs:

'These young ones [Africans] who have been educated disobey the Karanga laws! They change the Karanga customs because they mix our laws with European customs . . . They ruin the country . . . We cannot govern the country according to European ways! . . . I [Mwari] do not want to speak to these Europeanised Africans. The Europeans are the children of my sister [*vazukuru*]. I love them, but with regard to this law, I have no need of them. I do not want them to approach this place where I live, because they do not act properly. They always fight with the country' (Daneel 1970:78,79).

It was remarkable that at such a time Mwari should qualify black-white relations in terms of the *sekuru-muzukuru* (maternal uncle-sister's son) relationship, which in Shona kinship is the most cordial relationship, least dominated by the seniority principle. Possibly this metaphor was used because of the unusual circumstance of a white attending the oracle. On the other hand Mwari may have been revealing what he/she considered to be the ideal for black-white relations. Mwari even indicated a certain fondness for the 'white *vazukuru*,' who were granted the customary privileges in the black uncle's house and yard. But the *vazukuru* did not observe the prescribed tribal code of proper conduct. They did not simply freely use their black uncle's (*sekuru*'s) possessions, as they were entitled to do, but actually alienated large parts of the land which Mwari owned and which his/her black sons controlled by virtue of their common descent and inheritance. Worst of all, the white 'nephews' denied their black uncles the fundamental rights and dignity to which the latter are entitled according to age-old custom. In a profound manner, therefore, Mwari was urging his/her white 'nephews' on the eve of war to heed the laws of the land and thus to help create a situation of peaceful co-existence safeguarded by the stability of the Shona kinship structure. At the same time Mwari in no uncertain manner rebuked and warned his/her wayward nephews (Daneel 1970:84).

Because of the secret nature of cult messages, little accurate information is available about the exact contents of messages transmitted at the Mwari shrines during the *chimurenga* period. Cult messengers throughout Masvingo Province, the priestly colony at Dzilo, as well as the priestess Gogo Intombiyamazulu at the Vembe shrine confirm, however, that Mwari's message did eventually become a full declaration of war.[5] Mwari is reported to have engaged in oracular intervention, the gist of his/her pronouncements being full condonation of militancy and support for the ZANLA and ZIPRA fighters in their struggle to regain the lost lands throughout the country; divine confirmation that this time *chimurenga* would succeed in replacing colonial rule with black majority rule; and a reminder to blacks generally that the successful outcome of the struggle hinged on honouring traditional customs, at the core of which lay the combined powers of Mwari and the ancestors.

From a cult point of view, one must distinguish between the different types of delegations that arrived at the Dzilo shrine. Many of the regular messengers (*vanyai*) were stepping up the frequency of their visits, carrying supportive oracular messages back to their local constituencies; senior officials of the black nationalist parties either visited or sent delegations; ZIPRA and ZANLA fighters operating in the Matopo area regularly consulted Mwari, and ZANLA emissaries from their operational headquarters at Chimoio in Mozambique reportedly visited the shrines to obtain mystical directives for the conduct of war. According to vaChinovuriri, who acted as go-between between spirit mediums and ZANLA high command at Chimoio, Mozambique, during the war, large ZANLA delegations were sent periodically to confer with ritual officiants at the holy places in Zimbabwe.

As the war escalated, cult messengers established more regular contact between district communities, the fighters they harboured, and the Matopo priestly colonies (according to traditional informants in the Zimuto, Gutu, Zvishavane, NaJena, Mwenezi, and Chivi districts). The following account by P, *munyai* of Chief Maranda in the Mwenezi district, gives an impression of the experiences of cult messengers in the outlying districts:

I kept going to Matonjeni regularly during the war. Chief Maranda sent me to ask for rain and to tell Mwari we are suffering in this war, when will the suffering stop? At the caves Mwari said: 'I also see the suffering. There is nothing we can do to prevent it. Venerate your ancestors! Tell Chief Maranda to venerate the ancestors and he will see the misery stop!' We obeyed and eventually the situation improved . . . Mwari always protected me during my travels [on foot] to Matonjeni. During the war the shrines were both holy and dangerous: holy, because of Mwari's presence; dangerous because so many people of different tribes congregated there for advice . . . When you go to Mantonjeni as a *munyai* you represent all of Zimbabwe, knowing that the message from the Rock is that of your great Mudzimu— the mediator between God and humans. Mwari's pronouncements are heard from the rocks both at Mantonjeni and at Great Zimbabwe. You can see it in the lightning crossing between the two places (Interview at Dzilo shrine, 13 February 1989).

From this account it is clear that in outlying areas regular contact with the shrine served to encourage both the local population and the fighters during a protracted period of desperation and suffering. At the shrines Mwari kept telling his/her people that the war effort would be successful. The *vanyai*, moreover, were instrumental in upholding ancestral beliefs and thus bolstering the authority of the spirit mediums by providing them with divine sanction.

Territorially widespread as the cult network was, it could obviously not maintain the same close interaction as it had done in the 1896 rebellion. Guerrilla offensives, apart from ones launched close to the shrines, were therefore not directed or instigated directly by the oracle of Mwari. Nevertheless, the indications are that the close involvement and pervasive presence of Mwari—in his/her African guise—was unquestioned in the minds of many of the fighters. The conception was that Mwari presided over the war council (*dare rechimurenga*) in the spirit world. Senior representatives on the council were, first of all, national hero ancestors like Chaminuka, Nehanda, and Kaguwi. Then came the *mhondoro* or founder ancestors—the senior guardians of the land (*varidzi venyika*) of each area or spirit province. In the spirit world the final authority behind the ZANLA and ZIPRA high commands and their fighting forces was the *dare rechimurenga*.

The picture is one of a liberator God, a God of justice, who hesitated neither to declare war on behalf of his/her oppressed people, nor to intervene militantly and directly in a protracted struggle through a spirit war council. Thus, in a national crisis, the deity of rain and fertility turned into a warlord in order to recapture the lost lands of the dispossessed and re-establish peaceful co-existence and unity amongst all his/her subjects. In both the sociopolitical and the ecological context, then, Mwari manifested him/herself as the liberator and healer of the land.

The Spirit Mediums

The link between the spirit war council and the fighting cadres was the spirit mediums. The most striking features of the medium involvement which evolved during the struggle are the following. First, at the front a kind of spontaneous war-mediumship emerged as large numbers of fighters became hosts to ancestral spirits. They would become possessed prior to or even during contact with the enemy to provide on-the-spot guidance for action in the form of revelations about enemy movements and strategic positions; mortar men and bazooka launchers would go into trance before they could accurately direct their missiles at enemy targets; and, in critical situations such as ambushes, guerrillas would become possessed spontaneously and then rescue the fighters from their predicament.

Second, senior spirit mediums in each district operated from their village bases when liaising between the spirit war council and guerrillas in the district. One such medium was vaZarira, female *svikiro* of Murinye, founder of one of the leading Duma chieftaincies. She gave the following (abridged) account of her wartime duties:

> The fighters required me to meet them out in the bush. But *sekuru* [literally 'grandfather,' that is possessing spirit] Murinye revealed that all meetings with the *vakomana vesango* had to take place at my homestead. So they came, sometimes groups of twenty-five at a time . . . We taught them about what lay ahead, what areas to avoid, where to go . . . They would come back regularly to consult the *midzimu*. As they seldom offered the spirit anything, I provided them with ancestral snuff (*bute*) . . . I [the spirit of Murinye] disciplined those comrades who had transgressed the laws of war by sleeping with women. My *mudzimu* told the comrades not to kill innocent people, wrongly accused of witchcraft [that is, collaboration with the enemy], because the blood of the innocent would plague us, the mediums. It would also cause the angered ancestors to withdraw their protection from the fighters . . . My *mudzimu* told the comrades that the *masvikiro* are cooperating with God because Musikavanhu, the creator, is one with Mwari of the Bible. Mwari, we [the mediums] said, was on our side as he was always on the side of the oppressed in the Bible. In the Bible it says that if you invade/take someone's land you are seeking your own death . . .

This narrative clearly illustrates the ancestrally derived authority of the *svikiro* over the fighters. It is the ancestor who determines the venue for consultation, not the fighters. It is the ancestor(s) who lay(s) down the laws of war, disciplines the unruly, urges moderation in dealing with suspect villagers, and verbalises both the spiritual justification for war and the constraints.

Third, many *masvikiro* were integrated with guerrilla detachments, either temporarily or on a regular basis. They moved around with the fighters in their own spirit provinces, throughout their districts and over even wider areas, providing them with ancestral directives for field operations whenever possible. Others were at the front, liaising between rural communities and guerrillas, arranging traditional rituals for the struggle, mobilising the populace, and mediating ancestral directives and control during *pungwe* meetings.

Fourth, one should also note the role of spirit mediums in the ZANLA camps in Mozambique. Here the mediums represented the concerted spirit war council. At Chimoio, for instance, groups of mediums resided at the four points of the compass, from where they regularly sent official go-betweens to convey ancestral directives from the spirit war council directly to ZANLA high command. Haurovi Chinovuriri, who was to become a leading figure in our traditionalist ecological movement, was one of these go-betweens at Chimoio. He kept a careful record of all the messages sent by the ancestral war council, through their mediums, to Mugabe's guerrilla commanders.

The main functions of the spirit mediums in the rural districts where fighting was taking place were the following: (1) establishing regular contact between the ancestral war council and guerrilla forces; (2) providing the fighters with proper ancestral snuff (*bute*), which they had to offer regularly to the *midzimu* in return for mystical protection, inspiration, and guidance. In this capacity the spirit mediums were the recognised agents of the revival of traditional religion; (3) helping the fighters work out effective operational strategies based on their intimate knowledge of the terrain and their extraperception of enemy movements in their districts; (4) laying down the ancestral laws for the struggle and teaching the fighters how to obtain advance information about enemy movements by observing the behaviour of certain birds and animals (tortoises, bateleur eagles, etc.) considered to be emissaries of the ancestors. This, and the value of dense bush as cover, made the guerrillas particularly sensitive to ecology generally and, after the war, also to the conservation of wildlife; and (5) using their tribal political influence in their communities to ensure collaboration between the *povo* and the guerrillas. The indications are that it was only after 1972, when the guerrillas in rural districts deliberately started using allegiance to the *masvikiro* as a 'doorway' to the people, that they gained massive support at grassroots level—a factor which ultimately swung the struggle in favour of the bushfighters.

The *masvikiro* also played a significant role in secret *pungwe* meetings. There they proclaimed—often in a state of possession—the claims of the guardian ancestors to the lost lands. At the grassroots of peasant society these claims apparently had greater mobilising and inspirational power than the socialist-Marxist ideology taught by the guerrilla political commissars on the same occasions.

Another important function of the *masvikiro* at *pungwe* meetings was to help identify, through ancestral intervention, the real traitors to the cause, the enemy collaborators. In this respect *pungwe* frequently served as religious cleansing operations, analogous to traditional wizardry eradication. The lives of many suspects were at stake. A trusted medium or group of *masvikiro* would pass judgment on behalf of the ancestors on the guilt or innocence of the suspected wizard (*muroyi*), resulting in execution, disciplinary measures, or acquittal.

An accurate assessment of the roles played by local chiefs remains problematical. Some of them moved to the towns to avoid harassment. Others were suspected of collaboration with the white colonial administration.[6] To my knowledge only two chiefs (Negovano and Mabika) in Masvingo Province were executed for alleged collaboration with the white administration against the liberation forces. Chinowawa's account of the situation in Zimuto, moreover, contains a number of cases of close collaboration among chiefs, spirit mediums, and guerrillas, partic-ularly in the field of traditional ritual. Besides opposition to and elimination of anti-*chimurenga* chiefs, there was therefore also an extension of the traditional joint responsibility for the land of both chiefs and *masvikiro*. The same type of re-sponsibility is resurfacing in traditionalist earthkeeping programmes.

A surprising development was the explicit exclusion of *nganga* assistance at the battlefront. Most ex-guerrilla commanders I have spoken to claimed that *chimurenga* espoused a form of ancestor veneration which eschewed magical practice and precluded *nganga* participation. As it was not possible for them to identify *nganga* who engaged in secret wizardry practices, and as they were con-stantly under threat of being poisoned by villagers on whom they were dependent for food, they tended to avoid *nganga* at the front. The use of any form of magic by guerrillas was condemned. Wounded guerrillas could only be treated by trained medical officers in the field, in hospitals, or by receiving herbal medicine or symbolic snuff from recognised *masvikiro* and faith-healing from AIC healers.

The exclusion of *nganga* is a controversial issue, meriting further study. I am not sure, for instance, whether this was not a provincial rather than a universal *chimurenga* phenomenon. I mention it here mainly because earth-healing activi-ties undertaken jointly by *masvikiro*, chiefs, and ex-combatants in Masvingo Province after Independence perpetuated the *chimurenga* tradition of excluding *nganga* participation. Whatever the roles played by *nganga* during the struggle, there can be little doubt that the traditional spiritual agencies which were a driv-ing force at the very core of *chimurenga* motivation and military offensives were the deity of Zimbabwe, Mwari—the liberator god of the oppressed—and the an-cestral guardians of the land who directed and protected fighters and harassed communities. Thus the all-embracing purpose of healing the earth through recla-mation of the lost lands was fulfilled.

THE AFRICAN INITIATED CHURCHES

The role of the Independent Churches in the liberation history of Zimbabwe still has to be written. For members of both Mission and Independent Churches it was largely a matter of surviving between the Scylla of the Rhodesian forces and the Charybdis of the freedom fighters. Notwithstanding the pressures they were sub-jected to, the Independent Churches increasingly supported the liberation strug-gle. Bishop Mutendi's overt criticism of ZANU and ZAPU during the late sixties proved to be quite misleading in view of prophetic developments in the 1970s. His early public renunciations of radicalised politics, presumably for the benefit of the Central Intelligence Department (CID) whom he knew to be monitoring his sermons, belied the direct assistance eventually given by ZCC congregations to the guerrilla fighters.

But the ZCC was not the only AIC which actively supported the liberation struggle in Zimbabwe. *Ndaza* Zionist and Maranke's Apostolic prophets through-out Masvingo Province and further afield played an increasingly prominent role at the war front as *chimurenga* escalated countrywide into a full-blown bush war. Just as traditional spirit mediums were providing the guerrillas with mystical ancestral guidance, prophets were also moving around with the fighters at the front, prophesying to them in the name of the Holy Spirit about enemy movements and other security matters. Thus the diagnostic and revelatory services of the prophets helped to determine strategy as the guerrillas improvised their tactics from one situation to the next. Like the traditional *varidzi venyika*, the Holy Spirit was considered to be a kind of 'guardian of the land' against the white intruders. It depended on the predilections of Christian and non-Christian guerrilla commanders whether they opted for traditionalist or Christian prophetic guidance. Some of them made use of both, cross-checking one against the other.

Apart from the 'fighter prophets' operating at the front, there were also those who stayed at their church headquarters or healing colonies, from where they provided the guerrillas with information, pastoral support, and faith-healing services. Battle-fatigued or wounded fighters sometimes lived at healing colonies or in secret caves nearby in order to receive regular healing treatment. There are known instances of mentally disordered freedom fighters who were admitted to ZCC and other Zionist communities for protracted periods until they recovered.

Possibly the most important *chimurenga* function fulfilled by some AIC prophets—similar to that of their *svikiro* counterparts—was to assist in community-cleansing operations during *pungwe* meetings. They, too, had to help the guerrillas to determine who were the sell-outs, the traitors to the cause, and their work in this context was also expressed in the traditional idiom of tracing wizards. Ritual affirmation or repudiation of *uroyi* charges in this instance was ascribed to revelations of the Holy Spirit. Thus the Holy Spirit of the AIC prophets was publicly seen to act radically and judgementally against opponents of *chimurenga*.

The role of prophets in *pungwe* courts could raise critical questions about arbitrary judgements, executions, and possible misrepresentation of the work of the Holy Spirit. In fairness, however, one should consider that it was in this very context that the Spirit usually revealed him/herself to suspect members of the community as a life-giving and protective force. I have established beyond doubt that prophets were often instrumental in preventing executions whenever it was apparent that villagers were using the *pungwe* to get rid of people they resented. In numerous cases suspect villagers were actually ordered to go and live in prophetic healing colonies, where the scrutinising, revelatory, and disciplinary power of the Holy Spirit could, over a period of time, bring the culprits into line with the requirements of their society—hence, by appealing to the ultimate authority of the Holy Spirit, prophets managed to introduce an element of moderation and sanity, often at grave personal risk, into *pungwe* situations where flaring emotions and the need for revenge in a war-torn society could easily claim innocent lives.

In Gutu South three *Ndaza* Zionist leaders rose to prominence through their active support of the guerrilla fighters. They were Peter Muponesi, a roving prophet operating in Gutu and Bikita; and Prophet Mashereketo and Bishop Prophet Musariri Dhliwayo, both of whom lived in Vunjere, south of Mount Rasa, which the guerrillas declared a 'liberated zone.' Our study focuses on the third of these prophets.[7]

Musariri, an illiterate orphan, was chronically ill as a youngster. He only started experiencing deliverance and good health once he joined the Zion Apostolic Church, and established himself as a prophet and preacher after he had taught himself to read and write. Then he followed a secessionist leader, Chindoza, into the Zion Apostolic Church in Patmos and settled on a small farm near Zinhata township in Vunjere (Gutu South), where he ministered to a few small Zionist congregations.

During the years preceding *chimurenga*, Zion in Patmos became a flourishing faith-healing colony. The sick and afflicted kept flocking to the popular bishop-prophet. The farm became a refuge for the needy, reflecting the compassion of Mwari. Harmony prevailed and the number of Zionist families grew. The Holy Spirit moved mightily in the healing miracles performed, in the rainclouds, the seed sown, the crops reaped. Growing herds of cattle, sheep, and goats showed that Christ's salvation was not reserved for the distant heavens. Patmos was the Zionists' own place of milk and honey, a veritable little black Canaan in Vunjere until the fury of *chimurenga* struck, with the arrival of the first five guerrillas at Zion in Patmos in 1977. Soon the exacting price of liberating Zimbabwe's lost lands was felt in Zion. Musariri saw his own prophecies of suffering come true in the little settlement. The guerrillas camping in the neighbourhood made increasing demands on the farm's produce. First the fowl run, then the goat, sheep, and cattle kraals were emptied, until only a few cows remained to provide the fighters with milk. Zion became destitute.

Nonetheless, Patmos kept functioning as a refuge for troubled members of the community, both guerrillas and *povo*. Sick and wounded comrades came to Musariri for prophetic diagnosis, prayer, and laying on of hands. There was no rest for the man of God. He prayed daily for the safety of the fighters. He prophesied about enemy movements and how these could be countered. He warned the guerrillas of ambushes. He sprinkled their AK-47 rifles with holy water, declaring their campaign a holy war against oppression. He preached that Mwari was on the side of the oppressed, that his 'whore son' Jesus (which was how many guerrillas referred to the alleged saviour of the white intruders) was the true liberator of all humankind. At night he sometimes prayed with Comrade Nyika for a speedy end to the suffering of the war. Patmos became a kind of operational base from where the liberation war was directed, guided, and inspired by the powerful Holy Spirit of Zion.

Pungwe meetings were a combination of political instruction and kangaroo court judgement. Musariri had no option but to participate. He was cast in the role of judge on account of the divine power and illumination he stood for. Depending on what the Spirit revealed in each situation, he found himself prosecuting or defending. Altogether too much was expected of him. He had to fast and pray constantly to stay in touch with the promptings of the Holy Spirit.

In a precarious balance of interests between the *povo*, who desperately tried to avoid victimisation, and the guerrillas, who were determined to purge society of the wizardry of collaborating with the enemy, the prophet found himself under constant pressure. A serious mistake could be costly, if not fatal. He was in fact empowered to do what he had never aspired to: in the name of the Spirit to take or to save lives.

Two *pungwe* meetings stood out in Musariri's war career—one an occasion when life was preserved, the other culminating in death (Gumbo/Daneel 1995, chapter 9). The first concerned Guymore, who had managed to escape from the Musukutwa battle scene with both his arms shattered. For months he received treatment in the Vunjere caves, where guerrilla medical officers, spirit mediums, and Zionist faith-healers tried in vain to check the spreading gangrene. Musariri himself spent many hours in the caves with the wounded commander, urging him in vain to stop his heavy drinking so as to stand a better chance of recovery. Eventually he died.

After the commander's death his fellow fighters cried out for revenge. The rumour was spread that members of the family which had tended the stricken hero towards the end had poisoned his tea. It was a nasty situation. When Musariri arrived at the *pungwe* the family had already been rounded up amidst vengeful shouts of 'Down with the wizards!' A family massacre appeared inevitable.

It was in this explosive situation that the Holy Spirit took hold of Musariri and revealed, first of all, that because of the sacrifices of fighters like Guymore the war would soon be won by black Zimbabwe; secondly, that no poison had been added to the deceased commander's food or drink and consequently there were to be no reprisals; and, in the third place, that the accused family were to reside for some time in Patmos so that they could receive instruction in the ways of Mwari. No question was raised about the authenticity of, and divine authority behind, the prophecy. The spectacle of glossolalia, prophetic gestures in a flurry of billowing vestments, preaching, and prophecy served to subdue the angry and grief-stricken comrades. A family was saved. Zion in Patmos satisfied the comrades that even if there were a hidden threat to the cause, it would be neutralised by the penetrating cleansing activity of the Spirit of Zion.

The other *pungwe* was an even more serious situation. Four fighters had died of food poisoning after being fed by the *povo*. When Musariri arrived on the scene, one of the fighters was still thrashing about in poison-induced spasms. Shortly afterwards he died. An ugly mood prevailed as the remaining fighters rounded up township and village people. A punitive massacre was about to take place among the terrified people. Only at great risk to himself did the prophet intervene. He requested a *pungwe* for the next morning on the pretext of first having another *Ndaza* prophet summoned to help him identify the *varoyi* responsible for the poisoning. This was agreed to, thus averting a random gunning down of civilians.

There was, however, no way of avoiding or postponing prosecution. The next morning the two prophets, after a night of fasting and prayer, pointed out seven *varoyi*. They were the women who had allegedly prepared the poisoned eggs served to the fighters. That, at least, was what the two prophets independently claimed the Spirit had revealed to them. All seven were summarily executed by the fighters. Although Prophet Musariri was convinced that he was only the instrument of a divine verdict, and thankful as he was that the community had escaped an even worse fate, the faces of the seven witches haunted his thoughts ever after.

During *chimurenga* Zion in Patmos evolved its own liberation theology—not detailed in books but a living reality, emanating directly from the Bible, to be danced and preached regularly in the midst of crisis. A central figure in this theology was the biblical liberator, Moses. Like many other black prophets, Musariri was considered by his subordinate clergy to be the Moses of the Zimbabwean black Israelites. Exodus 3 became the cornerstone of God's war message. As God had called Moses from the burning bush, so he summoned the black prophets of Zion. Only now *all* of Zion responded by taking off their shoes as Moses had done. This is still the practice today at all ceremonies of worship. Through this act Zionists express their total submission to the will and the war-call of Mwari. It is Mwari who creates, gives life and declares war. Mwari saw the plight of his black Israelites and he authorised and directed *chimurenga*, as he also directed Moses' every step. Through Mwari's inspiration Prophet Musariri, like Moses, laid down the laws of war.

The latter theme was worked out around Deuteronomy 20:2 and 3, which describes the role of an Israelite priest at the onset of war. Musariri and his preachers called on the men at arms to consult the man of God, to heed his divinely inspired laws prior to action. Focal in the biblical-cum-Zionist war laws was the message of Deuteronomy 20:10: 'When you draw near to a city to fight against it, offer terms of peace to it.' This text was contextualised to apply to the relations between guerrillas and villagers, with a built-in plea for moderation and tolerance. The spilling of innocent blood had to be prevented at all costs, as in Musariri's role as the preserver of innocent lives in the *pungwe* context.

The mandate of the black prophets lay in Christ's call to mission and discipleship (Mk 16:15–18). In Patmos the believers courageously proclaimed that Jesus was not really the son of a whore but the saviour of all people. In Africa he is the champion of the oppressed. He stands in the line of Moses and David. He led the oppressed black Israelites from the white house of slavery. His Spirit is the true *Mweya Mutsvene*, the Spirit of Zion, who showed the fighters how to conduct Mwari's war.

Musariri's prophetic activities appear to be representative of those of many AIC war prophets. They lead one to surmise that the pneumatology evolved by the Spirit-type churches during the struggle presented a warring Spirit, deeply involved in a just cause, inspiring the fighting cadres to overthrow the oppressive rule of an alien enemy, as well as resisting the enemy within their own ranks which, if left unchecked, could destroy innocent lives. During the war AIC liberation theology led to a close identification of the concepts of salvation and political liberation. Yet the struggle for political and socioeconomic liberation never obscured the vision of God's salvation in terms of eternal life. The perception and experience of the Spirit's direct involvement in providing peace and improved living conditions in this existence were certainly broadened and deepened, but this did not obscure the good news of future salvation. Many guerrilla fighters and people who sought refuge in the prophetic healing colonies were evangelised by the prophets whose assistance they sought. To such converts prophetic Spirit manifestations certainly meant both liberation from unjust rule and individual salvation, to be realised in the future.

Despite religious revival and church growth during the war years, there were also signs of retrogression. Paradoxically, greater concern for a liberating Spirit was often offset by a submerged or diminished Christology in both AICs and mainline churches. Not all church leaders had the courage or the standing among guerrilla fighters to publicly proclaim the saviourhood of Christ, as Musariri did, because the renaissance of traditional religion made many of the bush fighters oppose Christianity. Some of their units destroyed or closed down church buildings. They saw Jesus as the white man's god, the epitome of oppressive rule (Daneel 1989b:72f). Consequently they operated under the slogan, *Pasi na Jesu!* (Down with Jesus!). Many church leaders and congregations who continued to profess their faith in Jesus Christ had their Bibles and vestments burnt publicly by the guerrillas. Some were martyred, others were forced underground. Many church leaders today frankly admit that during the war years they continued to preach Mwari the Father, the one God who was known in Africa long before Christianity came, and that they prophesied or acted in the Spirit, but that they seldom spoke about Christ for fear of being branded traitors to the cause.

In view of all this it is clear that the Zimbabwean AICs made a significant contribution to the second *chimurenga*, and that many of them are justly proud of their share in the reconquest of the lost lands and the attainment of political independence. Their liberation theology, by virtue of its holistic nature, already contained the seeds of environmental engagement.

Mamoyo, the Rozvi mbonga who acted the voice of Mwari at the Wirirani shrine in 1967.

Vondo Mukozho, Mwari cult messenger who accompanied the author in 1967 to the Wirirani shrine in the Matopo Hills.

The cave-shrine at Wirirani.

Pfupajena laments the ravishing of the communal lands in the distance during the discussion that triggered "The War of the Trees."

Lydia Chabata, the AZSM's first nursery-keeper, explains her work to a delegation of earthkeeping chiefs and mediums assembled at the movement's first nursery behind the author's residence where the movement began.

Spirit mediums Tovera (left) and Mukaro acting out the mystical collection of seedlings during a tree-planting ceremony.

Spirit medium Tovera stands guard over the seedlings during the ritual proceedings. The bird in his hands represents ancestral presence and protection of the environment.

"Forward the War of the Trees!" Spirit medium vaZarira Marambatemwa encourages
fellow earthkeepers to persevere in the struggle.

CHAPTER 3

Earthkeepers' Declaration of War

ZIMBABWE IN ECOLOGICAL CRISIS AFTER INDEPENDENCE

Since Independence in 1980 the traditional religio-cultural revival has continued. In contrast to the colonial period, ancestor veneration has now assumed great prominence at public occasions, in religious instruction in schools, in church ceremonies, and at ceremonies commemorating the struggle held annually at heroes' acres throughout the country. The Mwari cult has expanded its sphere of influence, becoming less secret and more easily accessible to noncultists from further afield than before 1980. It has also become more directly involved in national politics through the petitions of senior politicians. It would seem, for example, that Mwari's oracular views were solicited during the period when reconciliation was being negotiated between ZANU and ZAPU. Even business delegations from as far afield as Lusaka in the north and Johannesburg in the south were reported (in a series of research interviews conducted at the shrine, 1988–1990) to have visited the Dzilo shrine to consult the oracle about business ventures. Traditionally conservative as it still is, the cult is apparently adapting to modernisation, expanding its services to meet the needs of urban society as well.

The imposition of a socialist-Marxist model of local government in the rural areas immediately after Independence curtailed the land allocation and customary judicial powers of chiefs. Consequently the positions of both chiefs and *masvikiro*, which were always closely linked in tribal politics, were downgraded and they lost some prestige. The *masvikiro* in particular, after their rise to national eminence as *chimurenga* heroes, soon became frustrated with their relative obscurity in the postwar period. The new political system, they felt, did not accord them sufficient recognition for the key roles they had played in the liberation struggle. Neither could they exercise effective spiritual authority over modern processes of land and community development. The rules of the game were changing and they had neither the funds nor the power of a common front to continue having a meaningful impact on national affairs.

A decade after Independence, therefore, many tribal dignitaries found themselves relatively isolated and despondent. Despite the government's gradual restoration of some of the chiefs' former judicial powers, they felt powerless to do much about the problems of their people—continuing landlessness, poverty, increasing population pressure on the already overcrowded communal lands, deterioration of the environment resulting in scarcities of fuelwood and poor crop yields, and so on. Thus they were psychologically primed for concerted action aimed at effectively addressing political and environmental issues and regaining some of their former national influence and prestige. This was how notions of re-grouping in an ecological association started taking concrete shape.

By comparison, the AICs in Masvingo Province found themselves in a much more advantageous position in the postwar period. As far back as 1972 they had formed an association through which they could raise funds and engage in concerted action: an ecumenical council of Independent Churches called *Fambidzano*. (For a comprehensive description of the history and activities of *Fambidzano*, see Daneel 1989a.) Consequently they could increasingly devote their attention to development projects. Quite a number of *Fambidzano*'s member churches received funds for community development and vocational training centres, small-scale industries such as carpentry and clothing factories, and agricultural and water projects.

Thus the focus of the AICs in the postwar situation shifted significantly from political to socioeconomic liberation. The Holy Spirit was increasingly seen as the liberator from poverty and economic despair, hence as intimately involved, through the AICs, in nation building. In this phase development projects and even educational centres at AIC headquarters—such as the multi-million dollar college erected by Bishop Nehemiah Mutendi, son of and successor to the late Samuel Mutendi, at Zion City in the Bikita district—became signs of God's blessing on his people, his concretised salvation in black holy cities. This was not an entirely new idea. It was rather the practical extension of a pneumatological trend already manifest in earlier times, namely the Holy Spirit's function as healer and life-giver, holistically encompassing everything that affects human wellbeing.

These post-Independence developments in both traditional religion and the AICs became apparent to me in the course of renewed empirical research in Zimbabwe from 1984 onwards. As founder of *Fambidzano*, and in the 1980s still honorary director of this movement, I was involved in raising funds for and implementing the Conference's first development programmes. It was soon evident, however, that development and so-called economic progress were not necessarily nature-friendly and that the prioritising of human liberation easily led to, or became an excuse for, over-exploitation of the environment. For all their holistic healing activities, the AICs apparently shared with the rest of Christianity a limited perception of the grace of God—grace which encompasses all creation as God's gift. During my discussions with AIC leaders we agreed that we had been unworthy of this gift. We had to confess, in the words of Carmody (1983:79), that 'the ruin of nature and the denial of God go hand in hand, because both over-exalt human beings.'

So the conviction grew among us Independents that we had to do something about the environment. It was felt, for example, that—while still seeing the Holy Spirit as saviour, liberator, and healer against the *chimurenga* background—we had to move from a predominantly anthropocentric and therefore exploitive soteriology towards a more universal, cosmic, and, by implication, altruistic approach which proclaims and promotes justice, peace and salvation for all of creation. Such a broadened soteriology would entail a perception of the Holy Spirit as Earthkeeper and translate into a church praxis of ecological reform.

Discussions with traditionalists—particularly the *masvikiro*, chiefs and ex-combatants, many of whom had played key roles in *chimurenga*—increasingly led to a reconsideration of the lost lands. My research into *chimurenga* convinced me that *chimurenga* was far from over. The lost lands had been politically reconquered, but ecologically they were being lost all over again. Ecological reform in the communal lands was essential to stem the process of deforestation and threatening desertification which was annually laying bare some 3 to 4 per cent of the country's total land surface. The traditionalists agreed with me that in postwar Zimbabwe liberation of the lost lands had taken the form of massive mobilisation of peasant communities to join in tree planting, wildlife conservation and the protection of water resources. If we were really going to heal the earth as a form of extended *chimurenga*, what better strategy than that of channeling Africa's religious genius and philosophy into the field of ecological reform? And what better task force than *chimurenga*'s mobilisers of the *povo*—who, as indicated above, were psychologically primed for constructive national action? What better ecologists than the traditionalists who were kept aware by the oracular Mwari and their ancestral guardians of the suffering and mindless exploitation of the earth? Who in the ravished land could better understand the following gut feeling?

> 'From the masses to the masses' the most
> Revolutionary consciousness is to be found
> Among the most ruthlessly exploited classes:
> Animals, trees, water, air, grasses.
> Gary Snyder

In 1988 our thinking on these lines crystallised into action: we declared war on deforestation and on ecological destruction generally. At our meetings the slogans *'Pamberi nehondo yemiti!'* and *'Ngatifukidze nyika!'* (Forward the war of the trees! Let us clothe the earth!) were coined and soon became the rallying cries of our struggle. *Chimurenga* resumed; the old and new forces of liberation were invoked, remobilised. At least, that is how our growing band of earthkeepers interpreted the environmental struggle in which we engaged. Only now the quest for the lost lands was no longer directed to political liberation and supremacy but to healing the wounded land.

This commitment led to the establishment of three interrelated institutions to guide and give continuity to escalating ecological activities in the rural communities of Masvingo Province. The umbrella organisation, responsible for finance, ecological policy and implementation, research, and conscientisation, is Zimbabwean Institute for Religious Research and Ecological Conservation (ZIRRCON). It evolved out of my original team of field research workers, who cooperate with ecologists and senior members of two sister organisations: Association of Zimbabwean Traditional Ecologists (AZTREC) for traditionalists, and the Association of African Earthkeeping Churches (AAEC) for the AICs.

The chronology of institutional development is as follows. In 1988 I invited the traditionalists to launch a new environmental movement in collaboration with my research team. Out of this joint endeavour grew the Association of Zimbabwean Spirit Mediums (AZSM), which in due course was renamed the Association of Zimbabwean Traditional Ecologists (AZTREC). During this formative period of constitutional and administrative development the pivotal role of my research team in the establishment of the new movement, together with its ongoing research programme, called for institutional redefinition. Hence the name 'ZIRRCON' was chosen to designate an organisational entity which antedated the existence of AZTREC yet expanded and gained influence in tandem with the latter. Attempts at negotiating an earthkeeping commitment with *Fambidzano* delayed the full-scale participation of AICs. As a result the AAEC was only formed in 1991.

There was nothing particularly new in our attempts to develop a 'green environment' in Zimbabwe. Other environmentally concerned organizations such as Environment and Development Activities (ENDA), Save the Children (REDD BARNA), and Coordinated Agricultural Rural Development (CARD) were already conducting tree-planting operations in the communal lands at the time when we launched our green revolution. Besides, government institutions such as the Forestry Commission, the Natural Resources Board, and Agritex have long been engaged in agricultural and environmental conservation activities. We were soon to cooperate and liaise with these agencies. We knew we would be operating in harmony with broad national policy, manifested in such moves as the institution of a national tree-planting day. Indeed, as soon as we were in a position to do so, we actively supported this annual drive, both by supplying seedlings and by mobilising grassroots communities to intensify their participation. Government ministers and senior officials repeatedly expressed public appreciation for these contributions.

What is decidedly new in our movement, however, is the conviction that the same spiritual forces which were so decisive in the *chimurenga* struggle are equally significant in the current ecological liberation/healing struggle, spurring on the masses to engage in sustained and meaningful environmental action. Ours, therefore, is a conscious, innovative attempt to harness the traditionalist and Christian religious heritage, specifically in relation to the multifaceted concept of national liberation and the historical struggle to achieve it. Accordingly our emphasis is on the empowerment of religious key figures—spirit mediums and church prophets in particular—through funding, organisational structures, conscientisation, and joint ecological ventures, with a view to spreading the nascent 'greening-of-Africa' revolution beyond elitist circles to become truly a people's movement.

The description of institutional formation and ecological activities in the rest of this chapter focuses mainly on the inception and early development of our earthkeeping movement.

THE ASSOCIATION OF ZIMBABWEAN TRADITIONAL ECOLOGISTS

THE DISCUSSION THAT TRIGGERED THE 'WAR OF THE TREES'

On a hot afternoon in 1987 I was sitting in one of the guerrilla *poshitos* (hiding places) high up the slopes of a mountain behind *svikiro* Mapfumo Pfupajena's house. From this same spot the fighters had watched the daily convoy of civilians, travelling with armed escorts, pass along the Victoria-Umtali road. On this occasion Pfupajena, diminutive, grey-haired, clad in white overalls, was sitting on a granite ledge opposite me, looking down in the direction of Nyika Halt. He had just shown me the secret cooking places in the caves where, during the war, he had led groups of guerrillas into hiding after skirmishes. Sitting up there, the now distant ravages of *chimurenga* sharpened our eyes to the scars of a wounded earth. Below us the ravished communal lands stretched mile upon deforested mile into the distance. Barren and naked in the scorching sun, it uttered a cry for liberation and healing . . .

'The elders told us towards the end of the war that after Independence we *masvikiro* should rest and ask the ancestors to rest also,' the old man said. There was defiance in his voice.

'Why was such an order given?' I asked.

'Perhaps the people just wanted peace after all the bloodshed. Perhaps the politicians were scared of the power we represent. Or maybe they found it difficult to admit exactly how much we, the *midzimu*, had contributed to creating the new Zimbabwe.'

His words revealed the frustration felt by many spirit mediums about their apparent loss of influence and prestige in the new political dispensation.

'And are you resting?' I asked jokingly, anticipating the crotchety old medium's reply.

'Of course not!' he said indignantly. 'Our task of guarding the land is never done. These days I keep going down to the Portuguese border to help our soldiers who are fighting the MNR bandits. Pfupajena, the Duma conqueror of long back, still guides our soldiers to protect Zimbabwe, just as he guided the *chimurenga* fighters to win back the land.'

'And what does Pfupajena say about the destruction of the land, about all that land without trees we see down there?' I asked.

'Ah you! You sound like an agricultural demonstrator,' Pfupajena laughed. Then his eyes narrowed in concentration as he measured out the dark snuff of the ancestors into his left palm. I knew the snuff ritual must precede any further discussion. So I sat gazing down on the neglected contour ridges, the shallow, grey, sandy soil where a few Shona cattle plucked listlessly at dry maize stalks. I have always wondered at the hardiness of these animals who survive on such meagre pasture.

At last, having inhaled the dark grains deeply, the old man continued: 'Like all the great ancestors Pfupajena is a guardian of the land. Because of that he urges all vaDuma to protect the forests. The groves round the graves of our ancient dead on the holy mountains—Gwindingwi, Rasa, Vinga, Mugabe—particularly need protection. In the holy groves no hunting or tree felling is allowed. But who still respects the laws of our forebears? Nowadays everybody follows their own heads. In the reserves there is nothing left, no trees, no wild animals . . .'

He shrugged his old shoulders at the futility. It was the same helpless resentment I have often felt when observing the denuded slopes of Mount Mugabe.

'Why do you and the other *masvikiro* not band together as you did in *chimurenga*—this time to fight the destruction of the land?' I wondered out loud.

The old man sighed. 'We have been thinking of that,' he said. 'Some years ago we even held a few meetings at Chitungwiza where Chaminuka used to live. But nothing came of it. We have no money. No transport. Nothing.'

I leaned forward. 'Maybe I can help. Come to my house in Masvingo next time you're in town. Then we can discuss starting an association, writing a constitution, organising things.'

The invitation was spontaneous, born of a dream gone musty after too many years of academic rationalism and lack of practical involvement. I could not foresee all the complications then. Only when those shrewd eyes of many winters sized me up, attempting to probe the genuineness of my offer, did I realise that I might be letting myself in for more than I had bargained for. Yet excitement gripped me as the old head slowly nodded assent. Part of me registered hesitation. How was I to work with men and women of an ancient yet resilient religion whose beliefs and worldviews differed so vastly from my own? Another part of me responded to the scent of adventure. This was uncharted terrain, challenging me to feel, experience, and possibly help reinterpret the spirit of Africa in terms of a modern commitment to nature conservation. I shivered in the noon sun blazing down on the mountain's rock face. From the depths of that ageless self that defines our common humanity came the realisation that a new phase of my life had just begun.

Below us the expanse of abused earth seemed to mock our resolve. The cynic in me conjured up a monstrous windmill with giant rotating blades crushing the little Don Quixotes trying to stop their endless, wind-driven assault. The passage ahead, I knew, would be rough and hazardous.

FORMATION AND DEVELOPMENT OF THE TRADITIONALIST ASSOCIATION

Soon after our conversation on the mountainside, spirit medium Mapfumo Pfupajena showed up at our research center in Masvingo, and discussions about the formation of a traditionalist association commenced forthwith. Reuben Marinda, who had originally established contact with Pfupajena in Bikita and had tape-recorded his *chimurenga* experiences, was put in charge of the intensive discussions with our aged friend and the preparation of a draft constitution, largely modelled on the first constitution we had written for *Fambidzano*. We promptly coined the name Association of Zimbabwean Spirit Mediums (AZSM) and set about defining rules for the new movement's activities. My own contribution at this early stage was merely to ensure that the basic ecological objectives—afforestation, wildlife, and water resources, which we had already singled out during the mountainside discussion as targets for our struggle—were clearly specified. Pfupajena, in his turn, made sure that the promotion of traditional customs, beliefs, and ritual were included among the main objectives of the AZSM.

Although the first draft was revised in subsequent meetings, the original AZSM constitutional objectives (Appendix I, pp. 295–96 below) remained essentially unchanged. They were crafted by the *masvikiro* as a 'declaration of war.' Once again the mediums were laying down the rules of combat, this time for an ecological *chimurenga*! Once again the holy mountains in Masvingo Province and elsewhere—the same places where ancestral guidance for guerrilla warfare was received and arms were hidden—were to become focal points, this time claiming public recognition and protection. The traditional religious element was evident in the choice of the wild fruit trees to be protected and planted: particularly the *muchakata* (cork tree), *mushuku* (wild loquat), and *mutobge* (*azanza garkeana*) that bear the fruit the ancestors 'eat.' These trees were protected in many areas prior to the erosion of customary law through Western influence. In this respect the AZSM was resuscitating and extending traditional ecological laws and practices. The mobilisation of peasant society in afforestation projects was envisaged as the main strategy for combating deforestation.

The aim of protecting water resources included practical measures such as keeping marshlands, springs, and rivers intact and unpolluted, preventing riverbank cultivation and restoring catchment areas by planting grass and trees. In traditional terms such projects would be designed to avert the departure of the *njuzu* water spirits. These spirits (which fall in the category of *shavi*—that is 'alien' as opposed to ancestral—spirits) teach traditional doctors and mediums medicinal knowledge and help to provide rain. Thus their goodwill has a direct bearing on the maintenance of ecological balance (Appendix 1, pp. 295–96 below).

The list of animal species to be protected—duiker, steenbok, rabbits, and snakes—reflected the concern of the mediums. Because of the scarcity of game in the communal lands surrounding Masvingo town, the *masvikiro* have become the protectors of small game only. Big game in this part of the world has become the preserve of commercial farmers and the government Department of Parks and Wildlife (Appendix 1, p. 296 below).

The clause on the promotion of African religion and culture reflected the concern of the mediums, as custodians of tradition, about the processes of modernisation, change, and religio-cultural alienation. Read in conjunction with the preceding clauses, it conveyed the AZSM's overall approach of *religious holism*. Respect for the elders and ancestor veneration were considered as much part of the process of environmental reform as the physical planting of trees and protection of wildlife. Crisis, whether sociopolitical or environmental, stimulates religious revival. Conversely, religious revival stimulates and directs socio-ecological crisis management.

Our differing beliefs were never an issue. Before meetings I would often read from the Bible, usually about God's concern for nature. Isaiah 41:18–20 became a favourite passage, also among tribal elders. Here Mwari speaks about rivers that will flow among barren hills and villages, about trees that he will cause to grow in dry places: cedars, acacias, myrtles, olives. Of course, in our readings we replaced these with our own *msasa, mitondo* (indigenous acacias), *mikamba* (mahogany), *mikurumbira* (teak), and indigenous fruit trees so as to express God's concern for our drought-stricken land. The words 'People will see this and know that I, the Lord, have done it' made the point: all our earthkeeping endeavours are, in the final analysis, inspired and sustained by Mwari.

After such scripture reading and prayer, the elders and spirit mediums would pass round their snuff horns. Sniffing snuff and sprinkling it on the floor prefaced the ritual of communing with senior tribal ancestors. In this way we respected and tolerated each other's religious identities.

The elders and ex-fighters took the opportunity to strengthen their bonds with the *varidzi venyika* (ancestral guardians of the land), just as they had done during the war years. Only now it was happening in a postwar context of racial reconciliation, of a realignment of the Zimbabwean liberation forces in an all-out campaign against the destruction of our land.

The first AZSM executive was elected in mid-1988 after the constitution had been finalised. It consisted of the following dignitaries:

Patron:	Chief Murinye
President:	Haurovi Chinovuriri
Vice President:	Spirit medium MuDende
General Secretary:	Ex-combatant Tafirei Amigo
Vice Secretary:	Bishop Reuben Marinda
Treasurer:	Spirit medium Lydia Chabata
Committee members:	Ex-combatant Cosmas Gonese ZIRRCON; Researcher Daniel Zvanaka; Co-founder of AZSM and director of ZIRRCON, Prof. M. L. Daneel

In the course of the 1990 annual general conference, substantial changes took place in the AZSM executive. The new president and vice president were respectively spirit mediums Mapfumo Pfupajena and vaZarira. Cosmas Gonese, who had meanwhile moved from Gutu to Masvingo, was appointed both assistant director of ZIRRCON and general secretary of the AZSM, a double office carrying a full-time salary. Several mediums and chiefs in the fast-growing movement were also elected as executive councillors. The executive changed the name 'AZSM' to 'AZTREC' (Association of Zimbabwean Traditional Ecologists), the Shona equivalent of which would be *bato remasvikiro nemadzishe* (literally 'association of spirit mediums and chiefs'). The twofold motive for this change was that the membership had clearly spread beyond the spirit mediums; and for fundraising purposes it was important to use a more neutral designation, since to Europeans the term 'spirit medium' certainly did not connote tribal historian and political authority, as it did to Zimbabweans.

First Steps in Ecological Action

To launch our tree-planting campaign late in 1988, we invited Christian Rasmussen, chief executive of the Lutheran World Federation in Masvingo, to address the AZSM on the development of nurseries and woodlots at suitable water points in the province. Rasmussen responded by not just addressing and advising the *masvikiro*, but also calling an LWF meeting on afforestation in Masvingo Province on 5 December 1988. A long-term tree-planting programme for the province was discussed. I quote from the minutes:

> It is agreed that afforestation must have the highest priority and time is soon running out, so that many parts of Masvingo Province will not be able to sustain habitation due to lack of firewood . . . The community plays such a great role that all groups of society must be involved, from the ministries at provincial and district levels, to councillors, chiefs, WADCO, VIDCO, government extension staff, spirit mediums, traditional leaders, and churches.

It is apparent that at the very inception of the movement steps were taken to ensure interaction on ecological issues between religious bodies and government institutions. The interaction included explicit mutual recognition and interdependence.

In the course of December 1988 the association launched its first tree-planting campaign. Some Z$2,000 was raised in Masvingo's white business community, hence a combination of black and white initiative—albeit on a scale that was little more than symbolic—in the cause of the environment. Chiefs and mediums who attended an AZSM meeting at my house in mid-December were sent to their home districts to arrange tree-planting ceremonies: the digging of holes, soil preparation, accommodation for the tree-planting team, food contributions, etc. Christian Rasmussen assisted us with the purchase of seedlings at the Forestry Services' nurseries and provided LWF vehicles to transport the trees to the outlying districts.

On 12 December the 'offensive' started when the AZSM executive, spirit mediums, chiefs, and well-wishers left Masvingo in a hired bus. The next day cypress tress were planted at the war heroes' reburial site at Gutu district headquarters, where a large group of Gutu chiefs, *masvikiro*, ward and village councillors, school teachers, and district administration officials had congregated. The ceremony included some excellent speeches by chiefs, who linked the sacrifice of the fallen *chimurenga* heroes with the AZSM campaign to further liberate the ecologically still lost lands. On 14 December a colourful ceremony was conducted in Chief Negovano's territory in Bikita. With full TV and press coverage, the traditionalists appeared in their leopard skins, plumed headgear, and a wide variety of ancestral vestments. Sacrificial beer libations, snuff rituals, and traditional dances provided a festive background to conscientisation speeches and tree planting.

The chiefs, headmen and councillors had emerged as the strategists and conscientisers who, through actual stocktaking of the ecological situation in their wards and chiefdoms, could assess fairly accurately the short- and long-term needs of the struggle.

Through spirit possession and addresses by the ancestors the mediums were invoking the spirit forces of the land. This mystical intervention in ritual activity triggered discussions about the reinstatement of customary ecological laws. Spirit medium vaZarira in particular had taken the lead in lecturing to audiences at ceremonies about ancestral prohibitions of tree felling in holy groves (*marambat-emwa*), while Tovera and Mukaro, merely by miming the protection of seedlings with slow gestures, reinforced awareness of an actual presence of guardian spirits.

Ex-combatants, through their narrations of the *chimurenga* past, transformed tree-planting ceremonies into *pungwe*-type instruction classes, in which the land-healing directives of the *varidzi venyika* carried indisputable authority. Gonese bluntly insisted on total obedience to the ancestral war council (*dare rechimurenga*) if afforestation in Zimbabwe was to succeed; and AZSM president Chinovuriri, through inspired lengthy accounts of *chimurenga* events, invoked the mystical sanction of the liberation struggle to provide unassailable legitimation for the war of the trees.

The enthusiasm of teachers and school communities held vast potential, either for AZSM participation in existing ecological programmes at schools or for the mobilisation of school communities as 'auxiliary forces.'

The pattern of warfare having been established, the 'green forces' returned to the rural battlefields during successive rainy seasons. After the first season's 5,000 trees, about 165,000 and 540,000 were planted respectively in the 1989/90 and 1990/91 rainy seasons. Because of severe drought the 1991/92 target of another half a million trees, as a joint effort by AZTREC and the newly formed AAEC (see below), had to be abandoned. Only about 120,000 trees were planted, mainly at schools and at church sites—although even here the normally stable water resources were drying up. At some woodlots, therefore, the survival rate of trees might have dropped from the 70 per cent frequently achieved in previous years to a mere 20 per cent. Pending rains and a fresh injection of funds, some 250,000 seedlings were kept in AZTREC and AAEC nurseries by way of a holding operation for the 1992/93 tree-planting season.

What the early history of ZIRRCON/AZTREC (and the AAEC) proved beyond any doubt was that the ecological mobilisation of rural communities on the basis of religiously inspired models (to be discussed in the ensuing chapters) was highly successful. Judging by the growing demand for trees in rural communities, the ZIRRCON movement could have planted more than a million trees each year if there were no financial and climatic constraints. During the years 1998–2000 however, the overall production of seedlings kept creeping up and came close to the ideal of a million trees per year.

THE ZIMBABWEAN INSTITUTE OF RELIGIOUS RESEARCH AND ECOLOGICAL CONSERVATION

ZIRRCON stems from a three-year period of empirical research (1965–1967) among Shona Independent Churches in the rural areas of Masvingo Province. This research led to many years of ecumenical engagement with the Independents, resulting in *Fambidzano's* theological training programmes and socioeconomic development projects. A similar pattern of sustained practical commitments between research team and grassroots communities studied evolved from another field research programme, initiated in 1984 to investigate the role of religion in Zimbabwe's liberation struggle. In this instance ecumenism assumed a different form: not just interchurch unity, but also close interaction between traditionalists and Christians, the two groups joining forces in the war of the trees.

As our research centre gradually expanded into an ecological operational base, the name 'ZIRRCON' gained currency and the institute became a recognised agency in Masvingo society. A constitution and institutionalisation proper, however, only came later when it became important to differentiate between the responsibilities and activities of ZIRRCON and its first affiliate, AZSM/AZTREC, and when the first, albeit unsuccessful, attempt was made in 1990 to register the affiliated bodies as social welfare organisations.

The main objectives of ZIRRCON were defined as follows:
- to promote empirical research into Zimbabwean religion: its history, beliefs, and rituals, both traditional and Christian (including studies of *chimurenga* and religio-ecological interaction in ZIRRCON-sponsored projects);
- to initiate new ecological conservation programmes through its affiliates, AZTREC and the AAEC;
- to liaise with government agencies and local government authorities involved in ecological work;
- to raise and administer funds for research and ecological projects, maintaining good relations with sponsors through responsible budgeting, expenditure control, and accounting;
- to make available research results through the publication of a ZIRRCON series (both academic monographs and popular books), occasional and seminar papers, ecological training material and, eventually, a quarterly bulletin;
- to plough back research expertise and field experience into grass-roots organisations such as AZTREC and the AAEC by running a ZIRRCON department to conduct training/conscientisation programmes in both traditionalist and Christian circles. This includes course development.

In the early 1990s ZIRRCON consisted of three departments: research, ecology, and financial administration. At that time the executive consisted of myself as unsalaried director and the following salaried staff: Rev. Solomon Zvanaka, assistant director and head of financial administration; Leonard Gono, ecological field operations manager; Bishop Reuben Marinda, general secretary of the AAEC; Haurovi Chinovuriri, general secretary of AZTREC; and Tarisai Zvokuomba, senior research worker. There were also a number of junior research assistants.

From a religious point of view the denominational composition of our 'command group' in the green revolution comprised the two *Ndaza* (Holy Cord) Zionists, the Rev. Zvanaka and Bishop Marinda[1]; and three Zimbabwe Reformed Church members (Gono, Chinovuriri, and me). Among these last three, I myself had strong AIC leanings after years of participation in both Spirit-type and Ethiopian-type churches (cf. Daneel 1987) and Chinovuriri still actively participated in the traditional religion. Tarisai Zvokuomba, an Apostolic prophet, having been converted to our new liberation theology of the environment, at an early stage started eliciting confessions of ecological sin from church members during our eucharistic tree-planting ceremonies.

Ecologically, ZIRRCON became remarkably successful. First of all it founded and helped to institutionalise its two sister organisations, AZTREC, which we have discussed, and the Association of African Earthkeeping Churches (AAEC) which we introduce below. These were the two 'military arms' which inspired and mobilised the green liberation army at the rural grassroots in terms of African philosophy and Africa's diverse religions. Working in tandem with these two organisations, ZIRRCON has, in the second place, performed impressively, particularly in its nursery development and tree-planting ventures. Acting as a unifying umbrella body, ZIRRCON's executive had regular meetings with the executives of its sister organisations and participated in their annual conferences, thus retaining the initiative in policy making and in planning project implementation. Insofar as ZIRRCON interacted continually with grass-roots communities, both directly and through the hierarchies of its sister organisations, ecological warfare in the field was characterised by both top-down and bottom-up modes of operation. The nursery keepers and tree planters depended on overall campaign strategies devised by ZIRRCON's triple executive body, which liaised at top level with government departments such as the Forestry Commission, the Natural Resources Board, Agritex, and National Parks and Wildlife. At the same time the executive relied on the grassroots communities' ecological expertise and experience, which codetermined the struggle. In the third place, ZIRRCON's fund raising and financial accountability have been considered sufficiently successful by sponsors to warrant sustained support.

THE ASSOCIATION OF AFRICAN EARTHKEEPING CHURCHES

CHURCHES PREPARE FOR ECOLOGICAL WARFARE

Several Christians were involved in ZIRRCON and AZTREC's core team from the start, and many church people participated in the traditionally oriented tree-planting programmes. This pattern, which stimulated inter-religious participation and interfaith dialogue, continued. It actually established a praxis of spontaneous ecumenism, revolving around mutual concern for the environment despite religious differences. Nevertheless, it was felt from the outset that the AICs should be enabled to develop their own ecological programmes. They control vast networks of congregations, composed largely of peasant families in rural communities. As indicated above, they also have rich traditions of enacted liberation theologies, which were also employed during *chimurenga*. After Independence the AICs continued the liberation struggle at a socioeconomic level by fighting poverty through rural development programmes (community development, small industries, agricultural projects, water projects, family planning, etc.). *Fambidzano* was instrumental in planning, fund raising, and assisting its member churches with the implementation of projects. Thus the AICs were well placed at the grassroots to contribute to the ecological liberation of the lost lands.

After years of close involvement in the building of *Fambidzano*, my first thought was to invite *Fambidzano* to join in ZIRRCON's tree-planting programme. Letters were written to Rev. Peter Makamba—my successor and general secretary of the Conference—and later a plea for environmental reform was directed to the administrative board. Some of the older AIC leaders on the board, co-founders of *Fambidzano* in 1972, were in favour of joining forces with ZIRRCON. Others were opposed because of ZIRRCON's close identification with traditionalists. In the end ZIRRCON's invitation to *Fambidzano*, which had remained open for a full three years (1988–1990), was spurned.[2] Tenuous relations with *Fambidzano* persisted long after this decision not to become involved with AAEC. Meanwhile the ecological performance of ZIRRCON/AZTREC had triggered the imagination of numerous AICs. Increasing numbers of AIC leaders, many of them affiliated to *Fambidzano*, approved of ZIRRCON's endeavours and sought affiliation. Entirely in accordance with the original ZIRRCON blueprint, Christian leaders started requesting assistance to enable them to conduct their own tree-planting ceremonies based on biblical principles, as AZTREC was doing in terms of traditional religion. In the course of the 1990/91 rainy season ZIRRCON delivered seedlings to the headquarters of four AICs, and the first church-directed 'green battles' took place. The churches who fired the first salvo in the new *chimurenga* were the following: Bishop Wapendama's Apostolic Church (Zimuto), Bishop Elijah Hore's Zion Sabbath Church (Masvingo district), Rev. J. Zvobgo's African Reformed Church (Masvingo district) and Bishop Ishmael Gavhure's First Ethiopian Church (Bikita district). It was no coincidence that the last three churches all belonged to the nuclear group which had taken the lead in launching *Fambidzano* all those years ago.

A 'Green Army' of Bishops and Their Followers

Given the opposition of *Fambidzano* described above, the official launching of ZIRRCON's newly recruited fighting force was not easy. The formation of the AAEC in Masvingo's Mucheke township on 8–9 March 1991 took place in a virtual state of siege. Makamba had mounted a demonstration by a number of leading women of *Fambidzano*'s Women's Desk at the bus depot to divert AIC leaders arriving from all over the province from attending our meeting. Some of Gonese's traditionalist supporters also participated in the demonstration, the strategy of which was to persuade Independents as they arrived to return home straight away, using money which Makamba was providing (by writing cheques on the spot). There was some coercion: *Fambidzano* bishops were threatened with expulsion from the conference or withdrawal of financial support for their churches' development projects should they proceed to Mucheke's new hall to attend our meeting. Banners proclaimed that joining ZIRRCON was tantamount to destroying *Fambidzano*.

Disconcerting as all this was to me as a former *Fambidzano* director, there were some lighter moments. When I drove up to the demonstrators and started moving amongst the women, they greeted me warmly and switched to a supportive chant: 'Plant your trees! We know you do not intend ruining *Fambidzano*!' A few of them drew me aside to explain their embarrassment at what was taking place. I, in turn, shared with them my concern about the obvious misrepresentation of ZIRRCON's motives. The joke of the day, however, was when a few bishops managed to beat Makamba at his own game: they collected their cheques from him, pretending they were returning home, then made a detour to our meeting and signed up for the ecological struggle—cheques in hand, mischief in their eyes. But humour could not dispel my sadness at having to cross swords with a former ally and fellow pilgrim. The war of the trees was indeed turning into a bitter struggle on all fronts, exacting a heavier price than I had anticipated.

Our first meeting was attended by a number of AZTREC well-wishers and groups of delegates from eighteen AICs, all of whom duly decided to proceed with the formation of an earthkeeping association. Against a backdrop of mounting opposition and destructive misinformation it was heartwarming to see the participants band together. The very fact that AIC leaders immediately started paying their joining and affiliation fees—not easy in a subsistence economy familiar with deprivation—demonstrated their determination to push ahead with our new venture.

After much discussion about alternative names for the association, we decided upon 'Association of African Earthkeeping Churches'—in Shona, *Makereke okuchengetedza zvisikiwa zvaMwari* (literally, 'the churches who keep God's created things' or 'the churches who protect God's creation'). In true African style, nearly all the churches present were represented on the first AAEC executive. This was in recognition of their role as pioneers or founders of the new movement.

The majority of affiliated churches were of the prophetic *Ndaza* Zionist type (i.e., the robed Zionists of the holy cords)—splinter groups of the Zion Apostolic Church and Zion Apostolic Faith Mission, respectively established in Zimbabwe by the pioneer Zionist leaders David Masuka and Andreas Shoko (Daneel 1971:302–315). Quite a number of these churches were and have remained affiliated to *Fambidzano*. Consequently the new body's relationship with *Fambidzano* was focal in the meeting's deliberations. Recognition of the direct link of our movement with the AIC prophets' role in *chimurenga* was apparent in the choice of Bishop Musariri, the war prophet who had played such a dramatic role during the *pungwe* meetings at Vunjere, as patron of the AAEC. Reminiscent of the late Bishop Moses Makamba, who had always graced *Fambidzano* meetings with opening and closing prayers, Bishop Musariri provided quiet, soft-spoken inspiration during our AAEC deliberations. Together he and I laid hands on and prayed for the kneeling members of the newly chosen AAEC executive. Thus—in the name of Christ, the universal guardian of all creation, and in the name of the Holy Spirit, the guiding power in our struggle—we consecrated the 'high command' of our ecclesiastical strike force.

In probably the longest speech I have ever made in Shona, I attempted to outline our religio-ecological battle strategy. The following summary of what I said outlines the major themes of the day and of the movement that it began. First, I read from Isaiah 43.

'Fear not, for I have redeemed you; I have called you by name, you are mine. When you pass through the waters I will be with you; and through the rivers, they shall not overwhelm you; when you walk through fire you shall not be burned, and the flame shall not consume you' (Isaiah 43:1–2).

I went on the say:

In response to what we have seen at the bus depot, I call upon you to be steadfast, because we ground our work in Mwari. He is the one who inspires and strengthens us, whatever numbers rise against us. He requires us in his Word to be fearless, just as he did of the Israelites. We don't want to see fearful people running away. *Fambidzano* started with a small number of supporters, only twelve churches, but through perseverance it has grown strong and influential over the years. Today we start here with a new association of only eighteen churches, but we want to see it grow rapidly to a membership of fifty or a hundred churches, all of whom should be planting trees.

In Isaiah 43:18f Mwari says: 'Do not ponder the old things . . . *Behold I am doing a new thing* . . . I will make a way in the wilderness and rivers in the desert, whereby the wild beasts and my chosen people will honour me!' In accordance with God's Word I tell you, too, that this association we are creating today is a new thing God is doing in our midst. Mwari inspires and builds. It does not belong to us but to God. Therefore, if we are courageous and persevere, this new movement will perform great deeds. Let us persevere in the knowledge that we are receiving a gift from God.

Our mandate for our new task comes from both the Old and the New Testaments. It derives from our faith that we belong to the body of Christ. As members of that body we are not only commanded to build unity amongst ourselves as fellow believers, and amongst Christian churches, but to build new relationships with the entire creation in an attempt to avoid destruction and preserve life for all creatures. Why do I say this? Because the body of Christ is not only the church. It is much more than that. Indeed, in Colossians 1:15–21 we read that Christ's body is the church, he is its head. But we also read that in him (through his initiative) all things hold together, in him all things are created. That makes him the true guardian of the land, the great guardian of all creation. This twofold interpretation of the body of Christ should be read together with Matthew 28:18, where Jesus says, 'All authority in heaven and on earth has been given to me.' We take this to mean that his presence and power pervades all creation, so we as members of his body have a responsibility for creation.

The implication of all this is that when we as Christians partake of holy communion we express our unity in the body of Christ, that is the church. At the same time we reaffirm our responsibility for the body of Christ, in the sense of all creation. The sacrament therefore makes us earthkeepers, stewards of creation. So we are repeatedly given a mandate in Christ to plant trees, to conserve wildlife and to protect the land's water resources. That is why you have heard me suggest that each of our member churches should conduct at least one tree-planting eucharist each year where the bread and wine are taken before planting the trees.

Frequent references were made to *Fambidzano* to establish in the minds of those present that the AAEC considers itself to be an autonomous movement, complementary to *Fambidzano*, with a separate set of constitutionally defined objectives—not a rival intent on destroying its competitor. Amongst other things I said:

Our aim is not to kill *Fambidzano*, as the demonstrators at the bus depot seem to think. Everybody knows that *Fambidzano* was my 'child,' which has matured and already for many years has been standing on its own feet . . . I want all of you to know that I have had good relations with Peter Makamba for a long time. When he succeeded me in *Fambidzano* he led the conference successfully for years. It is only in relation to this new task of ours that we do not see eye to eye. When I invited *Fambidzano* to plant trees he refused, saying: 'You have now started with the spirit mediums. So you want to place us (the churches) and the mediums in one basket . . . You have backslided as a believer.' Whereupon I told him: 'I am not a spirit medium myself, but a friend of the mediums.' My contention is that the mediums should wage war against deforestation in terms of their own beliefs and the churches should do so on Christian principles. Each movement should have its own religious identity but they should recognise the value of each other's contribution.

Go, therefore, you who belong to *Fambidzano* and report to your conference what has transpired here. Be loyal to *Fambidzano*! Be loyal to the AAEC! Let your wisdom refute the rumours that Daneel is trying to break *Fambidzano*!

I explained the relationship and interaction between the AAEC and AZTREC as follows:

Most of you know that I have been doing research amongst both traditionalists and the black churches for many years. I have helped the spirit mediums and chiefs to form an association called AZTREC. As you see, some of its representatives are here today. AZTREC has managed to fight bravely on behalf of a spoilt environment. So I say we respect their efforts, we fight alongside them and we do not obstruct or reject them in any way. Whatever our critics say, we proceed along the route of cooperation. The final judgment of our interaction lies with Mwari, not with us . . . Our support for the traditionalists as fellow fighters in a new revolution requires mutual respect and dialogue about our religious differences. Such interaction does not exclude Christian witness. Neither does it imply backsliding or compromising our Christian beliefs. In the first place we have to love, not judge! Let us also remember that many chiefs are staunch church members and that quite a few *masvikiro* regularly attend church.

The tribal elders appeal to Chaminuka, Kaguwi and other regional spirits as the *varidzi venyika*, because that is their continuing faith and the custom of the forefathers. We Christians, on the other hand, say that in Christ we ourselves are the guardians of the land. By planting trees our earthkeeping churches honour Christ, God and his creation. We shall plant trees throughout Zimbabwe and beyond, particularly in those areas where the earth lies naked. In doing so we shall learn from scratch what God's word says about his creation and we shall teach each other a new theology of the environment.

We now have three movements in one: ZIRRCON, AZTREC and the AAEC—movements with separate religious identities but with common ecological aims. We shall draft separate constitutions, without at any point forgetting to consider and redefine the nature of our interrelationships.

I then spoke of the AAEC as a liberation movement:

At first our country was liberated through the struggle of *chimurenga*. The war was fought by churches, by the chiefs and mediums, many of whom supported the guerrilla fighters. Much blood flowed before the country was free. Now we want to broaden the struggle, to open up a new front of *chimurenga*—one which will liberate not only humans, but the trees, the animals, the water of our country. These aims do not mean that we arrogantly consider ourselves capable of everything. No! We rely on Mwari and with his help we shall succeed in planting so many trees that the land can heal. Then, in liberating nature, we will once again find our own liberation. We want to clothe the barren landscape so that it may live and prosper.

We killed the land! We chopped down the trees. We enslaved and polluted the world! We, therefore, are the ones who have to heal creation. We share a common guilt: the white colonisers who caused the blacks to crowd the tribal lands, and we, the blacks, who chopped down trees indiscriminately without ever thinking of producing our own firewood in return.

Forward the war of the trees! Let us mobilise all our fellow Christians to use their hands to clothe the earth. Let us heal the earth by laying hands on the land and praying for it as we do for sick people. Let this healing anointment translate into nurseries full of seedlings and flourishing woodlots as far as the eye can see. It does not matter if we start in a small way, for our work as custodians of nature is part of the good news we proclaim: God's salvation of all creation. The growth of our trees will be reflected in the growth of our churches.

And finally I tried to articulate AAEC activities as part of an African and a global vision:

We have as our first target the churches of Masvingo Province. But we should soon move into the other provinces of Zimbabwe, to conduct training sessions there, using the lessons on environmental theology which we are already preparing. Regional tree-planting centres, owing allegiance to Masvingo headquarters, should be established in all the provinces of our country.

Eventually our struggle should extend to neighbouring countries: South Africa, Mozambique, Botswana, and Zambia. We can visit these countries and teach the people there about the sacredness of trees. The model of our liberating work will hold good for many countries in Africa. In South Africa I am already discussing with some university people and AIC leaders the prospects of launching similar ecological projects. You must remember that South Africa has got even more AICs than Zimbabwe. There are more than 5,000 Independent Churches with many millions of black members. How about some of you going down there and inviting their bishops to come and see what we are doing in Zimbabwe? Once South Africa has been fully liberated politically we can move to and fro easily, witnessing about our tree-planting eucharist which is the symbol of the salvation of all creation, the coming of a new heaven and a new earth. Just imagine our green army of churches expanding throughout the south and further north in Africa, re-establishing the forests which will draw the rain and save our wildlife!

Our AAEC has a message for all the world. We shall therefore acquire membership of the national Christian Council so that we can properly inform the World Council of Churches about our work. In turn we can learn from World Council publications and conferences about the world church's struggle for the 'justice, peace, and integrity of creation,' known as JPIC. Our strength and our contribution to the world church in the earth-healing struggle lie not so much in publications but in actually treating the patient, the earth. Even if ours is a small beginning let us set the example by practising our earth-keeping ministry with all our hearts!

Maybe all this is just a dream of mine. Maybe some of it will only be realised after my death. Nevertheless, that is the inspiration I have received. It is a vision which from today we shall all share. We shall not be daunted by whatever enemies rise against us, for we have a just cause grounded in God's Word.

Thus the first battle cry of the green struggle was sounded by an ecclesiastic 'high command.' The bishops and followers then returned to their respective headquarters to recruit more churches for the earth-keeping force and to prepare their followers for action.

THE RAPID EXPANSION OF THE ASSOCIATION

By the time the first annual general meeting was held on 4 April 1991, less than a month after the founding of the new association, the membership had risen from 18 to 35 member churches. This rapid growth and geographical expansion were to continue. By the end of that year more than 100 churches had joined: 81 from Masvingo Province, 11 from Matabeleland, 5 from Midlands, and 4 from Manicaland. Some 30 per cent of this total hold double membership (both AAEC and *Fambidzano*). By 1997 the membership had grown to 150 churches. *Fambidzano* had never shown such rapid and geographically widespread growth. Its peak membership a few years ago, some two decades after its inception, was 80, possibly 90, churches. The AAEC grew into a larger movement within one year. This comparison should not be interpreted as competition between the two movements. An element of competition is, of course, unavoidable, even healthy. But as I indicated at our first AGM, the ideal situation at which we should aim in the future should be the merging of the two movements. Such a union would be a massive stride forward for AIC ecumenism in Zimbabwe, and would give the churches involved a broader base for joint planning of projects.

President Machokoto's key address reflected level-headedness and sound leadership. First he made a plea for genuine ecumenical cooperation. 'What I ask of God,' he said,

> is a true sense of unity amongst us. We have to work together and avoid all forms of confusing conflict. Our unity must rest on convincing works. It is no use us coming here to enjoy our tea and meals without engaging in development and money-generating projects which show convincing progress. The basis of our work, according to God's Word, is love, a love which reveals itself in works. Having come here to engage in development, let us show our willingness and ability to work. Therefore each of you, as you leave here, go and prepare yourselves for tree planting. ZIRRCON's main task is to inspire and advise; not to provide everything required for tree planting. We, the churches, will have to make sacrifices for the cause to which we have pledged ourselves. Therein lies our unity . . .

Machokoto confirmed his willingness to cooperate with AZTREC by advocating recognition of the tribal elders: 'We must be fully prepared,' he said,

> to recognise the authority of our kraalheads and chiefs. For if we show contempt for them, where will we plant our trees? A Christian attitude is required towards the rulers of the land. Let our bishops in their eagerness to fight the war of the trees not antagonise the keepers of the land. If you are a church member yet try to place yourself above the laws of the land, you are not a true convert. Let us fully support our elders in this struggle of afforestation, so that the ZIRRCON-AAEC objectives may be realised in practice.

It should be pointed out that, although I appreciate the need for economic progress in a poverty-stricken society, I repeatedly reminded AAEC leaders that our association was not to be conceived of as a development funding agency. Aware of the predicament *Fambidzano* had faced all along because of limited funding which could never fulfil the development aspirations of all its member churches, I indicated that ZIRRCON-AAEC would be prepared to process some well-planned and deserving development projects, provided its primary aim of ecological repair was at no point overshadowed by other concerns. My original argument to induce *Fambidzano* to join in a programme of large-scale tree planting actually rested on the conviction that its nature-exploitive projects (agricultural and water schemes) should be augmented by compensatory, altruistic, nature-friendly and nature-repairing projects. Time alone will tell whether the AAEC will be able to strike a balance between exploitive and altruistic development ventures; whether the eagerness for economic progress can be curbed sufficiently for a healing ministry of earthkeeping to take root.

Soon after its inception the AAEC took on four nurseries, pushing the total of ZIRRCON nurseries in the 1991/92 season up to ten. The Forestry Commission handed over three of its nurseries to the AAEC:

- Mutirikwi nursery at Chief Shumba's homestead in Masvingo district, tended by Edwin Machokoto, brother of the AAEC president, and Makara Taoneichi. This nursery cultivated 52,000 seedlings during the first season after the takeover;
- Muchibga nursery at Chief Nyajena's homestead in Masvingo district, with nursery keepers Onias Hore, son of the AAEC vice president, and Dewa (47,000 seedlings);
- Chivi Central nursery at Chivi growth point, tended by Bishop Farao Murambiwa and Pedzisai Shoko (76,000 seedlings).

The fourth nursery, called Zimuto II and tended by Bishop Kindiam Wapendama and his home congregation, had already been developed with ZIRRCON assistance prior to the formation of the AAEC. It cultivated 16,000 seedlings in 1991.

A total of 191,000 seedlings produced by only four AAEC nurseries in their first year indicates sound organisation and ecological commitment amongst participant AICs.

Severe drought prevented ZIRRCON from planting the half of a million trees targeted for the 1991/92 season. Nevertheless, most of the seedlings (70,000) donated by ZIRRCON for the National Tree-Planting Day to schools and other organisations came from AAEC nurseries. The bulk, moreover, of the 120,000 trees actually planted during that season represented AAEC initiative. Nine AAEC ceremonies were held, six of them in Chivi, the most drought-devastated district of the province. Even though many of the trees planted did not survive because of the failure of water resources, the AICs demonstrated their will and determination to heal the stricken land under the most adverse conditions. Their preparedness to do battle against all odds augured well for Zimbabwe's green revolution. In addition, their preaching of earthkeeping sermons and experimentation with entirely new tree-planting liturgies signified adoption and enactment of a fully contextualised ecological liberation theology.

ZIRRCON is the leading member of the three affiliated organisations in such areas as fund raising, administration of funds, provision of transport, and the planning and implementation of programmes. There is regular interaction at all levels, at executive, departmental, and committee meetings and in the implementation of field projects. The general secretaries of AZTREC and the AAEC, for instance, are members of the ZIRRCON executive, where they act as liaison officers for their respective organisations. The ZIRRCON director reciprocates by acting as liaison officer and official representative of the Institute at the council and administrative board meetings of AZTREC and the AAEC. In practice, however, virtually all ZIRRCON staff members participate in the annual conferences and other meetings of the two sister organisations.

Members of the different departments and committees also interact regularly. Responsibility for the organisation of nurseries, tree-planting ceremonies, payment of fieldworkers out in the rural areas, arrangements for training programmes, liaison with government officials, etc., is shared on a day-to-day basis. During the 1990/91 rainy season, for instance, the late Leonard Gono (then still head of ZIRRCON's research department) and Cosmas Gonese (former general secretary of AZTREC) cooperated all the time—organising tree-planting ceremonies, arranging for the transport of seedlings and fencing materials—in what turned out to be a massive combined ZIRRCON/AZTREC afforestation drive.

At the same time the three organisations are semi-autonomous, each with its own identity, constitution, and code of conduct. Both AZTREC and the AAEC are entitled to raise funds on their own, in addition to the funding provided by ZIRRCON. Such funds are administered by their respective treasurers and finance committees, via their own bank accounts. All funds raised by ZIRRCON and ZIRRCON Trust, however, are administered by ZIRRCON's finance department. Thus, in view of its responsibility to sponsors, the major fund-raising agency is in a position to exercise strict control over expenditure and to play a leading role in the institutionalisation of our three-pronged religio-ecological movement. Having briefly outlined the relationship of ZIRRCON, AZTREC, and AAEC, we turn in following chapters to discuss the traditionalist ecological movement in greater detail.

CHAPTER 4

Traditional Belief Systems and *Chimurenga* Motives in Ecology

AN OVERVIEW

In this chapter we examine the evolution of AZTREC's ecological liberation struggle since the inception of the movement in 1988. In its redefinition of the struggle the healing of the ecologically still lost lands is paramount. In its constitution, as we have seen, this finds expression in the goals of afforestation, wildlife conservation, and the protection of water resources.

So far afforestation has been AZTREC's cardinal concern, and tree planting its main weapon in combating deforestation and other forms of soil degradation. This chapter focuses, therefore, on tree-planting ceremonies which channel traditional religious impulses into earth-healing activity.

The *chimurenga* background is still very much in evidence, partly because AZTREC decided to interpret its earth-healing programmes as an extended, diversified process of liberation, and partly because the modern revival of traditional religion and culture—which reaffirms the authority and influence of the traditional chiefs and mediums—is rooted in this anticolonial history. First, in every district where trees are planted and nurseries are established, AZTREC conducts its offensive from the same traditional spiritual base as the guerrillas, chiefs, mediums, and *povo*, namely the guidance of the *varidzi venyika*. It also sends regular delegations to the oracular shrines of Mwari vaMatonjeni to report on ecological progress and receive directives for the continuing struggle of *kufukidza nyika* (clothing the earth). Second, key positions on the AZTREC executive have been held by *chimurenga* veterans such as Chinovuriri, erstwhile liaison officer between mediums and ZANLA high command at Chimoio; Pfupajena, popular Duma medium on the Musikavanhu war front; vaZarira, the Duma medium who advised guerrillas in the Zvishavane area; MuDende, trained guerrilla fighter and medium; the guerrillas' consultant in Masvingo Province, Lydia Chabata, who became AZTREC's first nursery overseer; and Cosmas Gonese, former detachment commander Weeds Chakarakata of the ZANLA forces, who became the association's first general secretary.

Some of these *chimurenga* veterans have since joined Gonese's splinter group, AZTREC Trust. This is understandable in view of the emotional bonds forged between members of the schismatic group during the war years. This development has not prevented ZIRRCON-AZTREC from drawing on *chimurenga* history for inspiration in mobilising its green force. In traditionalist circles war heroes abound, whatever their status at the time. Consequently no single group in Shona society can lay exclusive claim to the inspirational legacy of the nation-wide struggle. Nevertheless, inasmuch as some of the Gonese defectors contributed significantly to AZTREC's initial ecological effort, particularly by harnessing traditional African forces for conservationist work, they are mentioned here for the sake of historical accuracy.

Chimurenga veterans like Chinovuriri, MuDende, Tovera Chaminuka and a large number of less prominent yet still active mediums, as well as the vast majority of chiefs in Masvingo Province, remained loyal to ZIRRCON-AZTREC. Hence the withdrawal of the Gonese defectors did not greatly affect the traditionalist contribution to the ecological drive of our movement.

AFFORESTATION AT THE BEHEST OF GUARDIAN ANCESTORS

AZTREC has proved beyond doubt its ability to mobilise peasant communities. Like other African peoples, the Shona live with their ancestors, whether they venerate them in traditional fashion or revere them Christian style. And when the ancestors call for the ravished land to be clad once more with trees, people in the rural areas respond. Senior members of Zimbabwe's Forestry Commission have admitted that they had never before witnessed such sweeping enthusiasm and commitment to ecological conservation in Masvingo's rural communities. To understand this enthusiasm for ecological reform we have to turn to the spirit beliefs and rituals which generated the vision and motivation for a better environment.

RITUAL TREE PLANTING

ZIRRCON-AZTREC's executive and annual general meetings are improvised *pungwe* meetings at which ecological warfare is planned with due regard to customary law and ancestral sanction. In other words, in discussing the performance of nursery keepers, the types of trees to be planted in new woodlots, preparations, fencing, aftercare and the like, ancestral involvement is assumed. True to the traditional African worldview, the wellbeing of society is considered to require the participation of all its members, both the living and the living dead. In this case the performance of the living earthkeepers is subject to either the mystical approval or the retaliation of the guardian ancestors of the land, depending on the living role-players' dedication and consistency in observing the generally accepted ecological norms. The wartime *pungwe* involved a demonstration of right-mindedness in response to the ancestrally sanctioned propaganda and codes of behaviour. In this sense AZTREC's workshops, instruction sessions, and conscientisation programmes are *pungwe* events based on a similar ethic, monitored on each occasion by the true representatives of the ancestors, the chiefs and the mediums.

Tree-planting ceremonies out in the rural areas are ritual events, modelled largely on the traditional *mukwerere* rain rituals (Daneel 1971:121–128). Like the *mukwerere*, AZTREC's *mafukidzanyika* (literally 'earth-clothing') ceremonies focus on the environment and the need for rain—in this instance for the newly planted seedlings to survive and grow. Accordingly they are held at the same stage of the seasonal cycle, the rainy season. Preparations for an AZTREC *mafukidzanyika* ceremony are very similar to those for a *mukwerere*, in that tribal elders expect villagers who participate in and benefit from the tree planting to contribute finger muller or sorghum for beer brewing. Elderly women, past child-bearing age, of the ruling lineage of the chief or headman in whose area the ceremony is held, are responsible for brewing the beer. The chief, or elders related to him, contributes one or more sacrificial beasts for the occasion and villagers are expected to make small donations to purchase additional food and drink. AZTREC sometimes raises funds to subsidise the larger tree-planting ceremonies, but encourages self-help by the communities. Thus the old custom of the entire community contributing to the ritual, thereby showing their respect to the guardian ancestors, is upheld. In the process a kind of multi-tribal 'ecumenism' is established, reminiscent of the *chimurenga* war council of the spirit world, in which regional and more exclusively tribal concerns were transcended by provincial or national interests.

But the wider 'ecumenical' spirit unity in ecological warfare at no point obscures or diminishes the role of the guardian ancestors of the region where the ceremony takes place. In the ritual addresses to the ancestors the senior regional spirits are mentioned by name and their mediation between their living descendants and the traditional creator God is relied upon, as is the case in all *mukwerere* supplications. After all, the local villagers, relating to AZTREC through their chief, medium and headmen, remain responsible to the local guardian spirits for faithfully fulfilling their duties in the newly planted woodlot, such as watering the seedlings, protecting them against domestic animals, and other forms of aftercare. The wide ecumenical perspective is therefore provided not so much by ritual address of specific guardian ancestors as by the creation of a new ritual context, which—through numerous conscientising speeches and the participation of tribal dignitaries from further afield—links the local spirit order with that of the entire nation in pursuit of a liberated environment.

AZTREC's *mafukidzanyika* ceremonies apparently transcend, even if only temporarily, the tribal political conflict manifested in the proliferation of immigrant *mukwerere* or *mutoro* rituals. Common concern for the environment and 'ecumenical' unity of spirit powers find expression in united action, in much the same way as the crisis management of *chimurenga* required nation-wide unity, superseding divisive tribal political rivalries. It is not clear at this stage whether our earth-clothing tree-planting ceremonies are in fact contributing to lasting solutions between ruling and immigrant elites. Yet in the ritual context of *mafukidzanyika* presiding chiefs and councillors (both immigrants and members of the chiefly lineages) demonstrate convincingly the will to form a common front in the war of the trees. In none of the numerous AZTREC tree-planting ceremonies conducted since 1988 have tribal political rivalries surfaced or marred the proceedings.

There can be little doubt that the tribally comprehensive *mafukidzanyika* rituals benefit the chiefs by enhancing their status and reinforcing their political authority. Some of them almost certainly view AZTREC as a means of restoring at least some of their former powers and dignity. Nevertheless, the fact that immigrant kraalheads and headmen have on the whole cooperated with the chiefs in the new ritual context and that there has been no overt protest in the AZTREC chiefdoms against tribal political misuse of the new association, suggests that what we observe here is much more than mere pragmatism or power play on both sides. Whether because of ancestral sanction and persuasion or ecological urgency, or both, the fact is that the new ritual engenders unity of purpose and resolve. Unlike the fragmentation of *mutoro* units, which emphasises clan autonomy and tribal diversity, AZTREC's improvised *mukwerere* rituals promote multitribal unity in a national, if not a continent-wide, cause.

MYSTICAL UNION AS A CONDITION FOR ECOLOGICAL COMBAT

At the start of each *mafukidzanyika* tree-planting ceremony there is a presentation of beer and snuff, together with a ritual address to the land's guardian ancestors. The senior chief, medium or tribal elder conducting the ritual proceedings congregates with other traditional dignitaries around the beer pots, which are placed next to the seedlings to be planted. Dressed for the occasion in official regalia (ostrich-feathered headdresses, necklaces made of bones, beads or carnivore claws, a variety of leopard, cheetah, civet, and rock-rabbit skins, etc.), the AZTREC mediums highlight the traditional nature of the ritual. The chiefs wear their bronze breastplates and white pith helmets, old colonial symbols of their political authority. While addressing the ancestors, the ritual officiant pours ancestral beer from a calabash down the sides of the beer pots and on the seedlings. Snuff is also presented to the ancestors, while snuff-horns are passed around amongst the tribal elders, symbolising communion with the spirit world.

On 22 December 1990, at an AZTREC tree-planting ceremony in Chief Nhema's area in Zaka district, a tribal elder, Mutengai Nhema, addressed the regional ancestors as follows:

> We have gathered here today in honour of you, our ancestor, father Nhema. Your children want to clothe the earth [*kufukidza nyika*] which is naked. We want you, our father, to bless the work your children will be doing here. We ask for rain because your children are being scorched by the heat of the sun. Give us the coolness of water! Even those who provide us with seedlings are asking your guidance in their work of clothing the earth; this land which you see is barren because of our chopping down all the trees.
>
> You, *mhondoro* [the senior 'lion' spirits], have no wilderness left in which to dwell. We want to return the forests to the naked land. [At this point snuff is given to the ancestors by sprinkling it on the ground.] Pass on our plea, you, oh Nhema and Pfupajena, to the unknown ancestors. You, our forefathers, also pass on our plea to Musikavanhu [God] so that the trees we plant will be watered sufficiently to survive. We ask you, in addition, to bring the numerous deaths out here to an end, to eliminate the [figurative] lion which is devouring many of our people.

We have brought you this calabash of beer so that you and the other ancestors can quench your thirst. Your children are ready to clothe the earth.
Notify the ancestors whom we do not know and Musikavanhu. Your children want to protect your holy shrines with trees so that you can rest in the
shade. We want to thank you that you have gathered us here. Don't forget
us. [At this point ancestral beer is poured down the sides of the beer pots
and on the ground.] Once again we give you snuff to share with our guests.

You, grandmother Chabata [addressing Lydia Chabata, then still nursery
supervisor of AZTREC], tell our guests that this snuff-horn is our ancestral
spirit. For it is the one we use when we approach our holy graves to tell the
ancestors about our problems.

After this address, spirit medium vaZarira, then still AZTREC vice president,
as always wrapped in her leopard skin, made the following speech:

I am fearful as I stand here addressing the descendants of Nhema, because I
am standing on the bones of our [Duma] ancestors. I call upon you, father
Nhema, as I am in your country, I being a Duma medium. I did not elect to
be a *svikiro*, but I was elected to be one while still in my mother's womb. As
I stand under this *muonde* [wild fig tree] I request vaNhema to be present
here because he used to rest under this very tree; here where he received
food from Matonjeni before he travelled to confer with Zhame. This indeed
is the tree where Nhema ate and rested, the *muonde* which provides human
beings with nourishing fruit.

I want to call upon vaNhema today. Whether he is in the cave [grave], up
in this tree here, or in the pool of water over there, we ask him to come and
witness what his children are doing in his territory. The problem of our land
is that it is like a woman whose dress was eaten by white ants. Surely such
a woman will not be happy.

If you are in the pool, vaNhema, lift up your head and observe what your
people are doing in your area. You have allowed us to come here today. Had
you not done so, nobody would have been present to plant trees.

We, the spirit mediums, have a problem with the way people are destroying the country. The holy shrines where our ancestors were buried are
being destroyed. These shrines [encompassing large tracts of wooded
mountain] sustained people with food and life. But the people themselves
destroy them. I am deeply concerned about our people not realising to what
extent our country—the country of our ancestors—is being destroyed.
Some people will say: 'The old woman is mad! Why should she involve
herself in tree planting?' You may have heard that my name is vaZarira. But
my nickname is *Marambatemwa* [the name traditionally used for holy
groves where all tree felling was prohibited]. I was nicknamed thus because
whenever I find a person felling trees, I fall ill and go home in a terrible
state.

If you go to the mountains you will find all the holy groves naked, because of wanton tree felling. These shrines used to be the fortresses and the

dwelling places of the ancestors and the ancestral lions [*shumba dzavadz-imu*]. Since we ourselves are the destroyers of trees, we have to restore the shrines through tree planting. Where there are no trees there are no rains, no springs, no marshlands. As this is our own fault, we, the children of Nhema, shall dedicate ourselves to clothing the denuded land. Forward, the war of the trees!

When we started this organisation people were asking: 'What are the *masvikiro*?' They did not know that we, the mediums, represent the ancestral guardians of the land and that we fight this war of the trees, helped and directed by the guardian ancestors.

The trees are a gift given to us by Musikavanhu through our ancestors. We are alive as people because of the trees. The trees clean the air we breathe. Our ancestors in earlier years were strong people with a longer lifespan than ours because they breathed clean air, while we breathe polluted air in the absence of trees. That is why many people are just dying these days.

In the past we were prohibited from moving in certain forests after dark. The elders warned that the lion spirits of our ancestors were active in those areas at that time. Nowadays these *mhondoro* are no longer seen because we have destroyed their habitat. Now, as you observe the barren land, note that all the *masvikiro* are shedding tears in the midst of such devastation.

Of interest here is the firm belief in the close link between apical ancestral spirits and the creator God and their common concern for ecological issues concerning the land. The closeness of God and the people's dependence on him/her as the ultimate owner of the country or universe are more pronounced in the *mafukidzanyika* (and *mukwerere*) context than in family rituals. The notion of a united council of tribal guardian spirits, operating under the direct guidance of Mwari and giving directives to the ecological fighters, is a clear parallel with the ancestral *dare rechimurenga* under whose authority the guerrillas operated. It should be noted here that whether God was addressed directly or through the tribal ancestors—an alternation also characteristic of rain rituals (Daneel 1971:127)—the names 'Zhame' and 'Musikavanhu' featured more regularly than Mwari. This could be attributable to Rozvi-Duma rivalry, as a result of which for a long time the Duma tended to frequent the high-God shrine of Musikavanhu in the Chipinge district rather than the Rozvi-affiliated shrines of Mwari in the Matopo hills. Both ritual officiants and tribal spirits in these ceremonies were obviously Duma.

In both rituals communication with the ancestors, the symbolic reaffirmation of mystical union between the living and the living dead, was featured as a premise of the ecological struggle. True to the Shona worldview, major environmental endeavours cannot be initiated without the guidance and approval of the mystical forces regulating land issues. The ritual officiants addressed the ancestors as the ones who had actually gathered the people for tree planting, and the ones from whom the new association sought guidance. It was the initiative of the ancestors that mattered. Ecological endeavour without their inspiration and directives would be futile as, to quote vaZarira, such action would be misdirected and result in destruction of the trees planted. Here fervent belief in the mystical powers of the regional spirits features strongly. They are the ones representing the traditional staff, the ancient seats of (tribal political) power, despite their temporary rejection by the colonial powers. They, therefore, are entitled to retaliate by withdrawing their protection from the trees planted, or to give their blessing to the green revolution.

Ancestral presence also has an ethical dimension. It is to the guardian spirits, whose privilege it is to rest in the shade of trees in the holy groves (*marambatemwa*), that public confessions of guilt about environmental destruction are made by the ritual officiants on behalf of all participants. In a sense, therefore, the ancestors are the ecological conscience of their living descendants. They are the ones who provoke confessions of guilt and instil resolve to remedy the situation, since they are the custodians of the land whose prerogatives are denied through wanton destruction of their forests. Their own wellbeing is being threatened by the irreverence of their living descendants who no longer heed customary ecological laws or show ritual respect. A direct result of such neglect is the barrenness of those areas where the *mhondoro* (lion) spirits used to dwell and the resultant disappearance of the latter—a withdrawal which leads to drought and agricultural decline in the community.

THE ROLE OF THE CHIEFS

As mentioned before, most *mafukidzanyika* ceremonies are characterised by a wide representation of traditional elders, government institutions, Cabinet Ministers, educational institutions, religious bodies and rural people. A strong sense of unity and common purpose marks ritual celebration, speech contents and tree planting. Shared concern for a fast deteriorating environment acts as a catalyst for joint action. It is striking, too, that much of the inspiration, ideology, and organisational drive for ecological warfare is expected to come from the traditional ecologists—the chiefs and *masvikiro*—in their age-old capacity as ritual and political representatives of the senior ancestral guardians of the land.

Gonese, former general secretary of ZIRRCON-AZTREC, said at one of the ceremonies: 'The arrangement of our association is for the chiefs and *masvikiro* to take the initiative against deforestation, because they represent the customs of our ancestors, they have the [ecological] knowledge to instruct the young, and they have the authority to prevent destruction. Their aim is this: *Let the holy places of the past once again be honoured as holy! Let the places where trees were chopped down be restored!*'

Significantly, this prominent ex-combatant here attributes a leading role to chiefs and mediums jointly, as if they are one. In his view, therefore, the controversy regarding the unequal contributions of these tribal authorities to *chimurenga* (as argued for example by Lan, in favour of the *masvikiro*; cf. Lan 1985:166–170) does not feature in the new *chimurenga* for a liberated environment. Both these role players are equally important and interdependent! Their combined efforts, moreover, are not those of isolated religious professionals but are fully integrated with the efforts of the people, the *povo*. For, as Gonese subsequently insisted, the restoration of the land and the return of lush forests depended on 'you, the people.' Gonese also postulated an integral relationship between the tree-planting ventures of the traditional authorities and those of the government. 'The government,' he said, 'has the same objectives in mind. Whenever there is a tree-planting cere-mony, President Mugabe is seen with a tree in his hands, which he then plants.'

The *mafukidzanyika* speeches of chiefs and councillors clearly reflect the need for united action to curb deforestation, appreciation for the endeavours of the new association, and willingness to establish new patterns of cooperation to heal the land. During the first round of tree planting in 1988 Chief Gutu said: 'Let us have an association which binds us, which unites us in strength; one which is recog-nised by our government and which we support at all times.' Chief Mukaro, also of Gutu district, expressed enthusiasm for tree planting 'because it satisfies our stomachs and fills our eyes and ears.' He thought that now there was new hope for the barren land because 'the chiefs and mediums are uniting and mobilising peo-ple as they did in the war—this time to fight the destroyers of the land.'

Councillor Shamhu Mavurenga called upon chiefs and mediums to lead the ecological struggle. 'In the past,' he said, 'the land always prospered when the chiefs and *masvikiro* together upheld the old customs and religion. Let them do so again, for the land belongs to the ancestors.' These words articulate a *holistic worldview* in which ancestral guardianship, sound government, religious interac-tion between the living and the living dead, and environmental protection are in-terwoven strands of the same fabric.

Paramount in the speeches of chiefs is the theme of the barren earth, the ram-pant destruction in their own areas. In Gutu, for instance, Chief Gutu expressed concern about the absence of many species of wildlife formerly found in the dis-trict. He complained about the desecration of burial sites where the dense copses of trees (holy groves) were chopped down. He claimed that, as a result, one could no longer hear the drumbeat of the spirit world on Mount Jerimanda at the onset of the rains, which used to be a sure sign of the land's prosperity. Chief Mukaro, of Gutu South, described the barren land there as follows: 'We have no poles left for building houses, no game to hunt, no fish in the rivers to catch, as they were all netted out.' Chief Makumbe complained, resentfully and sadly, about soil erosion in his densely populated region. 'All over Gutu you find eroded gullies [*mako-ronga*],' he claimed. 'The people even attempt cultivation in the *makoronga*. They chop down saplings for firewood, but these only produce smoke and no fire. So we have great expectations from AZTREC to bring us trees. In the past we had holy places where you could hear the drumbeat of the spirits, indicating the pleas-ure of the ancestors. But these places are quiet nowadays. So we request com-rades Chinovuriri and Daneel to stand fast in their work. Let them uplift our dis-trict: the trees, the dams, the animals.'

In all this, nostalgia does not stagnate in escapism. AZTREC's tree-planting programme has rekindled hope of finding a solution and restoring environmental vitality. The battle cry, 'Forward the war of the trees!' is elaborated in rousing speeches calling for support of AZTREC's work: 'If you people follow the instructions of the chiefs and the mediums the land will be built afresh.' 'Plant indigenous trees and the barrenness of the land will cease.' Chief Makumbe expressed confidence in the ability of AZTREC's chiefs and mediums to effect lasting ecological change. 'As we plant trees,' he asserted, 'the rains will abound, the *mhondoro* [here an umbrella term referring to all wildlife] will return and the *njuzu* spirits will inhabit the pools.' Chief Gutu, again, expressed the conviction that all ecological control at district level should be vested in the chieftainship, the seat of traditional political power. 'It is not enough,' he claimed emphatically, 'to see the District Administrator and the police [in preparations for tree planting], as I, Chief Gutu, am the one who controls the *zvidoma* [witch familiars], witchcraft mediums of this district!'

In the last two statements we observe, first, the chiefs' inclination to express ecological concern in traditional religious idiom; second, an indirect hint at their frustration over the curtailment of their powers, coupled with a veiled threat of retaliation in the claim of control over the forces of witchcraft; and third, confidence that AZTREC can succeed ecologically, with the implicit expectation that it will be instrumental in elevating the powers of the chiefs.

Christian chiefs and councillors are sensitive to religious pluriformity in the *mafukidzanyika* context. Said councillor Mavurenga on one occasion: 'Although the land belongs to the ancestors, it is not only a matter of *kupira midzimu* (ancestor veneration). We must all pray perseveringly for the wellbeing of our country, because Mwari is the God of us all—both Christians and traditionalists.'

Ultimately, however, all environmental remedial activity is directly or indirectly related to the ancestral world by chiefs and headmen, Christian and non-Christian alike. The attitudes of the senior tribal ancestors, the guardians of the land in each district or region—their anger at neglect and their protective goodwill when they are recognised and venerated by their living descendants—are considered crucial to the existing environmental situation and its future repair.

All the chiefs and mediums on the AZTREC executive are agreed, for instance, that environmental deterioration is due to the decline of traditional religion. Said Gonese: 'By not recognising the spirits you people cause destruction to the land.' He considered Zimbabwe's liberation and independence to be proof that the ancestors control the history and ultimate destiny of the country. A positive response to their ecological directives could heal the land in the same way as it had led to victory in war. True to the traditional religious revival of *chimurenga*, Gonese insisted: '*No progress whatever will be made if we reject the old customs*, if we ignore the rules laid down by our forefathers and propagated by our *masvikiro*. We need to follow the ways of truth by honouring our ancestors. This is the sole condition set by Chief Gutu and the elders for the people to engage in conservation. Progress in conservation will derive from agreement between the ancestors and the diligent ones who are prepared to work' [my italics].

MEDIUMS AND THE SPIRIT WORLD

Mafukidzanyika is an extension of traditional ritual in a modern context. Likewise, the ritual activity of the mediums is still couched in the traditional idiom even while addressing modern ecological issues. Thus medium vaZarira addressed the ancestors as being fully in charge of ecology. She considered them to relate, at the grassroots, to the old order of tribal political organization—the kraalheads, ward headmen, and chiefs as ecological authorities. These elders, representing traditional society in its entirety, need ancestral directives for environmental repair. The whole community, in its turn, is subject, in vaZarira's perception, to the creator God (referred to as Musikavanhu, Zhame, or Mwari) who still speaks from the oracular caves at Matonjeni and who still sends rain in response to the requests of cult messengers who annually visit Matonjeni on behalf of their districts.

In terms of this traditional worldview, vaZarira's concern about a partly defunct traditional religious system is understandable. On one occasion she lamented: 'Where have the *vanyusa* [Matonjeni messengers] gone? Why do many of them no longer travel to Matonjeni to fetch rain?' Like Gonese, she considered the breakdown of the old system to be directly related to ecological degradation. In this situation tree-planting rituals provide the mediums with an opportunity to propagate and resuscitate the old order. To them, AZTREC creates a forum where they can voice complaints, a platform from which to promote the revival of old beliefs and customs.

At the same time the inspirational and protective value of the old order in no way inhibits modern activities and objectives. Contrary to the old custom whereby *masvikiro* had to eschew Western utensils, clothing, and any form of modern transport so that they did not jeopardise their authority, AZTREC mediums propagate responsible use of vehicles and funds, the use of polythene bags and modern equipment in nurseries, fencing of woodlots, etc.—in the same way as modern weapons were part of the ancestrally supported strategy of *chimurenga*. Thus the ancestors themselves are conceived of as modernising or contextualising their directives for ecological action.

In their evaluation of the modern situation the spirit mediums are both critical of government, in so far as they consider it to be ignoring or destroying the traditional order which is essential for proper land use, and willing to cooperate if their religious identity and contribution are recognised. Said vaZarira in one of her *mafukidzanyika* addresses: 'Don't be disturbed when I ask for the return of the Mantonjeni messengers. This will happen when the government realises that the spirit mediums, the Matonjeni messengers and the chiefs are one in their work for the benefit of the land. Don't you remember that before the government cast the chiefs and *masvikiro* away [through the new system introduced after Independence], we, the bones of old [the ancestors], we, the *masvikiro*, were in the [colonially imposed] wilderness? But we have returned to our lands.'

VaZarira's criticism of the government conveyed the feeling that the spirit mediums were not afforded the prominence in independent Zimbabwe which their crucial role in *chimurenga* warranted. In her own deliberations with senior government officials, her visits to Matonjeni, and in the heightened expectations that the government would restore at least some of the chiefs' former powers—and, in the process, the political status of the mediums as well—vaZarira saw prospects of a return of the traditional religio-ecological order. As may be observed in her communications with the ancestors cited above, tree planting only makes sense in a society where unity between God, ancestors and living beings is constantly reaffirmed and maintained through ritual. In this perspective reconciliation and cooperation between the present government and the traditional representatives of divine and ancestral power become a cardinal condition for environmental wellbeing: ample rain, good crops, abundant wildlife, and afforestation.

The comments of prominent spirit mediums on religio-political development in Zimbabwe indicate the significance of AZTREC as both a religio-cultural movement and an outlet for political frustration. As has been pointed out, the ritual context of *mafukidzanyika* is much wider than that of either traditional rain rituals or the chief's council where traditional cult messengers deliver Mwari's oracular message for the district. In the presence of this more diversified new audience—encompassing traditionalists, church people, and government representatives—a wide range of subjects is dealt with: the significance of comprehensive ancestral directives for the whole country, the prospects of an alternative Mwari cult centre at or near Great Zimbabwe, traditional religious developments in relation to rural and national politics, and the persistent underlying theme of the integrality of religion and ecology.

Thus many people who seldom attend traditional rituals, who have partly forgotten the old customs and laws and who rarely hear anything new about the secretive old high-God cult are exposed to a fascinating range of religious information and directives. Religious rivalry is also bound to surface in the new ritual context. Tovera's claims to being the mouthpiece for a more widely diffused form of oracular revelation by Mwari is a case in point. On the one hand, Tovera's activities may be motivated by self-interest. On the other hand, his attitude towards Matonjeni could well reflect a general need among Shona Traditionalists to situate their own oracular centre outside Ndebele territory—nearer home and nearer that towering symbol of Shona accomplishment, Great Zimbabwe. These important religio-cultural matters, going to the roots of Shona society, link the past with the present, fill the AZTREC participants with a sense of dignity and pride and give purpose to the earth-healing struggle. In addition the link and sense of shared destiny between participant urbanites (politicians, government officials, educators, etc.) and rural folk are convincingly and visibly demonstrated.

When interpreting the roles of AZTREC spirit mediums, one should bear in mind that there is nothing unusual about these religious professionals speaking out boldly on politically oriented issues, even if it means treading on the toes of the highest authority in the country. In their world such criticism is mystically sanctioned by the ancestors, as long as it is generally felt not to be destructively subversive but to serve the interests of both society and the environment. VaZarira's insistence that the government should inform the senior ancestors at Great Zimbabwe about the outcome of the war reflects the *masvikiro*'s quest for official recognition of their wartime role, as well as their mystically affirmed claims to a greater say in running the affairs of a modern state, particularly those pertaining to land distribution, agricultural policy, and ecological control. All this is based on keen insight into current land issues and development matters—a highly critical assessment of Cabinet Ministers owning former white farms while the resettlement of destitute small farmers lags behind, and resentment about the neglect of peasant society in contrast to large-scale urban and industrial development.

Considering the role of the *masvikiro* in the AZTREC tree-planting context, the institution could well develop into a socio-politically and ecologically stabilising agency. It is certainly instrumental in bringing the frustrations and ambitions of key tribal political figures into the open. At the same time it creates new opportunities for both chiefs and *masvikiro* to regain part of their former prestige and to take pride in a sustained and widely acknowledged contribution to the progress of the country.

From the government's point of view, ZIRRCON-AZTREC could be a means of accommodating the needs and aspirations of traditional ecologists country-wide. Our support could force a major breakthrough in environmental policy making, legislation, funding, and mobilisation at the grassroots, giving new impetus and direction to Zimbabwe's green revolution and ecological endeavour. There can be little doubt about the vast ecological mobilisation potential of this movement once it spreads nation-wide.

MWARI'S ORACULAR INVOLVEMENT

Mukwerere rain rituals establish a local spirit link with Matonjeni through the ancestral hierarchies of ruling and immigrant clans, and relate to the local cult messenger's annual visits to Matonjeni for direct consultation with the rain oracle. In similar fashion the new *mafukidzanyika* rituals establish a twofold pattern of communication with the traditional Mwari. First, as illustrated by vaZarira's ritual discourse quoted above, the ritual officiant appeals to Mwari via the senior guardian spirits, with specific requests for rain and protection for the trees planted. Second, after completing the season's tree-planting programme, AZTREC delegations visit the shrines of Matonjeni to inform the oracular deity about recent developments and to obtain guidance and inspiration from the oracle for the ongoing struggle to heal the land. This development corresponds with the wartime recognition of the ancient high-God as the ultimate head of the ancestral dare *rechimurenga* (war council), and represents a new variation of the *chimurenga* practice of conferring directly with the oracular 'warlord' at the Matopo shrines about the progress and strategy of the struggle. In this instance the deity emerges as environmental liberator—yet another aspect of his/her traditional image as rain-giver—rather than as the sociopolitical liberator from white oppression of the war years.

Chimurenga delegations to the shrines were either the regular cult messengers (*vanyai*), who represented prominent spirit mediums and/or bands of guerrilla fighters in addition to their standard duty of requesting rain for their districts, or actual groups of fighters who consulted the oracle directly. By contrast the composition of AZTREC delegations to the oracle is innovative. Instead of a single *munyai* arriving at the shrine representing his paramount chief, senior spirit medium, and tribal elders who had commissioned him at the chief's council to carry the district's gifts to Mwari, a large contingent of chiefs, mediums, and fellow traditionalists, representing an entire province, now converge on the high-God's shrine. In other words, tribal dignitaries are much more widely represented in the AZTREC delegation than in the traditional unit sent to Matonjeni to request rain. The AZTREC delegation, moreover, represents an institutionalised new configuration of fighting cadres, reports on a different struggle from the previous one, and virtually compels Mwari to reveal another side of him/herself in response to yet another set of liberationist requirements.

Just as national crisis and changing circumstances elicited a specific form of oracular intervention from Mwari during the 1896 rebellions and the second *chimurenga*, revealing him/her as a deity of war and peace, so the urgent need for country-wide ecological reform—indicated by the wide range of spirit hierarchies represented in the AZTREC oracular revelation—promotes yet another mutation in the understanding and oracular revelation of Mwari. The features and message of Mwari have always been determined by the deepest collective needs of his/her people. Thus the image evoked by the AZTREC delegation is that of 'guardian of the tree planter,' the one who ultimately directs all ecological conservation, the liberator from environmental catastrophe.

The composition of these delegations is a clear departure from the age-old tradition of small-scale district representation at the shrines. As will be seen below, the oracular consultations also differ from the fairly stereotyped rain supplications and individual requests. Formerly, individual healers (*nganga*) and/or spirit mediums did visit the shrines occasionally, but the regular visits of AZTREC delegates are a novel development. It was quite moving, during the 1990 visit, to observe the expectancy of chiefs as they arrived for the first time at the cult centre, whose rich tradition they had only heard about from their local messengers and fellow tribesmen. Their attitudes at Matonjeni reflected awe, respect, and mystification, as if they were about to probe the mystery of their origins, the very heart of Africa. From the secret depths of the shrine cave, the rocks of Mwari, they were to hear for the first time the voice of Africa's creator God—or at least that of an ancient medium whose entire being was attuned to the revelations of the divine.

On this pilgrimage to their roots, the chiefs and mediums were in their finest attire. The chiefs wore suits and their white helmets and bronze insignia, while the *masvikiro* were dressed in black, draped with furry skins, and plumed headgear. During the afternoon and early evening, while arrangements were being made with high priest Chokoto for the late-night shrine ceremony, the tribal elders sat around the village at the foot of Mount Dzilo, meditating in silence or conversing in muted voices, all indicative of a profound sense of the presence of the supernatural—there among the massive black domes of Musiki, the creator. Even before the cave ceremony the value of a Matonjeni visit was apparent. The key figures of an earth-healing movement had come to report on their work; to find the real meaning of their down-to-earth, hand-soiling labour, thus imbuing their ecological venture with mystical significance; to have it elevated, in the presence of Mwari, to national if not universal import.

The following excerpt from an article (*Masvingo Provincial Star*, 19 January 1990) by Golden Makwena—a reporter who had participated in, and reported positively on, our tree-planting activities from the start—portrays the main features of the nocturnal shrine ceremony at Dzilo attended by AZTREC's largest delegation to date:

It was exactly 1:36 AM when a delegation of about 60 people who had travelled a distance of more than 500 kilometers, from Masvingo to Matonjeni in Matabeleland South were awakened by Cde. Chokoto Ncube, who is the High Priest and Keeper of the sacred caves at Matonjeni, right in the heart of Matopos.

Although Chokoto uses the Ndebele *mutupo*, Ncube, he is in reality a member of the Mbire Shoko people, the original priestly clan of Mwari over the centuries.

The delegation of spirit mediums, chiefs, headmen and a news reporter from this paper had awaited with an air of expectancy hanging around all night for this moment . . . The High Priest gave instructions as to how movement into the sacred mountains was to be done.

Everybody was told to remove his or her shoes and watches and no cameras or tape recorders were to be carried into the holy shrine. With hearts beating faster everyone obeyed without asking any questions and by 1:45 AM the delegation formed one long queue.

As soon as queue was out of the gates [of Chokoto's village] everyone clapped hands so to punctuate the High Priest's arrival. In a few moments the long line of people arrived at a dark place where Mwari's *dombo* [rock] was invisible although the moon was shining brightly.

Everyone was told to face the way he or she had come from, north [at Wirirani delegations always had to face east, from where, it is believed, Mwari's eventual return to his people will take place], and Cde. Ncube started clapping hands while he informed the holy place of the presence of the delegation in traditional manner.

After a few speeches a hoarse voice answered from the cave. Everyone's backs were to the cave. That it was a hair-raising experience was reflected in the movements of those who were no longer feeling at ease.

The senior *svikiro*, Zarira Marambatemwa, handed over the sum of $40 to the High Priest, who in turn told the 'voice' about the money and the intention of the delegation. The voice answered in appreciation and gave the *svikiro* an opportunity to narrate what had made them travel such a long distance.

Cde. Marambatemwa reported on the progress made so far by the Association of Zimbabwe Spirit Mediums since the last time they visited the sacred place [in 1989] and were given the blessings and go-ahead by the Guardian of the land.

The voice from the cave replied that the association's efforts to liberate the land ecologically were appreciated and they were promised good rains, guidance and success in the future.

It was around 4 AM when all business was finished at the cave and every-one descended from the mountain in single file after having been told not to look back at the cave. The delegation was also told to go into the large hut where they had slept and sing till dawn for their ancestors to acknowledge their presence at Matonjeni.

This was accepted and with the provision of eight drums [*ngoma*] and the additional two brought from Masvingo and accompanied by two horns [*hwamanda*] music reverberated from the hut like thunder.

From this newspaper report it is evident that the atmosphere at first was tense with excited anticipation, even a bit awesome when the 'hoarse voice' first came from the dark depths of the shrine cave. After a while, however, as discussion between the oracular voice and delegates progressed—via elaborate Ndebele and Shona interpretations, hand-clapping and repeated calling of Mwari's praise names—the atmosphere relaxed noticeably. Mwari was re-sponding to his/her people, approving the new association's earth-healing ac-tivities, promising rain, support, and future success. Mwari was addressed as the ultimate guardian of the land and responded in this capacity. Attention was paid to national political, ecological, and individual matters. The cult cere-mony appeared to focus more on informing the creator-guardian of the uni-verse about communal and private matters and receiving divine endorsement, inspiration, and encouragement than on lengthy and detailed divine responses to each request. At no point was Mwari's judgement questioned and when the delegation moved away from the shrine, deep satisfaction and a sense of re-laxed accomplishment were noticeable. The drumming, singing, and dancing that followed until the skies reddened in the east were the final ritual affirma-tion of mystical encounter between the creator, all life that had gone before and the still living creation.

Carefully recorded oracular sessions capture the actual discourse taking place during a cave ceremony in greater detail. On 10 January 1989, when our delega-tion paid the first official visit to Matonjeni, we spoke to the oracle of high priest-ess Gogo at the Vembe shrine. Sitting under a massive overhanging rock which had slid halfway down a mountain slope a few years ago, we were facing the east which, between 4 and 5 AM, held a promise of dawn. Sibanda, Gogo's husband, interpreted our Shona communications to the 'Voice,' while priestess Gogo her-self—sitting about three metres behind us in a pole enclosure, half hidden under the *dombo* of Mwari—interpreted back into Shona for our benefit what the en-tranced female Voice of the oracle transmitted from the cave depths in a mixture of ancient chiRozvi, Ndebele, and Kalanga.

Sibanda: Tovera, we have come with your *vazukuru* [sister's sons] from Masvingo who have arrived with their *mbonga*.

Author: We have come to observe your ways, how you deal with requests for rain, because there is drought in the Masvingo area. We have also come on behalf of the Association of Spirit Mediums. On these two issues we need your guidance.

Sibanda: Tovera, the delegation has come to request rain and to hear your comment on the *bato ramasvikiro*.

Voice: Each matter should be considered in its own right. If it is rain you are requesting, you must come towards the beginning of the year. That is the law which should be kept.

Author: And what are the requirements for delegations coming here? Must a blanket and some gifts be brought after consultation with the chiefs back in Masvingo?

Voice: You arrange for the required amount of finger millet; then send two people. But those who live far from here are also allowed to bring money as gifts when they ask Tovera for rain. All the people of this region will congregate here today. You can see them when they come and ask them how they perform their ceremonies here at the *dombo*. You are invited and allowed to attend with them.

Author: We thank you, Tovera! *Mbedzi! Dziva! Shoko!*

Voice: The people congregate here because they are worried about the drought. They know that at the onset of a new year they have to come here. These days, however, they tend to neglect this custom.

Author: Why is that so?

Voice: The people are ignorant. They forget. Only when they feel the heat of the sun do they come. Otherwise they forget.

Author: What then are the rules for such a gathering?

Voice: The rules are good. It is only a matter of proper worship. When the people approach this *dombo* they must beat the drums and dance. That is all.

Spirit medium MuDende [AZSM vice president]:   I have come to ask about the Association of Spirit Mediums, Tovera. Will it make good progress and be a success? Will the people follow the arrangements made by the executive to elevate [*kukwidza*, literally 'lift up,' that is, respect] the land? To heal the land? We request that this movement will become well established and prove itself publicly.

Voice: I want you to know that I am greatly pleased to see a white man approaching this place. It shows the eagerness of all people to heal the land. I am most thankful and expect the Association to achieve in a great way. Mwari does what he/she wants to the people.

Chinovuriri [AZSM president]:   We want to know about this Association because Mwari knows the outcome of it all. Many people ignore it because they are satisfied to simply spend their money, to stuff themselves with food, and then to forget [about the state of the environment].

Voice: I am very happy with the Association and what it is doing in the country. He [the white one] has been given this association by the ancestral elders, so that we can render a great service to the people to survive.

Author: I want to ask something else. Years ago when I first visited Wirirani, Shoko, Mwari told me that the whites are the *vazukuru* [sister's sons] of their black *vadzisekuru* [maternal uncles]. Now that Zimbabwe is liberated, is there something specific which Mwari wants to communicate about *kubatana* [cooperation or reconciliation] between blacks and whites?

Voice: I have been sent into the world to do the work of my Father. The Father has been given the whites and has shaken hands with their *she* [literally 'chief,' that is, main representative]. But I myself have not shaken hands with the Father. I only do my work on this earth. I am fearful of shaking hands with the Father, he who has told me to go and work in the world.

Author: So it is said that the messenger of Mwari was sent to the world but has not shaken hands with the Father.

Voice: The whites and blacks are one! When you have brought up a child and the child is mature, and you then give that person a command which the person refuses, what then can you do with that child? It means, no human being elects or appoints another; no human being should hate another. No! We are simply one as people, blacks and whites.

Author: Does Mwari see that there will be peace between the races now that the war has ended?

Voice: Nothing bad will happen between blacks and whites, for they are one!

Author: Is this message of racial unity also given to other whites when they visit the *dombo*?

Voice: No. This has not been discussed before. Whites do not normally come here. Only one or two from the newspapers have ever visited this place.

Priestess Gogo [spontaneously]: And what about the water, Tovera?

Voice: There are no fountains here, but when the rain is sent there will be enough water. These days there will be no rain.

Delegation: Mbedzi! Dziva! Shoko! [with hand clapping, sighs, and expressions of gratitude to conclude the ceremony].

At Dzilo we were heartily welcomed by high priest Jonas Chokoto, keeper and ritual officiant of the shrine, which had formerly operated under the tutelage of the late Simon and Adam Chokoto, Jonas's younger brothers, Simon's wife Kombo and the well-known Rozvi *mbonga*, MaMoyo (Daneel 1970:25). That night we had the following discourse with Mwari:

[Hand clapping and praise-names called repeatedly by way of introduction.]

Author: Mbedzi! Dziva! Shoko! I have brought you a gift, a sign of joy. I do so because in the distant past I also visited you when your *dombo* was still over there at Wirirani, when Simon and Adam were still officiating. They received me well on that occasion. And you, Shoko, said that I should come again. So I have arrived once more. It was in 1967 that I spoke to you at Wirirani—twenty-two years ago. I am happy to be back. We had a good journey here. Here is your gift, $29—a sign of joy and thankfulness for the safe journey.

In the past I came from Gutu, together with the Gutu *munyai*, by the name of Vondo Mukozho. Now I am accompanied by the elders of the Spirit Medium Association.

Priest Jonas Chokoto: There you are, Shoko! He is Muchakata Daneel, Shoko, and he says that he has come to bring thanks to the great Father [*babamukuru*]. So he has presented his gift of $29, Tovera, Dziva!

Voice: [via female Shona interpreter who lives in cult colony]: I am most thankful that you have arrived here. You are my *muzukuru* [sister's son]. I can see that you are troubled. Therefore I shall mediate properly on your behalf. [*ndichandoudzavo zvakanaka*, literally, 'I shall go and tell it properly']. I shall protect you. [*Ndichakutariri-rai*, literally 'I shall look after you.']

Delegation [with hand clapping]:   Mbedzi! Dziva! Shoko!

Lydia Chabata [AZSM treasurer]:   I am asking as a young child who is nonetheless entrusted with the work of the elders, the work of the Association of Spirit Mediums. I myself am a spirit medium. I am asking for a husband who will keep me and look after me wherever I go. This will give me security and status. I did great and responsible work while the war was on, Tovera. For many years I operated in the bush. After the war I looked for a husband who will care for me, but up to now I am without a husband. What kind of *svikiro* will I be without a husband? As a single person I will not be properly honoured. Yet even after the war I kept working, doing the work which the ancestors have sent me to do, to liberate the land.

In the second place I present the matter of the white man who is with us—Prof. Muchakata. He has left his own tribe in order to work with the black people. I ask you to open doors, wherever he is trying to raise funds, so that the necessary funds be found. Bless his dealings with all the *vakuru* up there [government officials] so that he will not meet with unnecessary resistance.

We are therefore seriously requesting your full support and guidance for our work. After all, it is your work, Shoko. We have gone without salaries throughout the war from 1976. We simply did our duty without any compensation. And now, in the AZSM, it is the same story all over again: work without full salaries! How long will this situation continue? It is as if you do not want me to have a husband, to work without a salary. Do you want me to become a whore?

Voice: I thank you for coming here. Your own senior ancestors of Chabata have preceded you in coming here. So we have been waiting for your arrival. If you had not come here, you would not have been able to make progress in any of these matters. But since you have come, you can now return with a relieved heart because all matters will go well from now on. Because I shall guide you in whatever you do. Go and do your work, for I shall be your guide in all matters at all times.

Delegation   [clap hands, give thanks, and, still calling Mwari's praise names, shuffle from the shrine in single file]

INTERPRETATION OF ORACULAR MESSAGES

I have deliberately included the recorded text of oracular sessions, simply because detailed accounts of what transpires at Mwari's shrines are rare. Priest Jonas Chokoto has repeatedly impressed on me that no other whites are allowed to converse with Mwari at the Dzilo *dombo*. Gogo also indicated during the session at Vembe that only a couple of white news reporters had ever attended, but that on those occasions Mwari did not make pronouncements on race relations. In view of the trust placed in me and the unusual privilege of participating as a white in one of Zimbabwe's most ancient, treasured, if still secretive, rituals, I have reproduced excerpts of the dialogue of the first cult session, concerning our green revolution.

Mwari's oracles constitute a source of broad insight which warrants comprehensive theological reflection. At this point, however, I offer only a brief interpretation, lest we digress too much from the main subject: earthkeeping. I hope eventually to make a more comprehensive historical study of Mwari's oracular revelations.

In the oracular ceremony the nature and gender of the divinity at Matonjeni is not clearly specified. Priest Jonas Chokoto addresses Mwari as Great Father. Insofar as Gogo identifies her own role with that of the incarnate Christ, she also refers to God as Father. Yet as Dziva or Dzivaguru (the Great Pool)—a name Jonas frequently uses when replying to the female Voice from the cave—God is somehow the Mother of Creation, the Great Pool of fertility, the One who speaks from the cave, the womb of the earth, in a woman's voice. The interpreting priestess at the shrine always either speaks in the first person, impersonating Mwari, or refers to 'the Voice' which says this or that, with the result that no fixed gender is attached to Mwari. The ambivalence is probably also attributable to the fact that the Shona language does not have separate pronouns for different genders. Yet the anthropomorphic attributes of an androgynous deity—both father and mother— seem to be implicit in the proceedings.

A strong undercurrent of femininity and fertility is noticeable not only in the popular image of Mwari as rain-giver and guardian of all creation, but also in the contents of oracles. For instance, the warm response to Lydia Chabata's plea for a spouse, the keen interest in her ancestors, and the promise of Mwari's guidance and protection in her female world emanate from the understanding of a woman and a mother rather than from a male deity.

Despite his/her presence at the shrine, Mwari remains the unfathomable, the unknowable—the *mysterium tremendum*, to use Rudolf Otto's term. He/she is too mighty, too remote from human conceptions to be captured in manipulable definitions. Such an awareness is reflected in the 'fluctuating identities' of the Voice and interpreting priestess. Note, for instance, that Gogo sometimes intimates immediacy and presence, which strengthens the assumption that the Voice is that of Mwari him/herself. At such times she speaks in the first person, as the deity. But at other times she also identifies with the Voice, as if the communicating being of the oracle is an intermediary, possibly a spirit at the apex of the ancestral hierarchy, who intercedes between living beings and a remote deity. On occasion she even opts for a third possibility—that of herself as 'messenger of the Father' who is sent to work in the world. Here she uses biblical terminology, reminiscent of the words of Jesus Christ. In this regard it should be noted that priestess Gogo is an avid Bible reader, so that we have here an interaction of traditionalist and Christian influences. From the oracle it is not quite clear, however, whether Gogo was momentarily relegating the tricky issue of race relations to the more remote Father (in heaven?), the one who had 'shaken hands' with the whites and therefore knew the answer to my question, or whether she was suggesting some analogy between the incarnate Christ and her own role as a kind of 'mediator' between Mwari and her fellow human beings.

At Dzilo the proceedings were also characterised by shifting identities. Sometimes the Voice speaks directly as Mwari, Tovera, Shoko, Mbedzi, or Dziva—hence as approachable through personal praise-names or the clan name (*mutupo*) of the priestly Mbire-Shoko lineage. Then it suddenly comes across as an intermediary between God and the delegation: 'The voice is labouring on your behalf, interceding for you in prayer . . . I am also crying as you are.' So the revelatory Being can be interpreted one moment as God, the ultimate power of all creation, and the next as possibly the most senior ancestor of all humanity, the ultimate mediator responsible for approaching the unknowable creator deity.

Shifting identities in no way appear to confuse issues during ritual procedure. Africa in its wisdom shrouds the near-impossible presence of the divine in infinite mystery. It refuses to be trapped into conjecture and final definitions, probably considering these presumptuous. Somehow Mwari draws near, listens to and responds to the needs of his/her creation.

Christian influence on the traditional perceptions of Mwari appears to be undeniable; although, during discussions, cult officiants at Matonjeni understandably disclaim any form of syncretising conceptual interaction so as to safeguard the unique African identity of the cult. Opposition to the mere suggestion of Christian influence on the cult is attributable to the resurgence and reinforcement of traditional belief systems during the *chimurenga* years, when it became fashionable among traditionalists to reject Jesu Krestu as the deity of the white colonialists. After all, to many people the Matonjeni cult represents the final bulwark, even if only symbolic, against the religio-cultural encroachment of white 'civilisation' on the inner soul of black Africa. There is also antagonism and rivalry between cultists and prophetic AIC movements, notably Mutendi's Zion Christian Church, because of the latter's claims to mediate for rain on behalf of church-affiliated chiefs—claims which directly challenge the ancient power base of Matonjeni (cf. Daneel 1970:64f).

Mutual influencing can, however, take place in subtle and profound ways. On the one hand it is possible for tradition-oriented Christians still to see the Christian Mwari predominantly as a God of fertility, to be approached by 'cult specialists,' the clergy, on behalf of the entire church, while individual matters remain essentially the domain of the family ancestors. In the traditional setting, on the other hand, Christ can become a role model for ritual officiants, as seems to be the case with priestess Gogo Itombiyamazulu. Many traditionalists, moreover, have little trouble incorporating Jesus Christ into their religious world-view as the senior *mhondoro* spirit of the white tribe, the mediator who is as close to Mwari as the African national ancestors, Chaminuka and Nehanda, are. Christian influence might also have stimulated a more pronounced image of the oracular deity as Creator, Father, and Liberator—observable in both Jonas Chokoto's and Gogo's perception of Mwari as Great Father (*Babamukuru*), despite the continuing suggestion of a shrouded, mysterious Being.

I deliberately raised race relations with the oracle because of the will in ZIR-RCON-AZTREC to promote interracial reconciliation in our ecological struggle; also because Mwari's pronouncements way back in 1967, when I first visited Wirirani, included admonitions about racial harmony between his/her black people and their sister's offspring—their *vazukuru*, the whites (Daneel 1970:84–85). Mwari's assertion at the Vembe shrine that whites and blacks are one and that peace should prevail between them accords with the oracle's earlier urgings, at the onset of the *chimurenga* struggle, that racial equality should be achieved and that the discriminatory disregard of the *sekuru-muzukuru* kinship obligations—as perpetrated by the white immigrant *vazukuru* on their black *vadzisekuru*—should cease. Mwari's reference at the Vembe shrine to children who mature and then follow their own ways might still be a veiled criticism of the inclination of the 'unburnt pot,' the white people, to 'handle' and 'twist' the world after their own design.

Mwari's approval of and conciliatory attitude towards a white man attending shrine sessions project the goodwill of the cult community, just as the deity's emergence as an ecological liberator is a result of the determination of God's people to start healing the earth. Accepting a white man as a participant at the shrine certainly does not imply waiving the secret nature of the cult, or any change in the role of Mwari vaMatonjeni as the preserver of black African custom and culture. The shrine gates have certainly not been thrown wide open to white observers and participants. My own involvement could already have struck a false note—for all Mwari's conciliatory gestures—in the cult tradition. It should, according to the cult officiants concerned, be considered a special privilege brought about by unusual circumstances. White participation at one of the most exclusive of black Africa's rituals is not to be taken lightly. It requires an attitude of humility and respect as one feels the heart throb of the mysterious holy of holies at Mwari's sacred rocks.

At both shrines Mwari responded quite positively to our enterprise. During the cave ceremonies, because of the initiative taken by the green delegation, Mwari's rain-giving image mutated, as it were, into that of an ecological liberator, the one whom we petition to be the ultimate guide, protector, and affirmer of the green revolution. Note, for instance, vaChinovuriri's recognition at the Vembe shrine of Mwari as the originator of our ecological enterprise in Masvingo Province. Yet simultaneously he hands over 'your work out there, Shoko' to Mwari as a self-initiated endeavour of the people, a distinctly human activity which still requires divine affirmation. In the oracular encounter the dynamic and flexible image of the divine can be ascribed both to Mwari's self-revelation from the mystical beyond and to human perceptions or intervention in regard to the concrete and socially justified needs of this existence. The concept of the divinity is born anew and remoulded in the endless cycle of divine-human encounter.

An element of uncertainty about the future and a need for divine affirmation characterise the attitudes of delegates reporting on their fledgling movement for the first time. Funds have not yet been secured and government attitudes to our green revolution have not yet been fully gauged. The response to inquiries on these issues at both shrines is positive and confirms future divine guidance, support, and protection. But whilst guaranteeing successful fund raising for tree planting, the oracle does not describe detailed battle strategies or predict exactly the future attitudes of people and the expansion of the movement. As happened during the war years, the details of the struggle are taken care of by the ancestral war council, while the oracle more generally inspires perseverance as a condition for ultimate victory.

Divine affirmation of our earthkeeping struggle at Matonjeni has a psychologically motivating effect. It provides a tangible link with the ultimate liberating power behind *chimurenga*, the real source of the new state under black rule. As a result the complex and often frustrating task of tree planting and experimentation with indigenous species, the survival rate of which can be dishearteningly low, are elevated to a mystically sanctioned undertaking of national significance. Oracular recognition also stimulates a wider vision of ecological reform among the chiefs and spirit mediums. It strengthens their determination to persevere with their voluntarily accepted task of improving their environment.

To many chiefs and mediums who had never been to Matonjeni before, the trip to the oracle was an adventurous highlight after weeks of demanding work, organising and establishing new woodlots in their own chiefdoms. Communing with the very source of their tribal political powers—powers which have been radically and disturbingly curtailed by President Mugabe's government—offered the chiefs an outlet for their frustrations, possibly also a new sense of destiny in the new Zimbabwe as their imaginations were fired to innovate and lead fellow Zimbabweans in Mwari's expanding war of the trees. Shrine visits also stimulate discussions among delegates about divine presence at the caves and the attributes of the traditional Mwari in relation to Mwari as portrayed in the Bible. To many of them these are merely varied manifestations of one Universal Creator. Without suggesting that Matonjeni must become a hybrid of traditional and Christian practice, I felt that relating to the oracle, understanding the cult, and having dialogue with its cultists were more in keeping with Christian tolerance and witness to the presence of the cosmic Christ than radical rejection and dissociation would be.

In a sense, oracular support is the logical outcome of practising earthkeeping on holistic religious and African philosophic lines. The old high-God is the final power which unites and approves the disparate yet interrelated ecological directives of a wide network of guardian spirits. Thus the concerted activities of AZTREC are elevated to almost unassailable mystical and national significance, resulting in greater overall resolve at the distant district levels. In the process religio-cultural consciousness and identity are placed in historical perspective; research is promoted; and partly obscured theological issues concerning Christian missionary impact, conceptual change in God concepts, and the resilience of African traditional religion are brought into the open.

CHIMURENGA HISTORY AND THE BIRTH OF A NEW MYTH

Traditionalist tree-planting ceremonies present the tribal elders and war veterans with an ideal platform for recounting their *chimurenga* experiences and drawing on the religious motivation of the war to inspire ecological action and commitment. Drawing on the rich heritage of *chimurenga* religion enables the elders to introduce a dimension of myth and mystical empowerment which appeals to the imagination and reinforces the call and sanction of both guardian ancestors and creator God. In the process a new myth is born, in which *chimurenga* history is reinterpreted in the context of the green revolution in such a manner that cultural, religious, and nationalist-patriotic motivational forces converge in a powerful imperative to participate in environmental reform.

The late Haurovi Chinovuriri, first president of the AZSM and subsequently general secretary of AZTREC, was a passionate exponent of the continuity between the liberation war and our ecological struggle. During the war he had been personally involved in the establishment of ZANLA camps in Mozambique. For several years, while acting as intermediary between the spirit mediums and ZANLA high command at the Chimoio camp, he was able to observe at close quarters the impact of spirit counsel on the determination of guerrilla strategy. Because of this war background and his prominent position in the movement, Chinovuriri was AZTREC's main war historian and mythologist during *mafukidzanyika* rituals.

Chinovuriri always maintained that the early contacts between guerrillas and mediums represented the origins of our earthkeeping association. When the guerrillas accompanied the aged medium, Nehanda, from Dande to Mozambique, and when ancestral directives for military strategy were faithfully recorded in 'the book of the *masvikiro*,' the foundations of our earth-healing movement were already being laid.

A favorite topic of the myth-maker was the intervention of spirit mediums during the massive raid of the Rhodesian airforce on the ZANLA camp, Chimoio, in Mozambique. On occasion he recounted: 'It happened exactly as MuDende had told us. The preparations for defence against the enemy attack were made according to the directions of the *masvikiro*. We were ready for them. So many aircraft were shot down in the attack that Samora Machel could build a big township from aeroplane parts alone. Among the aircraft shot down were three Mirages . . .'

I could not but smile at the hyperbole of Machel's township built of aeroplane parts. Informed historical accounts do not confirm such a loss of aircraft—in fact, they record a crushing defeat, in military terms, and destruction of the ZANLA camp (Moorcroft and McLaughlin 1982:151–157). Chinovuriri's account, however, turned a devastating experience into a powerful myth capable of informing and inspiring earthkeeping ventures in rural communities for generations to come . . .

Chinovuriri told how the remains of Mbuya Nehanda's *svikiro* were kept in a special grave in Mozambique during the war. Afterwards her bones were carried by Chinovuriri, Takawira, and others, travelling on foot all the way from Chimoio in Mozambique to Dande in northern Zimbabwe. This was in direct obedience to the instruction of Chaminuka, Zimbabwe's national war ancestor, that the fallen fighters should be properly buried in all districts of Zimbabwe. This injunction triggered the reburials at heroes' acres all over the country, with the approval of President Mugabe and Vice President Muzenda.

Chinovuriri's narratives were in harmony with the call of the chiefs and *masvikiro* during *mafukidzanyika* ceremonies to heed the ecological directives of the ancestors and Mwari. But he also showed that AZTREC is providing a public platform for a reconsideration of *chimurenga* history, the outcome of which will stimulate ongoing, ritual manifestation of spirit forces country-wide. The ancestors themselves, through Chaminuka, were presented as having laid down a postwar religious programme—pilgrimages to the traditional holy places in the country—so as to maintain the national unifying power of traditional religion which dominated during the war years (in contrast to localised lineage or tribal concerns which often characterise traditional ritual life) for the benefit of the entire nation. In the pilgrimage to the holy places the new ecological liberation theme introduced by AZTREC acquired special significance.

The new myth stipulated, furthermore, that political liberation is not yet complete. There is still an imbalance between the traditional spirit world and the ruling powers of the day, painfully evident in the persistent drought. Restoration of the national balance, it was suggested, could only be achieved if the necessary rituals were performed at the ancient citadel of Great Zimbabwe, the symbol of national wellbeing. AZTREC, it was hinted, should be instrumental in bringing about this event, which will give due recognition to the true spirit owners and guardians of the land. Insofar as the envisaged harmony between spirit powers and government will propitiate the forces that are withholding the life-giving rains, and so restore nature as well, both political and ecological liberation motives are realised to some extent. Here one discerns once again the holism of Africa's religion and worldview. Good politics, harmonious intertribal and race relations, a thriving subsistence economy (based, for AZTREC's peasant participants, on stable climatic conditions and a healthy environment), and ritual reciprocation between the living and the living dead—all of life hangs together in a seamless totality.

Like dreams, myth and ritual symbols inform religious life and facilitate adaptation to changing circumstances. AZTREC's new myth, as developed by Chinovuriri, was historically based. Yet, couched in mystical terms, it assumed and affirmed supernatural sanction of innovation in the form of ritualised ecological and nation-building appeasement of the ancestral world. On the one hand, the new myth confirmed and embellished the old tradition built into *chimurenga* history. The national ancestors as symbols of resistance, and the holy places (particularly Great Zimbabwe) as symbols of national progress and good government, were retained and extended to the new struggle.

At the same time the emergent myth acquired new dimensions, articulated by Chinovuriri but also willed and approved in the *mafukidzanyika* context, as if a groundswell of the collective unconscious was irresistibly breaking through the hiddenness of the unknown. New was the 'edited' rendering of *chimurenga* battles, such as the air attack on Chimoio, in such a way that ancestral intervention could be seen to provide real solutions: protection against military might, liberation from white political and cultural domination, and the building of a new society in which imperialistic presumption had been vanquished (symbolised by Machel's township built from destroyed enemy aircraft parts).

New, too, was the admission of a white participant to an essentially black African enterprise. Chinovuriri on a number of occasions likened my role in founding the AZSM to that of a 'chief.' By saying that I was not made a chief only recently, but was one already in my mother's womb, and that I could therefore not escape this chieftainship even if I wanted to, he was in a sense contextualising my role, identifying it with the problematic position of the chiefs in post-Independence Zimbabwe and referring to the inevitability of destiny. It could be that the white participant was being persuaded subtly to stick to his guns should the going get rough. Yet the ease with which, in terms of broad classification, an erstwhile 'enemy' of the liberation cause could now be accommodated as fellow combatant indicates flexibility in the new myth—the will to take responsibility for a new programme of racial reconciliation and to change attitudes for the sake of a racially open-ended revolution.

Even more significant was that the new myth recounted the past in such a way that Zimbabwean nationalist sentiments could take the form of an ethos—an ethos which defines progress not only in terms of repossession of the still 'lost lands' held by whites, or in terms of the good life (financial rewards, consumer products), but in terms of *altruistic labour invested in environmental reform.*

AZTREC delegation of chiefs and mediums arrive at the Dzilo shrine to confer with the Shona high-God about the War of the Trees.

The drumbeat at Matonjeni elicits spirited and, at times, spirit-possessed dancing in honor of Mwari.

High priest Jonas Chokoto in the courtyard of his homestead; the Dzilo shrine stands in the background.

AZTREC chiefs plant seedlings next to the grave of Jonas Chokoto, an act of commitment to the country's earthkeeping struggle.

Earthkeeper Muchakata assists with tree planting and then celebrates the establishment of a new woodlot with spirit medium vaZarira Marambatemwa and Chief Murinye, patron of AZTREC.

CHAPTER 5

Reviving and Reinterpreting Traditional Ecology

AN OVERVIEW

Traditional African ecology, like everything else in Shona society, is inseparably linked with traditional religion. Environmental protection is sanctioned by the creator God and the guardian ancestors of the land. Trees symbolise ancestral protection and/or various forms of continuing ancestral involvement in the community of the living and their habitat. Birds and animals are considered a legitimate food resource for humankind. But strict rules were laid down for the protection and survival of all species and, as was poignantly illustrated during *chimurenga*, certain animals and birds are considered to be direct emissaries from the spirit world to the community of the living. Water resources were protected through the prohibition of riverbank cultivation and elaborate rules regarding the prudent use of marshlands, springs, and fountains. In the event of abuse, mystical retaliation could be expected: animal predators or snakes threatening human life at the site of the spoilt water resource, or the departure of benevolent water spirits.

The traditional 'nature reserves' were the holy groves (*marambatemwa* or *madambakurimwa*). Here the close proximity of chiefly burial sites and surrounding tracts of sacred land—sometimes encompassing large mountain ranges with thickly wooded slopes—epitomised the sanctity of creation and the guardianship of apical ancestors, mandated by the creator deity, over all natural resources. In the *marambatemwa* all trees and plants, all wildlife, and all water resources fell under the mystical tutelage of the senior spirits and whatever guardian animals and reptiles—*mhondoro* lions (real or psychic), baboons, leopards, snakes—they chose to use. This guardianship was exercised in close cooperation with their living representatives: the chiefs, tribal spirit mediums, and ward headmen. Harvesting of natural resources in such groves, if any (for example, the felling of limited numbers of fuelwood trees, game cropping, or the use of water resources), was strictly controlled by the chiefs and mediums, following ritual interaction with the guardian spirits. Often it was a special prerogative of the chiefly house.

Factors such as population growth (and its corollary, increased pressure on communal lands); acculturation and the erosion of customary values; Christianity's deprecation of traditional religion; modern land husbandry; and the curbing of the judicial, land allocating, and hence ecological powers of chiefs, have greatly weakened the motivation for communal ecological control, or it has been assigned much lower priority in the struggle of peasants to survive in an environment of diminishing resources. In some cases traditional holy groves have become virtually extinct or have been limited to smaller patches of land as increasing numbers of tribespeople had to be accommodated in the congested tribal territories. In other instances the breakdown of customary law and tribal authority simply led to a gradual invasion of holy forests, resulting in unchecked tree felling, land clearing, and hunting.

Yet all was not lost. Traditional ecology has all along formed an integral part of the religiocultural heritage and identity of Zimbabwe's African people. Despite considerable neglect of customary law in some instances, and ineffective implementation of ecological strictures in others, African wisdom regarding the environment remained a force in peasant society. Many chiefs and headmen stubbornly insisted, against seemingly insurmountable odds, on the protection of the *marambatemwa* in their areas of jurisdiction. Far from being swept aside by the processes of modernisation, political change, and much-vaunted agro-economic progress, or merely voicing nostalgia for the good old days, they kept functioning as religiocultural custodians and protectors of the earth. Hence, with the advent of AZTREC, a core of traditional leadership was available, ready to appeal to the same spirit powers in the ecological crisis as the guerilla fighters and spirit mediums did during the struggle for independence.

But AZTREC's green revolution was not simply a revival of traditional religion and ecology, as the *mafukidzanyika* tree-planting ceremonies described in the previous chapter seem to suggest. Things have indeed changed. Some chiefs, for instance, are committed Christians and a number of spirit mediums participate in church life. Thus their appeal to the guardian ancestors of the land in the war of the trees may be intended not so much to promote traditional religion and renewed dependence on the old spirit world, as to stimulate the ecological responsibility and activity exemplified by the ancestors in the old order. In other words, revival of the old system involves reinterpretation, even of the interaction and equilibrium between the living and the living dead, and the attribution of new meaning to traditional beliefs and practices in a changing situation. As the institution which empowers chiefs, mediums, and other traditionalists to wage the ecological war on traditional lines, AZTREC is responsible for assessing this somewhat uneven process of revival and reinterpretation of the old order, guiding it along lines considered appropriate by the participant chiefs and mediums themselves, and relating it meaningfully to existing ecological programmes in the country.

AZTREC's activities and plans already reflect traditional conservationist sentiments and values attributed to trees and wildlife. Some of these, and their relevance for modern ecological warfare at Africa's grassroots, will be discussed in terms of AZTREC's threefold ecological objectives.

In contrast to what we have been discussing above, the rest of this chapter is not confined to past and current religio-ecological realities and achievements. Here I wish to pay attention to future prospects, plans which may or may not come to fruition in the actual practice of our movement. As the founder and former director of ZIRRCON, I do so partly on the strength of many years of close identification with Shona traditionalist friends and the traditional religious insight derived from this experience, and partly because of a need to leave our earthkeeping movement at least a profile of the green dream that is dreaming me. Whereas my proposals are often taken seriously and acted upon by fellow green revolutionaries, the process of reinterpretation, ritualisation, and contextualisation itself has a habit of finding its own course—a course following the rutted, unpredictable surface of the land we are trying to heal and the age-old wisdom of the people, rather than the imaginings of an involved yet culturally still alien *murungu.*

Whatever the limitations of my own role in AZTREC, the resilience and adaptability of traditional religion as an ecological motivational force in the modern era are indisputable and something to be reckoned with. My proposals in this chapter in no way represent mere romantic notions harking back to a bygone age. The resurgence of traditional religion as a unifying force during the *chimurenga* period clearly illustrated its ability to adapt and effectively deal with critical situations in modern warfare. Both Mwari, the creator, and the guardian ancestors of the historic past gave mystical directives for the use of modern weaponry against the common enemy. By the same token they are now considered to be inspiring and directing modern ecological warfare. Some of the spirit mediums, for instance, convey ancestral directives on the use of modern fencing materials for the protection of woodlots, while the oracle of Mwari proclaims support even for a modern fund-raising drive on behalf of his/her earthkeepers. Thus, because of the flexibility and continuing importance of traditional religion, there is no reason that the guardian ancestors of the *marambatemwa* will not mystically sanction AZTREC's envisaged modern wildlife programmes such as fencing of sanctuaries, restocking of game in the communal lands, and engagement in anti-poaching operations. Neither is there reason to doubt that a conceptual remodelling of the role of the *njuzu* will lead to modernised ritual which will render the latest water conservationist measures both culturally acceptable and sustainable in Shona peasant society.

THE SIGNIFICANCE AND SYMBOLISM OF TREES

Traditionally it was the responsibility of chiefs and headmen to delineate areas in their territory for cultivation, grazing, and tree felling. The senior spirit mediums played a crucial role in monitoring and policing the harvesting of fuelwood, communicating ancestral approval or disapproval, and bringing trespassers to trial in the chief's court. Both chiefs and mediums were responsible for the perpetuation of customary conservationist laws, peculiar to their own territory and reflecting the specific wishes of their apical ancestors. As environmental custodians they did not hesitate to uphold and strengthen the fairly common belief that trespassers in forbidden territory would be chased away by ancestral *mhondoro*, leopard, or whatever animal or reptile the ancestors chose to scare off wayward tribespeople.

Originally, Shona Traditionalists maintain, virtually all large trees (*miti mikuru*) were protected, as they belonged to the *samarombo*—ancestors who were believed to dwell in tree branches. Special permission, which entailed the chief's ritual supplication of the *samarombo*, had to be obtained prior to felling such trees. If this was not done, tree felling meant fighting the *samarombo*, thus disturbing the equilibrium between the living and the deceased in the local community. To avert the wrath of the *samarombo* or the *midzimu enyika* (ancestors of the land), trespassers were fined by the chief. A fine consisted of a sacrificial goat or cow and beer. If, however, the ancestors—through persistent affliction of the community—rejected the conciliatory ritual conducted on behalf of the community by the chief and *svikiro*, the ecological offenders would be ostracised. Hence the protection of *miti mikuru* was a distinct feature of traditional ancestor veneration.

Different species of trees have their own religious connotations. Some of the better known ones in Masvingo Province are the following:

- The *mubvumira* (from *kubvuma*, literally 'to approve'; wild syringa, *kirkia akuminata*) symbolises ancestral approval of the coming of age of their agnatic kin and the consequent geographical expansion or segmentation of villages in the land under their guardianship. For instance, when the head of a family is informed by an adult son that he wishes to build his own homestead within the confines of the existing village or to establish a new village in the ward, a cutting from a *mubvumira* tree is planted by the father at the proposed new site. If after some months the cutting shows signs of healthy growth, it is interpreted as ancestral approval of the son's ability to take responsibility for his own household and of the site he has chosen.

- *Muzeze* (*peltoforum africanum*) branches, which are adorned with bright yellow flowers during the rainy season, are used for purification after burial rituals. Handling a corpse is contaminating and could cause the contaminated person to be afflicted with dream visitations from the deceased's lonely spirit before it is elevated to ancestral status in the *kugadzira* ritual (Daneel 1971:101f). Thus it is essential that all parties who have handled the corpse participate in the concluding rite, during which purificatory water is sprinkled on individuals from *muzeze* branches.

- The *muchakata* (wild cork tree; *parinari curatellifolia*) is the ancestral tree most commonly used for ritual purposes. Of all the 'big trees' it is the one which is always left untouched when bush is cleared for crop cultivation. In a sense this species is sacrosanct, untouched even by agricultural expediency, which sometimes justifies the felling of some of the 'holy trees' mentioned above. It is generally agreed in the communal lands that only madness, in the sense of complete alienation from the accepted mores of society and the spirit world, could cause people to chop down *muchakata* trees. For this tree, more than any other, symbolises ancestral care and protection.

In addition, a wide range of wild fruit trees are also associated in varying degrees with the land's guardian ancestors. The *mushuku* (wild loquat), for instance, is often found in large numbers on wooded mountain slopes in holy groves. These may be harvested only sparingly for fear of incurring the wrath of the *midzimu* at the depletion of their own 'food supplies.' Where *mushuku* woodlands have been cleared for settlement, people living there often complain about offended *mhondoro* spirits making their lives miserable.

The persistence of these beliefs and their impact on the preservation of traditional ecological systems call for further study. AZTREC's concern for indigenous trees has, however, helped trigger discussion in traditionalist circles about both the cultivation of the 'holy trees' of old and renewed application of ancestrally inspired ecological laws. It appears as if the war of the trees has brought into the open many long-obscured ecological values and ancient beliefs. The explicit identification of ZIRRCON-AZTREC's key figures with such values is a clear indication of our confidence in their recruitment and mobilisation potential. The use of tree names by the combatants in the ecological *chimurenga* is likewise expressive of Africa's abiding wisdom about the sanctity of creation.

During Zimbabwe's liberation struggle the guerrilla fighters used nicknames which they either chose themselves in order to identify with skills or qualities required on the war front, or which were conferred on them by fellow fighters after feats in combat. A major consideration was anonymity in order to protect their families. In the war of the trees key figures followed suit, in this instance using tree or tree-related names to add drive and meaning to the struggle.

The most obvious and appropriate nickname was that of *Marambatemwa* (literally 'refusal to have the trees felled'), which I personally gave to senior spirit medium vaZarira after I had heard her urging people to honour and protect the traditional holy groves during a *mafukidzanyika* ceremony. Living up to her new name, which soon became current throughout the ZIRRCON-AZTREC movement, *Marambatemwa* became a veritable crusader for the holy groves, making it the main theme of her speeches at all the tree-planting ceremonies she attended.

I myself adopted the name of *muchakata* (wild cork tree), not to invite the ancestor veneration for which the tree is known, but to show respect for traditional custom and to cater, as the *muchakata* does, for the needs of both humans and animals. Protection in this instance implies shade and rest for the fighters of the green revolution: my attempts to help provide some financial security and ecologically relevant policies to sustain the fighting cadres, just as the ancestors—approached under the *muchakata* during rain rituals—are expected to mediate rain and thus agro-economic sustenance in a rural subsistence economy. Perhaps the paternalist in me subconsciously prompted the choice of this name, seeking to secure a kind of sacrosanct status in a position which can be highly controversial and, because of its exploratory nature, open to harsh criticism.

Key figures in the AAEC also use tree nicknames. Rev. Solomon Zvanaka settled for the *muzambiringa* (grapevine) because of the image of Christian unity presented in the New Testament description of Christ as the vine (John 15). As a conciliatory figure, Rev. Zvanaka, ZIRRCON's current director, is indeed a promoter of unity among AAEC adherents. Bishop Machokoto, former president of the AAEC, goes by the name of *mushuku* (wild loquat), the image in his case connoting ample provision for the AAEC churches he was leading, for in a good season Mwari provides a rich harvest of delicious *mushuku* to thousands of people throughout the province. Bishop Marinda, general secretary of the AAEC, maintains that his family name of Marinda (literally 'graves'; that is, keeper of the ancestral graves) indicates adequately the involvement of his agnatic kin in keeping royal Duma graves over many generations. As 'grave-keepers' the Marinda family tradition includes guardianship of holy groves, the difference in the AAEC context being that the bishop is a fellow keeper of the modern *marambatemwa*—the woodlots planted by participant churches.

For all their genuine meaningfulness, these nicknames obviously do not have the same significance that nicknames had in the life-and-death situation of the national liberation struggle. Nevertheless, the use of tree names in our earthkeeping activities makes us more aware of our rootedness in traditional ecology and our kinship in a new struggle. It enables us to be much more observant of the qualities of individual trees than before. It also encourages frank comment on the character traits we observe in each other which correlate with, and are fostered by, identification with the trees of our choice. It nurtures a growing sense of our communion with creation— seeing trees and plants not only as an exploitable resource but as brothers and sisters whose sanctity requires respect. Such awareness instils humility to counter the arrogance caused by a perverted sense of human dominion over creation.

All this is not a reversion to traditional 'animism' (the notion that all creation is animated by magical or spirit forces), as our reconsideration of customary beliefs concerning the interaction between certain tree species and the ancestors may seem to indicate. Rather, our attitude entails attributing recognisable and inspiring cultural value to our ecological struggle, a way of contextualising our quest. The keenness of fellow earthkeepers to identify tree species and to engage in searching discussions about the flora and fauna of our country as we ceaselessly travel the countryside on our many errands—planting trees, monitoring woodlots, managing nurseries, conducting workshops—is a direct result of dreaming this new dream, living a new myth as we listen to the whispers of our friends, the trees.

In addition to the kind of quasi-ecological 'conscientization' that my colleagues and I attained by identifying with trees, the phenomenon of sacred groves, when retrieved by AZTREC, became important, in our new *chimurenga*. In the communal lands the sacred groves indeed constitute a large proportion of the remaining closed-canopy forests. If ZIRRCON-AZTREC were to undertake a systematic survey of *marambatemwa* and inspire chiefs, spirit mediums, and district (village and ward) councillors to renew their commitment to the protection of their sacred groves, this would be a massive stride forward in grassroots conservation, over and above the introduction of our 'modern' *marambatemwa*: woodlots and orchards.

From a pilot study already conducted by ZIRRCON's research department it is evident that all chiefdoms in the province contain several groves, some well preserved, some partly defunct. Traditionally the ideal seems to have been that each *dunhu* or ward should have at least one such grove, the state of a well-kept grove symbolising socio-ecological wellbeing and the stability of the entire community (humans—the living and the living dead; wildlife; trees; plants; water resources). Without a *marambatemwa* or *madambakurimwa* in honour of the local lineage progenitors, and via them the senior guardian ancestors of the land, community life was incomplete, if not untenable and futureless. The chief ritual officiants responsible for propagating and enforcing the ecological laws concerned, and for communing with the senior ancestors, were the chiefs and/or ward headmen, as well as the spirit mediums of the senior ancestor(s) buried in the grove. Contravention of a shrine's laws, for instance through tree felling or hunting, was punishable with heavy fines or, in the case of severe mystical retaliation, ostracism of the offender from the ward community.

The Duma people in particular are noted for their elaborate traditions of sacred groves. In Gutu South, in Chief Chiwara's chiefdom alone, there are at least four major shrines with surrounding wooded groves. In earlier centuries the embalming or mummification of Duma royalty took place at these shrines, and selected families of shrine keepers (for example Bishop Marinda's family) evolved their own histories of shrine protection from one generation to the next. The Vinga shrine on Mount Vinga is the most important, as it contains the graves of Dumbukunyuka and several other Duma dignitaries. This shrine is a symbol of Duma unity. In periods of crisis, such as war or drought, Duma chiefs used to consult the medium of Dumbukunyuka at this shrine. The Vumba shrine comprises a large *mushuku* forest adjacent to Mount Vumba, a forest which is believed to be protected by a large *njuzu*-affiliated snake which lives in a pool near the top of the mountain. Third in order of importance is the Chiunga grove, the place where Dumbukunyuka lived and died. Whereas Pfupajena was the courageous warrior-conquerer who expanded the boundaries of the Duma realm, Dumbukunyuka was the wise leader with prophetic insight who stabilised Duma hegemony and outwitted his foes. When the Rozvi eventually killed him, he is said to have disappeared underground and to have risen after some days at a place where his tribespeople could collect his corpse for its final passage to the Vinga shrine. The fourth shrine grove is that of Mount Vunjere, named after NeVunjere who lies buried there. Because of its dense growth, it was used by the ZANLA guerrillas during *chimurenga* as a safe refuge for regrouping, nursing their wounded, and spells of rest. Situated within the woodlands of the Vunjere farmland, which the bushfighters declared a liberated zone towards the end of the struggle, the Vunjere grove became a base from which extensive guerrilla operations were launched.

Against the background sketched here, what can ZIRRCON-AZTREC do to help Zimbabweans preserve and/or restore their ancient religio-ecological sanctuaries, groves which together comprise a large area of open- and closed-canopy natural forest of great biodiversity? My proposals at present are the following:

- A systematic survey of all *marambatemwa* in Masvingo Province should be undertaken. This should include each grove's history of origin (that is the roles of tribal progenitors and rulers), as such histories reveal tribal identity and aspirations which have a bearing on ecological motivation.
- On the basis of such a survey the ZIRRCON-AZTREC executive could determine which of the major shrines in the province should receive special attention and support. The selection could be guided by the chiefs and mediums of each district who, as keepers and advisers, have intimate knowledge of the groves in their respective areas.
- Once consensus is reached, specific objectives, rules, and programmed action can be determined and implemented. For instance, deforested areas in selected *marambatemwa* can be rehabilitated through reforestation, with local communities taking responsibility not only for the actual tree planting but also for establishing indigenous tree nurseries from which they can draw seedlings for their own annual restoration programme.

- Such activity could reinstate natural forest and game sanctuaries in the communal lands. For example, if ZIRRCON-AZTREC can persuade Forestry and Parks and Wildlife to assist with preliminary feasibility studies, it should be possible to launch a joint project of transforming at least a few of the largest sacred groves in the country into state-subsidised, tradition-oriented nature sanctuaries. Such a scheme would accommodate both the state's wildlife objectives, supervised here by Parks and Wildlife yet basically controlled by grassroots communities, and traditionalist religious sentiments of drawing inspiration and guidance from the local guardian ancestors.
- A balanced combination of state support and grassroots action could elevate the major *marambatemwa* in the communal lands to a level of national significance, as genuine symbols of ecological hope and efficiency at the epicentre of environmental devastation and soil depletion caused by overpopulation and the consequent overuse of all natural resources. Such nature reserves could become religio-cultural centres of African achievement, variously interpreted by participant workers or observers in terms of their own individual religious persuasions, yet springing from their common African roots.

The heartbeat of AZTREC's ecological programmes so far has been its nurseries and woodlots, spread fairly evenly over all the districts of Masvingo Province, with Chiredzi and Mwenezi as recent additions. From an early date the chiefs and mediums declared their wish that we should continue planting exotics, such as eucalyptus, tipuana tipu, and lucaena, but that the emphasis should be on indigenous trees, the 'trees of the people' (*miti echivanhu*). So, with the assistance of spirit mediums, tribal elders, and school communities, the pairs of nursery keepers appointed to each nursery collected seeds, prepared the required potting soil in polythene bags, and started cultivating a wide variety of tree seedlings.

It is difficult to determine to what extent AZTREC key figures' explicit support of the *varidzi venyika* (guardian ancestors of the land) was decisive in the choice of indigenous trees for the war of the trees. As neither Forestry nor the traditional authorities had ever planted indigenous trees to any significant extent, there was no obvious example to go by. However, the tribal elders were inclined to choose the types of tree which would satisfy their own, often neglected, religio-cultural needs and those most likely to meet with ancestral approval. Thus it was no coincidence that, for our very first indigenous tree nursery (developed at my house), spirit medium Lydia Chabata of her own accord chose ancestrally significant trees such as *muzeze* and *mukamba*, as well as *mushuku* (wild loquat) and *mutobge* (custard apple), both of which she claimed would produce food for the ancestors to eat. For my part, I insisted on extensive cultivation of the acacia species—*msasa, mutondo, muvuzhe* (mountain acacia), and in particular the *mudziyavashe*—to establish the prospect of large-scale fuelwood production, one of our main priorities. Thus AZTREC's choice of indigenous species was determined by a mixture of traditional religious and practical motives.

These motives became even more varied and comprehensive as more species were added: *mukurumbira* (teak), in addition to the *mukamba*, as long-term investments in commercial timber; lucaena for both cattle fodder and fuelwood; and all sorts of fruit trees (mango, citrus, guava, pawpaw, peach, etc.) for the establishment of orchards in rural areas.

Of late some of our nursery keepers in the Chivi district have been experimenting with baobab and *muonde* (wild fig tree), but the *muchakata*, for all its religious significance, is not cultivated. Perhaps because of successful protection and self-perpetuation it is commonly seen in maize fields in the province and consequently is not felt to be threatened in any way.

Whatever the tree species selected for cultivation and planting, the prominence in the movement of age-old religious values is evidenced by the constant talk in AZTREC circles about the traditional value of trees, the use at *mapfukidzanyika* ceremonies of various nicknames based on traditional tree symbolism, and the invocation of ancestral approval and protection of all trees planted in AZTREC woodlots. It is even possible that to those rural participants who no longer experience the ancestors as a consistent force in their lives, indigenous trees will increasingly acquire traditional cultural value. Should the envisaged reforestation of damaged *marambatemwa* areas get off the ground, it is likely that the motive for selecting and planting trees will be quite specifically religious. At all events, the correlation in people's minds between the traditional sacred groves and our modern woodlots (also regarded as *marambatemwa*, because of religiously imposed strictures and the controlled cropping of trees under traditional authority) could culminate in the attribution of new religious meaning to AZTREC's 'sacred groves.'

PROTECTING AND INCREASING WILDLIFE RESOURCES

Because of ZIRRCON's preoccupation with tree planting during the initial phase of its existence, as well as lack of funds and specialist staff, little has been done about its second objective: wildlife conservation. Nonetheless there is considerable enthusiasm for game conservationist programmes in AZTREC and AAEC. At both the executive and the field-training level there is consensus that ZIRRCON should try to raise funds for wildlife research; for a specialised wildlife component in ZIRRCON's ecological and research departments; for game restocking programmes in the communal lands, as implied in the foregoing discussion of the rehabilitation of nature sanctuaries (*marambatemwa*); and for introducing contextualised game conservation texts, based on customary hunting philosophy and praxis, into the syllabus of our training programmes.

These objectives are somewhat ambitious and their realisation will certainly require more substantial funding than ZIRRCON can rely upon at present. Nevertheless, they reflect the common will of a wide spectrum of African rural communities and are particularly relevant in terms of shifting game conservation responsibility from the bureaucratic, if not elitist, level to the grassroots of rural African society. For this reason alone it is worth considering briefly what we have resolved and planned so far.

Soon after the formation of the AZSM in 1988, I introduced the idea of the new movement acting as a link between black and white farmers in commercial farming areas with a view to game farming. The target area at that stage was the Gutu commercial farming community, where I had close ties with a number of farmers, particularly the late Toy Nel and his family of Chibakwe Farm, who have operated a successful game project for many years. The idea was to launch game farming on a mutual aid basis in a locality where black and white farmers on adjacent farms could develop a 'cooperative' along predetermined lines of interaction. At the time the Gutu chiefs and mediums, together with a number of ex-combatants serving on Gutu's rural development committees, strongly supported the proposals.

Despite the paucity of game in the overcrowded communal lands of Masvingo Province, a hunting tradition still exists in rural society. Discussions with tribal elders in particular reveal nostalgia for the past when game abounded in their districts, pleasure in the narration of wildlife and hunting stories, and eagerness to discuss customary hunting codes. In Gutu district the hunting feats of the Rufura tribe's founding ancestor, Mabwazhe—particularly his killing of the rogue rhino in the Rozvi king's territory in the eighteenth century—have attained mythical significance. Courage, fierce independence, and economic enterprise among Rufura tribespeople are viewed by many as character traits imparted supernaturally by their hunter ancestor.

Some of the traditional hunting laws inevitably relate to the holy groves. These include the prohibition of killing any animals in such areas, unless an annual hunt is called by the chief as grove caretaker, with the approval of the guardian ancestors. As representatives of the ancestral guardians, the chief and the senior medium are entitled to certain portions of the meat of animals killed in or near a sacred grove. This reveals close interaction between guardian spirits and hunters in the observance of traditional game-culling codes.

I have listed some of the most common game laws which, according to chiefs and mediums, existed prior to the colonial period. These include the restriction of hunting to the winter season; prohibition of killing young animals or females in foal; a quota system for individual hunters; constraints on hunting for commercial purposes; and the entitlement of the chief in the hunting area to specified portions of meat in honour of the guardian ancestors. Birds and animals such as bateleur eagles and tortoises, considered to be 'emissaries' from the spirit world, were protected. Spirit mediums were appointed guardians of threatened species like ant-bears, pangolins, and bush babies (Appendix II, p. 297).

Quite a number of these customary laws coincide with those currently applied by National Parks and Wildlife in hunting concession areas. Detailed research could well reveal considerable variation in these laws from one district to another. Significant, however, is the persistence of a core hunting code in peasant society as part and parcel of oral tradition. The code ties in closely with traditional religion and, despite the scarcity of game in the communal lands, is still held in high regard, particularly by traditional elders in respect of their sacred groves.

In view of all this I have no doubt about the viability of reintroducing game into the communal lands, starting with some of the larger *marambatemwa*. These can be game-fenced and stocked, following feasibility studies and intensive discussions with rural communities, district councils, and the chiefs and mediums of AZTREC.

A considerable amount of spadework has already been done, including preliminary feasibility studies at Mount Rasa and discussions with councillors and communities about the establishment of a game sanctuary at this mountain. Senior officials of the Worldwide Fund in Harare have been supportive of ZIRRCON's proposals and initiatives in this field, and we hope that the combined efforts of these two institutions will soon culminate in the realisation of some of the ideals outlined above. The development of a *marambatemwa* game sanctuary at Mount Rasa could well have far-reaching consequences for the reintroduction of game in Zimbabwe's overpopulated communal lands.

Once the wildlife section of ZIRRCON's ecological department is in place, an attempt will be made to study the overall situation of wildlife conservation in this country. Prevailing conditions in the Chirisa game park in Gokwe, in the hunting camps of the Zambezi valley, and in the Matusadona, Hwange, Gona-re-Zhou, Kyle, and Mushandike parks, particularly in terms of game populations and anti-poaching operations by Parks and Wildlife, should be surveyed. This should be done in cooperation with the conservationist and government departments concerned. ZIRRCON requires accurate information in order to define a meaningful role for its members in the protection of endangered game species. From time to time the poaching of rhino (for example the discovery of 13 rhino carcasses in the Gona-re-Zhou park and 17 carcasses in the Zambezi valley reported in December 1988), preventive rhino dehorning measures, the introduction of rhino-breeding units, and the culling of elephant are discussed at ZIRRCON-AZTREC executive meetings. Participant chiefs, mediums, and a number of ex-combatants have shown great interest and motivation to become actively involved in the anti-poaching campaign. It is generally agreed that the war of the trees should be extended as soon as possible to include a war against poachers—specifically rhino and elephant poachers, but also fish poachers, such as the illegal netters of fish in Lake Kyle, the Sanyati Gorge, and other locations at Lake Kariba.

Considering the focal role in *chimurenga* of spirit mediums acting on behalf of the guardian spirits of the land in each district, and their representation of the ancestral war council in uniting and mobilising people against a common enemy, it seems feasible to officially incorporate influential mediums—even if only experimentally at first—in the anti-poaching units of Parks and Wildlife. As many of the *masvikiro* are still convinced of their age-old calling to protect wildlife and pride themselves on their *chimurenga* involvement, they will be only too willing to carry on the fight against those who are destroying our game population, particularly rhino, for personal gain. These men and women are admirably qualified to fulfil a mystical watchdog function, seeking in the process to establish the kind of justice between human beings and wildlife which the guardian ancestors require. In actual fact this is part of the struggle against the destructive *uroyi* (wizardry) of greed!

The deliberate introduction of the supernatural realm into this area of African life could help motivate communities to become active in uprooting evil, in this instance through the detection, exposure, and ostracism or capture of poachers.

PROTECTING AND INCREASING WATER RESOURCES

AZTREC's chiefs and mediums are already actively protecting water resources through the prohibition of riverbank cultivation, strict application of customary laws concerning the protection of fountainheads, and the siting of eucalyptus plantations in places where there is little risk of damaging the sponge of underground water reserves. To arrive at realistic and more comprehensive objectives in this field, however, will require surveys of the availability and state of water resources in Zimbabwe's rural areas, and related efforts such as the control of fishing and water pollution.

Some projects for AZTREC's future consideration are the following:
- *Anti-siltation measures.* Lake Kyle is one of the major water resources in Masvingo Province, both for Masvingo town and the irrigation schemes of the Lowveld sugar cane industry. Much of its catchment area is being impaired by deforestation, gully formation, lack of contour ridging, and harmful cultivation practices, particularly in the Gutu, Zimuto, and Masvingo districts through which its feeding rivers flow. Siltation can be curbed through stricter control of grazing and soil cultivation in the communal lands—a task in which AZTREC can assist agricultural extension agencies like Agritex. In deforested areas where squatters have been removed, plantations of indigenous and/or exotic trees could be introduced as part of ZIRRCON-AZTREC's annual tree-planting drive, subject to agreement with Masvingo's town council and provincial land-use committees.
- *Gully reclamation.* Peasants in the communal lands are confronted with escalating levels of soil erosion. Gully formation caused by flood water in the fields and water chains is integral to this serious depletion of arable topsoil. Part of the solution obviously lies in supervised improvement of farming methods, such as correct ploughing practices, contour ridging, and properly planned soil cover (trees and grass) in and around arable lands. It is conceivable that existing land husbandry programmes could be augmented by experimental projects in which peasant communities take responsibility for the reclamation of gullies by planting not only trees but also different grass species in order to arrest soil erosion. Ridges and small dams can be built in gullies to help curb the soil-eroding flood water.
- *Protection of river banks* against bush clearing, cultivation, and gold panning should become a formal priority of the chiefs, spirit mediums and tribal elders who are active in AZTREC. Exposure in news media of major offences could be one means of rendering the prohibition effective and demonstrating the determination of the movement to exercise its ecological watchdog function.
- Ecological staff could assist rural communities with the *planning and implementation of dam building schemes.* In addition to planting woodlots near

dams, they could promote bird life and water vegetation, as well as help to stock dams with fish and control netting.

- As the *masvikiro* and chiefs extend their responsibility in this area, they could *reinterpret their traditional water conservationist duties* in terms of preserving the aquatic dwelling places, the underwater cities of *njuzu* spirits in rivers, pools, and dams. Thus they could define their tradition-oriented contribution in the modern context more precisely. Youth programmes at the conference centres in the envisaged *marambatemwa* sanctuaries will give tribal elders an opportunity to teach young people about the sanctity of water and the customary rules for the preservation of water resources in specific groves. They will be able to draw on a rich store of *njuzu* stories about rain making, flooding rivers during good rainy seasons, the protection of aquatic medicine resources, and so forth.

Judging by the frequent references at *mafukidzanyika* tree-planting ceremonies to the *njuzu* and the guardian ancestral spirits in connection with rain making and environmental wellbeing, the mystical powers associated with all water resources still exercise a powerful sanction in traditionalist circles for all supportive and protective human endeavour in this field. The *njuzu* spirits, like the tribal ancestors, relate directly to Mwari at the cult shrines of Matonjeni. AZTREC's delegations to the shrines with rain requests to Mwari assume both the support of these water spirits for their visits and divine empowerment of the spirits to interact with human beings to ensure respectful use of life-giving water and the protection of all *njuzu* abodes.

Just as the *mafukidzanyika* ceremonies are evolving from a preoccupation with tree planting, it is likely that new forms of indigenous ritual will develop in relation to water projects. Thus the launching and completion of dam-building projects could well be accompanied by *njuzu* ceremonies featuring traditional *shavi* dances. In this instance the drumming, songs, and dancing will serve to strengthen the ties between living beings and a living water world, the commitment of participants to mystically sanctioned laws concerning the use of water, and, more generally, the resolve of our earthkeepers to protect water medicines and water itself as medicine for healing the land.

CHAPTER 6

Environmental Custodianship and Earth Community

ZIRRCON's contribution so far has been but a drop in the ocean, if one considers the magnitude of environmental problems worldwide and the requirements for responsible stewardship in Zimbabwe. Yet ZIRRCON has managed to place environmental concerns fairly and squarely in the liberationist tradition of peasant society. Its declaration of a 'war of the trees' has revived the sentiments and unifying forces of *chimurenga* to give special historical meaning to the struggle of liberating the agriculturally depleted, beleaguered soil. Earth-healing endeavours form a platform which pays tribute to the heroes who fought colonialism, and simultaneously creates opportunities for heroic exploits in a new struggle, which largely explains the fascination and staying power of ZIRRCON's cadres of green fighters. Pragmatic and exploitive motives are no doubt present in the ranks of ZIRRCON's earthkeepers. After all, who in peasant society does not a want a steady income to supplement the vicissitudes of subsistence farming? And which villager in a denuded environment will not want to capitalise on firewood or timber for building and carpentry in accessible woodlots? But much more than mere pragmatism must be at work for these same people to persist year after year with time-consuming afforestation projects even when black frost wipes out their seedlings, entire woodlots are decimated by livestock starved for good grazing, and any number of hitches thwart outright success. Our movement indeed employs cool-headed agro-economic reasoning for waging a war of afforestation. But its long-term sustainability and success will continue to lie in the people's love of the land and their willingness to sacrifice and suffer in their attempts to restore that which essentially spells 'home' to them.

Despite the geographic limitations of its contribution and the relative lack of Western-style ecological expertise, ZIRRCON has managed to strike a healthy balance between instructive conscientisation and earth-healing action. Not satisfied with rousing meetings, conferences, and workshops—valuable and indispensable as these occasions may be—the movement has engaged in decisive action from the outset. Thus it created a tangible guideline or 'myth' for itself, symbolised by nurseries and woodlots, on which it could build and which in itself provided an example and motivation for continued earth-healing action. ZIRRCON's staying power and future growth hinge largely on this combination of convincing action and inspired teaching.

To evaluate ZIRRCON's contribution purely in terms of ecological achievements is to misunderstand the religio-cultural mould in which all its activities are cast. AZTREC has been a vehicle of traditional contextualisation of the idiom in which earthkeeping concern is expressed. Is it succeeding in setting a new religio-cultural course for environmental endeavour? As we conclude the first part of our study we have to consider a few related questions as well:

- What is the significance of African religion for ecological action in the 'global village'?
- What can we learn from it and how can it shape our attitudes as we are increasingly drawn into a religiously pluriform league of earthkeepers from many parts of the world?
- What, moreover, are the theological implications of the ZIRRCON model of traditionalist and Christian counterparts sharing ecological mission? My answer to these questions is not a thoroughgoing theology. I merely offer some observations which I consider significant for an eventual theological evaluation.

TRADITIONAL CUSTODIANS OF THE LAND AND
RELIGIO-ECOLOGICAL INNOVATION

The most outstanding feature of AZTREC's work is the ability of the traditional custodians of the land to appropriate and revitalise Africa's age-old religio-ecological values in a modern programme of environmental reform. AZTREC has demonstrated convincingly that where the authority of the traditional leaders (chiefs and mediums) is still relatively intact, they are capable, once motivated and empowered, of mobilising rural society for large-scale environmental programmes. Appropriation and revitalisation of traditional values, as we have seen, are based on holistic worldviews, but are much more than a mere reversion to, or revival of, the old religio-cultural order. Through AZTREC's persistent ecological engagement, the spirit guardians of the land are now seen not only as insisting on observance of customary ecological laws to preserve the holy groves, but as demanding a much more aggressive and geographically extensive process of healing and clothing the barren land through reafforestation and related programmes. In other words, the religious dynamics of inspirational interaction between the living, the living dead, and the creator God are currently informing and initiating new but still basically indigenous patterns of ecological curative action to remedy humanly inflicted imbalances and destruction.

How, then, is the traditionalist appropriation of the old religious order, the building on old foundations, introducing innovative change? I mention a few significant examples. First, the *mafukidzanyika* tree-planting ceremonies resemble the *mukwerere* rain rituals in their dependence on the guardian ancestors of the land. Yet the ancestral demands have changed in that the right-mindedness that they demand in return for mediating abundant rains and good crops involves more than just the traditional respect and veneration symbolised by libations and ritual addresses. In the new ritual context they in fact require their living descendants to create the actual conditions for good rainy seasons, namely ample vegetation achieved through reafforestation. This is an entirely novel notion in a belief system that traditionally required only the conservation of abundance, which nature itself could keep regenerating before the problems of overpopulation, land pressure, and deforestation got out of hand. What is happening, in a sense, is that African rural society's growing knowledge, acquired from modern education, about ozone depletion, the hothouse effect of deforestation and air pollution and its possible impact on climatic cycles, is being meaningfully related to the African cosmic order, which is still kept in balance through mystical sanction and appropriately ritualised human response. The environmental viability and success of AZTREC lies in 'modernising' the mystical sanction of the ancestors within an earthkeeping praxis which in some respects transcends traditional conservationist customs, without alienating people from their ecological roots.

Second, even the mystical spirit world appears to be regrouping in AZTREC's version of the war of the trees. As in the war years, the senior guardian ancestors of chiefdoms and districts are collaborating in the spirit war council (*dare rechimurenga*) presided over by Mwari. Such change is evident in the broad representation of spirit hierarchies at tree-planting ceremonies, where the parochial ward and chieftaincy interests reflected in *mukwerere* rain rituals acquire wider significance in a regional and national perspective. The involvement of Mwari, the oracular deity, in particular underscores this trend. AZTREC pilgrimages to Matonjeni strengthen our traditionalist constituency's awareness that their struggle has national, even universal, implications. Such widened horizons bolster sustained ecological commitment.

In the third place, traditional perceptions of evil are imaginatively applied to environmental destruction in the development of an indigenous ethos aimed at ecological repair. The will of traditional authorities in AZTREC to impose drastic sanctions on environmental trespassers—as also happens in the AAEC—surfaces in the stigmatisation of such offenders as *varoyi venyika* ('wizards of the land'). Customary law has always included punitive measures against *varoyi* because of the threat they pose to the wellbeing of individuals and society. Hence branding wanton tree-fellers and cultivators of riverbanks as *varoyi* creates a situation in which effective disciplinary measures can be taken against transgressors of an emerging green ethos.

The traditionalist model of earthkeeping developed by AZTREC is certainly worth considering for the development of inculturated environmental strategies elsewhere in Africa. It enables traditional authorities to harness African cosmologies and worldviews for sustained ecological action. Through its mobilisation of grassroots communities in afforestation programmes, AZTREC has achieved what the Forestry Commission of Zimbabwe, by its own admission, has not been able to do, despite its greater financial stability, salaried staff, and other resources. In my view AZTREC convincingly demonstrates that the institution of the chieftaincy, including spirit mediumship, is capable of orchestrating comprehensive environmental reform in Africa. For the chiefs and mediums to contribute their own ecological creativity, they require a platform that is organisationally and financially independent of government and environmental institutions.

CONTRIBUTIONS OF AFRICAN RELIGIOUS VALUES TO EARTH HEALING

Part one of this study has attempted to probe the cosmological roots and belief systems of the Shona as a motivating force in the mobilisation of inculturated earthkeeping. The insight it generates may be significant for the development of a relevant eco-theology or environmental ethic in the global village. Numerous anthologies comprising contributions from all parts of the world reveal acute awareness among academics of the value of the 'primal' religions, alongside other world religions, for a radical rethink of the prevailing anthropocentric ethic in industrial consumer societies with its devastating impact on natural resources. Generally, they do so by giving examples of the role attributed to 'primal' religions with a view to replacing this anthropocentric ethic, understood as an emphasis on human wellbeing at the expense of nonhuman life and the resources of the earth, with an ethic of responsibility and respect for all creation.

Positive as current appraisals of 'primal' or 'indigenous' religions and their significance for the development of a global environmental ethic are, we are left with the problem of generalisation and application when one moves from local rural contexts to global industrialised ones. I agree with the call to have the earth as prophet and the indigenous peoples as teachers. But how do indigenous peoples' rituals for the renewal of human-earth relations gain recognition in consumer cultures in which economism (McDaniel 1995:150) and individualism are the main tenets of urban religion, at the expense of bonding rituals? And exactly what inspiration is conveyed by the primal consciousness which could or should help modern society recapture a sense of community? I do not profess to have complete answers to these questions. Neither do I, as an outdoor, rural person, have adequate tools to gauge the relevance of the AZTREC story for urban society. Nevertheless, because of a shared destiny and common humanity in the global village, the AZTREC experience and its religiosity have validity and impact beyond its own geographical confines. Narration of the experience, as I have attempted in this publication, may in itself be a challenge and an inspiration in the common quest of earthkeepers worldwide to heal the earth.

To this end I shall highlight and evaluate some of the values of African religion as they surfaced in the AZTREC experience. Although I hesitate to suggest universal application of locally contextualised values, it may be helpful if in some instances I briefly indicate the shaping influence African religion has had on my own existence, steeped as it still is in the Western culture and life style. In so doing it is just possible that my brief outline of a few religio-environmental themes (sense of place, sense of community, renewal of human-earth relations, and awareness of divine presence) will crystallise into meaning in the reader's globally related, if totally different, context.

SENSE OF PLACE

McDaniel (1995:194) correctly distinguishes one of the characteristic attitudes in 'traditional native paths' as 'authentic spirituality (which) lies in being bonded with, and indebted to, a specific geographical place or life-community, on which our survival depends and which partly forms our own spiritual identity.' He draws on the American Indian awareness of the relationship between personal spirituality and specified locality to illustrate the direct correlation between the development or shape of our own inner beings, our souls, and our loyalty or bondedness to local places. 'We find ourselves,' he says, 'when we come home to our local bioregions, when we let them form us and make us more human' (McDaniel 1995:197). And: 'We make contact with the Great Spirit when we know and love where we are' (McDaniel 1995:195).

This spirit-related sense of place contrasts sharply with what the same author calls the culture of 'consumerism' and 'indoorism.' Indoorism contributes to a mentality which isolates 'nature' as something 'outside'—to be enjoyed occasionally, but essentially remote from indoor life—and establishes indoor experience as normal reality. To many Christians religion in such a culture is text-based and human-preoccupied, in the midst of sermons which 'stress human-divine and human-human relations at the expense of human-Earth relations' (McDaniel 1995:196). Consumerism, in its turn, emphasises material progress and upward mobility as if these are morally justifiable trends, regardless of the alienating implications for a sense of self and of place.

These negative features of predominantly urban cultures are challenged by 'traditional Native ways':

In the first place they invite us to have more worship services outside, in the great cathedral of the open sky, where we can honor our kinship with the animals and the wild plants. Equally important, however, they invite us to recognise that our spiritual identities are partly formed by the very geographics and life communities in which we are situated (McDaniel 1995:196).

McDaniel's observations are similar to those I made in my earthkeeping encounter with African religion, particularly as regards the definition and function of religious values within a specific geographical space. It is not coincidental that the Shona people's overriding concern during the political liberation struggle and in our current war of the trees was and still is the lost lands. This concern is rooted in a religiously inspired sense of place. The land is the people, the animals, the plants, the entire earth-community—unborn, living, dead. In other words, the land is the totality of known and unknown existence. Invasion of the land by foreigners and destruction of its resources for human gain or 'progress' make the people living there rootless serfs and aliens. Through internal and external displacement, they lose touch with the dwelling places of their ancestors, hence with their own cultures and history. In the dried-up riverbeds, the deforested plains and dwindling wildlife they sense a loss of that which shaped their inner beings, their souls. Thus recapturing the land politically and restoring the land environmentally are integral processes in the individual and group experience of spiritual rebirth, revival and growth.

To rural Shona it is not the local village or chiefdom which spells 'home.' The village is too limited a setting for the lineage or extended family group to acquire full significance. The chiefdom, again, encompasses too wide a geographic region for individuals to be intimately associated with all of it. 'Home,' therefore, is the local ward (*dunhu*) with its cluster of villages, its ruling council of interrelated kraalheads under the tutelage of the ward headman (*sadunhu*), and the extended network of relatives: uncles, aunts, grandparents, in-laws, and their respective nuclear families, all living within walking distance of each other in the same locality.

Membership of *dunhu* society and involvement in the subsistence economy of Shona peasantry have a built-in spiritual dimension, informing all peasant activities. Whatever one's formal or institutional religious persuasion—be it Christian, Islamic, or whatever—tilling the soil or keeping livestock on the land of a ward community involves belonging. This requires the kind of interaction with the Creator, as well as the deceased keepers of the soil and their living representatives, that etches itself upon the soul. One cannot, for example, desecrate the weekly *chisi* rest day of the ancestors by tilling the soil and hope to escape retaliation from either the guardian ancestors of the soil or the peasant community of the *dunhu*.

Rootedness in such a rural Shona 'home' inevitably qualifies the religiosity and cultural tradition of generations of families. The Chagonda clan's special relationship with Mount Rasa in Gutu East comes to mind. As descendants of the famous rainmaker Marumbi, whose rain-making stones affirm a close link with the rain-giving deity at Matonjeni, the successive generations of Chagonda people see themselves as the mediators of rain, not only for their own ward but for the entire region. To the extent that they please Mwari and their ancestors by protecting the vegetation and animal life on the slopes of their sanctuary, Mount Rasa, they contribute to the equilibrium between the living and the spirit world which is necessary for good rainy seasons. At the foot of Mount Rasa the villagers recognise the abiding presence of mountain acacias covering the mountain slopes, the early morning calls of guineafowl and pheasants, the flight of eagles, and the warning sounds of rock rabbits high up on cliff ledges. All these are symbols of spirit presence, signs of spiritual wellbeing, and promises of life-sustaining agricultural stability, as long as the mountain and its resources are not abused. Here respect for the ancestors and their individual histories is equivalent to love of place, which to the Chagonda ward community means awareness of mountain presence and responsibility for its environs.

As has happened elsewhere in Africa, the Shona's earthbound religious values have been eroded by various factors. Population growth, coupled with restrictive land legislation, has exacerbated the pressure on the land, deforestation, and scarcity of fuelwood. As a result it became impossible for kraal and ward headmen—whose powers, like those of chiefs and spirit mediums, were curtailed under colonial rule—to impose the old ecological codes of conduct. Many *marambatemwa* were desecrated as kinsfolk, desperate for land and a stable supply of fuelwood, cleared the bush in previously forbidden areas. This was not just an unwanted invasion of the cherished 'home' territory of ward dwellers but also an abuse of the symbols of their inner worlds of reverence and veneration. Survival on limited and overexploited land, it seemed, became the norm instead of peaceful wellbeing in a balanced interplay between peasants, ancestors, the land, and their life-giving Creator.

Nonetheless the change in religious values appears to have been less dramatic than one may have expected. I have always been struck by the rural rootedness—spiritual, economic and ecological—of Shona urbanites. Even second- and third-generation city-dwellers tend to maintain their ties with and their religiously defined responsibilities for their home villages in the communal lands. Their relatives keep farming the family fields and many of them return home periodically when family or ward rituals are performed. City life therefore remains an economically induced adjunct, while the prospect of eventual retirement in the rural home community makes the harsh urban realities bearable. Even though they develop a new dependence on the money earned in town, a new house in a suburb, social ties in urban clubs, associations or churches, still the rural sense of place and ritually defined obligations to the upkeep of the earth community in the home setting persist. To many it becomes a cherished value in the midst of economic flux, a value to be preserved and to fight for.

It was the tenacity of this earthbound religious value and the attitudes it generated in the lives of my Shona friends, as it surfaced in both the political and environmental liberation struggles, that struck a chord in my own existence. Personally, I had pleasant memories of an adventurous childhood at Morgenster, a sense of security derived from the mission station where my parents lived and worked for nearly forty years. I at least had a fixed home base, a somewhat idealised sanctuary and anchorage, during many years of life and travel abroad. But thoughts of Morgenster were an inward sentimental trip, treasured for its ongoing value in my own life but with no real obligations beyond self. It was only when I was confronted with the reality of the lost lands as they figured in the lives of countless guerrillas, elders, and displaced villagers during and after *chimurenga* that my own sense of place acquired firmer contours. As I became more aware of the comprehensive significance of *marambatemwa* for the Shona's sense of place and home, reflected at each AZTREC tree-planting ceremony in the mediums' supplications and the nostalgic pleas for environmental repair by chiefs, headmen, and councillors, my own earthbound faith grew into expanding vision, action, and commitment.

In the process of inner change, sketched in the first chapter of this book, I started to consider Morgenster mission and the mountain on which it is situated as my *dunhu* home community, with its own holy grove, its well-kept graveyard housing missionary ancestors who had influenced my life and those of the people still working there, and its *marambatemwa* forests of wild loquat and acacia trees on mountain slopes. At tree-planting ceremonies my anger and frustration at the relentless denudation of the mountain's face by squatter intruders enabled me to relate to the chiefs' and mediums' nostalgic laments over the nakedness of their own home territories. During weekends at Masvingo my academic indoorism of reading and writing made way for regular pilgrimages to the mission. For quite a while I felt no need to see friends in the community of living people there, but preferred to relate to the diminished forests, granite hills, rivulets, birds, and the ancestors I had known so well as a child. Often I stood on the holy ground of my own place, communing with and sensing the presence of the men and women now resting in the small graveyard. Part of me was battling with a transition from pietistic faith with its heavy emphasis on soul salvation and individual spiritual growth—the strategy of my Protestant missionary ancestry at whose graves I stood—to a more earthy faith which sought peace in relating the good news of redemption and resurrection to all the earth. Somehow I needed spirit affirmation to initiate a mission of earthkeeping, to set a new course—a course deviating from, yet augmenting, the original course of mission marked out by the forebears of my *dunhu* home community. I had to reinterpret the inspirational message from the ancestral cloud of witnesses (Heb 12:1–2) of the mission, to seek the face of Christ the Earthkeeper, and then proceed along the new course with the benediction of the pioneer missionaries who had given spirit content to my sense of place in childhood. It was quiet where I stood among the tombstones, smelling the fertile soil and mouldering wild loquat leaves, hearing the distant call of bulbuls.

I was still mystified, seeing only in part, observing a dim image in a mirror (1 Cor 13:12). But in communing, sharing, the love of place was confirmed and waxed strong. I knew that *sekuru* Louw, pioneer missionary and founder of Morgenster, would applaud our attempts to cultivate and plant *mudziyavashe* fuelwood trees. He had taught me the value of these trees in my boyhood. He was still teaching me. I remembered how Cinie Malan, his wife, had written a list of indigenous trees in the vernacular in the back of her Shona grammar book, one of the earliest developments of Shona as a written language. She could have listed cultural or religious key terms. What made her decide on trees? Did she anticipate the eventual need for an earthkeeping mission? Then there were the resting places of Coen Brand, leading educator, and Dr. Tommie Steyn, MBE, famous eye doctor of Zimbabwe, both of whom had taught me, together with their own sons, to love the bush. They had once seen the same beauty on Mount Mugabe that I was looking at. Through my eyes and senses they were still seeing and feeling the environs of our home right now. There was peace about the earthkeeping mission after we had spoken . . .

Having related to the earth community back home, I felt free to develop a ministry of earth healing, for in Christ all things hold together (Col 1:17). Now I could operate further afield, with the inspirational back-up of a home base, just as my missionary ancestors had developed educational and medical networks throughout Masvingo Province from that same base. I had to revise my own sense of place after all the talk and research about Zimbabwe's lost lands. I had to contextualise for myself the cosmic holism of my Shona friends, find the *dunhu* community of my youth, and internalise the religio-ecological values of both worlds before I could shoulder the kind of environmental responsibilities which the escalating war of the trees entailed.

Although I kept travelling alone to Morgenster for this kind of eco-spiritual experience, these pilgrimages were never isolated, mystical events. My sense of place was in transition, informed by the values of fellow Shona earthkeepers as they themselves were rediscovering their own relatedness to the earth in their own home communities. Most of them had an advantage over me: they had deeper roots in the lands of their forebears, going back several generations. Moreover, unlike me—an alien missionary not expected to have a lasting environmental responsibility at Morgenster—they, traditionalists and Christians alike, all had ongoing ecological duties in their *dunhu* home territories.

What I did share with the Christian communities of the AAEC was the attempt to give Christian content to the ancestor-related sense of place that we encountered in our AZTREC counterparts and detected within ourselves. I understood and respected the eco-spiritual ways of AZTREC chiefs and mediums. But I had to find my own mode of communion with the Christian ancestors who had influenced my understanding of creation and spirituality in my youth. There are indications that fellow Zionist and other AIC tree planters were and still are going through similar processes of reinterpretation. In the final analysis it appears as if participation in the war of trees has brought about a general awareness among our earthkeepers—irrespective of religious affiliation—of our primordial ties with the earth. All of us still share the primal vision with our non-Christian forebears, the intuition of being bonded with the entire earth family, the universe, and its Creator. This awareness exacts humility and faith. Then, by rediscovering and taking greater responsibility for one's individual roots in the soil, the broader perspective of earth-care, beyond the local situation, starts unfolding.

SENSE OF COMMUNITY

A cornerstone of the Shona understanding and ordering of community is the pervasive interaction between the living and the living dead. Existentially this is the most consistent and demanding, and ritually the most comprehensive, component of Shona—if not all African—religion. Without the ancestors, life, in all its passages, joys and vicissitudes, is just not possible. The ancestors, like their living descendants, play a vital role in society and have a definite impact on community life. Theirs is an extension of life here and now. The two spheres of life—the seen and the unseen—are interdependent. If the ancestors' benevolence and protection against evil forces are forfeited, the meaning and stability of the societal group are at risk. By the same token the equilibrium of ancestral existence in the spirit world is disturbed or spoilt if they are not remembered, honoured, and respected by their living kin in prescribed rituals.

This interdependence is manifest in both family and wider lineage or ward rituals. If, for instance, the union of a new couple is to be blessed, the procreative powers of the bride's matrilineal ancestors must be ritually recognised by including a *ngombe youmai* (motherhood cow) in the *roora* (bride price) paid by the groom's wife-receiving relatives. If this is not done, barrenness or miscarriages are often attributed to the omission and the anger of the spirits of the wife's mother or grandmother, who have a legitimate claim to the motherhood cow. Ritual amends for the omission highlights the significance of two interacting kin groups—the wife-providing and wife-receiving lineages—respecting each other's privileges and responsibilities for the sake of in-group harmony. It also illustrates the ongoing responsibility of the living towards the spirit world and the spirits' obligation to maintain order among families through mystical intervention.

Another example of how the core of community life is ritually reinforced is the *kugadzira* (literally 'to set right'), the home-bringing ceremony in which the spirit of a deceased relative is elevated to the status of ancestorhood (Daneel 1971:101f). If the home-coming spirit is the head of a family, the deceased's name-bearer officially receives both the name of the father—a ritual which suggests close identification with, if not living personification of, the departed person—and full responsibility as ritual officiant for the extended family in its relations with the ancestral world. In the course of the ritual the entire family situation (outstanding debts, land issues, unsettled conflicts, *roora* payments, individual problems, health, etc.) is reviewed in the presence of the new name-bearer and, by implication, of the spirit who, on becoming a proper *mudzimu*, accepts mystical protective responsibility for the family. Different groups of participant relatives—aunts, uncles, in-laws, sons and daughters of the deceased—publicly address the name-bearer and indicate how they propose resolving unsettled family problems.

The *kugadzira* ritual therefore entails a thorough stocktaking of family affairs. Mystical involvement in family life is reaffirmed; the kinship code of behaviour, represented by the family ancestors, is reinterpreted and applied to pertinent issues in the presence of all interested parties. A sacrificial beast, the *gono guru* (great bull), is dedicated to the home-coming spirit in anticipation of future family rituals. Subsequent illness or misfortune among relatives will trigger the next round of ritual activity (including the sacrifice of the *gono guru*), and the close interaction of kin, the living and the living dead, will once again be demonstrated publicly. Rituals of this nature certainly serve to strengthen close family ties. The mystical dimension of ancestral presence and activity imparts indisputable authority and stability to the inner dynamics which holds the family group together.

Similar deference is shown to the apical ancestors of the ward or chiefdom when multilineal communities meet for the seances of senior spirit mediums at *mukwerere* rain rituals. Tribal political or ecology-related rituals in the wider family context are therefore marked by the same mystically reinforced sense of community. At these ceremonies the regulation of community life in relation to agro-economic activity, the state of the environment and the rhythm of the seasons—according to customs upheld by the senior guardian ancestors—are up for review. Assessments are made of the observance of *chisi* (ancestral rest days), proper care of water resources and observance of the rules for the use of arable fields and grazing areas. Serious misdemeanours may be referred to the chief's court, which reflects the interwovenness of eco-religious praxis and customary law. The ancestors' perception of the way in which their descendants keep the land influences the nature of their mediation with Mwari, the Shona high-God, and the kind of rainy season that can be expected.

In rural communities, structured according to a worldview of a seamless totality of interacting forces (humans, wildlife, the seasonal forces of nature, the Creator, etc.), a ritually determined agenda for earth healing is already functioning. Ideally, therefore, a true sense of Shona community entails a code of earth stewardship. Processes of modernisation, acculturation, and land pressure have eroded these values and impaired their application. Yet the AZTREC story shows that the underlying sense of community has survived in Shona society and that it still provides a mobilising focus for earthkeeping.

This reverence for the ancient African keepers of the land at ceremonies where natural resources are being renewed should convey a message of hope to the global fellowship of earthkeepers. For it suggests that the brazen, exploitive excesses found in all human cultures—particularly in 'progressive' economism, self-seeking individualism, and consumerism—can be replaced by altruistic earth concerns. What is needed is to rechannel Western performance-oriented attitudes by considering the cosmic history of the earth; recognising the relatively late appearance of human beings on planet Earth; and respecting all the ancestors of humankind who appeal to their fellow pilgrims as stewards of the earth. Thus a new sense of cosmic community which seeks to balance human use of creation with service to it is indeed possible.

The ritualisation of earth-care in AZTREC's *mafukidzanyika* ceremonies promotes continuity in tree planting and attitudes of determination and commitment in the tree-planting community. To the extent that appeasement of the earth's guardian ancestors is focal in earth repair, the personal interaction between earthkeepers, living and dead, and the entire earth community is enhanced. Ritualisation, moreover, elevates the driving force of earth-care to a level beyond the often controversial motives of leading environmentalists. Once the motivation for action is perceived as mystical or divine in origin, hence beyond dispute, and once the earthkeepers' acceptance of such motivation is consolidated by regular ritual activity, the perpetuation of earth-care is safeguarded irrespective of ecological setbacks and disappointments. Ritualisation of earth healing, whatever the religion practised, promotes holistic perceptions of the human community as an integral part of creation. This kind of respect and love for the earth counteracts the mindless exploitation and destruction of its beauty and resources.

Ancestral involvement in the protection of holy groves and *dunhu* home territories stimulates compliance with customary ecological codes and the redefinition of ethics in accordance with changing environmental conditions. In spirit medium vaZarira's address to the Negovano senior ancestors, for instance, one finds explicit recognition of ancestral authority over all land issues, symbolised by the 'ruling staff' dating back to ancient times. It is at the ancestors' behest that new conservationist measures are undertaken: cultivation of seedlings in nurseries, planting of trees in woodlots, protection of riverbanks, springs, game species, and so forth. Ancestral bondedness to the earth qualifies the personalties of the earthkeepers with the soil, rivers, trees, birds, and animals. Repeated ritual recognition of the relationship inspires the earthkeepers' code of conduct—a code not neatly defined in individual contemplation, but born from the healing activities of sweating bodies and dancing feet. According to this code, moreover, wanton earth destruction—heedless bush clearing, felling ancestrally protected trees, hunting protected species of game—or refusal to share responsibility for the earth is sinful, an intolerable 'land wizardry' (*uroyi hwenyika*) which disrespects the in-terwovenness of all creaturely life.

AZTREC's *mafukidzanyika* ceremonies ritually affirm the inseparable whole-ness of creation: the interface between Creator, humans, other creatures and the expanse of land and waters. When vaZarira, for instance, introduces a tree-plant-ing event in Chief Nhema's territory, her address to the guardian ancestor, Nhema, first of all links the ancestor with the Creator, Zhame, by referring to the *muonde* (fig tree) where Nhema used to find nourishment prior to his visits to the shrines at Matonjeni. This attests dependence on the sustaining and life-giving Creator. Then the earlier theme of identification between ancestor and earth com-munity is elaborated. 'I want to call upon vaNhema today,' the medium says, 'Whether he is in the cave, up in this tree here, or in the pool of water over there, we ask him to come and witness what his children are doing in his territory . . . if you are in the pool, vaNhema, lift up your head and observe what your people are doing in your area.' Later, as the ritual proceeds, vaZarira leads the tree planters in addressing the seedlings as kin. In submitting the seedlings to the soil the spirit medium hands over to Nhema, the ancestor, what he requires. In the ritual context Nhema is the soil, personified.

The identification of guardian ancestors with all creation remains focal in the *mafukidzanyika* re-enactment of the cosmic cycle. This is the crucial dimension which triggers and gives meaning to tradition-oriented earth-care. Personifying the earth—water, land, birds, all creatures acquiring an anthropomorphic charac-ter—introduces an indisputable element of human respect and responsibility for the earth community as kin. This contrasts with secular Western cosmologies, which tend to reduce the environment and its resources to soulless, exploitable commodities. In its ritual 'humanisation of nature' AZTREC therefore appeals to the conscience of a consumer society, locally and abroad, to heed the sanctity of all creation, the 'personhood' of all vegetation, birds, and animals, so that what-ever harvesting, cropping, or mining takes place will be done with the respect, gratitude, and humility expected in any interhuman or human-divine encounter.

AZTREC's earthkeepers have somehow managed to reinterpret Shona sym-bolic language in their relationships with trees. Now not only the specific ances-tor who mystically sanctioned a new village settlement is identified with the *mub-vumira* (ancestral approval) tree, but a host of living tree planters, individually identifying with the trees as their kin whose names they adopt. *Chimurenga* im-agery and constant preoccupation with trees, moreover, tend to make the occa-sional ritual identification between symbol and what it represents—in this in-stance tree and tree planter—more pervasive and permanent. Tree planters become the trees they are related to! They deliberately develop those character traits that they see symbolised in the tree of their choice. In the late Leonard Gono's case he sacrificed himself as *mabvamaropa* ('that which produces blood') for the earth cause. He became *Mabvamaropa*, not only in the ritual context of tree planting but in all of the life he lived. While he fought the killer disease that eventually claimed his life, his resilience matched that of tough kiaat wood. In his old age my adoptive father, Chief Murinye, is increasingly becoming *Muuyu*, the baobab tree, ancient and imperturbable patron of the traditionalist tree planters, more unwavering than when I knew him as a young man, adamant that nobody in his chiefdom will ring the bark of a *muuyu* and thereby bring it down. And those chiefs and headmen who call themselves *Murwiti* (black ebony) have noticeably hardened and are applying stricter measures to combat random deforestation. They are polished black iron, black ebony, in their relentless campaign against unscrupulous tree fellers.

To me it has been a novel experience to be called and recognised as *Muchakata*, the cork tree. This *chimurenga* name is often used in jest, as are those of fellow tree planters. Leonard, for instance, reminded me once with a wicked grin that there is also a downside to being called *muchakata*. 'Why?' I asked. 'Because the *muchakata* spreads a pretty nasty smell at the time of year when it sheds its fruit,' he said. This caused great hilarity in the group. Lightness and humour served to strengthen our kinship ties with tree brothers and sisters. I found myself much more alert to the presence of fellow *michakata* as I travelled up and down the Masvingo-Harare road on ZIRRCON errands. I noticed, and then became attached to, some dense copses of cork trees in whose shade a few kudu bulls often rested. During the drought in the early nineties I felt the pain of my elders as their roots reached for the receding water table in the sandy soil just north of Masvingo. In vain. Slowly they withered and died. They do not have a strong taproot that reaches deep into the soil to keep providing them with moisture when the rains stay away. As a nomad with shallow roots because of endless travel I, too, am vulnerable, forever at risk on unsafe roads. But I also share with fellow *michakata* the urge to protect and sustain the life of our earth community. When I look at the dense, dark green foliage of a healthy *muchakata* I feel encouraged not to quit but to keep facing and to help shoulder the problems of our earthkeeping struggle. *I am Muchakata!* I cast some of the shade where earthkeepers nowadays work and rest. In their talk and laughter and in the cooling wind I feel the numinous, the movement of Spirit where all our labour, pain, and joy start. And when our first *marambatemwa* game sanctuaries take shape one day—an ecological impossibility in the most densely populated rural lands of Zimbabwe!—I hope still to cast a shadow where kudu, impala, duiker, and klipspringer can rest without fear.

Sharing kinship with the earth community has also heightened my own experience of being protected and cared for. The granite kopje next to the Harare road on the outskirts of Masvingo town houses a little colony of dassies (rock rabbits), sentinels of our Shona ancestors. When I drive past them on a trip to Harare, I notice those dark, observant eyes peering knowingly at the road and the passing vehicles. Invariably I stop, watch them and address them: *'Imi varidzi vemugwagwa, mutichengete parwendo yedu!'* (You guardians of the road, protect us on our journey!) Sometimes Shona friends accompanying me are puzzled and a few have questioned my petition from a Christian point of view. I usually explain that as an adopted descendant of the famed hunter Mabwazhe, founder ancestor of the Gumbo people in Gutu, and as a childhood dassie-hunter myself, this is my way of praying to God for a safe journey, a prayer which both Mabwazhe and Mwari will understand. To me the watchful eye of the dassie is God's way of alerting me to the dangers of a road which carries far too many drunken and unlicensed drivers. This is certainly not a magic formula for road safety. There is no absolute safety anywhere in this world. Nevertheless, every time I return from Harare and drive past my dassie family in their granite home, I speak to them, thanking God for a safe journey despite the risks I take through driver's fatigue.

And the *chapungu*? To me the bateleur, with its exquisitely trimmed black and white feathers, slightly flared wingtips, and serene, sure flight, has always been master of the skies. Impatient to settle on a glide path which follows the up-draft of air currents, the *chapungu*'s wing flap is short, swift, and powerful; the whistling sound can be heard from a distance. But once those pinions are stretched, there is quiet and calm as the eagle wings its way upward and sideways into the skies with graceful ease. If I could fly I would want to fly like *chapungu*. Fascination and fantasy of flight have awakened new respect and awareness of Mwari, here revealed as *Wokumusoro* (the One above) of the Shona through the centuries. It touches my being when I stop my car by the roadside somewhere in the lowveld of Zimbabwe to rid my mind of overload and I watch *chapungu* gliding circles of greeting above me. I watch wing flap and flight path. If air turbulence causes *chapungu* to make nervous corrections to his flight, I feel warned against the complacency wrought by millions of kilometres of air flight and overland travel. I feel warned from Beyond against taking life for granted. And I proceed with care. But those wings, mastering all air currents, also remind me of the goodness and freedom of liberated life which, despite the poverty and suffering that always surround us, calls for celebration. So my feathered brother writes the good news with wingtips against blue skies—the good news of Christ's salvation of all creation.

My relations with *muchakata*, dassie, and bateleur illustrate that they do not have the same ancestral connotations for me as for many of my fellow earthkeepers. Coming from a Protestant Christian background, I have contextualised the meaning of Shona symbolism and my own rootedness in the earth community in a way which makes sense to me as a Euro-African among African earthkeepers. What may strike Western readers as ecological sentimentality or romanticism is to me an existential, instinctive natural theology in the Franciscan rather than the Calvinist tradition. It is fascinating to probe the New Testament meaning of 'in Christ all things hold together' (Col 1:17) through the grid of Shona culture and religion. It is not an easy passage in any framework, for Christ's fulfillment of culture, as I understand it, involves a transformation which keeps qualifying the individual's relations with fellow human beings and with the earth community. Shona religion offers an imaginative way of encountering Christ the Earthkeeper through kinship with, in my case, *muchakata, mbira*, and *chapungu*. It has given me a glimpse of how many of my Shona fellow earthkeepers perceive Christ's presence holistically. However, the insight gained from that experience entails a twofold challenge: first, to attempt to translate Christ's lordship over all creation into Shona ecological praxis as a form of healing service to the earth community, as opposed to human domination based on a misconception of humanity as the 'crown of creation'; and second, from within such service to rethink the environmental implications of Christ's salvation for mission. Complex as this may be, it derives not only from scriptural revelation but also from the realisation that God has not left him/herself without witnesses in creation and in the world's religions (Rom 1; Acts 14).

This account of my own experience is not meant to propagate a specific line of religio-ecological action in the global village. I wish through tangible illustrations to make the point that the indigenous religions of this world, and those of Africa in particular, have a potential for reconnecting human society with earth community. Exposure to indigenous religions could enable those of us living in urban consumer societies to rediscover the religious values of our own ancient forebears. Reaching out for their presence could help us to overcome the addictive hold of indoor city life as we redefine our own basic notions of community, develop new kinship ties with mother earth, and find the commitment to earth-care which accords with our own convictions and circumstances.

COMMUNION WITH THE CREATOR

Of all AZTREC's rituals, the communion of its leaders with Mwari the Creator at the cult shrines in the Matopo hills is probably the most profound affirmation of the close bond between Creator, human society, and earth community. We have noted that the oracular messages pronounced at the cult caves do not spell out a green vision or a specific ecological strategy for Africa. Nevertheless, in its intensity and reverence for Mwari, the ritual activity expresses environmental commitment, awareness of divine involvement in the life cycle of creation, and the need for ongoing divine-human encounter to spark, empower, and legitimate the struggle.

AZTREC's annual pilgrimage to the cult shrines places the earthkeeping quest in both a historical liberationist and a national context. Communion with Mwari as an extension of *chimurenga* evokes memories of resistance in various periods of oppression: first the Ndebele, then the white invaders. In response to these oppressive forces, Mwari emerged as a god of national crisis who demanded freedom and justice for his/her people throughout Shona territory, who motivated the hero ancestors (Chaminuka, Kaguvi, Nehanda, and others) to take up this cause. In line with this tradition, Mwari urged the wartime leaders Robert Mugabe and Joshua Nkomo to unite their cadres against the common enemy and, after Independence, to unite their parties in governing the country. AZTREC earthkeepers feel called by this liberationist legacy to engage the common enemy of earth destruction and to unite all healing agencies, of whatever religious persuasion, in the war of the trees under the spirit guidance of Mwari, the ancestral war council (*dare rechimurenga*), and its spirit mediums.

This combination of national, political, religious, and ecological motives makes AZTREC's annual pilgrimage to the Matonjeni shrines meaningful. An essentially conservative African deity, Mwari has all along insisted on the preservation of indigenous beliefs, customs, and culture in the face of acculturation and modernising change. Communing with him/her therefore reinforces a sense of pride in Zimbabwean nationhood and in healing service rendered to Mwari's stricken earth, in a manner not always experienced in the hurly-burly of daily life back home. To those who have suffered serfdom and obscurity under the colonial regime, participation in the still semi-secret oracular rituals at Matonjeni—the ultimate bulwark against foreign intrusion and a source of genuine Africanness which has virtually escaped Western contamination—is a spiritually rejuvenating experience of retrieving wholeness in the Creator's presence. Human wholeness in this instance assumes divine recognition of the earthkeepers' dignity, the legitimacy of their quest for social and material wellbeing, and the restoration of life-giving relations between humans and the earth community.

Apart from the emotional satisfaction and inspiration derived from oracular revelations at the cult shrines, AZTREC's Matonjeni visits also illustrate the adaptability of African religion to changing circumstances. Instead of stagnating and declining in the face of social change and aggressive Christian expansion, indigenous religion has gone through a historical process of periodic revival and reinterpretation, resulting in the emergence of a traditional *theologia africana*. Mention was made of conceptual mutations as Mwari was understood to respond and urge resistance to various forms of oppression. There can be little doubt that oracular involvement in both *chimurenga* periods—the 1896 rebellions and the bush war preceding Independence—engendered and strengthened the image of Mwari as a deity of justice and liberation. AZTREC stands in this tradition through its awareness of national crisis, in this instance not socio-political but environmental, and through its regular visitations, which offer a new angle on the oracle's involvement in a regionally widespread dilemma. In religio-historical perspective AZTREC's contribution lies in interpreting the Creator as an immediate presence, an immanent personal power in creation; perhaps more readily available and sensitive to the needs of peasant society than the God conveyed by the *vanyai* who petitioned for rain in the past.

Not that this contribution implies radical conceptual change. Early descriptions of Mwari (for example W. J. van der Merwe, *The Shona Idea of God*) did not portray the same remote *deus otiosus* character ascribed to some African divinities. As sky-God (*Wokumusoro*, 'the One above') Mwari may in some respects have been perceived as a distant, transcendental Supreme Being. But he/she was also *Watangakugara* ('the one who sat/existed first'), Runji (the 'needle' who 'threaded' the earth with lightning), and Dzivaguru ('Great Pool,' symbol of fertility). The attributes associated with these praise names are those of an anthropomorphic, feminine, and immanent being, a Creator bound to and living in creation; a closeness which may also include panentheistic notions of divine power permeating the living and inanimate phenomena of nature. It is possible that both the transcendence of Mwari as *Wokumusoro* and his/her presence in the 'Great Pool,' *Dzivaguru*, are respectively represented symbolically in the Zimbabwean soapstone bird and the crocodile on the stylus below it, a centuries-old relic found at the Great Zimbabwe ruins.[1]

Traditionally the conception of Mwari's remoteness as a transcendent being was probably not so much spatial; it was rather a case of the deity being crowded out of people's daily lives because of their overriding ritual preoccupation with the ancestors. Crisis management during periods of national upheaval tended to refocus on the immediacy and active presence of the deity. AZTREC's activities add yet another dimension to this pattern of periodically intensified contact between the oracle and its widely dispersed constituency, and the concomitant resurgence of communal awareness of, and faith in, the Supreme Being's direct involvement in this existence. AZTREC's distinctive contributions to the reinterpretation of Mwari the Creator's involvement in creation are the following:

First, the *mafukidzanyika* tree-planting ceremonies as ritual improvisations of the *mukwerere* rain rituals assign the Creator a prominent role. Instead of merely requesting the apical ancestors of the region to forward a plea for rain to Mwari at Matonjeni, as in the traditional *mukwerere*, Mwari's immediacy and presence in the local tree-planting context are emphasised. The old route of appealing to the oracular deity via an entire hierarchy of ancestors and through visitations to distant shrines is still acknowledged and upheld. But, as we have noticed in the ritual addresses of spirit medium vaZarira and fellow tribal elders, Mwari is assumed to have drawn close as an insider to his/her own creation. Talking about the Creator as an immediate presence and communing directly with him/her through prayer are highly innovative features. This spontaneous, direct worship possibly derives partly from Christian influence and partly from a sense of urgency in peasant society caused by droughts and other signs of environmental deterioration. At all events, the ease with which such innovation is accommodated and experienced as genuinely consistent with the ways of the forebears indicates the versatility of African religion and its ability to absorb foreign religious influences without losing its identity.

Second, AZTREC's active resistance to random tree felling invokes a responsive and retaliating deity as the source and enforcer of an emergent, if still basically traditional, ethical code for environmentalism. Mwari is not only the Great Pool (*Dzivaguru*) who resists desecrating pollution and erosion-prone cultivation of riverbanks; he/she is also proclaimed to be present in trees. Consequently Mwari experiences anger and pain when trees are felled with a disrespectful, exploitive attitude which disregards the sanctity of creation. In contrast to such abuse, the earthkeepers' address of seedlings as kin during planting ceremonies reflects communal right-mindedness and acceptance of stewardship in the earth community—respect for the guardian ancestors and an imaginative form of worshipping the Creator. Here the immanence of God in creation emerges from a theologising process triggered by action rather than abstract reflection. The liberator God who heeds the suffering of oppressed and deprived people, as *chimurenga* history bears out, now incarnates him/herself in the ecologically stricken land in agony at the abuse of trees, grasses, animals, birds, and the soil itself, and demands justice for the entire earth community. There is simply no place for divine remoteness in AZTREC's earthkeeping world where the abused kin of creation so obviously voice the outrage of a disturbed Creator.

Third, regular visits to Matonjeni by AZTREC delegations instil a new sense of the accessibility of the divinity. Chiefs and mediums in Masvingo Province who wish to make impromptu visits to the shrines, in addition to AZTREC's official annual pilgrimage, may use ZIRRCON's vehicles. Their one-and-a-half-day outings to the shrines, some 300 kilometres from Masvingo town, are very different from the journeys formerly undertaken by *vanyai* on foot over many days. The adventure and hardship encountered by elderly cult messengers on their annual journeys to and from the shrines obviously contributed to the mystique of the cult and helped establish an image of a creator high-God too distant for regular communion with individual tribespeople.

There are indications that the cult has lost some of its exclusiveness and secrecy since Independence. Thus AZTREC is not alone in promoting a new form of cult accessibility in peacetime. Senior politicians and official representatives of political parties visit the shrines more regularly than before. African businessmen from as far afield as Lusaka in Zambia and Johannesburg in South Africa are now known to send delegates to confer with Mwari. Ordinary people with personal requests also frequent the shrines more readily than before and bigger 'gifts' (money contributions) are required by the cult officials for oracular sessions. In some respects, therefore, the cult appears to be becoming commercialised.

Nevertheless, the traditional system of communicating with Mwari is sufficiently unspoilt for the visiting earthkeepers to experience a religious comfort zone, a sense of belonging. As the champion of African cultural and moral values and the maintenance of societal order through the agency of headmen and chiefs, Mwari speaks in an idiom understandable to chiefs and mediums. He/she is the chief of creation! To the chiefs who confront new agro-economic and ecological challenges at a time when some of their land-allocating and judicial powers have been curtailed by government, the Matonjeni oracle represents a sympathetic, politically relatively inviolable forum where they can vent their frustrations. As the God of Africa, Mwari listens and understands. He/she prompts new vision and hope through presence and supportive affirmation of human and earth needs rather than through prescriptive revelations or guaranteed solutions. Mwari's presence remains an enigma, but at the Matonjeni shrines it is tangible, close, emanating from cave entrances and granite rocks.

The three points I have raised here may not suggest any dramatic development in the cult's history, besides perhaps enriching and adding a new dimension to the already rich and diversified image of the traditional deity. As an ecologically interested high-God and provider of rain, Mwari has always been the potential or implied guardian of creation. Now, however, he/she emerges explicitly as liberator-earthkeeper, present in and supportive of current earth-care programmes not only during oracular revelations at selected locations in the deep of African nights, but throughout the territory of AZTREC's operations and beyond.

As for my own attendance as privileged participant-observer of the Matonjeni oracle, I have always been deeply moved by the experience. The trip into the heartland of the Matopo hills—past the historic site where Cecil Rhodes and the Ndebele warriors held their *indaba* towards the end of the previous century, and past an endless array of towering granite rocks framed by green mountain acacias—is in itself a powerful reminder of the God of history, the biblical Creator who promises a new heaven and a new earth.

Then, in the course of an evening in the cult community, one is made aware of the unbroken communion between Creator, people of the now-time and of the distant past, and all the animate and inanimate denizens of the earth. The preparations by dim fire light in a large smoke-filled hut are simple. There is no furniture to speak of; only a low buzz of voices hiding excited expectation, subdued laughter, sharing *sadza* (stiff porridge), wild spinach, and water. The sharing of a simple meal in a world warm with welcome and trust is in itself an act of worship. Waiting for midnight heightens expectation, allows quiet for fatigued contemplation in a circle of relaxed faces.

When the priest's call comes, all shoes are removed and all modern gadgets like watches, torches, bangles, and tape-recorders are left in the hut as people move out, mute and in single file, to the shrine's cave entrance. There is no impressive, humanly constructed temple, no sculptured images of Mwari or the ancestors, no regalia except the dark cloth worn by the priests and priestesses as a sign of respect to Mwari, no symbols of human achievement. Communion requires a bare, unpretentious gathering of Mwari's people in his/her presence. As you sit down on stone or soil the moon and an expanse of stars light up the 'temple,' a massive overhang of granite rock behind you; in the wetlands below choirs of crickets and frogs remind you of Paul's proclamation to the Athenians: 'God who made the world and everything in it, being Lord of heaven and earth, does not live in shrines/temples made by man, nor is he served by human hands, as though he needed anything, since he himself gives to all men life and breath and everything' (Acts 17:24–25). Only here the same truth about God the Creator is enacted with discerning wisdom in a non-Christian ritual: the God of Israel who revealed himself on Mount Sinai did not leave himself without witness in the Matopo hills and on other holy mountains in Africa.

The female voice of Mwari from the cave depths addresses you in an ancient Rozvi dialect, conjuring up the passage of ages and bygone African dynasties. Responses to Mwari's voice express utter respect, piety and dependence. Here, as in Romans 1:20, there is the realisation that 'since the creation of the world his (Mwari's) invisible nature, namely his eternal power and deity, has been clearly perceived in the things that have been made.' The rock formations from which the voice comes testify to divine power and sovereignty. In addition Mwari speaks not only about the human order, politics, and progress but also about rain and crops, the state of the land, its trees, animals and all its denizens. Quality of being, justice and peace—Mwari's revelations infer—the entire life cycle of creation is at stake. When the wholeness of the earth community is disturbed by the hubris and avarice of human beings, all of life is threatened. Mwari's judgement of such human failure finds expression in severe drought or individual misfortune, the primary aim of which is not to make human beings suffer indefinitely but to restore, through human endeavour, the broken life cycle of the earth community.

Back in the priest's hut after the encounter with Mwari in the starlit 'temple,' another form of human communion unfolds. Rejoicing and abandon replace the seriousness and weightiness of worship as seven drummers draw the returning delegation into traditional dance. Drumbeat and stamping feet honour the ancestors and celebrate the restoration of creation's wholeness. Swaying bodies and glazed eyes also tell a story of abandoning the hurts and illusions of life . . . until fatigue takes over and the dawn sky reddens above inert bodies in the priest's courtyard.

Animated discussions about future earthkeeping activities mark the AZTREC delegates' return trip. To me this is a clear indication that whenever there is genuine renewal of the bond between God and the people of this earth—in whatever religious context—the chances are that there will be a reappraisal of the sanctity of creation and, with it, new patterns of commitment to earth-care. This is the inspiring yet unassuming message of Matonjeni to the earthkeepers of a religiously pluriform global village: seek ye first the kingdom of God, in communion with the Creator of all the world, with each other and with all the living or voiceless denizens of creation, if there is to be abundance of life, justice and peace on earth!

MISSION IMPOSSIBLE?

ZIRRCON's earthkeeping endeavour qualifies as 'mission' in a twofold sense. First, the entire movement is characterised by an overriding preoccupation with the implementation of environmental reform. In this sense the war of the trees is the operational method of an ecological mission, whose achievements can be measured in accordance with secular ecological criteria.

In the second place, the mystical motivation and drive behind ecological endeavour qualify the entire process as religious mission, the basic tenets of which can best be assessed in terms of African traditionalist or Christian theological criteria.

As a Traditionalist 'Mission'

Although the word 'mission' was not used in this volume to characterise AZTREC's endeavour—largely because of its loaded and fairly exclusive Christian connotations—it is appropriate to speak of an 'African traditionalist mission.' African religion admittedly lacks the dimension of aggressive proselytising, conversion, and recruitment which characterises Christian mission. Yet AZTREC's green warfare resembles Christian mission because, in contrast to normal ATR practice, Mwari is believed to send traditionalists into the world for a purpose wider than the interests of their own clan or tribe. They, too, measure the relative success or failure of their mission of ecological stewardship in direct relation to the mystical source of their endeavour. Hence the repeated appeal to the ancestral guardians of the land to observe, inspire, and recognise the tree-planting work of their living descendants and AZTREC's annual deliberations on the progress and problems of the green struggle at Mwari's Matopo shrines.

AZTREC's use of the term 'mission' has several implications. First, the experience of a revitalised life cycle between God, humans and cosmos along traditional cosmological lines stimulates a recognisable and acceptable religious revival which heightens meaning and quality of life. To many traditionalist peasants who have had only limited opportunities to rise above relative rural obscurity, involvement in a ritually sanctioned and much publicised enterprise of convincing regional and national significance is no mean achievement.

Second, the idea of being commissioned by Mwari to engage in environmental mission strengthens the conviction that the process of environmental degradation can be arrested, or even reversed. Such conviction revives the hope in agrarian circles that a viable subsistence economy is still feasible.

Third, religious inspiration contributes to ecological commitment and responsibility in caring for existing projects. I have indicated that mystical directives to restore the land correlate directly with increased involvement in tree-planting ceremonies and give clout to committees responsible for the all-important care of young trees in new woodlots. It is my conviction, even though I do not yet have statistical data to prove this point, that ancestrally driven care and protection of woodlots produces an above average survival rate of trees planted compared with similar grassroots ventures in Africa. The observable success achieved in the field, despite numerous setbacks, conveys the message that the mission is difficult yet possible!

Fourth, the idea of mission enhances sustained commitment. Mystical persuasion keeps alive the realisation that the environmental crisis is a lasting condition, a kind of terminal illness in Africa and the rest of the world. Consequently the struggle to heal the earth, at the behest of Mwari and the ancestors, will continue indefinitely. Apparently there can be no final battle which settles the score once and for all, as happened at Independence with the ending of white colonial rule and the introduction of a new political dispensation. Success in environmental healing can be achieved and must be achieved. Mission is possible, in that patches of land and earth community can be restored and kept in harmonious balance. But the paradox remains. Success is relative, subject to the exploitive and predatory nature of human beings, in the same way that human health remains subject to destructive and debilitating forces in this existence. At no point is healing final and conclusive. Environmental mission therefore remains, in a sense, incomplete, impossible! In this dialectic between the possible and the impossible the earthkeeper may be tempted into cynicism or fatalism, to abandon a struggle in which victory remains forever unattainable, hence the significance of a mandating and inspirational agency which is considered to understand the earth and the human condition from within, yet also operates from a detached position beyond it. Regular ritual communication and renewal of mandate with this source of inspiration contribute to understanding of the earthkeeping task in hand and to the earthkeepers' perseverance in the face of heavy odds.

The deity at Matonjeni has in some ways always been a commissioning power, in other words a God of mission. Whether Mwari's people are petitioning for favourable agricultural conditions and reliable seasons, for liberation from oppression or for political change and social justice, they always had to comply with oracular directives in order to attain the desired end. Allied as it is with an emergent Christian ministry in eco-mission, AZTREC contributes to a purposeful extension and elaboration of traditional mission in the cult. Aimed at sustained environmental repair and traditionally perceived justice in the distribution and management of the land, this mission—as interpreted and practised by AZTREC—is likely to become as integral a feature of the Mwari cult as the traditional procurement of favourable rainy seasons.

THE PERSPECTIVE OF CHRISTIAN MISSION

A vexing problem arises when one tries to assess the nature of ZIRRCON's environmental mission in Christian terms. Above all, is it legitimate for Christians to share a mission of earth-care as closely as the AAEC churches and AZTREC traditionalists are doing, and still retain the true spirit and essence of New Testament missionary outreach? Does the Christian/non-Christian ecumenism evinced, for instance, in intensive multifaith interaction and dialogue during tree-planting ceremonies and Matonjeni visits—for all the mutual respect for divergent religious identities—necessarily jeopardise the exclusiveness and inherent radicalness of Christian witness? Is it possible to obey Christ's classic commission to his disciples in Matthew 28:19 to go forth, proclaim the good news of salvation and baptise converts in the name of the Father, Son, and Holy Spirit, in a context where the cosmic implications of salvation seem to obscure the call for personal redemption? In other words, does eco-mission shared between Christian and non-Christian partners, as implemented by ZIRRCON, unavoidably result in syncretist compromise at the expense of a Christ-centred focus on conversion, hence an enterprise to be repudiated theologically as 'mission impossible'?

These are questions which I, as a missiologist and the initiator of our earthkeeping movement, have grappled with and continue to ponder. I have often wondered whether my close identification with chiefs and mediums, my support for their visits to Matonjeni and participation in the oracular sessions of the cult, have at all confused my AIC colleagues and fellow Christians of other denominations, or have hindered rather than furthered Christian witness. There were the times when I wondered whether my inquisitiveness as a researcher had led me deeper into African traditional religion than the missionary in me was strictly prepared for. Addressing the ancient Mwari of Africa during oracular sessions, in particular, filled me with a sense of awe and reverence, but also with trepidation at betraying the gospel message in the eyes of people inclined towards such an interpretation of my religiously inclusive behaviour.

Be that as it may, and despite my experience during Matonjeni visits of walking a knife-edge between two religious worlds, the challenge of Christian mission, of proclaiming and enacting the good news of Christ's salvific work in this world, was never absent, never obstructed, never entirely unheeded. In other words, ZIRRCON's eco-mission, with its emphasis on interreligious dialogue and joint environmental action, at no point superseded or snuffed out my very real awareness of Christian identity and witness. Christian mission, it appeared, could maintain its Christ-centred focus, its concern for both human and cosmic salvation, even while extending its energies to the field of earth-care and collaborating with non-Christian fellows in mutual respect and trust.

What, then, are the dynamics of this seemingly contradictory religious process? My attempt to answer this question does not profess to be an exhaustive treatise of the theological issues involved. But a few pertinent observations should shed some light on the nature of our Christian mission as it unfolds in the ZIRRCON context. I include them at this point for the sake of those Christian readers who may be alarmed by my positive appraisal of the earthkeeping role of traditional religion to the point of willingness to learn from African indigenous wisdom and cosmology.

The soteriology of the AICs affiliated to the AAEC has evolved from a preoccupation with the healing ministry of Christ. Salvation was accepted as integral to the good news, but its manifestation in the here and now, in the form of human healing and liberation from the threatening powers of evil—wizardry in particular—became a central feature of conversion, recruitment, and church growth. African prophetic healers became the icons of African Christianity, mirroring Christ the healer to their followers; they engaged full-time in exorcism and related faith-healing activities, and developed their churches as healing colonies. AIC missionary proclamation invariably makes its appeal for conversion in an endless variation of witness sermons, testifying to revelations of the Holy Spirit as manifested in the praxis and history of these churches.

Mention was made of how, during different historic phases with changing needs, this healing praxis was moulded into liberation ministries of socioeconomic and political significance. Against this background the AICs had little difficulty envisioning earthkeeping as yet another extension of Christ's, and therefore of their churches' mission. Through my own and several AAEC leaders' emphasis on texts like Colossians 1:17 ('in Christ all things hang together') the image of Christ the Earthkeeper, replacing and fulfilling the role of the ancestral guardians of the land (*varidzi venyika*), has emerged quite vividly in participant AICs. The implications for an AIC understanding of ecclesiology and the mission of the church in this world will be discussed in part 2.

The point to be made here is that the emergence of Christ as Earthkeeper and a distinct concern for cosmic healing (that is, ecological mission) have not detracted from the centrality of Christ the Saviour and the concomitant call for human repentance in the AIC understanding of mission. One dimension enriches and stimulates, rather than stifles or ousts, the other. If anything, the ecumenical interaction between member churches of the AAEC in their earthkeeping mission, together with their ongoing encounter with traditional religion in AZTREC, has stimulated their missionary outreach—both dialogue and witness—to their non-Christian partners. Not all 'green' bishops are prepared to attend and participate in AZTREC's tree-planting rituals. Some of them explicitly state that they do not want to jeopardise their Christian discipleship and testimony in the eyes of their own followers through such cooperation with non-Christians. There are also a few church leaders who, on the same grounds, have resisted the use of tree names as an indication of their involvement in the green struggle. This diversity of views in the Christian camp receives due recognition and respect. Nobody is coerced into ecological partnership with non-Christians.

The majority of AAEC leaders and their followers, however, attend AZTREC ceremonies and are satisfied that united action in the war of the trees in no way exacts a price of religious compromise or syncretist acquiescence. They sit among traditionalist elders, even discuss ancestral directives as transmitted by the spirit mediums, contribute to discussions on the planning of AZTREC projects, and help with the actual planting of trees in the course of day-long *mafukidzanyika* ceremonies. They only withdraw temporarily when the ancestors are being addressed and refrain from drinking sacrificial beer as witness to their Christian allegiance. In this way they feel they are sharing environmental mission and maintaining a respectful Christian presence among their non-Christian fellow fighters. This presence does not intrude offensively on the traditional world of veneration and worship. From my observation of numerous AZTREC ceremonies I am satisfied that the chiefs and mediums on the whole experience this form of religious dissociation by the AICs, not as judgement or personal rejection, but as genuine and acceptable religious differentiation. Consequently a mood of sharing and openness to ongoing dialogue prevails.

The interreligious context is equally relaxed when AZTREC representatives attend and participate in the *maporesanyika* tree-planting eucharists of the AAEC. There is a marked difference, however, in that the Zionist, Apostolic and other bishops leading the service preceding holy communion take the opportunity to engage in what could be called missionary proclamation. The good news propagated concerns the healing of humans and of the barren earth. Repentance in Christ is requested for both individual soul and cosmic salvation and appeals are made to Christian and non-Christians alike. The ceremony, moreover, blends human and cosmic healing in symbolic activity. After taking the sacrament the celebrants extend Christ's life-giving communion to the earth by placing seedlings in the soil, and soon afterwards partake of Mwari's healing powers through the hands and prayers of faith healers interceding on behalf of the earthkeepers themselves. Some of the chiefs and other AZTREC members who are active or lapsed church members participate in either holy communion or faith-healing ceremonies, or both.

The missionary witness and outreach of the AAEC's tree-planting eucharist qualify and augment the emergent trend of interreligious dialogue. The same chiefs and mediums who commune with the African deity at Matonjeni form part of the audience at AAEC eucharistic celebrations and listen, together with Christian earthkeepers, to Christ-centred gospel preaching. The *maporesanyika* context thus affords Christian earthkeepers an opportunity of witnessing to the uniqueness of Christ's saviourhood, to the exclusive claim that there is no other name by which salvation can be obtained, without adopting an intrusive or offensive stance which could alienate their traditionalist partners. Having helped to set this trend in our tree-planting eucharists, I frequently use the opportunity to convey my convictions about an ecoministry inspired by Christ and the Holy Spirit in an attempt to establish a truthful dialectic between Christian message and African religion. Thus we have an interface between learning from the ecological religious wisdom of Africa and addressing it from within a contextualised mode of African Christianity—both respectful dialogue and missioneering witness. The interreligious encounter leaves scope for the integrity and self-respect of representatives of both religions in the war of the trees and establishes the kind of rapport which allows me to identify with the Mwari cultists at the Matopo shrines without undue risk of being misunderstood by ZIRRCON's Christian constituency.

In conclusion, some comments about general revelation as a basis for a theology of religions and its bearing on missionary proclamation will further clarify my own and ZIRRCON's ongoing association with the Mwari cult. It was mentioned earlier that there is some consensus among Christian-oriented AZTREC chiefs and myself that the Matonjeni cult and Shona religion generally are a manifestation of the concern of the Bible's universal Mwari for his people in Africa. Such a viewpoint, reinforced by a periodic respectful Christian presence at the shrines, can easily lead to simplistic identification of Mwari of the Bible with Mwari of Matonjeni, resulting in a syncretised belief system in the cult community and in the AZTREC constituency. This is the risk you take if you want to create scope for meaningful dialogue and joint ecological stewardship from a vantage point of respect for other people's religious convictions. Responsible dialogue from the angle of Christian discipleship should retain its witness character, even as it seeks to shake the attitude of intrusive arrogance and triumphalism which has so often obstructed rather than illuminated the message of God's grace in Christ among non-Christian faiths. The theological background to this viewpoint is as follows.

In the Reformed missiological tradition J. H. Bavinck's theology of religions, to which I subscribe, is one of the most useful and convincing in its openness to all forms of religion, as well as its consistently sensitive application of biblical criteria to Christian/non-Christian encounter. Religion to Bavinck is a manifestation of the biblical God's concern for all humanity and therefore a result of God's general revelation. General revelation is not the presentation of divine truth which humans discover through reason, as in natural theology. It is rather a form of personal encounter brought about by God's will, a claim by the Creator on all creation whereby he makes his presence felt in the lives of all humans: 'From age to age,' says Bavinck (in Visser 1997:118), 'He (God) addressed man and called him to repentance and conversion. The history of mankind is more than just a long account of what man has done, created and invited; its deepest mystery is the story of God's concern with man and man's response to God's revelation.'

Bavinck bases his assertions about general revelation on five clusters of biblical texts: Job 33:14–15, about the closeness of God to humans through visions and dreams; John 1:4, 5, 9, about the universality of God's light which is not overcome by darkness but enlightens all people; Acts 14:15–17, where, in the midst of all the disparate ways of nations and their distortions of truth in religion, God did not leave himself without witness; Acts 17:26–27, where the search of humankind for God is qualified in the first place by his care for all people; and Romans 1:18–20, which elucidates the process of human suppression of truth despite divine revelation of God's power and divinity in creation.[2]

To Bavinck Romans 1:18–32 is the biblical cornerstone of an understanding of God's general revelation. In *Religieus besef en Christelijk geloof* (1949) he makes a profound theological and psychological analysis of these texts. Here he finds

evidence of God's endless involvement with all human beings,[3] of human awareness of being touched in some measure by God's revelation, and of the human
tendency to rebel and flee from God. Bavinck analyses the human response to
general revelation in terms of the suppression of truth (Rom 1:18) and the substitution of God's truth with untruth (Rom 1:25), a process which does not defeat or
obscure truth totally as it keeps prodding human consciousness. In Bavinck's
(1966:122) own words:

> Man has repressed the everlasting power and the divinity of God (Rom.
> 1:20). It has been exiled to his unconscious, to the crypts of his existence.
> That does not mean, however, that it has vanished forever. Still active, it re-
> veals itself again and again. But it cannot become openly conscious; it ap-
> pears in disguise, and it is exchanged for something different. Thus all
> kinds of ideas of God are formed; the human mind as the *fabrica idolorum*
> (Calvin) makes its own ideas of God and its own myths. This is not inten-
> tional deceit—it happens without man's knowing it. He cannot get rid of
> them. So he has religion; he is busy with a god; he serves a god—but he
> does not see that the god he serves is not God Himself. An exchange has
> taken place—a perilous exchange. An essential quality of God has been
> blurred because it did not fit in with the human pattern of life, and the image
> man has of God is no longer true. Divine revelation indeed lies at the root of
> it, but man's thoughts and aspirations cannot receive it and adapt them-
> selves to it. In the image man has of God we can recognise the image of
> man himself.

Bavinck argues that although all religions should in principle be measured in
terms of the suppression and substitution of God's truth noted in the first chapter of
Romans, the history of religions and missionary experience suggest that they are
not in all respects similar. There are 'culminating points' in some non-Christian religions which reveal a greater influence of God—a compassionate divine preven-
tion of complete repression and substitution of the truth[4] not found in all religions.
Bavinck discerns such 'culminating points' in Islam and Buddhism. Greater famil-
iarity with African religion might have caused him to identify a similar culmina-
tion point in the African—more specifically Shona—perception of the creator
God. Be that as it may, Bavinck's analysis of Romans 1:18f is considered profound
by such prominent Dutch missiologists as J. van den Berg and J. Verkuyl. According to Visser (1997:139), Kraemer initiated this interpretation,[5] but Bavinck
worked it out in greater exegetic and psychological depth. Visser discerns similarity between the views of Calvin and Bavinck, but suggests that the latter's approach has a more substantial theological and anthropological foundation.

Barthian theology breathes a different spirit. Aimed as it is at the recognition
and retention of the absolute uniqueness of the special revelation through Christ,
it opposes all forms of theological relativism and natural theology. To Barth (in
Visser 1997:95, 143) all non-Christian religion is merely *Angelegenheit des gott-
losen Menschen* (an issue of godless people). General revelation exists, he says,

but the revelation of Christ illustrated that humans have been incapable of hearing God's voice through this medium. Instead of generating genuine encounter, general revelation leads to idolatry. Non-Christian religion, in this reasoning, represents only monologue. Missionary outreach, in consequence, is a matter of projecting the gospel into an unprepared, empty context. (*Das Evangelium geht ins Leere!* says Barth.)

By contrast Bavinck insists that general revelation establishes a process of dynamic dialogue between God and human beings. The concrete result of this is a 'universal religious consciousness' (Bavinck 1949:11, 12; 1966:29, 30), traceable in five features which all religions share to a greater or lesser extent: people's sense of cosmic relationship, acceptance of religious norms, the dialectic between activity and passivity, a thirst for redemption, and awareness of a higher power (the Great Unknown) in the background (Bavinck 1949:72–75; 1966:111–112). This positive theology of religions implies that missionary outreach has to proceed cautiously, in recognition and sensitive understanding of the human-divine encounter and dialogue which preceded Christian presence. All Bavinck's publications on non-Christian religions[6] attest an attitude of respectful probing of the religio-cultural world in which the gospel message is proclaimed.

Mindful of human rebellion against God and the human tendency to suppress and replace the truth of God's general revelation (Rom 1:18f), Bavinck maintains a precarious balance of sensitive understanding in dialogue with representatives of non-Christian faiths on the one hand, and proclamation of Christ's good news which calls for conversion on the other. The latter dimension is worked out in great detail around two key concepts: *elengchein* (Greek for 'rebuke,' 'persuade,' 'convince,' found in texts like Jn 16:8, Mt 18:15, 1 Tm 5:20, and Rv 3:19) and *possessio* ('to take into possession'). Missionary proclamation is an 'elenctic' process, based on the Bible as an 'elenctic' book. It always assumes and connects with the divine-human encounter which has already taken place prior to Christian proclamation, so that existing religious notions can be unmasked (the main connotation of the term *elengchein* in Bavinck's interpretation) and recognition of the flight from God in former religious activities can precede conversion in Christ.[7]

To Bavinck the term *possessio* means the religio-cultural interchange when communicating the gospel and establishing the Christian church. As the church indigenises itself in the local context it does not merely assimilate local culture in a bid for relevancy. That way lies syncretism. Instead, it 'takes possession' of the local culture, cleanses it through confrontation and transformation, and thus develops a visible manifestation of Christian discipleship, sufficiently continuous with the old culture to be recognisable yet essentially different and new.[8] Although Bavinck does not use the terms 'inculturation' and 'contextualisation' in this connection—these concepts became current in missiological debate at a later date—he provides a solid theological foundation for their emergence and development.

As a former student of Bavinck's[9] I have always been impressed by his penetrative insight into non-Christian religions, combined with compassionate yet humble concern for the proclamation and enactment of Christ's good news in their midst. From all I heard and saw of this remarkable theologian it was clear to me that as a 'transparent' Christian he managed to fuse convincingly his practical missionary vocation (in Indonesia and the Netherlands) and his academic missiological reflections as they appeared in his numerous publications. His influence on my own ministry among the Shona Independent Churches and traditionalists was enduring and far-reaching.[10] Building on the main tenets of Bavinck's missiology, I have of course developed some emphases of my own and contextual insight peculiar to the African situation.

I mention only a few of these. First, it is important in Christian mission to realise that the confrontational elenctic of unmasking the flight of humans from God even as they seek him applies as much to Christians as to non-Christians. The gospel is a two-edged sword which exposes the hubris and limitations of individuals of all religious persuasions, of both message bearers and their audiences. Christian triumphalism, therefore, only has legitimacy as an expression of God's sovereignty and grace; never as a claim to the inherent merit or superiority of a particular form of human faith. Second, Bavinck's theology of religions assumes the presence of the triune God of Scriptures in all religions, a theological position which enables one to qualify Christ-centred elenctics as an expression of fulfilment theology. This is not the fulfilment of relativism which accepts all religions as building blocks in a global religious 'monolith,' with Christianity at the apex, the 'crown' of all religions. Instead, it refers to the revelation of Christ incarnate, whose presence in this world ushers in a new dispensation, fulfilling the old order by way of sustained encounter and change. Third, I have attempted to study the historic process of Christian confrontation and transformation of African religion in the mission strategies of Shona Independent Churches,[11] using some of the interpretive tools provided in Bavinck's theology. In doing so I was able to uncover the inherent theology of religions in the faith-healing ministry of AIC prophets, where interreligious dialogue and 'unmasking' of old precepts in the name of Christ and his Spirit are integral to a spontaneous, Bible-oriented attempt to inculturate or contextualise the church in Africa (Daneel 1974, chapters 3, 4).

Given this theological framework, how does one explain sustained collaborative involvement in the non-Christian cult at Matonjeni? Is it possible to combine the roles of participant observer (researcher), fellow earthkeeper (partner in ecology), and messenger of the good news (Christian missionary) in a situation where mutual respect and sensitive understanding between myself and cult officials appear to preclude any form of rigorous elenctic discourse?

In all honesty, my natural inclination is to advocate the continuance of the old cult. Aware of its significance in Zimbabwe's liberation history and its sustenance of the rich religio-cultural heritage of its African constituency, it seems only fair to me that it should continue rendering a service which keeps people in touch with their religious and historic roots. Against the backdrop of colonial intrusion and Africans' resultant cultural alienation through an imported 'civilisation,' it is difficult not to be supportive of the Mwari cult, even if this does not tally in all respects with my Christian convictions.

If one considers the cult theologically as a product of God's general revelation, as an institution which unwittingly suppressed and replaced the true revelation of

God's power and divinity in creation, it becomes even more difficult to adopt an attitude of sheer confrontation as if one is dealing with flagrant evil. I have found it more correct to treat my priestly hosts at the shrines with due respect, to conduct my inquiry with genuine interest in their beliefs to the point of learning from them, and to inform them openly about my conviction that in talking to their Mwari during oracular sessions, I was addressing Mwari, the Creator and Saviour of all creation as I have learnt to understand him from the Bible. I have related to the cult officials as partners in our common quest for the wellbeing of the earth community and as fellow pilgrims in this world, who have already heard and absorbed on their own some aspects of Christ's special revelation through the gospel message and who therefore share with me the elenctic process of being addressed in the light of Christ's lordship, irrespective of our different beliefs and religious affiliations. In conversation it was apparent that we could accommodate our religious differences without having to judge or withdraw from each other as fellow human beings created by God.

Engaging in elenctic discourse as a privileged attendant at secret cult activities for purposes of observing and understanding the deeper soul of Africa remains complex and stressful. The chances of being misunderstood, of being seen as just another pretentious intruder who seeks to impose his 'superior' religion (against the sensitive historical background of Mwari's opposition to the white conquest of Africa) were and still are very real. Mission impossible? Humanly speaking, yes. But there is a way, however subtle or unexpected, in which Christian witness emerges, even in the most unlikely circumstances. After all, acceptance of the Christ figure renders all believers emissaries, missionaries, whether they acknowledge this or not. Thus it happened in 1967 towards the end of my first visit to Matonjeni, the morning after attending the oracle, that I felt compelled to invite the entire cult community to share in my religious life as I had shared in theirs. My invitation accorded with the African custom of reciprocity. All the key figures and their families attended.

I read from Acts 17—Paul's discourse with the Athenians at the Areopagus—about the 'unknown God' behind their religious practice. Identifying with my audience, I did not attempt any form of preaching but discussed the revelation of Christ, who came and was present as the fulfilment of all our religious groping, both Christian and non-Christian. I remember explaining the light which we had already received through God's revelation in creation, a light which we were incapable of perceiving in full. We know yet do not know. Nevertheless, the closeness of the Mwari we had sensed all along enabled us to develop religious practices. These were like fires at night which provided us with some light and warmth for survival . . . until daylight came, illuminating all the earth, in Christ's revelation and resurrection. I explained the resurrection of Jesus on lines similar to Stephen Neill's (1991:66) observation: 'not simply as the resuscitation of a single man, but as the rebirth of the entire universe; what the gospel offers (as a result) is not a new understanding of self in an unchanged world but an invitation to adventure in a world in which all things have become new.'

In explaining Christ as the fulfilment of all religion, I pointed out that he could not possibly be the *mhondoro* (senior tribal ancestor) only of the white race, comparable to Chaminuka, the hero ancestor of the Shona, as popular opinion at the cult centre seemed to assume. As Son of the Mwari of all creation and heir to all power in heaven and on earth (Mt 28:18) he was the *mhondoro* of all races on earth. He favoured no race above others, had wrought salvation for all and invited discipleship. In conclusion I did not press for conversion. But I felt relieved that after several days of intense involvement in the religious affairs of the cult, I could share something of my own religious convictions and allegiance with people who then for the first time had trusted a white man to enter their own holy of holies.

The response to my message and prayer was warm, appreciative. Gone were the first five days of tension and uncertainty in the cult colony when it was still unclear whether Mwari would allow the presence of a white man at the shrine. (For a description of the eventual breakthrough, see Daneel 1970:10–11.) There was friendship and an invitation for me to return. In missiological perspective, a new adventure in interfaith dialogue and elenctic encounter was underway.

During subsequent visits to the shrines, without and with ZIRRCON delegations, I have refrained from lengthy biblical expositions. Elenctic encounter, I realised, also takes place during discussions at the shrines about divine revelations and cult practice, when there is opportunity to explain similarities and dissimilarities between Christian and indigenous African beliefs. Witness, on the other hand, can be even more effective when maintaining a regular presence at the shrines, caring about the people there, taking their religion seriously without indulging in confrontational dialogue whenever the opportunity arises, and saying a brief Christian prayer over a meal shared with a priest or priestess. When Jonas Chokoto, chief priest at the Dzilo shrine, died recently I was out of the country and could attend neither his burial nor his home-bringing (*kugadzira*) ceremony. Nevertheless, in honour of our partnership in earthkeeping I later accompanied a delegation of chiefs and mediums to the shrine and helped them plant a number of fruit trees at the late priest's homestead. I personally planted a tree at the head end of Chokoto's grave and addressed him as friend and fellow believer in the presence of cult officials and his son who had succeeded him. Somehow I had to give public recognition to the inner peace, piety, and quiet dignity I had observed in this man's life—qualities which reminded me of the good news of Christ's new dispensation of life and light.

Yes! Christian mission alongside non-Christian partners is possible. The route is uneven, uncharted, full of surprises, and at times discouraging. Because we only see in part in this existence (1 Cor 13:12), it is sometimes difficult to read our theological compass. We make mistakes. But because of Mwari's grace and the sheer adventure of life itself, the challenge is worth facing.

Bishop Machokoto, first president of the AAEC, addressing an audience on the need for a united earthkeeping endeavor between Christians and Traditionalists.

Bishop Krinos Kuudzerema of the Zion Apostolic Church lays hands on and prays for a mother and child at Ndaza "Jerusalem," Gutu, in 1965.

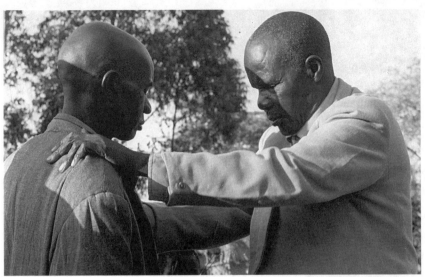

The late Bishop Samuel Mutendi, founder of the ZCC in Zimbabwe, laying hands on a patient in Zion City, Bikita, 1965.

Blind Prophetess Mai Febi of the African Apostolic Church of Johana Maranke sprinkles children and new-born babies with holy water as protection against evil forces, at Mfararikwa, Maranke, 1965.

PART II

African Initiated Churches: Environmental Mission and Liberation in Christian Perspective

Introduction

THE EARTHKEEPER'S CALL

In the beginning
earth was formless and void
and the Spirit of God moved over the waters.
God said: "Let there be light!"
And there was light.

After *chimurenga*
the earth was scorched and barren
and the Spirit of God urged prophets:
"Cry, the empty gullies, the dying plains—
clothe naked land of the forebears!"
And hope returned.
Healing hands, young leaves of trees.

Heeding the call
they came:
black multitudes
churches of the poor:
billowing garments . . .
red, white, blue, resplendent green
bearing holy staves, cardboard crowns.
Cursed descendants of Ham
rejects of white mission,
lift the fallen banner of Spirit
kingdom's cornerstone
where souls of people, tree souls meet.

Prophets shouted:
Repent! Confess!
I bare earth with axe and fire
rape forests without return
sledge-rip gullied meadows
turn earth's water to trickling mire.
Confess and baptize . . .
the wizards, the land!
Oust demons of neglect.
From Jordan emerge
with bonded hands, new earth community.

Touch childless womb, touch hapless soil
—seedlings of love.

Proclaim new heaven,
new earth in black Jerusalem
"Come Mwari!
Come Son! Come Spirit!"
Bare feet touch sacred soil
where rhythmic bodies sweat and sway,
where weary traveler
finds cool in shade
rustle of leaves
fountains spring
clear water of life.

The African Initiated Churches in Zimbabwe indeed heeded the prophetic call to earthkeeping. They joined forces with practitioners of traditional religion—the chiefs, headmen, spirit mediums and ex-combatants of Zimbabwe's political liberation struggle—and formed their own Christian wing of the green army. This they called the Association of African Earthkeeping Churches. Over nearly a decade this body has grown into an imposing ecumenical association, currently counting some 150 member churches and representing an estimated constituency of two million adherents. In the space of a few years, they have engaged in nursery development and the planting of millions of trees. New earthkeeping rituals were introduced. Countless sermons were preached and numerous sacramentally related green activities were performed, all pointing to the evolution of a grassroots eco-theology.

The second half of this book presents a profile of the emergent AIC theology within the green struggle. Hopefully it will not merely be an exercise in self-assessment with and for the AIC communities engaged in earthkeeping, but will also challenge the church in Africa and abroad to reconsider and restructure its ministry to the environment.

METHODOLOGICAL REFLECTIONS ON AIC EARTHKEEPING THEOLOGY AS A COMMUNITY-BASED CONTEXTUALIZATION MOVEMENT

When one theologizes as an ecologically motivated insider and also a cultural outsider who tries to see things with African eyes and feel things through the throb of dancing black feet, one needs to consider the methodological implications and limitations.

AIC theology by definition is *spontaneously enacted theology*. It is not an academically systematized theology, the preserve of 'professional' theologians who retreat Western-style to reflect on their research and then record their reflections in writing. Quite the opposite. AIC reflection and response to life-situations in a given context are first of all in the form of community events and find expression in emotionally uninhibited dance, song, vivid proclamation and social action, all based on predominantly literal interpretations and applications of Scripture. Given this characteristic of AIC theology, it is appropriate that the first section of part II focus mainly on church praxis—that is to say, on patterns of activity emerging in what is felt to be the church's new ministry of healing and liberating all of creation. Here, too, the basic dynamic in theological innovation derives from spontaneous community response to comprehensive (anthropological and ecological) needs in peasant society, instead of being imposed by written dictates from above. Admittedly, key figures like myself and fellow founders of the AAEC have helped to give some organizational direction to new developments, as will be described below. But the starting point remains in the reality that we Independents of Zimbabwe experienced the movement of God's Spirit in direct relation to both the church's task and a devastated environment. This movement of the Spirit, moreover, correlated with our sharing of scriptural insight against a common, if diversified, background of *chimurenga*, which eventually converted into concerted church activity—earth healing through tree planting.

Enacted, sung, and danced in direct response to African needs, AIC theology—for all its lack of books written by the actual participants—is *contextualised theology* par excellence. In his discussion of the varieties of local theology, Schreiter (1985:7-16) distinguishes between three different models: the translation, adaptation, and contextual models. To relate AIC theology, my involvement in its interpretation, and specifically the current eco-theological development in the AAEC to other local theologies, let us briefly discuss the earthkeeping movement in the light of Schreiter's models.

For Schreiter, translation models are the theological procedures generally adopted in traditional cross-cultural missionary situations. To be properly understood, church ceremonies, worship, catechetical instruction, and gospel proclamation need to be translated into the recipient culture. This translation entails a twofold procedure: freeing the Christian message as much as possible from its previous cultural association, and then translating it into the new situation. 'An underlying image directing this procedure,' says Schreiter (1985:7), 'is one of kernel and husk: the basic Christian revelation is the kernel; the previous cultural settings in which it has been incarnated constitute the husk. The kernel has to be hulled time and again, as it were, to allow it to be translated into new cultural contexts.' Variations of this model can be found in attempts to rid Western Christianity of Hellenistic categories, in the post-Vatican II liturgical adaptation of Roman Catholic rites to local customs, and in countless Protestant attempts to translate the Bible using concepts which are considered to have linguistic equivalents in local cultures.

This model has two major weaknesses. First, it stems from a positivist understanding of culture. Since it is the foreign missionary or Bible translator who is analyzing the culture, the focus is not so much on the culture investigated as on finding parallels with a previously contextualised Christianity. Second, the kernel-and-husk theory tends to assume a supracultural setting in which the message is translated into a new cultural situation. Consequently the interwovenness of revelational kernel and cultural husk, also in the Bible, is not sufficiently recognized to deal with the theological complexities involved.

Adaptation models take local cultures more seriously and often emerge at a more advanced stage of local theological development. In this kind of model expatriates and local leaders cooperate in attempts to construct local philosophies or world-views which correspond with Western philosophical or theological systems as a basis for a local theology. Schreiter (1985: 9) writes:

> Placide Tempels's *Bantu philosophy*, first published in 1944 from his experience in the Belgian Congo, is an early and good example of this approach. In this book Tempels takes the then prevalent Neo-Thomistic philosophical framework and redevelops it with equivalent categories from Bantu peoples. The understanding was that this could form the basis for a sub-Saharan Christian theology much as Neo-Thomism had formed the basis for a European theology.

In its refined, more advanced form the adaptation model involves training local leaders to study their own religio-cultural heritage in Western categories and on that basis to create existentially relevant theologies. African theologians such as John Mbiti and Charles Nyamiti are examples.

A major advantage of this model is that when local theologians use Western categories and methodological frameworks in their writings it facilitates understanding and dialogue between Western and other, mainly 'third' world, churches. The limitations, however, are obvious. This kind of theology is mostly addressed to academics who do not necessarily represent the same constituency as does the local church. Consequently the role of local communities in the theological process is neglected or remains somewhat obscure.

Contextual models differ from the first two in that reflection focuses less on the faith received than on the local socio-cultural context. In this category Schreiter distinguishes between an ethnographic and a liberationist approach. The former is particularly concerned with cultural identity. Here a local theology starts with the needs of the local people and not with questions asked by other Christian churches or those raised in systematic presentations of the faith. Small Christian community movements have been vehicles for this kind of theologising, resulting in enhanced identities. This theological method, however, has a number of limitations. Concern for identity and stability often causes conflicting notions in the environment to be ignored for the sake of harmony and continuity. The ethnographic approach easily falls prey to cultural romanticism and, as a result, fails to come to grips with sinful aspects of cultural histories. Sophisticated cultural analysis, moreover, tends to exclude the most crucial component of the theological process—the communities themselves. Yet Schreiter (1985:14) maintains that these limitations can be overcome if a lively dialectic between gospel traditions and local cultural traditions is maintained.

Whereas the ethnographic approach is concerned with cultural identity and continuity, the liberationist approach focuses on social change and discontinuity:

Put theologically, liberation models are keenly concerned with salvation. Liberation models analyze the lived experience of a people to uncover the forces of oppression, struggle, violence, and power. They concentrate on the conflictual elements oppressing a community or tearing it apart. In the midst of grinding poverty, political violence, deprivation of rights, discrimination, and hunger, Christians move from social analysis to finding echoes in the biblical witness in order to understand the struggle in which they are engaged or to find direction for the future. Liberation models concentrate on the need for change (Schreiter 1985:15).

One of the most positive features of this approach is that it unleashes Christian witness and action in communities by linking their existential needs with the saving word of God. Limitations are the inclination to concentrate on the needs of people to the exclusion of biblical witness and the experiences of other churches. In addition there is a risk that reflection sometimes takes place only after action instead of forming the basis for it.

METHODOLOGICAL REFLECTIONS ON MY PERSONAL ROLE IN THE MOVEMENT

The translation and adaptation models raise the question whether my own theological reflection—couched as it is in Western categories, and aimed partly at interpreting AIC theological development to both Western and African academics—can do justice to AIC theology. Is this vibrantly celebrated theology not distorted in the process of writing, and does my attempt to verbalize and systematize realities to which I remain in part an outsider not overshadow community enactment of that theology? In other words, is my theologising among the Shona Independents not susceptible to the pitfalls of the adaptation model? Schreiter (1985:18–20) warns against the dominance of professional theologians in the development of a local theology, insofar as their role imposes a new hegemony on already oppressed communities. Nevertheless, he points out that if the professional theologians participate in the community's experience they could create bonds of accountability between local and world church.

I hope that my role among the AICs fulfils a meaningful bridging function between Independents and the wider body of Christian believers. Nonetheless the following aspects of this function should be noted when assessing the environmental theological developments presented in this study.

First, much of my work in Zimbabwe corresponds with Tempels's immersion in and interpretation of African culture and world-views. A significant difference, however, is that among AICs I operate as a theological freelancer, seeking to interpret and participate in their theological development as a kind of adopted insider rather than working as a missionary of a Western church. It is in that capacity that I try to construct an indigenized philosophical framework as a basis for a Christian African theology. In addition, it should be noted that as a participant observer and fellow Independent I have welcomed the role of 'theological innovator' in the AIC context. Here my pietistic evangelical roots in the Protestant Calvinistic tradition are discernible. At the same time the Independents, with their zest for religious celebration, have taught me to be dogmatically 'footloose'—to dance at the point where precise systematic reflection gets blurred by the urgency of life and action. Consequently I have been much more involved in initiating and participating in new AIC movements—focusing on ecumenical theological training, socioeconomic development, and ecological endeavor—than in producing Tempels's kind of comprehensive, culturally adapted, and systematized theological reflections.

Second, the prominence of my position as founder and co-architect of the AAEC, in which I have been given the role of and the title 'Bishop Moses,' inevitably reflects in the theology developed by the movement. Central features of eco-liturgical innovation (for example, the trend towards environmentally related conversion, 'ecological' baptism, public confession of ecological sins, and the introduction of a tree-planting eucharist) derive directly from my proposals and insight based on research and participatory experience. These proposals, made at executive meetings and conferences or in tree-planting sermons, are 'experimented' with in church praxis, assessed in terms of grassroots response and then adopted or rejected through community consensus reached during tree-planting ceremonies rather than in the more reflective context.

Third, at this stage I cannot assess accurately the enduring impact of my influence on theological developments in the AAEC context. Other observers will be able to judge this aspect at some future date with greater objectivity than I am capable of. I am confident, however, that sufficient safeguards are built into AAEC theologising to prevent it from becoming a one-man show.

Fourth, these safeguards consist of the following: The AICs by their very nature will not permit an adopted outsider to do their theology for them. My proposals are accepted only to the extent that they fit and help extend the existing theology of the AICs. The reward for me as a fellow AIC innovator is to see some of our new ideas being absorbed and contextualised in AIC ceremonies, there to emerge in surprising variations and shapes based entirely on the intuitive creativity and improvisation of AIC communities themselves. In other words authentic innovation is and remains the responsibility and prerogative of AIC communities. Schreiter (1985:16–17) aptly describes 'the community as theologian': '. . . the Holy Spirit, working in and through the believing community, gives shape and expression to Christian experience . . . [therefore] theology is certainly intended for a community and is not intended to remain the property of a theologian class.'

Fifth, the emphasis on community enactment of AIC theology does not, of course, rule out authorship by a nuclear group within the community, which gives voice to (and produces written reflections on) the theology of the community (Schreiter 1985:17). A lot of discussion and planning of possible earth-healing liturgies take place at AAEC executive meetings and conferences. Thus a substantial cross-section of AIC leaders take part in reflection and help to direct the new earthkeeping ministry, the war of the trees. Leadership participation at this level of theologising is vitally important because of an AIC ecclesiology—particularly in the prophetic movements, constituting the bulk of AAEC membership—which elevates the founder and succeeding leaders to a point where they virtually, as iconic embodiments, *become* the church. Given this ecclesiological trend, AIC communities expect their bishops, both in the ecumenical context of the AAEC and in their own churches, to take a strong and convincing lead in the movement's environmental struggle. The bishops do so by preaching their growing ecological convictions to the AAEC's ecumenical conference audiences, calling on their flocks during ordinary church services and newly liturgised tree-planting ceremonies to help liberate the environment, and generally guiding whatever innovation their followers may spontaneously enact during such ceremonies.

In addition, an integral part of AAEC theological innovation is the interaction between ZIRRCON and AAEC. As a result certain key figures have been authorised to produce publications on behalf of the entire movement for a variety of purposes. Thus Bishop Marinda has been commissioned to write two handbooks in the vernacular—one on AIC environmental theology and another on an AIC theology of development—to be used as prescribed material for AAEC conscientisation courses; and Rev. Solomon Zvanaka is producing a traditional 'theology' of the environment for AZTREC's ecological training programs.

My drafts of *African Earthkeepers* were followed with keen interest by the AAEC. When sections of these drafts were read out to bishops, their critical and stimulating feedback created a theological workshop situation. This in itself is a relatively new development in the AIC context, for a large number of them are barely literate. AIC leaders are now not only aware of the value of ZIRRCON's monitoring and ongoing research service, but are themselves increasingly joining in reflection on the interaction between Scripture and ecological warfare and of the telling on paper of their own story.

Having briefly described the AAEC's multifaceted process of theological development, I must emphasize that my account of AIC theology is purely introductory. It is quite impossible to do justice here to the entire tapestry of richly varied church ceremonies, the roles of all the leading figures, and the rich theological themes in a mass movement of this nature. Nevertheless, my descriptive analysis of the emergent AAEC theology is an attempt to complement my own earthkeeping experience and observations with a probing scrutiny of the communal psyche of the movement. To this end I studied the tape-recorded tree-planting sermons of both Spirit-type and Ethiopian-type AIC leaders, a few of which are included here in Appendixes 3 and 4 (pages 298–319). This gave me some idea of how leading earthkeepers relate scriptural passages to the dynamics of their green struggle. I also used interview material to gauge the attitudes and convictions of some prominent AAEC figures regarding the newly introduced eco-liturgical activities in the field. Only fourteen respondents (mainly bishops and a few *Ruwadzano* women leaders) were included in this brief survey, conducted under my supervision by Tarisai Zvokuomba. Although by no means exhaustive or fully representative of AAEC leadership, this survey does provide valuable insight into influential role-players' assessment of the environmental ministry which they are helping to initiate. At any rate, an empirically based analysis of this nature enables one to distinguish characteristic features of the theological consensus emerging from the AAEC's earthkeeping praxis.

Finally, with reference to Schreiter's contextual models of theologizing, it should be noted that the AICs' contextualization incorporates in its own unique way both the ethnographic and the liberationist approaches. Prophetic healing practices in particular illustrate their intense preoccupation with African culture, traditional religious beliefs, and world-views. Dialogue and interaction at this level are generated by the existential need to relate the good news of God's word to the living realities of Africa and are not prompted by Western-style academic or theological motives of cultural analysis. At the same time the experience of colonial oppression, religious paternalism, poverty, and lack of socioeconomic opportunities caused the AICs to develop into liberation movements with strong undercurrents of intuitive—even vehemently proclaimed and largely unwritten— liberation theologies.

The existential nature of the AIC's *people's theology*, moreover, makes it less prone to the weaknesses which Schreiter identifies in both the ethnographic and liberationist models. Here cultural analysis or experience neither obscures the community's contribution to a local theology, nor leads to cultural romanticism. The AIC community by and large remains the creator of its own theology, and an ongoing dialectic between a strong prophetic tradition and local culture results in confrontation and transformation of those traditional practices considered to be sinful, rather than in uncritical accommodation of such practices for the sake of cultural continuity and identity. Here, too, the people's needs in the struggle for liberation tend to color or even distort Bible interpretation and spontaneous action often precedes theological reflection. Despite these shortcomings the Independents' committed search for scriptural guidance and the promptings of the Holy Spirit counteract theological deviations or inconsistencies. Thus the contextual model of the AICs, comprising the integration of both religio-cultural identity and relevance with a tradition of struggling for sociopolitical liberation, forms an ideal vehicle for a ministry of environmental stewardship.

CHAPTER 7

The Church as a Healing and Liberating Institution

To understand current ecclesiological developments in the AICs participating in the AAEC's earthkeeping programmes one needs to look at the development of AIC images of the church since the inception of these movements in Zimbabwe early this century. First, a background of Western denominationalism and poor theological training within the AICs has led to a somewhat fragmented, superficial ecclesiology, lacking in a careful, dogmatic formulation and historical perspective on the development of the church through the ages (Daneel 1987:269f). Second, African culture and social structures naturally left their mark on AIC ecclesiology. Customary law and kinship codes gave rise to legalistic trends, so that many Independents saw their churches primarily as new 'tribal' communities with essentially modified codes of conduct. Sundkler (1961:310–323) observed a growing tendency among South African Independents to turn religious groups into new 'ecclesiastic tribes.' Oosthuizen (1968:82) in his turn judged that ethnicity had corrupted the AIC perception of the church: 'The whole tribe is the church without any idea of personal decision. Its basis is purely ethnic, i.e., based on blood relationship.'

I argue, however, that if tribalism dominates to the extent suggested by Sundkler and Oosthuizen, there could be no question of a Christian ecclesiology among the Zionist and 'messianic' churches, and these movements would have turned into modern versions of tribal religion. The qualifications 'family churches' and 'tribal churches' are misleading insofar as they do not adequately recognise the Independents' insistence on a new Christian identity for their institutions and the transformation of traditional beliefs, social structures and customs which marks their enacted theology. My argument against one-sided generalisations of this kind is as follows:

> We do not deny that the old tribal system conditions and even subtly dominates in certain important areas within the (Independent) church, but this does not justify unqualified generalisations which assume that adaptation and indigenisation (in AIC ecclesiology) imply no more than a simplistic reversion to the old order (Daneel 1987:271).

There can be little doubt that the prophetic movements—numerically the biggest component of all southern African AICs and of AAEC membership—are popularly perceived as healing/liberating institutions. This perception relates closely to the holism of African religions, in which both liberation (i.e., expelling destructive and unwanted powers) and healing (i.e., restoring wellbeing) feature prominently. It also evolves from prophetic concern with individual and societal maladies in the African context, in the form of a distinctly African interpretation of the healing ministry of the biblical Christ—an interpretation which, as we shall see, is reflected in the establishment and periodic redefinition of healing colonies at prophetic church headquarters.

I will trace briefly the development of healing liberation, a major theme in AIC ecclesiology, in relation to changing needs and historical contexts in Zimbabwe. This will help to clarify the subsequent discussion of the AICs' perception of the attributes of an earthkeeping church.

HISTORICAL PERSPECTIVES

FAITH-HEALING 'HOSPITALS' AS A MAJOR ATTRACTION

The first phase of rapid AIC growth in Zimbabwe, from the 1930s to the 1960s, was characterised by a process of religiocultural liberation. This process (Daneel 1998:36–42) involved emancipation from the tutelage of mission churches, a re-evaluation of indigenous culture and religion in AIC worship and ceremonial life, and the introduction of faith-healing practices which offered Christian therapeutic solutions to sickness and affliction as experienced in terms of African world-views. It was during this phase that the image of prophetic churches as 'hospitals' emerged. The AICs' replacement of both traditional African healers (*nganga*) and mission church doctors by prophetic faith-healers represented a significant break-through at the rural grassroots by instilling the perception of the church as a heal-ing institution. The centrality of this image is illustrated by the fact that faith-healing became their most potent recruitment mechanism, an outstanding attraction which, more than any other single factor, drew thousands of people into the prophetic fold (Daneel 1974:186f).

This ministry consisted in diagnosing illness or misfortune, with the prophet representing the revelatory and protective powers of the Holy Spirit. Healers took into account the traditional causation of illness, be it wizardry, vengeful *ngozi* spirits seeking retribution, displeased ancestral spirits, afflicting demonic spirits, or some other spirit agent operating in collusion with one or more living enemies of the patient. Once diagnosed, the afflicting power would be exorcised or neu-tralised through a host of ritual ceremonies, including water purification, tying with holy cords, laying on of hands, burning of holy papers, and prodding with holy staves—all symbolically illustrating the protective and liberating powers of God. Healer-prophets operated both in the privacy of the 'hospital' and during church services.

Thus the entire church was kept constantly aware of its healing ministry, not only by the ever-present healer-prophets at services, but also by the testimony sermons of healed patients reinforcing belief in a compassionate, responsive God.

The main image of the prophetic church that arose during this period was that of a safe refuge in a troubled world: a place where a strong, communal sense of protection and belonging prevailed, where evil was overcome and health restored both in individual lives and in society at large. The destroyer of human life—qualified as 'satan' or 'demon,' but personified by the traditionally familiar and threatening images of *muroyi* (witch or sorcerer), hating enemy, afflicting spirit, etc.— was experienced as being vanquished by the superior, liberating power of God. Despite the preaching of eternal life in heaven, the emphasis was decidedly on ecclesiastic mediation of tangible salvation here and now. In a very real sense salvation meant pastoral and psychological liberation from oppressive evil at African Mount Zions or Jerusalems. Here the men or women of God, the founders of churches, together with their bands of faith-healers, embodied for their followers a truly inculturated incarnation of Christ the healer—a visible and understandable manifestation of a caring divine power.

CHURCH AS SOCIOPOLITICAL HEALER AND LIBERATOR

Because of African holism the interpretation of a prophetic healing ministry was inevitably very wide. Illness was viewed not only as individual psychosomatic afflictions but also as sociopolitical conflicts and crises which had to be resolved in terms of a very real—if somewhat vague in theological definition—perception of God's expanding kingdom. Thus in AIC ecclesiology the prophetic churches' ministry of healing quite naturally came to be extended to burning social and political issues.

Clashes with the colonial authorities over land issues and attempts to 'heal' related societal conflicts stimulated the enactment and verbalisation of AIC liberation theologies, in which principal prophetic leaders started featuring as Moses figures to help solve the problems caused by discriminatory land allocation, or started preaching a scripturally based legitimation of black nationalist political aspirations (Daneel 1998:40–41). During the *chimurenga* years (1965–1980) the latent image of the prophetic church as a sociopolitical healer/liberator came to the fore quite dramatically as the AICs were drawn into large-scale, if secret, participation in the struggle. Increasingly the prophetic healers and their followers were called upon to help 'heal' the land allocation problem by supporting the guerrilla forces in their struggle against what were perceived as alien and intruding land usurpers. Although prophets still devoted attention to threatening mystical forces in individual lives, as described above, the focus had shifted to the fight against a twofold enemy: first, the white oppressors, who had to be pressurised into surrendering land rights and political domination; and second, the enemy within—black collaborators who backed the white regime and army and therefore threatened unity of purpose and action in the rural resistance movement.

The diagnostic and therapeutic thrust of many prophets had a direct impact on guerrilla field strategy, for the Holy Spirit was felt to respond positively to black demands in the liberation struggle. As a kind of 'land guardian' the warring Holy Spirit was considered to be inspiring and directing guerrilla activity, at the same time curbing internal destructive powers to preserve life in a torn society as in the activities of Bishop-prophet Musariri.

Church development was certainly not a homogeneous process during the *chimurenga* years. Instances are known of Zionist church buildings being burnt down by guerrillas who considered the church leaders concerned to be uncooperative or defiant. Yet in many cases prophetic church headquarters acquired a new dimension of offering protection and relative safety in life-endangering circumstances. God's presence at the African Mount Zions and Jerusalems translated into provision of food, faith-healing services, moral support through prayer or Spirit-inspired revelatory sessions, caring for wounded or mentally disturbed fighters, and the like, enabling both harassed bush fighters and suspect or threatened members of society to survive and find some meaning in life in the midst of suffering and deprivation. By identifying with people traumatised by war, the 'men and women of God' in their holy cities contributed actively to the political struggle.

CHURCH AS DELIVERER FROM POVERTY

The establishment of the ecumenical AIC movement *Fambidzano* in the early 1970s brought radical changes for its member churches. With their ecclesiastic isolation broken and their leadership's progress through some basic theological education patently manifest, the AICs felt themselves increasingly empowered and encouraged to deal with educational and economic development issues. For the first time they were able to capitalise on a united ecumenical front in development planning, fund-raising, and project implementation. Whereas *Fambidzano's* ecumenical focus during *chimurenga* was mainly on the development of TEE (theological education by extension) programmes, it shared the nation's concern for social restructuring and economic upliftment in the aftermath of the war. During the 1980s, therefore, the image of black churches as liberators from poverty, economic stagnation, and agricultural unproductivity started to predominate.

Through the introduction of a Women's Desk, *Fambidzano* advanced the process of female emancipation, particularly in rural society. Not only did talented women achieve prominence in theological training, income-generating small industries, and farming, they also started running their own antenatal and postnatal care clinics and launched family planning clubs. The largest AIC headquarters in the country, Bishop Nehemiah Mutendi's Zion City in Bikita district, includes an impressive multimillion-dollar complex of primary and secondary schools, hostels, and a large college (Daneel 1989, chapter 8).

All these socioeconomic and educational projects were closely interwoven with church life. In a sense some of the larger AIC headquarters started resembling the mission stations of Western-oriented churches, whose mission policy makers had all along adopted a comprehensive approach, integrating evangelism with education, medical services, agriculture, and industry. The introduction at AIC 'holy cities' of a wider range of professional workers than before, particularly in the educational field, did not, however, lead to fragmentation of purpose, as if farming, teaching, and commerce belonged to a more secular realm than worship and spiritually oriented church ceremonies. On the contrary, all farming and irrigation activities were surrounded and supported by Christian ritual.

School communities were drawn into the daily Bible reading and prayer sessions of the holy cities and women could preach about problems and successes in their industrial projects during the main church services. As a result, the AICs' socio-economic liberation programmes became integral to their healing ministries. This reinforced the holistic outreach of the church and the characteristic notion in the prophetic movements that Christ the healer-liberator looms large in all sectors of life through his bands of black iconic leaders, both men and women, who concretely mirror his concern for all humanity. Even though not all the needs of participant church members could be met, the holy cities became beacons of progress and relative security in a struggling subsistence economy which, after Independence, suffered crisis upon crisis as a result of severe drought. Although individual salvation and eternal life in a future heaven were still being preached, the good news increasingly included economic realities and opportunities, prospects of material improvement which to many people came as a gleam of hope in their overgrazed, eroded areas with diminishing farm produce.

CHURCH AS ENVIRONMENTAL HEALER AND LIBERATOR

The formation of the AAEC in March 1991 brought an even deeper understanding of the church's healing ministry in the ranks of the AICs. This time the focus shifted to the healing of a suffering creation, in which God's initiative manifests itself in human care for the environment. A new partnership in the divine-human encounter, with an overriding emphasis on Christian stewardship of nature, was taking shape. In the same way that the church's socioeconomic liberatory task had been clarified and broadened in the ecumenical context of *Fambidzano*, its earth-healing ministry—the plans and afforestation programmes—found its definition and impetus in the ecumenical context of the AAEC.

Considering the historical links between *Fambidzano* and the AAEC, one can say that the two ecclesiastic perceptions—the church liberating humankind from poverty and deprivation, and the church healing an abused earth—are integrally linked. Even at an early stage of *Fambidzano*'s socioeconomic development programmes I was already raising questions about how we could offset the exploitive dimension of improved agricultural production by ploughing back into nature what we were taking out for the advancement or progress of human beings. Christian environmental stewardship, by its very nature, should provoke such questions and seek to strike a balance between legitimate use and altruistic environmental management, or service rendered to the environment. The value of reflecting on such issues in an ecumenical context is that new insight and planned action influence a much wider cross-section of church communities than would happen otherwise.

How, then, is the earth-healing ministry of the AAEC churches interpreted by the key role players themselves? Tree-planting sermons provide illuminating clues. AIC leaders use these occasions as 'teaching sessions' to instruct and mobilise their followers. Their spontaneous expositions of what could be called an emerging theology of the environment probably provide the most accurate data for

interpretation at this stage. In January 1991, for example, Bishop Kindiam Wapendama, leader of the Sign of the Apostles Church, and as an AAEC executive member one of the most ardent advocates of a Christian green movement, preached as
follows at a tree-planting ceremony at his church headquarters in Zimuto district:

> Mwari [God] saw the devastation of the land. So he called his envoys to
> shoulder the task of deliverance. Come, you messengers of Mwari [ZIR-
> RCON/AAEC representatives], come and deliver us. Together with you, we,
> the Apostles, are now the deliverers of the stricken land. Let us go forth and
> clothe [i.e. heal] Mwari's stricken land. This is not a task which will enrich
> you. No! The deliverers were sent by Mwari on a divine mission. He said:
> 'You go to Africa, for the land is ravished!' Peace to you, people of Mwari!
>   Deliverance, Mwari says, lies in the trees, but in the first place the people
> have to obey. Mwari therefore sends his deliverers to continue here on earth
> with his own work, with all the work that Jesus Christ started here. Jesus
> said: 'I leave you, my followers, to complete my work.' And that task is the
> one of healing! We are the followers of Jesus and have to continue his heal-
> ing ministry. You are the believers who will see his miracles in this afflicted
> world. So let us all fight, clothing the earth with trees! Let us follow the ex-
> ample of the deliverers who were sent by Mwari. God gave this task to a man
> of his choice. Because this man responded, the task is proceeding as you can
> see for yourselves today.
>   It is our task to strengthen this mission with our numbers of people. You
> know how numerous we are. Sometimes we count ten thousand people at
> our church gatherings. If we work with enthusiasm we shall clothe the en-
> tire land with trees and drive off affliction [evil] . . . Just look at the dried
> out and lifeless land around you. I believe that we can change it. Because of
> our repairing the damage, because of our doing penance for our guilt in land
> destruction, God will heed our wish and give us plentiful rain.

Bishop Wapendama's exposition is representative of viewpoints frequently expressed in the tree-planting services of fellow AIC earthkeepers. God takes the
initiative to restore the ravaged earth, but the responsibility to deliver the stricken
earth from its malady lies with the Christian body of believers, the church. *This
mission is clearly seen as an extension of Christ's healing ministry, which his disciples must fulfill in this existence.*
    As a full participant in AIC earth-healing programmes, I have used preaching
opportunities at tree-planting eucharists to point out the integral link between the
church's ecological healing ministry and Christ's presence in creation. In 1991,
for instance, my sermon at the Topia headquarters at Norumedzo, Bikita, included
the following message:

> You have congregated here to participate in holy communion. This is the
> occasion where you use bread and wine in remembrance of the death of
> Christ on the cross. In this commemoration the body of Christ is central.

1 Corinthians 11:29 emphasises the importance of recognising this truth . . .
Hang on to the idea that we should know the body of Christ. In Colossians
1:15–17 the body of Christ is explained in a special way. He is the image of
the unseen God, the firstborn of all creation. All things were created in him
and for him, the seen and the unseen. Because of this all things hang together in Christ. Through Christ's death and resurrection all power in
heaven and on earth has, moreover, been given to him (Mt 28:18). From all
this we conclude that Christ is not only Lord of creation, but that his body is
all of creation. All created things are part of his body. The implication for us
as stewards of creation is that if we fell trees indiscriminately we are actually 'killing' the body of Christ.

In Colossians 1:18 we read that he [Christ] is the head of the body, the
church . . . Two main points therefore emerge in these texts from Colossians: first, the body of Christ is the entire created world; second, his body
is the church, the body of believers. In the past when we celebrated holy
communion we tended to remember only the one aspect of this twofold
truth, namely that we celebrate our unity in Christ's body as the church.
We neglected the other aspect of Christ's body. So I wish to remind you
here today that whenever you celebrate holy communion, be mindful that
in devastating the earth we ourselves are party to destroying the body of
Christ. We are *all* guilty in this respect. Both the whites and the blacks
are exploiters of the environment . . .

[Then follows an explanation of how, through tree-planting, the eucharist can
also accommodate the abused part of Christ's body.]

What we have done in the eucharist in the past is still there. It is good and
not wrong. It is just that we are reminded these days of something we have
neglected. We are healing and restoring that part of Christ's body which we
have unwittingly abused. That is the message I leave with you today: *Clothe
the barren earth! Heal the earth! It is fully part of our lives as Christians.*

Not all AIC leaders in the movement agree with a Christology which identifies
Christ's body with creation and defines earthkeeping as a form of mending his
body, the earth. Bishop Farawo, leader of the Zimbabwe Zion Apostolic Church
and a leading light among AAEC nursery keepers, for instance, defined his views
as follows:

The earth we abuse is not Christ's body, for it is the creation of Mwari. Yet
creation is like a person, the image of the body of Christ. Look at the trees.
They breathe like humans. So if we fell them we hurt the Spirit of God, because his Spirit is in the trees . . . Earthkeeping is like an expression of
Christ's body. Tree planting during the eucharist is not really part of Christ's
body, but it pleases Christ because we are clothing his earth; remedying the
barren areas and gullies which have been caused by abuse.

Diverse as AAEC views of an eco-related Christology may be, there is general agreement about the church's environmental liberatory and earth-healing mission throughout the movement. True to the AIC tradition of developing an enacted rather than a systematic written theology, this conviction finds its most consistent expression in church praxis. Two illustrations will suffice.

First, tree-planting ceremonies—as developed by member churches within certain broad AAEC guidelines, which leave ample scope for improvised experimentation—all bear the stamp of a contextualised healing ministry. The theme of curing the earth's deforestation malady keeps recurring. As is evidenced in the tree-planting eucharist discussed below, environmental degradation is compared to the havoc wrought in human life by a vengeful *ngozi* spirit. The seedlings represent the modern equivalent of the *mutumbu* (literally 'corpse') offering traditionally given to the family of the *ngozi* to appease the destructive spirit. Planting the seedlings is an act of reconciliation between creator-God, humankind, and creation. This, therefore, is the ecological parallel of the prophetic church's faith-healing practice, in which exorcism or appeasement of life-threatening spirits has always been prominent.

Consider in addition the eucharistic liturgy (see below) for tree-planting, which consistently underscores the church's therapeutic responsibility for an over-exploited environment. When, for instance, the leading bishop sprinkles holy water over the 'Lord's acre' (the plot allocated for the establishment of a new woodlot) he says:

> This is the water of purification and fertility.
> We sprinkle it on this new acre of trees.
> It is a prayer to God, a symbol of rain,
> so that the trees may grow,
> so that the land will heal
> as the *ngozi* we have aroused withdraws.

It is no coincidence that water, the age-old symbol of purification, of healing and life itself, should feature so prominently in the ritual preparation of the acre to be 'healed.' Sprinkling holy water over infants protects them against the onslaught of evil spirits. Sprinkling cleanses the sick of contamination; liberates unwilling hosts from plaguing spirits; and generally prepares barren women for childbearing and all those suffering affliction for spiritual, physical, and mental wellbeing. Holy water, prayed over by the prophet-healer, is the most potent symbol of God's reign, a divine rule capable of healing and restoring all of life. Thus the sprinkling of holy water over the seedlings and the 'Lord's acre' signals the casting out of the soil's denuded barrenness, of the vengeful spirit which provokes drought (in a sense this spirit also corresponds with the wrath of God, who punishes remissness in nature stewardship), and prepares the soil for full recovery under the cover of new trees.

In the second place, and probably the most convincing sign of an expanding and changing theological praxis, there is the impact of an earth-healing ministry on AIC headquarters. The shift in the focus of healing was reflected in the political and socioeconomic programmes and activities at church headquarters during the historical phases mentioned above. In the same way current earthkeeping is causing the evolution of yet another type of healing colony. In a sense the new and trend-setting model of an earthkeeping centre is the ZIRRCON-AAEC headquarters in Masvingo town. Without any pretence of representing a kind of super church headquarters which controls or dominates an extensive ecological 'strikeforce' of some 150 participant churches, the ZIRRCON-AAEC administrative centre nevertheless figures as a central earthkeeping nexus. This is where ecumenical church conferences take place, where ecological policy and project implementation are planned, and where AAEC officers are employed full-time to reflect and write on earthkeeping, develop training materials for conscientisation courses, and provide infrastructure for nursery development, woodlot monitoring, wildlife management, etc.

Taking their cue from this development and operating within an expanding network of earthkeeping churches, several prophetic leaders are becoming acclaimed earthkeepers in their own right. They are extending the existing healing colonies at their headquarters into 'environmental hospitals.' The 'patient' in this instance is the denuded land and the 'dispensary' (i.e., the faith-healing 'medicinal' arsenal of holy cords, holy water, staffs, paper and other symbols of divine healing power) becomes the nursery where the correct medicine for the patient, in the form of a wide assortment of indigenous, exotic, and fruit trees, is cultivated. The entire church community—both at headquarters and in outlying congregations, residents and visiting patients—now becomes the healing agent under the guidance of the church's principal earth-healer. Consistent aftercare of budding woodlots provides proof of the church's dedication, the woodlot itself becoming the focus of testimony sermons and a source of inspiration for an expanding ministry, as the testimonies of healed human patients in the past contributed both to a reaffirmation of belief in God's healing powers and to the church's recruitment of new members in its expansionist drive.

EMERGING ATTRIBUTES OF THE EARTHKEEPING CHURCH

From tree-planting sermons, interviews, and new patterns of activity within the AAEC's participant churches, one gets some idea of what the leading AIC figures consider the most significant attributes of an earthkeeping church to be. I shall give only a brief profile of what in the long run could develop into a full-blown environmental ecclesiology.

AN ECUMENICALLY ROOTED MINISTRY

Against the background of *Fambidzano*'s ecumenism as well as the geographically wide scope of earth-healing envisaged, it was evident from the outset that ecclesiastic endeavour was not intended for just one or a few environmentally interested churches, but for a massive Christian movement operating from a common ecumenical platform. From the outset the first AAEC president, Bishop Ma-chokoto, propagated the need for strong ecumenical foundations in our common ecological struggle. 'What I asked of God,' he said, 'is a true sense of unity amongst us. We have to work together to avoid all forms of confusing conflict. Our unity must rest on convincing work . . . The basis of our work, according to God's Word, is love, a love which reveals itself in works . . . We, the (AAEC) churches will have to make sacrifices for the cause to which we have pledged our-selves. Therein lies our unity . . .' My own expositions of a *divine mandate* for our work, with reference to Isaiah 43, as well as its christological basis (Daneel 1998: 101–102), implied wide ecumenical interaction.

This call for united action provides a key to interpret the ecumenism developed by the AAEC. Representing a predominantly peasant society which confronts the hazards and threats to subsistence on a deforested, overgrazed, and overpopulated land, the AIC bishops and their churches did not join forces to realise some ab-stract ecumenical ideal or for the sake of church unity as an end in itself. It was rather an ecumenism shaped by churches sharing a newly identified and common commitment—that of healing the earth. In a sense, therefore, the realisation of a common quest, the action in the field, give expression to the love in unity to which Bishop Machokoto referred. One can say that the escalating 'battles of the trees,' the development of nurseries with many thousands of seedlings, as well as the preaching and ritual celebration of tree planting and tree watering in the newly established woodlots, ameliorate interchurch conflicts. The earthkeeping church is purged from within of isolation and self-centred ambition as it bonds with other churches in an all absorbing ministry of environmental stewardship.

Not that all the differences and conflicts of the past have suddenly been re-solved. The prophetic churches tended to accuse the non-prophetic movements that they were not fully Christian because they did not heed the work of the Holy Spirit, and the Ethiopian-type churches in turn accused the Zionists and Apostles that their prophecies were products of traditional ancestral or alien spirits, not of the Holy Spirit. It is rather that these old conflicts pale into insignificance as the green revolution unfolds, at the annual conferences, executive meetings, and in the joint labour and ritual celebration of earth-healing ceremonies. Thus a new comradeship transcending traditional ecclesiastic divisions has started to evolve between creator-God, earthkeeping humanity, and the trees, plants, and wildlife. A new myth, arising from the common subconscious of Africa, blending with Christian perceptions of a realised, observable salvation for all creation here and now—and manifested in AAEC church life—is emerging.

Apart from being drawn into closer union with other AICs, the earthkeeping church is also challenged to participate in spontaneous ecumenism by interacting in a common cause with traditionalists, that is, with AZTREC. Once the AIC bishops felt secure about retaining their own brand of Christian identity in the green struggle, they were eager to promote wider religious unity, or at least mean-ingful cooperation, with their AZTREC counterparts, the chiefs, spirit-mediums, and other traditional authorities. Said Bishop Machokoto, the AAEC president, in his key address at the inception of the new ecumenical movement:

We must be fully prepared to recognise the authority of our kraalheads and chiefs. For if we show contempt for them, where will we plant our trees? A Christian attitude is required towards the rulers of the land. Let our bishops in their eagerness to fight the war of the trees not antagonise the keepers of the land. If you are a church member, yet try to place yourself above the laws of the land, you are not a true convert. Let us fully support our (tribal) elders in this struggle of afforestation, so that the ZIRRCON-AAEC objectives may be realised in practice (Daneel 1998:109).

This plea certainly does not imply a sweeping compromise of the prophetic AICs' general confrontational approach to the ancestral religion represented by their traditionalist co-fighters in the green struggle, the chiefs and spirit-mediums. Yet the call for submission to the laws of the land and for cooperation with the chiefs reveals a growing tolerance and a preparedness to move beyond the stereotyped prophetic restraints of in-group dynamics in the interest of a stricken environment. Instead of withdrawing from the traditionalist practitioners of ancestor veneration to demonstrate its rejection of 'heathenism,' the prophetic earthkeeping church now underscores at least ecological solidarity with its traditionalist counterparts in the green struggle.

AN EXTENDED MISSIONARY MANDATE

The good news proclaimed and enacted by the earthkeeping church clearly extends beyond soul salvation and faith healing aimed at the wellbeing of human beings, as tended to be the case in the AICs in the past. As propounded by Wapendama, the healing ministry of Christ remains focal to the church's mission but it now includes, more explicitly than before, the deliverance and salvation of Mwari's stricken land. The good news is that the barren land will be clothed, that is, be protected, by trees and plants. This form of salvation becomes manifest to the extent that the church fulfils its role as the keeper of creation, a mission in which its entire membership is harnessed as active agents instead of just a few specialised 'missionaries.'

Not that ecological specialisation is not appreciated in the church's environmental mission. Wapendama himself is an expert at germinating seeds of indigenous trees. His sermons reveal an extensive knowledge of trees: the correlation between healthy vegetation and proper living conditions for human beings, the importance of trees' 'perfume' for the breathing of all of nature, the interaction between trees and humans in seasonal change, the impact of bore-holes and barren lands on underground water resources, etc. Thus, like Farawo, Wapendama is a specialist healer—both of humans and of nature—competently heading his 'environmental hospital' and mobilising his followers on the basis of knowledgeable and exemplary environmental commitment rather than empty calls to comprehensive service.

Overall it is evident that the church's liberatory task is extended without hesitation from the sociopolitical to the environmental sphere. Without obscuring the futuristic dimension of people yet to be saved in the coming kingdom—as currently preached in AAEC churches—the earthkeeping mission focuses on salvation in this existence by materially improving the quality of life of all creation, protecting nature and curbing mindless ecological destruction at the behest of God him/herself. In addition identification with *chimurenga* tradition stimulates militancy, determination, and pride of accomplishment. It also fosters peoples' sense of ownership of the process, in contrast to colonialist or postcolonial government programmes.

ECOLOGICAL LAWS AND DISCIPLINE

In its application of what amounts to a new ecological ethical code, the earthkeeping church shows keen awareness of the need for well-defined church laws to prevent the wanton destruction of nature. Virtually all AAEC respondents concurred that such laws are necessary, that they should be drawn up and enforced by the church itself. Bishop Farawo proposed that ecclesiastic legislation should first of all prohibit wanton tree felling, because 'the trees mourn when you chop them down.' Disciplinary action, he claimed, had to assume the form of prophetic elicitation of tree-felling confessions, whereafter the church council should force wanton tree-fellers to plant and care for new trees as a form of punishment and recompense for the damage done. Tawoneichi claimed that new church laws should ensure aftercare of trees planted to secure a high survival rate. Reacting to the neglect in some AAEC woodlots, he stated: 'This law is necessary because it leads your heart in the right direction. If you ignore this law you are outside the Bible. Christ said, "without love you cannot obey my laws." So the church's tree-laws will be obeyed by those who love Christ.' Bishop Chimhangwa insisted that all church laws on earthkeeping should be written up in church books at once, thus reinforcing the gospel message of the earth's salvation. He considered many people still to be ignorant of the 'gospel of the trees' (*evangheri yemiti*). Consequently 'the threat of the destructive axe must be repelled.' It was suggested that even earthkeepers in the AAEC league still kept special axes for tree felling hidden in their houses, which they used secretly whenever it suited them. Mrs. Chimhangwa, the Bishop's wife, felt so strongly about unchecked deforestation through illegal use of the 'destructive axe' that she suggested the church should have trespassers thrown into jail until the urgency of environmental protection was fully understood.

The exercise of discipline by churches was most forcibly advocated by militant earthkeepers by requiring prophetic exposure of ecological sinners in various ritual contexts. This represents a contextualised reinterpretation of traditional evil, in terms of destructive wizardry perpetrated against the land—a subject to which we shall pay further attention below.

In contrast to the general consensus on the need for effective church laws and disciplinary measures against earth destruction, a few warning notes were sounded by individuals who saw the this-worldly emphasis of the green struggle as a threat to conservative other-worldly perceptions of spirituality. Said Mrs. Miria, wife of Bishop Farawo: 'No! Tree-protection laws are the domain of the government. We do not go to a heaven of trees when we die. We leave the trees down here on earth. Prohibitions about trees apply only to the order of this world, the life of the flesh. If we care for the land we are merely concerned with the life of this world. Heaven has its own laws!'

STRUCTURAL AND LITURGICAL CHANGE

Preoccupation with earthkeeping duties in some instances leads to a change in Christian group behaviour and individual lifestyles. Mention was made above of earth-healing colonies, which imply structural changes at church headquarters insofar as prophetic healers, together with their followers, become absorbed in ecological programmes. The demands of seed collection, full-time nursery care, liaising with schools and surrounding communities on issues like woodlot establishment, management, and aftercare, and networking with staff members at ZIRRCON headquarters certainly introduce patterns of activity based on, but quite unlike, those of the stereotyped prophetic faith-healing colony focusing mainly on human needs.

More significant than the outward changes in the organisation of some church headquarters is the willingness to adopt liturgical innovation, new symbols of salvation, and patterns of worship that fully express the church's dedication to renewal in its neglected task of environmental stewardship. It may be too early to assess the full implications of such renewal for the processes of conversion, recruitment, and baptism in the earthkeeping church. Yet significant developments in ritual procedures, such as public confessions of ecological 'sins' and the use of imaginative liturgies for tree-planting eucharists, are already in evidence. These reflect an awareness that theological redefinition should be manifested in green liturgies and worship if ecclesiastic reorganisation and successful implementation of earthkeeping ministries are to be effected. The nature of such rituals and liturgies will receive attention in the next chapter.

CHURCH LIFE, NOT SCHOLARSHIP, AS VEHICLE OF THEOLOGICAL REORIENTATION

Being engaged in ecumenical ecological programmes with an expanded missionary mandate, the earthkeeping church necessarily also has to monitor and assess this new activity. This is a spontaneous, reflective process relating to and emanating directly from praxis—there where tree planting and tree nurturing take place in a newly ritualised context. Instead of appointing theological committees or experts to theologise and produce written texts, as often happens in the West, the African earthkeeping church allows its key figures to relate praxis to scriptural truth, justification, and inspiration at the point of action. Often the result is a kind of re-enactment and improvisation of biblical history, in which African church leadership or the Christian community identify with biblical figures and/or events.

Some of the details of an emerging environmental theology, particularly as it relates to the perceived involvement of a triune God, will be discussed in the following chapters. Here I merely sketch a few characteristic Old Testament themes as they feature in earthkeeping discussions and tree-planting sermons.

The creation story and Adam's ecological responsibility in the Garden of Eden are virtually always given prominence in green sermons. Textual interpretation and contextual application vary considerably, yet common traits are noticeable. Rev. Sauro Masoro's sermon was a classic example of the straightforward manner in which humanity's earliest perception of ecological stewardship as portrayed in Genesis 2 is directly linked with current AAEC preoccupation with trees. Preaching in the shade of a *muchakata* tree, the Zionist minister proclaimed that the people present and the tree under which they were sitting were one. Without the tree the people would not be able to breathe, a fact which he considered to be underscored by God's first creating the Garden of Eden as a necessary condition for living before he could create a human being to inhabit it. God's act of creation, therefore, implies total interdependence between humans and vegetation, something which was not sufficiently recognised in the past. Genesis 2:9 was given immediate relevance when he insisted that 'the *muchakata* fruit we eat from this tree you see here is medicine which heals us. The *matamba* fruit we eat is medicine which heals us. Even if we eat a mango, guava, or orange, it is still healing medicine to us.'

In this AIC 'Garden of Eden' theology Adam and Eve do not figure as the crown of creation, or as rulers over nature, but as the equals of animals and birds and fully identified with their life. In conversation, Zionist Bishop Machokoto even went so far as to say that 'human beings were created for the purpose of caring for all of creation,' thus interpreting the meaning of human existence basically in terms of ecological stewardship, service to creation. Seen thus, there is a joyous relationship between humans and plant life, which Machokoto described in terms of communication and mutual respect. The trees, being addressed as brothers and sisters by tree planters during tree-planting ceremonies, now acquire a sense of dignity and value, knowing that they are no longer objects of mindless destruction by humans.

To the present-day earthkeeper the cardinal sin against God is disrespect for his presence in nature and mindless provocation of his protective jealousy of his forests—contemporary symbolic extensions of the Garden of Eden—as evidenced by the deforested regions of the Chivi district where Bishop Farawo himself leads the church's war of the trees. The Bishop does not judge and reject Adam's sin, moreover, but identifies with it, giving it particular poignancy in a rural context where environmental destruction reflects God's anguish and withdrawal. Absolution and deliverance, it seems, relate directly to restoring Mwari's creation, thus restoring harmony and closeness between Creator and human beings.

Other frequently mentioned Old Testament figures are Noah and Moses, both of them liberators and 'men of God' in their own right. What virtually amounts to a new Africanised mythology is developed around Noah's ecologically salvific work. His ark, in the earthkeeper's view, contained *all* animals and seedlings of all plants. ZIRRCON or the AAEC churches are likened to Noah's ark in that they become the protectors of Mwari's creation in the deluge of environmental destruction.

The uniqueness of Moses's call to liberate Israel is seen to derive from the fact that God addresses him from a burning bush and gives him a wooden staff as symbolic affirmation of his task. Great importance is attached to God's choice of a tree as a symbol of divine presence and power during Israel's exodus.

In some interpretations God's presence in a tree signifies equal status between humans and the rest of creation, the implication being that both are equally dependent on divine liberation from enslavement. Said Rev. Masoro:

> The Israelites complained to Moses that he alone was conversing with Mwari. They, too, wanted to communicate directly with God. So God said: 'Let them wash and prepare themselves before we converse.' But God did not speak out in the open plains. Whenever he spoke he was hidden in a *denhere* [clump of trees]. And the people had to lie prostrate in his presence. This shows that the tree and the human being are one [in status and need of deliverance].

From the ecological significance of the Old Testament figures Adam, Noah, and Moses, the attention often switches directly to Christ, the true source of all life and guardian of all creation. Union with Christ (Jn 15), poignantly expressed in the imagery of the vine and its shoots or the *muchakata* tree with its branches laden with fruit (suggestive of the original harmony between God and humans in the garden of Eden), provides life and, to the earthkeeper, empowerment to heal creation. Said Rev. Masoro in concluding his tree-planting oration: 'We cannot bear fruit if we are not in Christ, the true vine. If we do not go and ask for trees to plant we shall not have the trees which heal and clean us.' Pragmatic as this motive for tree planting may seem, it nevertheless flows from new life in Christ. Obedience to Christ inevitably implies Christian responsibility for all creation, especially tree stewardship.

Having considered some of the characteristic features of the African earthkeeping church, one can say in summary that prophetic healing colonies are extending their ministry to incorporate earth-healing. In the process some church headquarters acquire the features of 'environmental hospitals' with built-in healing responsibilities for the entire church community. In its new mission the church propagates salvation for all of creation, with a clear emphasis on the realised eschatology of a revitalised creation here and now. Individual spiritual growth is directly related to, measured and fed by participation in earthkeeping programmes. Ecclesiastic unity acquires a new dimension as churches overcome isolation on account of the common cause of serving God's creation. New laws and disciplinary measures against earth destruction strengthen their resolve, which in turn finds expression in green liturgical innovation. The accompanying process of theological reflection is spontaneous and fairly straightforward, if subtle and intuitive in some respects. New theological insight crystallises in the action of church people as they trace their own response to God's inspiration to ecological figures and/or events in the Bible. Through a growing perception of human guilt in environmental destruction people's position in creation is reappraised as one of humility and complete identification with all creatures rather than of triumphalist subjection.

Bishop Zvanaka and Principal Tarisai Zvokuomba (third and fourth from right) attend a beer libation of chiefs. Christian earthkeepers do not drink sacrificial beer for the ancestors but may take and pass on the calabash to a participating traditionalist as a sign of respect.

Bishops Zvanaka, Marinda, Masuka, and Moses pray over sacrament species and seedlings in preparation for the tree-planting Eucharist.

Sacramental empowerment culminates in tree-planting. Ruwadzano women often plant the bulk of the seedlings in new woodlots.

Women assert themselves as earthkeepers. Ms. Raviro Mutonga, chair of ZIRRCON's Women's Desk, reminds members of a women's club of their responsibilities.

Women take leading roles during maporesanyika tree-planting ceremonies.

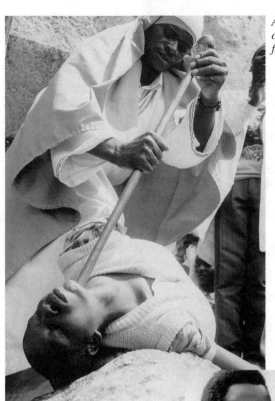

Apostolic prophet-healer ex-orcizes spirits from an af-flicted patient.

At sunset the mission to heal the land and to heal people unite as Bishop Solomon Zvanaka lays hands on a fellow earthkeeper — hands that still carry the soil of a day of tree-planting.

CHAPTER 8

Green Rituals and Liturgies

Confession of sins has always played a prominent role in the healing and sacramental ceremonies of the prophetic AICs. During faith-healing ceremonies the healer-prophet urges patients to confess their sins. Not only is this a way of placing the afflicted under the care of the Holy Spirit, but revelation of the dark side of the patient's existence also enlightens the healer-prophet about the cause of affliction, the area in the patient's life which requires therapy (Daneel 1974:214f, 292f). The confessions of converts prior to baptism symbolically illustrate the neophyte's acceptance of the authority of the church, represented during the ceremony by the prophet listening to the confessions, as well as the final mystical authority of the Holy Spirit which induces such confessions.

Public confessions prior to taking the sacrament of holy communion are in a sense a mass demonstration of right-mindedness and obedience to God. In the Zionist and Apostolic movements such confessions form part of an intricate process of cleansing the church community so that it can appear worthily before the holy God during the most revered and intimate ritual expression of divine-human encounter. In the Apostolic movement of Maranke and Mutendi's ZCC confession ceremonies consist of nightlong vigils, during which prophets reveal the hidden sins of unrepentant hearts and vaPostori judges at the symbolic fires of judgment spend hours assessing whether the self-confessed or prophetically accused wizards (witches and/or sorcerers) are sufficiently prepared or repentant to take the sacrament. As uroyi (wizardry), with its destruction of human life and social relations, is indisputably evil, and the muroyi in many ways becomes the personification of the biblical Satan, one can understand the prophets' intense preoccupation with this phenomenon when it comes to cleansing the church in anticipation of union with the body of Christ (Daneel 1974, chapter 4; 1990:220f).

CONFESSION OF ECOLOGICAL SINS, CONVERSION, AND BAPTISM

Some AAEC-affiliated prophets are already applying their newly gained insight into ecological stewardship to their moral guardianship over their churches. In the baptismal context they are increasingly revealing that the Holy Spirit expects novices not only to confess their moral sins in a society of disturbed human relations but also their ecological sins: felling trees without planting any in return; overgrazing; riverbank cultivation; and neglect of contour ridges, which cause soil erosion—in other words, taking the good earth for granted and exploiting it without nurturing or reverencing it.

At 'Jordan' it makes sense to the newly converted to confess ecological guilt, there where the barren, denuded plains, erosion gullies, unprotected riverbanks, and clouds of wind-eroded dust are clearly in evidence. Crossing the River Jordan in baptism after such confession means more than just individual incorporation into the body of Christ and the prospect of personal salvation in heaven. It also requires the new convert's commitment to helping to restore creation as part of God's plan and as a sign of genuine conversion and repentance in recognition of the gift of God's grace.

To many Independents baptism is also a healing ceremony in which baptisands drink the life-giving water of Jordan, filled by the Holy Spirit, for individual cleansing and curative purposes. It follows that the ceremony offers a unique opportunity for interpreting the Spirit as healer of both the people and the land. Baptism, therefore, becomes yet another feature of an extended ministry of healing, a changing ecclesiology. In that case, the drinking of Jordan water symbolises a shift from the baptisand's personal benefit from the Holy Spirit's healing and salvific powers to a ritual affirmation of solidarity with all creation, a new commitment, through individual conversion, to earth-healing.

It is not clear to what extent this reinterpretation of conversion and prophetically induced confession of ecological sins at baptism has really taken root in AAEC churches. However, discussions on the subject at AAEC executive meetings and the incorporation of these views into training material used at AAEC workshops point to growing consensus on what a contextualised ethical code in terms of eco-confessions should imply.

Easier to assess is the AAEC prophets' struggle against ecological sins in the context of numerous tree-planting eucharistic ceremonies, in which ZIRRCON staff members and I participate regularly. During the public confessions, which form part of the green liturgy preceding the taking of bread and wine, a core group of 'green prophets' from a wide range of Zionist and Apostolic churches increasingly brand offences which cause firewood shortage, soil erosion, poor crops and the absence of wildlife as a form of wizardry (uroyi)—the gravest of all sins, threatening not only human survival but all other forms of life. This trend has not yet developed into a practice of separating unrepentant ecological varoyi from the other communicants, paralleling the pre-sacramental cleansing praxis of the Maranke Apostles (Daneel 1974:293f). Nevertheless, as the resolve of the earth-keeping churches hardens and prophets become more and more convinced that the Holy Spirit rather than human beings motivates and guides the green struggle, unrepentant ecological varoyi in the AICs will increasingly find themselves barred from the eucharist. Discussions with prophets, who are becoming Christian 'guardians of the land' in their own right, indicate that they are increasingly convinced that the Holy Spirit is in fact inspiring the struggle against environmental evil, and that they generally have a clear perception of who the earth-destroying wizards in their society are. These varoyi are considered to include people in resettlement schemes who endanger the common good by indiscriminately felling as many trees as they can for a quick profit from selling firewood; who refuse to accept the principle that firewood can only be used by those who plant the trees that supply it; who resist government conservationist measures and the tribal elders' prohibition of tree felling in the traditional holy groves (maram-batemwa) of the ancestors; and destroyers of river banks.

The identification of ecological sin with wizardry and the insistence on public confession underscore a significant new development. They enable the church in its green struggle to identify the enemy outside and within its own ranks. Identification of the wrongdoers in turn enhances and crystallises the church's ethical code and control system. This development is reminiscent of the chimurenga struggle, in which counter revolutionaries and collaborators with the Smith regime were branded wizards. The task of the AIC war prophets, alongside the traditionalist spirit-mediums, was to elicit confessions from suspects during secret pungwe meetings as part of a process of identifying the wizard-traitors and singling them out for punishment. Unifying the battle ranks and cleansing the guerrilla cadres of internal subversion in terms of the idiom of wizardry indicated a relentless will to succeed and survive, for uroyi is an evil which brooks no compromise.

In the earthkeeping churches the nuances regarding wizardry are inevitably more varied and subtle than during the war. In contrast to the execution or torture of war traitors, wanton tree-fellers or poachers of wildlife will, upon prophetic detection, either be temporarily barred from taking the eucharist or, in the event of repeated transgression of the earthkeepers' code, be excommunicated altogether. The key figures in the AAEC are only too aware of a common guilt which, in a sense, makes all of us 'varoyi'—earth destroyers. To this they readily admit, which in itself is a sure sign of accepting collective responsibility for environmental restoration. There is a vast difference, however, between admitting guilt prior to committed participation in conservationist programmes, and deliberate deforestation or related destructive action in the face of a protective environmental code. It is this attitude of selfish environmental exploitation, regardless of the will of the community and the destruction caused to nature, which the prophets condemn as the evil of uroyi, to be stamped out at all costs.

Discussions about ecological uroyi and how to combat it stimulate emotional expressions of views which, probably more than any other kind of discourse, outline the underlying convictions in AAEC circles about the real nature of an earthkeeping church. Said Bishop Nhongo:

> The church is the keeper of creation. All churches now know that they must empower their prophets to expose [through Spirit-induced confessions] the varoyi who kill the land. These people who wilfully defile the church through their destruction of creation should be barred from holy communion. If I was the one who owned heaven I would have barred them from entering. The destroyers of the earth should be warned that the blood which they cause to flow [of trees, animals, etc.] will be on their own heads.
>
> This is the law of ZIRRCON! All churches are now earthkeepers, healing the earth. Those who obstruct this work must be expelled. Their destructive characters will cause them to attack and obstruct the fighters of the war of the trees.

Bishop Nhongo confidently proclaims the church as 'the keeper of creation.' The church's mission includes laying down and implementing strict rules against earth destruction. Strict environmental church laws imply authorising the prophets to expose ecological wizards during public confessions. Such exposure is but the first step in a process of church cleansing, so as to effectively mobilise the Christian green army, eliminate subversion and realise environmental goals. Paramount is an element of judgment and punishment so that—as in chimurenga—the enemy outside and within can be clearly discerned. The Bishop's somewhat tongue-in-cheek suggestion that, if he had a say in the matter, the destroyers of nature would be barred from heaven underscores the seriousness with which ecological sins are viewed.

A TREE-PLANTING EUCHARIST

The best example of eco-liturgical innovation in the AAEC churches in the process of giving ritual expression to an emerging environmental ethic is the introduction of a tree-planting eucharist. According to the member churches' annual calendar, a tree-planting eucharist only takes place once during the rainy season, so it does not drastically change or supersede established liturgical procedure regarding the sacrament of holy communion, popularly known in the prophetic movements as Paseka (paschal) ceremonies. Nevertheless the practice of tree-planting eucharists is of great interest, for various reasons. First of all, the participation of diverse churches in each ceremony and the sharing of ritual officiant roles on an interchurch basis strengthen environmentally focused ecumenism. Second, the integration of eucharist and tree-planting makes environmental stewardship, which in Christian tradition has often been treated as peripheral, part of the very heartbeat of church life and biblical spirituality. Third, this ceremony highlights characteristic trends of an emerging AIC theology of the environment. And, fourth, the new liturgies introduced are imaginatively contextualised in terms of African religious holism and worldviews. Thus an earthkeeping model is developed which could well challenge AICs elsewhere in Africa to assimilate environmental stewardship through similar liturgical innovation.

Consider, for example, the tree-planting liturgy drafted by Zionist Bishop Reuben Marinda, former general secretary of the AAEC, at the request of the executive after careful consideration.

Preparation for the eucharist starts with digging holes for tree planting in the vicinity of an AIC headquarters or in a local congregation. In some instances the woodlot is fenced and referred to as 'the Lord's acre.' General ceremonial procedure is in the hands of the principal church leader who, under supervision of the AAEC president and general secretary, assigns various functions to dignitaries in his/her own church and other participant churches.

While the communion table, covered with a neatly pressed tablecloth and bearing the bread, wine, and a number of tree seedlings, is being prepared, groups of dancers dance around the bulk of the seedlings to be planted, which are stacked nearby. Dance and song bring praise to Mwari the great earthkeeper, encourage the green fighters to be vigilant in the struggle, and even entreat the young trees to grow well. The service itself consists of several earthkeeping sermons by AAEC bishops and ZIRRCON staff members. It invariably also includes speeches by visiting government officials and representatives of the departments of Forestry, Education, and Parks and Wildlife, as well as the Natural Resources Board.

The sacrament starts with the public confession of ecological sins referred to above. All communicants, church leaders included, line up behind a band of prophesying prophets to confess their guilt and receive prophetic admonition as they slowly file past the prophets before picking up a seedling and moving to the communion table to partake of the sacrament.

We shall now consider in some detail the contents of the eucharistic tree-planting liturgy as read (in Shona) by Bishop Marinda at a ceremony of Bishop Mupure's Zion Christian Church of St. Aron on 1 February 1992.

By way of introduction all participants were welcomed to the Lord's acre, where the trees to be planted and the planters would share the same status as brothers and sisters in the Lord's presence. Mwari is the one who declares to his church people the value of their friends the trees:

> They will provide you with shade
> to protect you from the heat of the sun.
> They will give you fruit, for you to lead healthy lives.
> These trees will clothe the barren earth,
> protecting it against soil erosion,
> preventing it from turning into a desert,
> keeping the moisture in the soil.
> Look at the stagnant water
> where all the trees were felled
> Without trees the water holes mourn;
> without trees the gullies form
>
> for the tree roots which hold the soil . . .
> are gone!
>
> These friends of ours
> give us shade.
> They draw the rain clouds,
> breathe the moisture of rain.
>
> I the tree . . . I am your friend
> I know you want wood
> for fire
> to cook your food,
> to warm yourself against cold.
> Use my branches . . .
> What I do not need
> you can have.

I, the human being,
your closest friend
have committed a serious offence
as an ngozi, the vengeful spirit,
I destroyed you, our friends.
So the seedlings brought here today
are the bodies (mitumbu) of reparation
a sacrifice to appease
the vengeful spirit.
We plant these seedlings today
as an admission of guilt
laying the ngozi to rest,
strengthening our bonds with you,
our tree friends of the heart.

Let us make an oath today
that we will care for God's creation
so that he will grant us rain.
An oath, not in jest . . .
but with all our heart
admitting our guilt,
appeasing the aggrieved spirit,
offering our trees in all earnest
to clothe the barren land.

Indeed, there were forests,
abundance of rain.
But in our ignorance and greed
we left the land naked.
Like a person in shame
our country is shy
of its nakedness.

Our planting of trees today
is a sign of harmony
between us and creation.
We are reconciled with creation
through the body and blood of Jesus
which brings peace,
he who came to save
all creation (Col 1:19–20).

At this point Bishop Marinda digressed from the liturgical text by giving an exposition of Genesis 2:15–17. Corrupted by Satan, he argued, man became an enemy of God and nature by cutting down all the trees. 'As a result the weather patterns of the entire world changed. Man became the destroyer of the rain forests, the killer of the world's ecosystems.' God retaliated by sending severe droughts. 'Look, the rivers are dried up and all the fish have gone, because we cut away all the vegetation on the river banks, causing the river beds to fill up with sand.' Against this background of human sin against nature and God's judgment, an urgent appeal was made once again to confess environmental sins. Christ, the one who holds everything in creation together (Col 1:17), atones for such sins. As Lord of creation he works salvation for humanity. 'Humans, in their turn, have a duty to extend salvation to all of creation [as Christ's co-workers].'

In addition to the people's role of extending Christ's salvation to creation, Marinda also presented an intriguing interpretation of how Christ saves all of creation. Through the ultimate sacrifice on the cross, Christ brought all burnt offerings of Old Testament times—the destruction of sacrificial birds and animals, as well as the firewood used for this purpose—to an end. Hence 'through his death on the cross he also saved the animals, the birds, and the trees.' In the liturgy this theme is further elaborated with reference to Jesus' action against the merchants in the temple in Jerusalem. 'When Jesus heard the lowing and the bleating he knew the poor creatures were crying to be saved from the cruel merchants.' By lashing the merchants Jesus saved the birds and animals from the cruel fate of being sacrificed.

The liturgy then turns to the ecological strife caused on earth by Satan:

> There was war in heaven, says the Bible.
> Michael and his angels . . .
> He was hurled down,
> that ancient serpent called Satan
> he, who leads the whole world astray.
>
> So the devil is deceiving the whole world
> causing man to fight creation.
> Possessed by the demon
> man is destroying nature's beauty.
> All living things suffer—
> the trees, the animals, water.
> It shall continue
> until man extinguishes
> all life on earth.
> If we continue to kill the trees
> we hurt ourselves
> by hastening the end of the world.
> If the world is ultimately destroyed
> it will be the doing of man.

In a further elaboration of ngozi beliefs the liturgy explains the meaning of mutumbu payment and sacrifice. Replacing the sacrificial animals to appease the aggrieved and vengeful spirit with sacrificial trees to pacify the aggrieved land and its creator is 'the only way we can seek forgiveness for having caused the nakedness of the land.'

Then follows the celebration of sacramental bread and wine. Holding seedlings in their hands while receiving the sacrament, the communicants then proceed to where the holes have been dug in the new acre of God (woodlot). Prior to the actual planting, the Bishop walks through the woodlot sprinkling holy water on the ground and on the seedlings, saying:

> This is the water of purification and fertility.
> We sprinkle it on this new acre of trees.
> It is a prayer to God, a symbol of rain
> so that the trees will grow,
> so that the land will heal
> as the ngozi we have caused withdraws.

'Holy soil' which has been prayed over is then scattered in the woodlot to the words:

> You soil . . .
> I bless you in the name of Christ
> for you to make the trees grow
> and to protect them.
> Provide the trees with sufficient food
> for proper growth.
> Love the trees and keep their roots
> for they are our friends.

The Bishop then leads the green army into the Lord's acre to do battle against the earth's nakedness. The seedlings are addressed one after another as they are placed in the soil:

> You, tree, my brother . . . my sister
> today I plant you in this soil.
> I shall give water for your growth.
> Have good roots
> to keep the soil from eroding.
> Have many leaves and branches
> so that we can
> breathe fresh air
> sit in your shade
> and find firewood.

To the Western mind this liturgy may sound simple and fairly trivial considering the enormous, near impossible task of halting deforestation, desertification, and soil degradation. In the African cultural and linguistic context, however, as part of spontaneous ecological ritual activity, it is a powerful statement of Christian commitment to the healing of all creation.

The close identification with water, soil and trees—elevating them ritually to the status of communication with human beings—reflects African religious holism. Here the intuition of the past is taken to a level where mutual dependence is eloquently and meaningfully verbalised. In this overtly declared friendship, subsequent to admissions of human guilt in the mindless destruction of nature, mutual responsibility is reaffirmed: the new trees to provide shade and unpolluted air to sustain healthy life for humans, and the earthkeepers to water and protect their budding friends in the Lord's acre. The liturgy assumes responsible aftercare by the community of believers commissioned to do so—in itself a strong incentive to the woodlot keepers not to let the green army and its monitoring agents down. This imaginative encouragement of proper aftercare—normally the Achilles' heel of most African tree-planting endeavours at the grassroots—is already proving effective at sustaining responsibility for the sometimes monotonous chores in the wake of the more exciting ritual experience of tree planting.

Impersonating the vengeful ngozi spirit in terms of earth destruction is as potent a way of accepting full responsibility for deforestation as the confession of ecological wizardry. The ngozi is an aggrieved spirit of a murdered person or someone who has been the victim of a grave injustice prior to death (Gelfand 1959:153; Daneel 1971:133–140). In customary law and traditional religion the ngozi, which wreaks havoc in the offender's family through illness and death, has a legitimate claim to full compensation in the form of up to ten sacrificial beasts called mutumbu (literally 'corpse' or 'body,' since they pay for the corpse of the deceased). In some cases the offender's relatives also provide the ngozi with a young wife, who must sweep and tend the small hut specifically erected for her disgruntled 'spirit-husbands.'

Presenting the trees to be planted as mitumbu compensation for the ngozi spirit provoked by wanton tree felling is an illustration of thoroughly contextualised appeasement between humans and environment. The ritual, moreover, expresses compassion for the badly abused friends: trees, soil, water, and, by implication, all of life in nature.

The ngozi concept has several subtle connotations in the liturgy. It reflects the ruthlessness of the supposed human stewards of the earth who attack nature with a vengeance, like that of the ngozi, hence the seedlings are legitimate sacrificial substitutes for the stricken tree trunks or 'corpses.' Then, in sprinkling the water over God's acre, the words 'It [the water] is a prayer to God, a symbol of rain' implicitly suggest that God him/herself turns ngozi against the ecological offenders by retaliating with severe drought. This interpretation tallies with the still persistent and widespread traditional belief that the creator-God punishes transgressions against nature and the guardian ancestors of the land, who are responsible for ecological equilibrium, by withholding rain. In the admission of guilt, the ritual plea for termination of divine discipline, the renewal of human resolve to heed the environment as ordained by deity and ancestors, absolution is found. God responds by sending life-giving rain. Transformed as they are in the Christian liturgy, some of these traditional notions are still in evidence.

Sprinkling holy water and soil over the barren earth earmarked for repair is a symbolic act of earth-healing. It accords entirely with prophetic faith-healing practice as described above. As such, it is further proof of the ecclesiological shift which extends healing beyond human suffering to the healing or liberation of all creation.

Both the liturgy itself and Bishop Marinda's commentary make a powerful statement about the evil forces at work in earth destruction. Having deceived humanity and having alienated men and women from God, Satan is the main perpetrator of evil against creation. A frustrated being chased from heaven, Satan is presented as destroyer and foremost ecological enemy from the very beginning (Gn 2). This focus, however, does not minimise human guilt as demon-possessed human beings cause all of creation to suffer. Such madness raises the prospect of extinguishing all life on earth. 'If the world is ultimately destroyed, it will be the doing of man,' says the liturgy. By implication the tree-planting eucharist in its entirety epitomises fighting Satan and the demonic blindness to the needs of nature which has been induced in humans. Thus, during the eucharist, all participants are given the opportunity to confess their particular ecological blindness under the sway of Satan. And what more poignant way of doing so can there be in Africa than to own up to the particular kind of wizardry against creation in which one has indulged!

Christ emerges in the liturgy as the complete antithesis of Satan—the one who heals, protects and brings harmony. His blood effects reconciliation between humankind and the rest of nature. His salvation, through humankind, extends to all creation. The reference here is to Colossians 1:17–20. Although at this point the liturgy is not explicit about the twofold interpretation of the body of Christ (i.e., the body as church and the body as creation), the central concept underlying this Christological feature, much discussed in AAEC circles, is that 'in Christ all things hold together.' The sacramental activity which unfolds around this concept apparently suggests that the view propagated by myself and fellow Independents during eucharistic ceremonies is gaining currency, namely that at the point where the believers give expression to their unity in the body of Christ as church, by partaking of the bread and wine, they accept responsibility for the repair of the cosmic body of Christ, to which they also belong and which they, too, have abused. Consequently, in partnership with Christ who, as head of the believers, is the real *muridzi venyika* (guardian of the land—in contrast to or in fulfilment of the traditional concept of ancestral guardianship), they proceed in unity as the church to heal the stricken body through tree-planting.

In the tree-planting eucharist this close identification of Christ's body with the abused and barren soil makes sense. Traditionally the ancestral guardians of the land belonged to the soil. They are the soil! Their ecological directives issue from the soil, as expressed in the literal saying, 'Ivhu yataura' (literally 'The soil has spoken'). In a sense Christ in this context is both guardian and the soil itself. New conceptions of Christ's lordship and his salvation of all creation can develop from this essentially African expression of his pervading presence in the cosmos. In African peasant society at any rate Christ's reign as *muridzi* (guardian) of the land is an essential part of the good news, for he is the one who is believed to consciously strike a balance between exploitive agricultural progress and altruistic, sacramental restoration of the land.

Here, in Christ's lordship, the Independents give ecological expression to what Moltmann (1985:227) calls the messianic calling of human beings:

> In the messianic light of the gospel the appointment (of humans) to rule over animals and the earth also appears as the 'ruling with Christ' of believers. For it is to Christ, the true and visible image of the invisible God on earth, that all authority is given to human beings at creation . . . It is to 'the Lamb' that rule over the world belongs. It would be wrong to seek for the dominium terrae, not in the lordship of Christ, but in other principalities and powers—in the power of the state or the power of science and technology.

In all this there is no pretence that we earthkeepers are the saviours of creation, for that we can never be. But as believers and disciples of the one who holds all things together, we are erecting not merely symbolic but physical signposts of life-giving hope in a creation suffering while it awaits redemption. For, as Duchrow and Liedke (1987:61) correctly state:

> Spirit-endowed beings do not save creation, but creation looks to us. The way that we cope with its suffering shows how much hope there is for creation. When we increase the suffering of creation its hope sinks. When we sharpen the conflict between human beings and nature, and also the conflict between humans, then creation lapses into resignation. When, instead, in solidarity with nature and our fellow human beings, we reduce suffering, then the hope of creation awakes into new life.

Such a solidarity between humans and nature is precisely what the AAEC hopes to achieve. Through the movement of the earthkeeping Spirit new unity is being established between formerly opposing churches and between a pluriformity of religions in society, giving rise to an ecumenism of hope. In the participating holy cities and Jerusalems, hope takes concrete shape in the form of a healing ministry that attempts to cover and nurture the afflicted land. Serious attempts to expose and discipline those who continue raping the earth embolden the green combatants to intensify the struggle. Replacing the trees in sacramental recognition of the lordship of Christ—the ultimate guardian who reigns over, yet suffers within, the stricken earth—brings life and celebration to creation.

CHAPTER 9

Toward an African Theology of the Environment 1

Mwari the Creator as Insider

In this and the next two chapters I attempt to trace a profile of the AIC theology undergirding and stimulating the praxis of an earthkeeping ministry as it takes shape in the AAEC context. Inasmuch as the theological discourse represents reflections on and elaborations of trends already identified in the previous two chapters, we are not dealing with a written, fully systematised theology. Instead, our sources are verbalised and enacted conceptions and convictions which emerge spontaneously during tree-planting ceremonies and are integral to AIC theological praxis. Through repetition by leading figures and affirmation by participant church communities these convictions become *theological guidelines* for the core activities of the entire earthkeeping movement.

I shall also endeavour to highlight the relevance of AIC environmental theology for African Christian theology generally as articulated in the world of publications and Western-oriented academia. Black African theologians have done little towards producing a comprehensive Africanised theology of the environment. Hence the earthkeeping AICs may well provide both the incentive and the basic building stones—derived from biblically intuited and envisioned praxis—for the development of such a theology. In addition some insight will be drawn from recent works by Western theologians engaged in eco-theology. Their inclusion serves only to relate the AICs' contribution meaningfully to the growing concern about a deteriorating environment among churches worldwide.

It is remarkable how some trinitarian notions or beliefs currently emphasised by Western theologians as being pertinent to a realistic theology of creation—although varying greatly in their expression—implicitly or explicitly underlie the earthkeeping ministry and sacraments of the AICs. I shall indicate how the call for God's full presence in his creation (Moltmann 1985:13; Wilkinson 1990:280) coincides with an outstanding feature of AAEC environmental work—that of experiencing God the Creator as insider, present in and in control of creation. To fully appreciate the significance of this theological development, the undefined but very real traditions of a remote Creator God among the Shona require brief consideration.

A REMOTE CREATOR?

THE DISTANT ONE OF TRADITIONAL RELIGION

Traditional concepts of God in Africa have contributed to a certain remoteness and transcendence of God the Father in African Christianity. Traditionally the general image of Africa's Supreme Being was that of a creator who, although the foundation of all that exists, was not considered to be directly involved in all the day-to-day details of maintaining and controlling it. The Shona concept of *Wokumusoro* (the One above) to some extent expresses Mwari the creator's remoteness from creation. The function of organising and maintaining creation was largely attributed to the ancestors, whose veneration became a dominant feature of traditional religious activity. In some instances God's remoteness was ascribed to human error which had disrupted the divine-human relationship. Western observers in particular have emphasised silence, perhaps mystery and detachment, as outstanding characteristics of the traditional divinity in Africa. With the exception of Mwari, the oracular deity of the Shona, and the divinities worshipped by the Dogon, Ashanti, and Ambo, the God of Africa has been characterised as a *deus otiosus* or a *deus remotus*. As Taylor (1963:85) observed concerning the apotheosis of Kyala: 'Beginning in this world as part of the human hierarchy of the living and the ancestors, they (the gods) are eventually, as we might say, pushed through the sky-light and lost sight of.'

Against this background it is understandable that Western missionaries, apart from using the traditional names of the African Supreme Being for God in their biblical translations, tended to direct their indigenising policies mainly to the accommodation or confrontation of the more dominant ancestor rituals. Thus the pertinent questions arise: Did the church in Africa succeed in drawing the remote one convincingly into the ambit of day-to-day human life? Did he/she acquire recognisable features as the insider?

MISSIONARY TRADITIONS

In considering these questions we briefly look at the two most prominent missionary traditions—those of the Roman Catholic and the Reformed Protestant churches—that have played a major role in the Christianising of the Shona in Masvingo Province, where the AIC environmental theology is currently unfolding.

The Roman Catholic tradition of natural theology allows for far-reaching accommodation of or adaptation to the varied cultures of humankind. In contrast to the Reformed view of human nature as totally corrupted by sin, Catholicism holds that some uncorrupted seed is present in creation. As a result the Catholic Church assimilates what it considers to be good customs among people, not necessarily by way of radical transformation but by synthesising indigenous and Christian truth. Papal decrees have enhanced missionary strategies based on accommodation and assimilation and even assigned the church the function of guarding the positive aspects of indigenous culture.

There can be little doubt about the salutary impact of assimilate rites. In rural areas the church appears to have come closer to the people; it has lost some of its alien Western character and has gained in popularity. One of the most convincing proofs that the Catholic Church has become inculturated in Shona society is its ability to maintain a reasonably stable membership, without great loss through schisms or individual defections to the AIC movement and other churches.

Yet considering the traditional religious preoccupation with ancestral involvement in everyday life—at the expense of a remote creator-God—there is considerable ground for controversy over the Christian nature of the assimilated Catholic rituals (see for example the polemics between Rubio, Kuehne, and Oscar Niederberger, in Daneel 1971:276) and for concern about interpretive confusion. In the liturgy of the burial rite, for instance, no clear distinction is made between Christian and non-Christian ancestors. All the deceased person's ancestors are addressed collectively and they are all accorded a mediating function on behalf of the deceased.

One should not indulge in glib generalisations about what could amount to a popular yet superficial accommodation strategy. Representative empirical evidence is necessary for a balanced assessment of the full impact of Rome's missionary policy on the Shona Catholic Church. Nevertheless, recent research into the spirituality of the liberation struggle has indicated a marked difference among Shona Protestants and Catholics as regards dependence on the guardian ancestors of the land and their spirit-mediums for mobilising resistance against the Smith regime. Protestants by and large considered such dependence a sort of spiritual backsliding, while Catholics tended to condone it as a form of traditional religious renaissance endorsed by their church. Several former guerrilla commanders who are active Roman Catholics tended to equate Christ's salvific work with the liberating activities of the Shona hero-ancestor Chaminuka during the struggle. Although such religious differentiation may reflect the difference in official mission policies between the two church traditions, it is possible that in a protracted war situation the attention of thousands of members of both mission churches was thoroughly absorbed by the ancestors.

In the Reformed tradition, Calvinism took a more pessimistic view of human nature than Rome's natural theology. As a result, Reformed missionary theology tended to present individual conversion as a radical break with the past and treated the process of church indigenisation as a total transformation of all aspects of indigenous cultures and religions (Bavinck 1949:126, 174; 1954:234, 245). This approach tended to exclude adaptation in the form of identifying and incorporating constructive elements of traditional customs. Instead, it consistently promoted a policy of discontinuity which inhibited dialogue between representatives of Western and African cultures and led to a negation of indigenous practices by the early mission church policy makers.

Although Dutch Reformed missiology in South Africa was influenced by German theologians in its insistence on church indigenisation (Warneck 1987:22; Van der Merwe 1967:52), the early Dutch Reformed Church (DRC) missionaries among the Shona lacked the strong theological interest of German missionaries like Bruno Gutmann and Christiaan Keyser. Hence Rev. A. A. Louw, the pioneer missionary operating from Morgenster, and his colleagues propagated a radical break with Shona culture to those who accepted the Christian faith. In the course of time, however, some leading DRC missionaries actually engaged in research to acquire deeper insight into traditional worldviews. This led to such valuable publications as *The Shona Idea of God* by Prof. W. J. van der Merwe, and the development by individual missionaries of an exorcist ministry which took the traditional spirit world seriously.

But the general trend was towards elimination and a measure of negation of Shona beliefs, rather than sympathetic interaction and dialogue. Attitudes to the ancestor cult, in particular, concentrated so exclusively on actual or imagined features of worship—idolatry and satanic perversion—that little or no room was left for remoulding by assimilation, or for substituting parallel Christian rites within the church.

The implication of this policy was that the good news of the missionaries seldom addressed the full range of existentially significant issues in a rural subsistence economy. What was good news at the mission stations and at the schools and clinics erected by the missionaries was not necessarily good news in the village. Religiously, church members tended to live in two worlds. They would attend Sunday services and prayer meetings at the mission station, where God indeed seemed to be present for the protection and advancement of his people. Back in the villages, however, the threat of wizardry, destructive forces, and crippling droughts was as real as before. Here God did not always appear to be the insider. Because the Christian message insufficiently penetrated this world, many church members continued to propitiate the ancestors, to surround their homesteads with a 'stockade' of magically prepared objects to ward off evil, to participate in traditional exorcist and witchcraft-eradication activities, etc., in an attempt to secure their wellbeing.

INCULTURATION AND REHABILITATION IN AFRICAN THEOLOGY

Since about 1970 African theology has burgeoned in an attempt to give expression to Christianity in African religio-cultural terms, to relate Christianity meaningfully to Africans' view of reality, and to integrate it with their worldview. According to Ukpong (1984:510) 'the final goal [of African Theology] is to help the African live out Christianity authentically within his cultural milieu and to integrate his religious personality.' Adopting a new theological methodology, these theologians evaluated the Bible and Christian tradition with greater openness to African culture. As the latter is allowed to determine the course of theologising to a greater extent, the result is an existentially oriented, contextualised theology rather than a rationally systematised, doctrinal theology in the Western sense.

As a form of contextualised inculturation, African theology should be characterised as religio-cultural liberation. It presents a new approach in the face of a history of colonial subjection, Western racism, and imperialism. Enforced acculturation has caused a deep, traumatic split in the African soul—'religious schizophrenia,' as Desmond Tutu put it—with an accompanying identity crisis. Against this background African theology forms part of Africans' attempt to overcome alienation from their cultural heritage. Reaction against colonial conquest provides self-respect as a necessary condition for the search for a new, liberating identity. Hence there is a preoccupation with, and a re-evaluation of, indigenous traditions—not a return to the fleshpots of Egypt, as Witvliet (1984:111) puts it, but the necessary and demanding first phase of emancipation from Western religio-cultural enslavement. A characteristic feature of this form of liberation theology is the rediscovery and appreciation of those tenets of African culture which were rejected or ignored under Western domination. Rehabilitation of culture, tradition, and history is thus the hallmark of this first phase of liberation.

How does this rehabilitation of traditional religion affect theologians' views of biblical and African concepts of God? Is the *deus otiosus* brought into the inner circle of humankind or does he/she remain the remote outsider? Does Scripture remain normative or is the gospel message smothered in African religion and stripped of its own liberating power?

When responding to such questions one should bear it in mind, first of all, that against the background of colonialism—which all too often was mirrored in missionary policy, praxis, and attitudes—African theologians, in their reflection on traditional religion, invariably tend to be passionate apologists. They are understandably concerned with their own religious roots. What they find there shows continuity with the Christian faith rather than the discontinuity which the missionaries tended to emphasise. The God of Africa and the God of the Bible are essentially one. As Kibicho (1968:235) puts it: 'I think it would be right to conclude that the Kikuyu conception of God compares well with the Hebrew conception of the Old Testament, perhaps at the latter's highest level of development.' This favourable comparison, which features in numerous variations in monographs on the African understanding of God (e.g., Idowu's *God in Nigerian Belief*; Danquah's *The Akan Doctrine of God;* Nyamiti's *African Tradition and the Christian God*; Mbiti's *Concepts of God in Africa*; and Setiloane's *The Image of God Among the Sotho-Tswana*) implies rejection of the idea of a *deus otiosus* or a *deus remotus* as a misleading generalisation contrived by Western observers. Such elevation of the African concept of the Supreme Being, moreover, is based on a prefiguration paradigm in which traditional religion represents a *praeparatio evangelica* in its own right, comparable to the Old Testament. Like the latter, African religion finds its fulfilment in the gospel of Christ and does not fall under the judgment of discontinuity preached by the missionaries.

In an article on the encounter between the Christian faith and African religion, Mbiti (1980:817f), for example, states emphatically that the God of the Bible is the same as the God already known in the pre-Christian framework of African religion. This God revealed himself not only on the Old Testament Mount Sinai but also on Mount Fuji and Mount Kenya. Consequently Mbiti rejects the Western theological distinction between 'general' and 'special' revelation as unbiblical. God's revelation should not be restricted to the biblical account of it. 'One important task, then,' writes Mbiti (1980:818), 'is to see the nature, the method, and the implication of God's revelation among African peoples, in the light of the Biblical record of the same revelation.' By implication, therefore, the historical account of God's involvement with the people of Africa is considered to be on a par with his involvement with Israel.

Setiloane, in turn, suggests that African religion should reject the Western portrayal of the Christian God, for the West has lost the experience of God as *mysterium tremendum et fascinans* and has substituted for it a *deus absconditus*, or a saviour only of individual souls. To Setiloane, therefore, the Sotho-Tswana hesitancy in the presence of the mystery, Modimo, is more acceptable than the glibness with which the Christian evangelist speaks of the 'Lord' (Setiloane 1976:85f).

Contributions from theologians such as Setiloane (1976), valuable as they are in establishing an independent theological orientation by way of religio-cultural liberation from the virtual monopoly formerly exercised by Western theology, also cause some concern. African Protestant evangelical theologians like Byang Kato, Adeyemu, and Tienou have serious reservations about the use of traditional religious notions as a basis for the development of an African theology. Bosch (1974:118–119) was of the opinion that 'Africa has not yet produced many scholars who are equipped to produce a truly incarnational theology emerging from a profound encounter between the Bible and the African world.' In his view francophone African theologians have been overly committed to speculative theology and anglophone theologians to apologetics. The need currently is for an African theology which takes both the biblical revelation and the African world seriously, 'an authentic theology of religions . . . that moves beyond isolating certain aspects of African life and thought for which sanction from biblical revelation is then sought' (Bosch 1974:118–119). This is precisely what is taking place, not in the written reflections of sophisticated African theologians, but in the spontaneously enacted theology of many AICs.

MWARI AS INSIDER

In contrast to African theologians' attempts to trace a continuity between the God of Africa and the God of the Bible and to repudiate or ignore the very real dimension of God's remoteness in traditional religion, the Independents in practice appear to acknowledge both continuity and discontinuity. The Shona prophets, for example, recognise the continuing significance of the traditional high-God cult and still take seriously the remoteness of Mwari, which is also the name for God in their Bibles. Through improvised rain rituals, tradition-oriented yet radically changed, they endeavour to bring the distant God, traditionally approachable only to a few cult officials, into the ambit of daily living. This ritual attempt represents the line of continuity. For in Zionist sermons and ritual, Mwari, the distant one of the Matopo hills, is now introduced as the recognisable one, much closer to the individual than formerly.

There are several ways in which the traditional high-God was drawn close and in which his image changed the Shona prophetic communities. First of all, he was drawn close as rain giver and provider of crop and human fertility. In other words, he remained recognisable in his traditional function, the difference being that he became much more accessible than he had been through oracular pronouncements in former manifestations. In the second place, he became prominent in adapted ancestral rituals, such as the consolation ceremony (*runyaradzo*) substituted for the traditional home-bringing (*kugadzira*) ritual. As a result of the Zionists' elimination of all addresses to the ancestors and their attempt to suppress their mediatory function, the role of Christ came to feature more prominently and was further highlighted by the iconic leadership of the Zionist bishop. This contrasts favourably with the way Christ is to some extent overshadowed by ancestral mediation, for instance in Roman Catholic rituals (above). In the third place, healer-prophets took over the position of the traditional healer (*nganga*). Their faith-healing ministry in the name of the Holy Spirit incorporates diagnostic and therapeutic activities in which traditional magic and medicine are replaced by the healing power of a manifestly present God. Fourthly, a special ministry of exorcism and witchcraft eradication brings the real African perception of evil and sin into the open and confronts it directly with the liberating and reconciliatory power of God. This prophetic ministry differs vastly from the missionaries' rejection of witchcraft and their preaching of individual immorality and sin against God, in a manner which seldom penetrated to and directly addressed the African experience of destructive evil in society.

THE ZIONIST GOD OF THE CROPS

In the prophetic Zionist and Apostolic churches it is as the immanently present guardian and protector of crops that Mwari the creator enters peasant society most forcibly and pervasively. Prophetic intuition at this point runs parallel with what present-day Western theologians signal as significant for a theology of creation or ecology. In his attempt to establish guidelines for such a theology Jurgen Moltmann (1985:13) stresses God's immanence in the world. 'An ecological doctrine of creation,' he says, 'implies a new kind of thinking about God. The centre of this thinking is no longer the distinction between God and the world. The centre is the recognition of the presence of God in the world and the presence of the world in God.'

Moltmann explains how the Old Testament presents Yahweh as a deity different from the world, to contrast his nature with the pantheistic matriarchal and fertility cults of the Canaanites. In this world 'God's context is transcendence, and the world as the work of His hands is turned into immanence. Nature is stripped of her divinity, politics became profane, history is divested of fate. The world is turned into passive matter' (Moltmann 1985:13). This view obviously accorded with the modern processes of secularisation and seemed to justify the ruthless conquest and exploitation of nature by modern Europeans. According to Moltmann, however, a modern ecological doctrine of creation must perceive and teach God's immanence in the world: 'God is not merely the Creator of the world. He is also the Spirit of the universe. Through the powers and potentialities of the Spirit, the Creator indwells the creatures He has made, animates them, holds them in life, and leads them into the future of His kingdom' (Moltmann 1985:14).

For many years Bishop Samuel Mutendi, founder of the Zion Christian Church in Zimbabwe, expressed similar convictions at his Zion City, admittedly against a theological background very different from Moltmann's, and in ritual activity rather than in written theology. He, too, attempted to proclaim the biblical Mwari as truly present and totally involved in all of creation—in a peasant society as the God of farmers and their vitally important subsistence crops. Both Mutendi and to some extent his *Ndaza* Zionist counterparts elsewhere in the country, realised that the immanence of the ancient God of the Matopo hills was not the same as the overriding pervasive presence of the biblical God, as was increasingly manifest in the black Zion Cities and Jerusalems of the AICs. The one who traditionally had remained something of an outsider because of the predominance of tribal and family ancestors in everyday religious life had to be brought inside, into daily life! And of course in the Zionist bishop's mind nothing could be more effective than confronting and transforming the old Mwari cult.

This was Mutendi's message of an immanent Christian God in creation. God as father and creator was experienced and preached as the God of ecology! In the presence of thousands of ZCC subsistence farmers the protective blessing of the divinity, traditionally called *Wokudenga* (the one in heaven), was conveyed directly to the seeds and the crops as a substitute for the generation of crop fertility by the oracular deity at Matonjeni. In a very real sense the Bishop reflected the incarnation of the biblical, ecologically active Mwari at Zion City. A subsistence farmer himself, as dependent on the agricultural economy as his followers, the Bishop identified with them totally in his petitioning of God. Unlike the white missionaries, whose livelihood at the mission station remained secure when the rains failed, the Zionist Bishop faced the same dilemma and hardships as his followers in periods of drought. When they suffered, he suffered. When they rejoiced over a bumper harvest, he led their celebration, their thanksgiving and their testimony sermons which proclaimed a caring God present in the midst of his people. Existentially, therefore, God as creator entered the lives of these Zionist peasants in the person of someone who shared their destiny, who felt what they felt, whose features they knew and who lived in their midst.

The Zionist presentation and experience of God as insider sheds new light on the relationship between the God of Africa and the God of the Bible. It complements the written theology of black African theologians referred to above, and in some respects could even function as a corrective to the reflections of academically involved theologians. Less intent than their more Westernised fellow theologians on championing the uniqueness and legitimacy of the African religious heritage in the face of an often deprecatory missionary tradition, the AIC prophets appear to be less inhibited in presenting the uniqueness of the Christian God, who both accommodates and judges the God of Africa. In his attempts to bring God inside, the ZCC Bishop at Zion City had no hesitation in facing the conflict which his attempts at Christianising the Mwari cult and contextualising the Zionist message of God's presence had provoked (Daneel 1970:69).

The Shona prophets' attempts in this respect resemble the penetration of the Old Testament Yahweh into the Semitic world. Bosch (1974:51f) gives a striking description of the continuity and discontinuity between Yahweh and El, a prominent Semitic God. In that assimilation and integration, too, there was continuity. 'El was king, creator and judge, the holy one, the One to whom the heavens belonged and the God of the heavenly council (Psalm 82). Yahweh absorbed all these characteristics and still emerged a uniquely different deity. Without being equated with El, he penetrated the Semitic world via El.'

Likewise, in the Shona prophetic movement, Yahweh enters a world already occupied by pre-Christian concepts of Mwari and, like El, he gives fresh content to these concepts to gain access to the Shona worldview. But there is also discontinuity, because the Mwari proclaimed by the Shona prophets makes different and more comprehensive claims on the individual than Mwari vaMatonjeni ever did.

Another point of discontinuity is that Mwari, Modimo, Nkulunkulu, and other African deities try, through their representatives, to maintain themselves in opposition to Yahweh. This is not to attack the African theologians' view that the traditional God of Africa is the same as the God of the Bible. The God of the Bible indeed did not leave himself unwitnessed in Africa! But the effect of his intervention in the thought world and lives of people outside the biblical revelation is, in a Christian perspective, incomplete and in need of change. Of this the Shona Independents are aware, existentially rather than doctrinally. As a result they consciously engage in transforming the old into something new. Theirs is a ritually enacted and dramatised theology of fulfilment in which the old deity is not embraced as if he has merely donned a new garment, but in which he emerges as the one whose existence was always surmised, who indeed was always present, yet who now manifests himself as the Totally Other.

THE IMMANENT GOD OF THE TREES

The earthkeeping ministry developed by the AAEC is an extension of AIC (particularly Zionist) theology with its central focus on an involved, pervasively present deity in peasant society. Mwari is the power behind all activities and developments in the black Holy City and Jerusalem headquarters of the prophetic churches. He is the one who cares for his people by providing or withholding rains. He is the provider of crops, life itself—as portrayed in Bishop Mutendi's work.

That Mwari the creator has emerged more decisively and imposingly in both the ritual and mundane life of his people in Zimbabwe is also due to far-reaching historical processes in the country. For all their limitations, as pointed out above, the Western missions did play a cardinal role, through their religious educational endeavours, in promoting perceptions in African society of a deity immanent in all of creation, all facets of life. Their numerous schools and Bible teaching created some conceptual clarity about the ever-present biblical creator, Jehovah. During the country's protracted liberation struggle, too, Mwari did emerge in the minds of the rural masses as the God of war, the God of liberation, the one who directed—through the ancestors and Spirit intervention—action in the battlefield. To many fighters he was the one who guided *pungwe* meetings, who inspired his 'war prophets'—both ancestral mediums and AIC visionaries—to direct military action and established a degree of justice in the midst of destructive upheaval (Daneel 1998).

Against this background and through deliberate interpretation in the AAEC local green movement as an extension of *chimurenga*, Mwari once again figures as the commanding God of war, the indomitable liberator. As the initiator of the war of the trees Mwari draws close in a very special way. In the struggle for the restoration of his creation he is not the absent, withdrawn deity, but the Old Testament Jehovah of the battlefields who summons, directs, and commands his emissaries in continual interaction between himself/herself, human beings, and all creaturely life.

What then are the main attributes of Mwari as proclaimed or described in the AAEC's earthkeeping ministry?

A Pervasively Present Creator

Both the Ethiopian-type and the Spirit-type member churches of the AAEC regularly refer to the consistent presence of Mwari as *Musiki* (Creator) in creation. At an Ethiopian-type tree-planting ceremony at Rev. Zvobgo's Shonganiso Mission, Rev. Mandondo showed profound awareness of divine presence in all of nature. He said in his sermon:

> You will see the miracles of Mwari if you persevere [in your earth-keeping ministry]. Up in the mountains I can see Mwari. In the rocks and the trees I see Mwari. There his strength and his works are revealed. If you go to Mount Selinda you will be shown trees called *miti mikuru* (great trees). Whose strength do those massive trees reveal? Mwari's, of course! There you will witness God's work. His work is clearly seen in the things he has created. Follow the river and observe the running waters. Whose do you think it is? Mwari's! But the works of God are now destroyed. We do not see them any longer. We ourselves are responsible for the destruction of creation. So let us restore God's works, accepting that the task is ours. Let us replace the trees we have felled. God will rejoice when he observes this.

This speech reveals a keen sense of God's pervasive presence in nature, in trees, rivers, rocks, in the wind and dampness of dense forests, of which lamentably so little is left, and in people. Although not explicitly mentioned, one finds here a recognition of the creator as mystery, the *mysterium tremendum* which Setiloane uses to qualify the Tswana's approach to Modimo. The awareness of the creator's presence in his creation is marked by reverence, even awe. Yet despite the sense of divine mystery there is no suggestion here of pantheist-style immanence—an IT-presence as Setiloane would have it. God is indeed immanent in the trees, in the dense forests, where his majesty and power are manifest. Yet he remains a personal being with anthropomorphic attributes: the transcendent one who is not far away, yet the other in the I-Thou encounter who observes the earthkeepers, rewards them as Laban rewarded Jacob for faithful service, lives among them, calls on them to restore creation, talks to them from inside the trees (as he did when he called Moses to liberate the Israelites), and rejoices at the sight of nature's renewal.

One need only listen to the muttered dialogues with God and with seedlings as they are being planted at tree-planting eucharists to be persuaded of a general respectful awareness of Mwari's presence among participating tree planters. The following excerpts from such addresses at Bishop Chimhangwa's tree-planting ceremony in Chivi district on 8 April 1993 bear this out:

Bishop Marinda: Mwari, Father, I have come today to plant your trees. I have come with the *mutumbu* tree to pay for my transgression [of earth destruction]. I place them here in your soil. You, tree, I place you in this soil. Grow! Become tall, wax strong! Even if the hail from the heavens hits you, I want you to remain alive . . . through the coming ages. My friend whom I love, I shall come to visit often to see you. Stay right here where I plant you.

Rev. Solomon Zvanaka: You, tree, I plant you. Provide us with clean air to breathe and all the other benefits which Mwari has commanded. We in turn will take care of you, because in Jesus Christ you are one with us. He has created all things to be united in him. I shall not chop down another tree. Through you, tree, I do penance for all the trees I have felled.

Participant policeman: You, tree, are my friend. Wherever I am I shall remember you and come and check to see if you are well. I cannot leave or forget you. I ask God to protect you so that you will not be eaten by the creatures of the bush or destroyed. Remember that I have felled many trees. Forgive me! That was before I was made to realise that you, tree, are my brother.

Tree symbolism, of course, is focal in ecological movements worldwide. Despite its relative isolation as a grassroots movement, the AAEC's preoccupation with trees has remarkable parallels elsewhere, particularly in eco-feminism. Says Kyung (in Hallman 1994:178) about commitment to the liberation of people and nature,

We would share the symbol of a tree as the most inspiring symbol for the spirituality of eco-feminism . . . The tree captures the life-giving thrust and power of the eco-feminist movement. Its roots go deep into the soil of mother earth, strengthening it against erosion yet sucking its life-giving moisture . . . The leaves transform death-dealing, poisonous carbon dioxide into life-giving oxygen. They provide shelter and shade for the life and growth of diverse insects, plants, birds, animals, and humans. Its fruit gives fruit for the body and its flower gives food for the soul. Then its leaves die and become compost to re-create the soil. This cyclic, rhythmic process of creating, nurturing, healing, and re-creating life symbolises the aspirations of cosmic spirituality of eco-feminism.

What Kyung captures here in sensitive, poetic language is quite similar to what the Shona earthkeepers of the AAEC intuit, experience, and verbalise, if in a somewhat more pragmatic and ideationally unsystematised manner. In both instances acute awareness of divine presence in all creation facilitates a deep understanding of the interwovenness or connectedness of all human and non-human life on earth. Without any access to the World Council of Churches' work and publications in the field of (JPIC) Justice, Peace, and the Integrity of Creation, the AAEC in its earthkeeping ministry is giving expression to the kind of insight formulated in the 1990 Kuala Lumpur report (by the subunit for Church and Society) on the relationship of God's Spirit to creation:

> Because of the presence and pervasiveness of the Spirit throughout creation, we not only reject a view in which the cosmos does not share in the sacred and in which humans are not part of nature; we also repudiate hard lines drawn between animate and inanimate, and human and non-human. All alike, and all together in the bundle of life, 'groan in travail' (Rom 8) awaiting the full redemption of all things through Jesus Christ, 'in the power of the Spirit' (Michaelson, in Hallman 1994:100–101).

Similar convictions characterise the ecological theologising of modern Western theologians. Moltmann, as we have seen, argues for an ecological doctrine of God's immanence in the world. Such immanence qualifies God not only as creator of the world but also as spirit of the universe. 'Through the powers and potentialities of the Spirit,' Moltmann (1985:14) says, 'the Creator indwells the creatures he has made, animates them, holds them in life, and leads them into the future of the kingdom.' The interconnectedness of all creation, according to Moltmann (1985:17), hinges on the interpenetration or *perichoresis* of the trinity, whereby 'God is in the world and the world in God.' Consequently there can be no such thing as solitary life. Our human bondedness with nature, through the Spirit, can therefore be described 'as a spiritual ecosystem. Through the Spirit, human societies as part-systems are bound up with the ecosystem "earth" (Gaia)' (Moltmann 1985:18).

The AAEC certainly has no extensively formulated ecological doctrine of creation, neither does it teach the *perichoresis* of the trinity! But the movement's biblically informed praxis of stewardship in most ways endorses Moltmann's views. Even a traditionalist headman, Mupakwa, is moved during a tree-planting eucharist at Bishop Musariri's homestead (on 17 March 1994) to call on all tree-planters: 'Come let us all move very close to Mwari, together with our land, so that our land will no longer be eroded,' and to claim that 'no human being sees all this, knows all this or controls all this (creation) . . . *Mwari is the one who holds all power and controls all life on earth.*' The closeness to Mwari, which assumes human response to and ecological safety in an ever-present creator, as well as the attribution of all powers of life to this deity, rests on recognition in faith that 'God is in the world and the world in God.' And even though a well-formulated trinitarian doctrine nowhere features as a conscious goal to qualify the theological basis of the AAEC's ecological ministry, repeated references to the trinity in tree-planting sermons, songs, and prayer reveal that the earthkeeping deity is an immanent insider as Mwari-Father, Jesus Christ and Holy Spirit.

During women's tree-planting ceremonies, staged by ZIRRCON's Women's Desk, the sermons of leading figures also emphasise divine presence and close identification of female earthkeepers with Mwari. At one such ceremony conducted in Chivi district on 20 December 1993, Raviro Mutonga—chairperson of the Women's Desk—preached as follows:

> You women who have come to assist our Women's Club of Doroguru, don't leave before you have eaten the goat's meat we have prepared. For it is you who were called by Mwari to come and plant and water his trees . . . You of the churches (women and men) came to do Mwari's bidding, to plant and water Mwari's trees . . . This is not a task to trifle with. It is the work of Mwari! God looked for assistance with his creation . . . So he created human beings to look after it for him. The bush with its trees and plants is much more important than we realised at first. Today we (women), having received seedlings, are the ones honoured with this task. We plant trees in the same way as Mwari did. In doing so *we draw closer and closer to him!* What do you say to that, mothers?

> [Response]: Oh yes, it is very good!

> [Then followed the praise song]:

> I've heard your message, Lord.
> I want to live with you
> in the wonderful place
> of your Son.

> [Chorus]: I come, I come

> To you, where there is home
> Receive me
> I've done your work
> Lord, receive me.

Mutonga's repeated insistence on the creator's authorship of human steward-ship of nature is more than just a straightforward ecological statement. In a pre-dominantly female setting, divine affirmation of women's responsibility, authority, and status in the upkeep and restoration of creation is certainly pertinent. As will be argued below, the creator who calls women and men to be earthkeepers is also the liberator who frees women from oppression, from the negative aspects of African patriarchy, as he opens up a new avenue of emancipation for and with them. The women's recognition of the sacredness of the relationship between God and creation (an earthkeeping task not to be trifled with!) and their drawing close to the creator as his assistants or co-workers, tacitly suggest that this is the domain particularly of women, that they represent and understand the cycles of fertility and new life, the protection and nurture of life itself—symbolised by the newly planted seedlings—in a way men cannot do. Though not spelled out, the immanence and closeness of Mwari here suggest understanding of either the feminine in Mwari (which has its antecedents in the traditional high-God cult) or at least his/her overriding care for all that concerns the fertility and life of mother earth.

The words of the praise song may still echo apocalyptic expectations of heaven as the wonderful place of Mwari's Son. Yet 'home,' where God is, in the context, of the restoration of the world as understood by the AAEC women, could also signify a growing awareness of this-worldly salvation; being with Mwari in the kingdom, the new heaven and earth already manifest in this existence.

In Zimbabwe, being one with the 'God of the trees,' being part of the fellowship of earthkeepers, means being hurt with or in Mwari at the sound and sight of chopping axes in dwindling woodlands; it means joining the 'all-embracing fellowship of suffering.' It means hours of back-breaking work in scorching sun and a feeling of powerlessness and futility when the rains fail and thousands of seedlings—representing years of toil in nurseries—wither and die. It means pain in the face of destructive opposition from those who hold salaried posts in 'conservation' yet have no heart for creation. It means being judged and rejected by those of the faith who seek the kingdom only in other-worldly spiritual growth and soul salvation. It also means suffering and deprivation when periodically there are no funds for salaries for diligent and faithful earthkeepers . . . when the entire future of our earthkeeping movement and endeavour hinges on Western sponsors caught up in their own neocolonialist 'benevolence' and bureaucracy.

Significantly, the image of a compassionate, jealous, and suffering deity implicit in the understanding and experience of the AAEC earthkeepers qualifies bath Mwari's transcendence and his/her immanence. As *Wokumusoro* he remains the sovereign, transcendent being whose reign over creation is all-powerful. At no point, however, does this 'transcendent' reign exclude or obscure his immersion in creation as compassionate guardian of the land (*muridzi venyika*), the divine fulfilment of both traditional notions of ancestral land guardianship and biblically informed conceptions of environmental stewardship. Pantheistic trends in his immanence as a power or life-force in trees and other natural phenomena are offset by the decidedly anthropomorphic attributes of the ever-present gardener who dwells among us as both spirit and personal being. In their own way the Shona earthkeepers recognise the divine-human encounter at the core of all their ecological activities. Whether as tree planters they succeed or fail, celebrate or suffer, the fundamental mutuality between Mwari, the creator-guardian, his earthkeeping churches and all creatures remains.

A Summoning and Empowering Deity

The excerpts from sermons quoted above and the previous chapter indicate how the immanent creator is repeatedly proclaimed as a summoning and empowering deity. Mwari calls and commissions human beings to engage in earthkeeping; he provides the mandate, the inspiration, strength, and endurance for such activity. Depending on the contexts of sermons and the motives of preachers, some variations can be discerned in the conceptualisation of the sovereignty of an all-powerful creator who has not relinquished control of creation, as well as the nature of interaction between that creator and the commissioned human keepers of creation. The following quotations are fairly representative of AAEC views:

Zionist Bishop Nhongo (interview): The war of the trees is the holy war of Mwari. Mwari commands this war. So we have to fight unreservedly.

Zionist Bishop Hore (interview): This is Mwari's war. ZIRRCON wages it in Mwari. He controls rain and drought. Without Mwari's approval and strength this struggle of trees will be in vain anyway.

Apostolic Bishop Wapendama (sermon): He [Mwari] called his envoys to shoulder the task of deliverance [of the stricken land] . . . It is our task to strengthen this mission [of God and of the church] . . . I beseech you to place yourselves in the hands of Mwari. He alone can give us the strength to endure in this struggle.

These statements pay tribute to the sovereignty of God. As the concerned owner of creation he is the initiator of all earthkeeping endeavour, who commands, controls, guides, and directs all attempts to heal the earth, in this instance his holy war of the trees. Bishop Wapendama's suggestion that the deliverance of the land is a form of *missio dei* with concrete implications for God's church—namely shouldering the responsibility of developing an earthkeeping ministry—is also implicit in the assertions of the others. For all its emphasis on God's initiative, his calling of green fighters, and his guidance and empowerment of the forces in the struggle, such a *missio dei* in no uncertain terms underscores the significance of human response and action. On the basis of God's empowerment and affirmation human earthkeepers can and must 'fight unreservedly' (Nhongo); 'ZIRRCON is the human institution which is waging a green war' (Hore); the members of the AAEC are 'strengthening the earth-healing mission' and 'enduring a demanding struggle' (Wapendama). Quite clearly human beings, by virtue of being creatures of God and belonging to creation, are called upon to be its stewards and, as Mwari's co-workers, to join in the struggle for its preservation and wellbeing.

Yet there is little here to suggest that humanity shares Mwari's all-powerful dominion over creation. As earthkeepers humans have a certain privilege and responsibility for other creatures, but their mission is to serve, not to reign over creation; to wage war, not to conquer nature, but to restore it obediently in full recognition of their dependence on the strength and guidance of the creator. Considering the regular confessions of ecological sins at AAEC tree-planting ceremonies, this understanding of humankind's role in keeping and restoring creation stems from awareness of human hubris and rebellion against the creator, as evidenced overwhelmingly by all the manifestations of earth destruction wherever tree planting takes place.

AAEC leaders participating either in traditionalist tree-planting ceremonies or in Christian ones with a large component of traditionalists do not hesitate to proclaim a universal divinity whose summoning and empowering outreach extends to all humankind. At a ceremony at his homestead on 17 March 1994 Bishop Musariri, patron of the AAEC, said in his sermon:

These two people, the chief and the priest, appear before Mwari as a pair. They are the caretakers of creation, appointed by Mwari. God chose them as guardians of creation. They lead the people according to Mwari's guidance . . . [In conclusion] . . . We are messengers of Mwari, guardians of his creation. Whatever criticism people level at me, this is the task I represent. We shall not waver! Not here at our dwelling place, or in the household of Mwari!

By proclaiming chief and priest God's chosen guardians of creation, Musariri was asserting divine legitimation for both earthkeeping movements: AZTREC of the chiefs and mediums, and the AAEC of the priests and prophets. By assuming that these movements are united in the ecological struggle Musariri is not only justifying current trends of mutuality and the formation of a common front in ZIRRCON's war of the trees, but is also hinting that Mwari's sovereignty overrides humanly created divisions and the conflicts of religious pluriformity. The creator is calling and empowering all his people—at any rate those who are religiously divided in the local situation—and with a kind of comprehensive ecumenism he sweeps religious animosities aside in the interest of a higher purpose: the restoration of creation. Chief and priest, traditionalist and Christian, are equals, caretakers of creation, in the presence of Mwari!

Musariri is not necessarily implying complete religious relativism or, with his open, reconciliatory stance, compromising the uniqueness of his own Zionist Christian faith. He is in fact aware that he can be and has been criticised on this score, hence his insistence that he, as patron of the AAEC, and his fellow earthkeepers will not waver, either in the rural villages or in the church, the household of God. The basis for such single-mindedness and courage, it would appear, lies in accepting that he himself, the priest Musariri, is called and guided by Mwari to act as caretaker and guardian of creation. He accepts, as pointed out above, that the task involves suffering.

How do the earthkeeping women respond to Mwari's authority? At a treeplanting ceremony at Doroguru on 20 December 1993, Raviro Mutonga of the Women's Desk said:

Nobody thought that this land right here is a place where trees will be planted. I myself thought it was a field in which I'll plant groundnuts this season. But see what Mwari does. He said: 'No groundnuts will be planted here! You will plant my trees!' People confuse each other by saying: 'ZIRRCON orders the planting of trees!' *I tell you: this is the work which Mwari commands us to do!*

We read from Isaiah 41:19 and 20:

> I will put in the wilderness the cedar,
> the acacia, the myrtle, and the olive . . .
> that men may see and know,
> may consider and understand together
> that the hand of the Lord has done this,
> the Holy One of Israel has created it.

So we women here today have a great task, in fulfilment of the prophecy in Isaiah. The trees we plant here are the ones mentioned in the Book.

Ms. Mangombe, one of the leaders of the Doroguru club, had this to say in affirmation of Mutonga's views on female earthkeepers: 'We as women are the first [after the problem caused by Eve in the garden of Eden] to return to this task of tending Mwari's garden. We women are chosen by Mwari for this important task and will be honoured for it. When planting Mwari's trees as a woman, ordained by Mwari to do so, I have to do it dressed in my church uniform. These are not in the first place my trees, or ours. It is God who waters or kills. He causes the trees to wither and die, or he provides life through rain.'

Both speakers invoke the commissioning authority of Mwari to claim a unique responsibility for women as earthkeepers. Mutonga combines her assertion that Mwari, and not ZIRRCON, commands tree-planting by citing a biblical text which attributes prophetic expectation of environmental improvement to God's initiative and glory rather than to people's. Mangombe assigns women a unique role as God's stewards in creation by alluding both to Eve's original rebellion against Mwari—as if saying that being the first to rebel, the first to repent establishes a kind of female prerogative in earthkeeping matters!—and to Mwari's special choice and ordination. To Mutonga, identification of the trees planted with those mentioned in the Book (the verses quoted from the Bible) probably means elevating the women's land-healing contribution on that day above the assertive and sometimes self-congratulatory patriarchy of ZIRRCON's male leadership. Mangombe's insistence on planting trees in her church uniform may have similar connotations: not only to honour and respect the commissioning creator, but also to earn recognition and respect in the male-dominated earthkeepers' world for the outstanding ecological contribution women have made all along, often without any acclaim.

It is not far-fetched, therefore, to suggest that in the women's world under consideration the commissioning deity is in fact a God of empowerment and liberation. There have been no deliberate attempts to flout ZIRRCON's male authority, and Ms. Mutonga operates with great poise and dedication within the parameters of the earthkeepers' leadership hierarchy. She is also fully aware that the movement's male leaders publicly acknowledge Mwari at all times as the prime mover and final authority of all ecological endeavour, citing the same biblical texts as she does. Nevertheless, there is a subtle difference here. For despite all their appeals to divine inspiration and guidance, the male earthkeepers have in fact been centre-stage in virtually all tree-planting ceremonies. They spend hours introducing mainly male dignitaries attending these ceremonies, extolling the achievements of male figures in building the movement, claiming impressive statistics of trees planted without always giving full recognition to the impressive work of women as caterers, nursery keepers, and tree planters, and allowing women proportionally much less time than men to give speeches or sermons at gatherings.

Small wonder, therefore, that at ceremonies staged by ZIRRCON's Women's Desk Mwari emerges as a liberator whose special calling validates and elevates the roles of earthkeeping women. Liberation from male domination, non-recognition, and marginality, even if not yet complete, is the existential reality of women appearing proudly in their neat church uniforms at the behest of Jehovah of the Book, he who makes it possible for women to be emancipated, powerful, and influential earthkeepers in their own right.

Finally, for all the women's sensitivity to and need for emancipation and justice, the image of God as one who empowers and liberates applies to the entire movement. In the understanding of the earthkeepers, the growing trees and their spreading shade are literally liberating the barren earth from the life-sapping blaze of the sun. To thousands of peasants who have no place in the halls of fame and power in the cities where national history appears to be made, taking a hand in the environment in a way that matters means liberation from obscurity and powerlessness. Pioneering an earthkeeping ministry and a new African theology in the often despised and rejected world of the AICs means being liberated to experience ecclesiastic recognition, maturity, and growth. To the politically and religiously somewhat marginalised chiefs, spirit-mediums, and commoner traditionalists in modern society, liberation means greater influence and meaningful service both to the devastated land and to rural society. Somehow Mwari the liberator calls and empowers the downtrodden, the poor, the oppressed, the marginalised and faceless masses to rise on behalf of the voiceless creatures and overexploited matter of this earth; and in so doing to find healing, wholeness, and fulfillment.

Rain-Giver and Judge

Steeped in Old Testament narrations of God's dealings with his people, the AAEC leaders' sermons paint a picture of intensely rewarding and/or retributive interaction between Mwari and the people living on his land. Whenever people do not repent or follow the divine commandments, God—as in Israel—ravishes the land through war, pestilence, drought, or floods. And when harmony is restored, the suffering is replaced by wellbeing and abundance. 'Once Israel has repented of its infidelity to God's commandments and returned to the right path, God will restore its fortunes. Then the land will flourish with abundant rain and bountiful harvests. The people will return from exile to its lands and restore its ancient cities. It will prevail over its enemies and reduce them to servitude, or, in a more universalist vision, the other nations will stream to Zion, be converted to its God, and peace and justice will prevail throughout the earth' (Ruether 1992:66,67; with reference to Zch 14:12–20 and Is 2:2–4).

This is the focus of the Shona earthkeepers' attention: establishing, as God's people, new forms of *eco-justice* in the already existing dispensation of his kingdom, and in so doing achieving a meaningful and prosperous life, at least relatively free from Mwari's judgment. The AAEC is not unaware of the New Testament texts dealing with the passing away of heaven and earth. But caught up in the afforestation struggle with all its practical and ethical demands on the earthkeepers involved, they understandably prefer passages from John (Rv 11, 19) which reserve judgment for those who destroy the earth, interpretations which insist that those who disrupt the union (of earthkeepers) in Christ (Jn 15)—the creator and real Earthkeeper—will be punished, and Pauline texts which underscore the restoration of the present world, to passages which imply judgment and complete destruction of the earth as a condition for radical apocalyptic replacement (Zerbe, in De Witt 1991:90). Eternal life in heaven for individual believers after death is certainly not a lost dimension. Yet in the earthkeepers' world, salvation is already seen and felt where nurseries and woodlots symbolise reconciliation between the God of Zion and his people, whose regular tree-planting rallies reveal the saviour's presence in his black Zion Cities and Jerusalems.

That Mwari features pre-eminently in the tree-planting context as the rain-giver, the one whose blessing and/or judgment can be gauged from seasons and harvests, is a sure sign that the traditional African concept of the oracular deity is still influencing the understanding of Mwari-Jehovah who reveals himself in the pages of Old and New Testaments. This again reminds us of the conceptual interaction between the Hebraic Yahweh and the Semitic El as the former entered the latter's world. It is to be expected that in a peasant society, where a subsistence economy hinges entirely on good rains and harvests and where for centuries the creator-God's most convincing act of salvation—despite his/her earlier remoteness—was to provide life-giving rain, such notions of God will persist and dominate, also in indigenous Christian circles.

To some extent Mwari the rain-giver is focal because of AZTREC's pre-occupation with Mwari the high-God at the Matopo shrines and the constant contact of AAEC participants, through close cooperation with the traditionalist movement, with the roots of the African faith. Note, for instance, the introductory remarks and conclusion of Chief Chivi's tree-planting ceremony at headman Gwenyaya's village—a ritual attended by large factions of both traditionalists and AIC Christians (27 August 1993). After invoking the ancestral landowners the traditionalist elder Mazodze said: 'We have started here by addressing the ancestors, but we have not yet prayed. So I give Bishop Chimhangwa an opportunity to pray. In so doing we place our tree-planting work at both [religious] ends. We indeed tell the ancestors but we also pray to Mwari.'

Although Mazodze was referring to the Bishop's Mwari of the Book, the implied cooperation between Mwari and the ancestors subtly evoked the image of the traditional rain-giver. The *mafukidzanyika* (earth-clothing) beer libation resembles the traditional rain rituals (*mikwerere*) too closely for the *mudzimu-*

Mwari interaction inherent in it not to remind one of the rain-giving Mwari vaM-atonjeni.

Chief Chivi's closing prayer had a similar bent:

> We thank you, Musikavanhu [literally 'creator of people'], you creator of all things. We your children whom you have permitted to live in your garden, are doing this [tree-planting] here for you. This task is accomplished by your children and grandchildren. See with your own eyes. See tomorrow, as you provide rain to water your trees. This we ask of you so that you will be mindful of our efforts tomorrow [in the future].

The chief adopted the Christian mode of approaching God through prayer. But it was no coincidence that he used the traditional name for God, Musikavanhu, who in earlier years was the rain-giver in the territorial cults of eastern Zimbabwe. To Chief Chivi this is the Jehovah of the Book, the same one Bishop Chimhangwa had appealed to. Yet as Musikavanhu he emerges in African garb: a father of children and grandchildren, concerned with African community life—the living and the living dead—and the God of peasants whose delight in proper earthcare will be reflected in the coming rain.

A perusal of AAEC sermons shows the extent to which Mwari the rain-giver preoccupies the minds also of Christian earthkeepers. Causality characterises the divine-human core relationships: the rain-giver responds directly with reward or judgment to his earthkeepers' performance! 'Trees bring life . . . trees bring rain,' Bishop Wapendama said. 'But since the trees have been felled in great numbers and the plains are naked, people nowadays are wondering whether floodwaters are not the water of Noah of long ago.'

To a mind-set where deforestation and desertification provoke divine judgment of a severity comparable with the deluge of Noah's time, tree protection and tree planting appear to be the only means of appeasing the wrath of Mwari. Said Wapendama in another sermon: 'I shall take responsibility for planting many more trees. I tell you, Mwari will give us plentiful rains because we are paying for the *ngozi* (vengeful spirit) which we have provoked through tree destruction.'

And yet the problem of how to interpret and accept chastisement remains when drought brings endless suffering. Having lost most of his livestock and all his crops during one of the most severe droughts in Chivi district, Bishop Chimhangwa grappled with the Old Testament narrative of similar occurrences in Israel at a tree-planting ceremony at Bishop Machokoto's village. Having likened the plight of his wife trying to find water with that of the Israelites when their water cisterns were empty (Jer 14:1–4), he said: 'My wife asked me whether we could grind the fifty kilograms of mealies which we had bought for planting into meal. She did this because we could not find mealie meal anywhere. That same day Minister Musika was at our village to assess the drought situation. The famine there is now so bad that the tortoises start climbing the trees.' In his appeal to his audience to save some water for the trees they had planted, Chimhangwa suggested that there was some consolation in knowing that others (the Israelites particularly) had also suffered with empty water cisterns. However, this did not deter him from voicing frustration, even lament and defiance, in the face of the relentless drought:

> We ploughed our lands and planted our maize and groundnuts. But there are no crops. Is that not a painful experience? If God were a person, don't you think I would have questioned him about this? Ah! It is impossible to question God! Peace to you, people of the Lord.

These words echo anguish and impotence at the chastisement meted out by the rain-giver who, in his mysterious, seemingly capricious way, appears to have turned his back on his troubled people—a desperate reality underlined on the barren plains of Chivi by the shimmering sun, cloudless skies and 'tortoises climbing the trees.'

ZIRRCON's more educated theologians—Bishop Marinda, Rev. Zvanaka, and myself—are contributing to this trend in an attempt to promote contextualisation of the emerging AIC earthkeeper's theology in Shona peasant society. Partly to coax our fellow earth stewards into greater effort and dedication, partly because of our own belief in a rewarding/judging deity, the causality in divine-human encounter is often proclaimed or implied. Note, for instance, Reuben Marinda's wording of the liturgy for the tree-planting eucharist:

> Let us make an oath today
> that we will care for God's creation
> so that he will grant us rain—
> an oath, not in jest
> but with all our heart.

The words 'so that' link God's rewarding rains directly with the earthkeeper's intentions and action in caring for creation. Mwari the rain-giver also features strongly in the sprinkling of holy water in new woodlots prior to planting. The church leader performing the ritual refers to the water of purification and fertility as a prayer to God, a symbol of rain.

The ritualised prayer to God is obviously for rain, so that the tree planters' labours may be blessed and the earth may heal. Are we dealing here with a narrow, even a manipulative perception of the deity which obscures the realisation that God's pervasive presence extends to all the richness of his creation? I do not think so. What else can an earthkeeper pray when commitment and perseverance culminate in entrusting carefully nurtured seedlings to the soil and life-giving rains are crucial for the next phase of greening God's earth?

Is this a flawed, one-sided, even heretical tree-planting theology in the face of the flux of seasons and the need to build peasant morale and motivation against heavy odds? Certainly, if one measures the inconsistencies, pragmatic motives, and variations of an unwritten theology of green action against the Reformation's neat formulae of *sola scriptura, sola gratia, sola fide*—Scripture, divine grace, and faith as the sole guidelines for Christian life and sound doctrine. We of the AAEC are indeed running a risk, at least at times, of losing sight of God's grace as we attempt to regiment the green forces by postulating a rewarding/judging creator.

The danger of succumbing to a kind of earthkeepers' self-righteousness, of trying to wrest from God some sort of this-worldly salvation based on human performance and merit is not illusory. In our attempts to accommodate and unite with our traditionalist fellow fighters we may also place too much emphasis on the rain-giver in his/her African garb—the oracular deity who provides or withholds rain in direct response to the annual pleas and gifts of regional constituencies at the Matopo shrines. Nevertheless, the centrality of Scripture in all AAEC deliberations, and numerous landmarks of experience along the route followed by the Shona earthkeepers (e.g., a rebellious and suffering bishop in the midst of drought admitting humbly that it is impossible to question God) permit the conviction that, despite imperfections, the truth will be served.

MWARI AS FATHER AND/OR MOTHER?

To what extent does AAEC theology display similarities with eco-feminist and other modern earth theologies in which the predominantly male deity of the Judaeo-Christian worldview is either replaced by Gaia, the ancient Greek earth goddess, or amplified by much greater emphasis on the female attributes of the Christian God? To answer this question we need to look at some of the characteristic features of such theologies.

Eco-feminism links the modern environmental crisis with male domination of women over the centuries. In Western male-dominated cultures males allegedly feared the dark, fertile, intuitive powers of the universe. This fear, it is argued, is manifested in patriarchal attempts to control both women (e.g., in the medieval witch hunts in Europe) and nature. Biblical religion appears to be hierarchic and patriarchal because of a history of Israelite confrontation with the female element in Canaanite fertility cults (McDonagh 1994:114). Whatever the reasons for the proclamation of male deity mainly by male priests and clergy, women's insight has been marginalised and their role suppressed. Thus, as Wilkinson (1991:194) says: 'Ecofeminists urge the rediscovery of an ancient alternative, which they believe to have preceded patriarchal theism: that is, a worship of the goddess, which does not exalt warfare and domination, but instead led to a nurturing culture in which men and women lived together in equal and complementary partnership.'

Eco-feminist critique has certainly sharpened the attention and sensitivity of Western theologians to both the masculine and feminine attributes of God and people. In an article entitled 'The Spirit of God's Femininity' a leading figure in the Roman Catholic *Theologie Nouvelle*, Yves Congar (cf. McDonagh 1994:116), traces the feminine attributes of God to the Old Testament prophets and wisdom literature. In support of this view McDonagh (1994:117) claims that the holistic view of God as Father and Mother evolves from the Old Testament wisdom literature specifically into the New Testament understanding of the Holy Spirit:

She is the principle of communion, binding all reality together. The Holy
Spirit is the source of all unity. All attraction, all bonding, all intimacy and
communion flows from the Spirit . . . In her the whole universe is linked together in one nurturing, enveloping embrace. She is the one who inspires all
fruitfulness and creativity—which are the signs of true bonding and intimacy. From her comes the great urge to heal what is broken, re-unite what
is separated, and recreate the face of the Earth (McDonagh 1994:119).

In the Protestant tradition others, like Moltmann, refrain from depicting God
as Mother, yet show great understanding for the holistic interrelatedness between
God, humanity, and the natural environment, which includes emphasis on an immanent and nurturing deity in creation and references to the earth as Gaia (Moltmann 1985:18).

Then there are theologians who are sceptical about the effectiveness of reinter-
preting the divine in terms of a gender switch. Ruether (1992:4), herself an eco-
feminist who agrees with much of the criticism of patriarchy and understands the
reasoning behind the introduction of Gaia as a new focus of worship, warns that
'merely replacing a male transcendent deity with an immanent female one is an insufficient answer to the "god-problem."' Instead, she convincingly insists that we
need a new vision of 'a source of life that is "yet more" than what presently exists,'
a vision of 'how life should be more just and more caring' (Ruether 1992:5).

Wilkinson (1991:278, 279) cautions that, although the characterisation of God
as mother highlights important biblical notions of divine nurturing and care, such
a definition 'makes it easier for us to make the dangerous mistake of equating
God with the earth, creation with Creator—and the Creator's immanence is not of
that sort.' Arguing on the basis of the Genesis narrative that the creator is distinct
from creation and not be confused with it, he quotes extensively from Rudy
Wiebe's novel, *My Lovely Enemy*.

When man speaks of 'God as Mother' her acts usually become so closely
identified with nature—the physical world everywhere—that he forgets the
image-ness and begins to think the words as physical actuality . . . But God
subsumes and is far beyond both Nature and Image. So it is better to contemplate the concept of GOD THE FATHER because no natural father
brings forth any life by himself. You are then forced to contemplate the creation of the world not as an act of physical birth out of God's womb (as
ecofeminists tend to imply), but rather as the act of being spoken into existence by Words coming out of God's mouth (Wilkinson 1991:279).

The AAEC's environmental theologians largely lack the sophistication and exposure to eco-feminist literature to deal explicitly with the wide range of definitions
and subtle distinctions. Our earthkeepers' reading of the Old Testament seldom focuses on the wisdom literature in such a way that Mwari Musiki (God the creator) is
portrayed as a female deity. We have indeed mentioned above that Mwari is immanent, the insider whose Spirit is in the trees and who therefore suffers when trees are

felled. But he is also the Other, a personal being distinct from the animate and inanimate objects of creation, who is present among his people and addresses them. And in this role he is regularly referred to in sermons as Mwari Baba (God the Father), Mwari Jehovah (God Jehovah), the masculine protector, keeper, and particularly father of all creation. The Apostolic, Zionist, and non-prophetic preachers of the AAEC would therefore tend to concur with Wilkinson and Wiebe's understanding of a masculine creator-deity—an understanding which is so richly differentiated, however, that it does not preclude some feminine allusions or comparisons when it comes to explaining Mwari's love and care for the environment.

In Shona traditionalist religious imagery the obvious parallel with Gaia, the Greek earth goddess, would be the creator as Dzivaguru (the Great Pool), a portrayal which has distinct connotations of feminity, fertility, potency, the mystery of life-force—in short, Mother. I have also indicated how the feminine attributes of the creator and rain-giver in the traditional cult at Matonjeni are in a sense reinforced by a female oracular voice addressing people from the shrines and by women occupying key interpretive positions during rituals (Daneel 1998:178f). Yet in the ongoing dialogue between AZTREC traditionalists and AAEC Christians the latter's insistence on proclaiming Mwari of the Bible and the conscious retention of a specifically Christian message of good news largely preclude references to Dzivaguru. Their motivation would resemble that which inspired the transformation of the Semitic divinity concept of El in the polemic between the Judaeo-Christian Jehovah and the Canaanite fertility cults.

Belief in a male deity need not, of course, exclude imaginative, inculturated reinterpretations of an earthkeeping deity, whose injunctions and care for creation derive from similar sentiments and solutions as those of the eco-feminists. Not only have the AAEC teachings of an involved creator contributed to greater awareness and acceptance of a sympathetic and nurturing dimension in divine-human stewardship; the AAEC has also launched programmes which promote women's empowerment and autonomous social organisation. Hence it is making a contribution, even if only a modest one, to overcoming oppressive patriarchy. A few examples will suffice.

At a tree-planting ceremony at Bishop Farawo's village on 7 February 1994 Bishop Marinda likened the work of the creator to the role of a *vatete* (paternal aunt):

> As we have heard today Mwari built a treasure of trees and wildlife into creation, of which we as people are the guardians. We, the people, said, 'We have been given this wonderful world by our Father Mwari.' Then we promptly forgot our responsibility as the protectors of creation. We became hosts to the *shavi* (alien spirits) of destruction. We destroyed the peace between ourselves and the creation for which we had to care. We were like lost children, claiming riches from their father, spending it all carelessly and then returning empty-handed.
>
> This world, as created by Mwari, can be compared to a virgin. You look at a girl who wants to marry. When this change in relationships is at hand

her *vatete* comes to adorn her with beautiful clothes. Her dress is decorated with beads. And when you see her, her skin glistens like that of a python. You know when you see a young woman clad like this that she is a virgin. She is a woman betrothed in an undefiled state. When she bears a child, say at Chief Ziki's homestead, the people will say: 'That one belongs to the chieftaincy.' But of the child born from the bush it will be said that the mother just arrived there with a stomach protruding like this [gesture of hand] in pregnancy.

God is the *vatete* who showed and gave us this world in all its splendour as a virgin: with its awesome, towering rocks, its densely leaved trees, laden with all kinds of fruit to feed humans, birds, and animals. God provided the abundance we are now trying to restore. We have carelessly spoilt the virginity of the earth, that which Mwari, our *vatete*, gave us. What we strive for is to give the earth back its virginity. Through the destruction of nature we have spoiled our relationship with created things and with our *vatete*, thereby causing the *ngozi* spirit [of vengeance] to rise. How do we repair such a breach in relations?

Audience: We pay!

Marinda: That is what we have come to do here today. We have come to pay with trees in order to restore relations with our *madzibaba* (fathers) and our *vatete*, Mwari.

We see the remnants of the earth's virginity in the wooded mountains. This world was ever so beautiful before we messed it up. The forests were thick. It harboured klipspringer, duiker, rabbits, rock rabbits, all of them in or near these mountain ranges. But these animals are all gone because we have destroyed their habitat. Maybe we will all end up living in the mountains when the plains are empty . . .

In the context of Shona kinship ties, Marinda's use of the *vatete* analogy to clarify Mwari's intimate, protective bond with creation is apt. The paternal aunt is the guardian of the procreative powers in the patriline of her brothers and father. By virtue of her bride price (*roora*), which assists a selected brother (the special tie is called *chipanda*) to pay *roora* for his wife, the *vatete* becomes 'owner' (*vamwene*) of the brother's offspring and has special authority over them. This authority includes safeguarding the virginity of her nieces, instructing and caring for them, and presenting them as virgins at marriage. Customary law stipulates that the *vatete's* significant role be honoured by the inclusion of *ngombe yovutete* (the aunt's cow) in the bride prices of the nieces in her care. Even after her death the *vatete* continues her important duties. If disturbed or dissatisfied as an ancestor she can prevent pregnancy by 'grabbing the womb' of a niece, an affliction which can only be remedied if the *ngombe yovutete* is produced and properly sacrificed in honour of the *vatete*.

Against this background, Mwari the *vatete* is woven into the intimate fabric of family life. He is more than just a remote, universal source of fertility. From within family life he/she takes care of procreation as the legitimate owner (*vamwene*) and custodian of those members of the family whom she has specially taught about the beauty and sanctity of life. As *vatete* Mwari could 'grab the wombs' of the female stewards of creation so that they, together with their menfolk, will suffer until they—the entire human family—do penance through sacrifice, in this instance by clothing the barren land. When Mwari presents the virginity of creation as utterly beautiful to the family of human beings, as the custodian aunt presents her *mhandara* (virgin) to her own family and in-laws, the beauty and importance of all creation acquires new meaning: softer, warmer, and perhaps more vulnerable to greedy exploitation, more in need of trustworthy custodians who understand the fragility and sanctity of the earth's virginity before the seasons of conception, birth, maturity, reproduction, death, and new life are full.

As Reuben Marinda's sermon indicates, Mwari is basically Baba, Father, but he sees with the eyes and feels with the caring being of a *vatete*—perhaps a bit more authoritatively than a mother would do to her offspring, yet with greater tenderness than the seniority, status and power of structured patriarchy tend to allow for.

Another example involves the role of women in ZIRRCON's Women's Desk. Here too, the vocabulary in women's sermons still largely reflects a masculine deity. It is not so much a matter of Mwari's gender. Instead, the crux of the good news is what Mwari as a just deity does for an abused earth and oppressed women. The women concerned experience engagement in earthkeeping and tracing Mwari's acts of justice in much the same way, albeit more intuitively, as Ruether envisages the search for a new life which should be more just and more caring.

Note, for instance, how Raviro Mutonga, chairperson of the Women's Desk, starts one of her tree-planting addresses:

> We women have our own things here. I am so happy because we know these things [mobilising empowerment, the ceremony itself, the new woodlot, caring for it, etc.] really are ours. How satisfying to know that no human being will be coming to interfere, to ask what it is we are doing [i.e., exclusion of domineering male authority]. You fathers who have come here today are in support of *our* endeavours. You have come here out of genuine interest . . .

The inference here is that Mwari is attributing a special responsibility for earthcare to women, that the men attending the women's ceremonies recognise this, and that justice is done by empowering women to play a leading role in the healing of the earth. Mutonga's introduction confirms feelings of self-worth, dignity and a sense of destiny among the neatly uniformed female tree planters as they set an example of committed, orderly, and emancipated militancy in the green struggle.

I have highlighted only one or two features of what could be termed a contextualised form of African eco-feminism. For now the story of women earthkeepers is being enacted at the grassroots by the growing membership of some eighty rural women's clubs. Hopefully the creative theology implicit in such development will yet be documented by these women themselves to enrich and give impetus to the labours of healing mothers of Eden worldwide.

An earthkeeper's exposition of Scripture in a tree-planting context. The Word of God is generally recognized as the criterion for Spirit-filled activity.

Zionist exorcism of demonic spirits during Jordan baptism illustrates faith in the cleansing power of the Holy Spirit.

Young children and students, mainly from rural schools, were recruited from the beginning of the War of the Trees to participate in tree-planting ceremonies.

CHAPTER 10

Toward an African Theology
of the Environment 2

Christ the Earthkeeper

In the 1970s Fashole-Luke (1976:148), referring to Mbiti's statement that all theology is essentially christology, commented that he found hardly any evidence of African theologians really wrestling with christological ideas. As a result he called for this subject to be given top priority in African theology. In recent years the situation has changed to such an extent that Nyamiti (1991:3) claims without hesitation that 'christology is the subject which has been most developed in today's African theology.'

One of Mbiti's early attempts to highlight christological features in African Christianity focused on the West African Initiated Churches (Aladura). He showed that these churches' main interest was in Christ's birth, healing miracles, triumphal entry into Jerusalem, death, and resurrection. From this he concluded that a Christus Victor was being propagated (Mbiti, in Schreiter 1991:20)—a tendency he attributed to the traditional myths of Africa which lacked a future dimension and held out no hope of human immortality.

> There is nothing in traditional concepts promising or hoping for a reversal of the experiences described in myths of the past. There is nothing to redeem man from the loss of immortality, resurrection, and rejuvenation. This never dawned on the thinking of our peoples nor did they ever conceive of a supra-human conqueror of evil among men (Mbiti 1968:55).

In view of this lacuna, the AIC portrayal of a Christus Victor, despite obvious doctrinal limitations and one-sidedness, conveys an extremely important message. The traditional void is filled by victory over the destructive powers that had prevailed in the past. The concepts of hope, victory, and salvation introduce new and enriching dimensions into the mythology and time concepts of Africa.

Other theologians, too, have noted the tendency to see Christ as the victor. A number of them claim that the AICs, particularly those known as messianic movements, accept a *theologia gloriae* at the expense of a *theologia crucis* (Daneel 1982). Bosch (1974:24), for instance, notes that Christ's incarnation and atoning death feature less conspicuously in African than in Western theology. He considers this to be an obstructive *theologia gloriae*, which could render Paul's claim of 'My power is made perfect in weakness' (2 Cor 12:9) even more incomprehensible and unacceptable in Africa than in Europe.

From our discussion of African christologies below it will be obvious that there is far greater awareness of the suffering and crucified Christ nowadays. A broader spectrum of christological theologising—including inculturated portrayals of Christ as ancestor, chief, master of initiation rites, healer, and so forth—makes it impossible and inappropriate to apply an either-or evaluative scheme in the sense of *theologia gloriae* versus *theologia crucis*. Nevertheless, Nyamiti (1991:18,19) correctly observes that the existing written African christologies have had little appreciable influence on the life of African churches. They are mainly systematic academic reflections on the mystery of Christ in the midst of African realities and need to be complemented with christologies that really function in the life of the African church. In this respect I consider the unwritten yet very real and distinct christological 'models' in the enacted theology of the AICs to be of great significance. The subject is too big and diversified for detailed consideration in this chapter. At most one could attempt to outline a few outstanding characteristics of an emerging AIC christology—that of Christ the earthkeeper, which is presupposed or manifest in our earthkeeping ministry. The importance of this exercise is, first of all, that it highlights an aspect of African christology which has received little attention from black African theologians so far. Secondly, it illustrates the extent to which AIC praxis complements and enriches not only African Christianity generally but written African christologies in particular.

CHRIST'S LORDSHIP AND THE MISSION OF THE CHURCH

Christology and ecclesiology are as inseparable as Christ, the head of the church, is from the communities of believers who constitute his body, the church (Nyamiti 1991:16). It is surprising, therefore, how often this integral link is overlooked or obscured in African theology. African christology generally, and Christ's lordship in particular, have been insufficiently related to the missionary nature of the church—a deficiency pointed out by Mbiti (1986:176–227). He maintains that although African theologians have written a great deal about the role of foreign missions in Africa—their evangelising, educational, and medical work—there is almost nothing about active missionary participation by the African church (Mbiti 1986:177). In a brief review of recent missiological literature he indicates that Ofori (*Christianity in Tropical Africa*, 1977) mentions only ten out of a total of 2,859 items in which African theologians deal with the subject; that Verkuyl's *Contemporary Missiology: An Introduction* (1978) contains not a single contribution by an African theologian; and that none of the contributions by African theologians in Horst Burkle's *Missionstheologie* (1979) approach missiology from the angle of the African church.

This theological omission is particularly serious in view of the fact that the church in Africa is probably expanding faster than anywhere else in the world, which suggests that there has been and still is an intense response to Christ's missionary/evangelising commission in African church praxis without a corresponding, supportive development in written theology. This again underscores the great value of the still largely unrecorded missionary traditions which the AICs have developed on the basis of their own understanding and experience of the biblical Christ figure—traditions which should be focal in future theological reflection on African christology and ecclesiology.

Let us briefly consider one such tradition, as it antedates and influences current AAEC developments in this field. In the Shona Spirit-type churches paschal celebrations culminate in the celebration of the eucharist. This is the context in which the church as a group concerns itself, directly or indirectly, with its outreach into the world. Christ's classic missionary commandment (Mt 28:18–19) often features prominently. Bishop Samuel Mutendi of the Zion Christian Church in particular used to challenge thousands of his followers, as they prepared for the climax of their festivities, with Christ's command to his disciples: 'I have been given all authority in heaven and on earth. Go, then, to all peoples everywhere and make them my disciples' (Daneel 1980:107f). The programme of the daily church council sessions included detailed planning of the countrywide missionary campaign which followed each *Paseka*. Regular prayer meetings focused on the Zionist church's outreach into the world. And Mutendi's mission-oriented sermons would culminate, immediately after the eucharist, in a send-off sermon aimed at inspiring a united and courageous Zionist response to the Lord's command.

In the ensuing campaign, teams of Zionists went on two-week or one-month missionary tours. These included pastoral care, faith-healing services, mass conversion ceremonies, baptisms, the establishment of new congregations and the expansion of existing ones, and, at the end, a report-back to the parent congregation at Zion City. Meanwhile at ZCC headquarters the people kept up a vigil of intensive intercession for Zion's mission to the world. There are many variations of these campaigns, also in the related *Ndaza* Zionist movements (the most strongly represented group of churches in the AAEC), but generally speaking the massive Zionist response to Christ's commission, triggered by sacramental celebration of his crucifixion and resurrection, derives from recognition of his kingship. This recognition is reflected in acceptance of the iconic leadership of the church's founder.

In his treatment of Matthew 28:18–19, the late Bishop Mutendi seldom dwelt on the actual meaning of the words 'all the nations' and he rarely specified the objective of missionary endeavour. Yet he assigned conversion, baptism and church growth paramount importance. He gave the text a specifically Zionist connotation by relating it to such texts as Isaiah 62:1 ('For Zion's sake I will not hold my peace, and for Jerusalem's sake I will not rest'). He also protested against some of his followers' halfhearted response to the church's mission, citing Romans 11:25 which refers to the hardening of the Israelites' hearts.

Ecclesiologically, the Bishop interpreted his movement as an extension of the pre-Reformation universal Catholic church and his leadership as rightfully continuing the apostolic succession. His missiology may not have been precisely defined. But his preoccupation with the great commission and his success in regularly mobilising his entire movement into a missionary force suggest acute

awareness of the fact that *all believers*—not just a select group of zealous followers—are missionaries, at the cutting edge of the church's movement in and into
the world. Judging by the Bishop's own insight and experience as a missionary,
he would have concurred with a definition of *missio dei* which included both a
sending, inspiring and guiding deity and a sent body of believers—the church, in
which humans share responsibility with God for establishing the good news of
shalom as a tangible manifestation of God's kingdom in a torn world.

In 1965 Bishop Mutendi sent off his missionary task force in a rather militant
mood. He likened their task to that of an Israelite battle force:

'When you go out to fight against our enemies . . . do not be afraid of them,
for the Lord your God, who rescued you from Egypt, will be with you' (Dt
20:1). The Zionists, too, had to advance like soldiers: 'Now that we
say, "Fire!" after *Paseka*, you must go out like one man to preach God's
word . . . You are going to fight Satan because you are the soldiers of God.'
[The Bishop also did not hesitate to contextualise his call in an oppressive
colonial situation, in which he himself had suffered. He said:] 'Let the cow-
ards who cringe when they see a white man sit down, because they will not
make good soldiers anyway. In the old days when I met with opposition
[from the government] all the elders backslided and left me out of fear.
Only John Shoko remained at my side and the two of us kept going. As
Jacob freed Israel, so a deliverer comes from Zion and the preachers are
sent forth in the world. The followers brought in [to Zion City] will be like
the sand of the sea.'

Against the background of his own resistance to white rule and periodic deten-
tion by the white government, Mutendi was implying that the good news to be
proclaimed during the campaign included liberation from the colonial yoke. His
identification with Israel's struggles suggested that he accepted being cast by his
followers in a Moses-like liberator role in the then only anticipated *chimurenga*
struggle. His reference to a 'deliverer from Zion' also reflected a form of self-interpretation of his own leadership in Zion City, modelled on Christ. The growth of
the black Zion of Africa undoubtedly was integral to the expansion of God's kingdom on earth.

Although Mutendi himself never presumed, as a black Messiah, to usurp
Christ's position, some of his followers tended to see him as a Christ-like deliverer—a 'man of God,' as he was popularly known among ZCC members. He
preached, and lived, much more than just a purely spiritual message. To a large
extent he was to his followers the creator of a new order, free from oppression and
white control. In this sense he was an iconic leader (Sundkler 1976:309–310; Daneel 1988:109f)—the epitome of the Christ figure in rural peasant society. To the
ZCC, Zion, the church, and God's kingdom were parts of a totality. Response to
Christ's missionary command, as voiced by the black icon in Zion, therefore,
meant the expansion of Zion and the building of Zion City as divinely authorised
activity within the kingdom of God. Limited as this interpretation of the great

commission may be, it accords with the characteristic realised eschatology of African Zionism. The new heaven and the new earth have to be experienced here and now, and the contribution of humans, in partnership with Christ, plays a key role.

This theology does not necessarily rule out individual salvation in Christ and faith in some form of eternal life in heaven. Bishop Mutendi in his posthumous state is believed to stand at the gates of heaven, where he mediates admission for deceased ZCC members as a kind of preliminary introduction, pending Christ's mediation and God's judgment. Many ZCC mission sermons, moreover, contain appeals for conversion based on texts such as Hebrews 13:14 which view the sufferings of this life almost exclusively in terms of a search for the 'city yet to come.' Emphasis on the future nature of God's kingdom thus maintains the eschatological not-yet as a necessary counterbalance to preoccupation with the enactment of salvation here and now (Daneel 1980:112–113).

The AAEC's tree-planting eucharists are extensions of Zionist paschal traditions in that they, too, provide a platform for a specific christological and ecclesio-missiological thrust. Significant parallels are noticeable. The lordship of Christ, for instance, remains the basis for whatever missionary work is attempted. The difference, however, is that another set of biblical texts is used, either in conjunction with or independently of the classic missionary command, to highlight Christ's incarnated presence as earthkeeper or protector of all creation. Instead of triggering the expansionist soul-saving drive of a particular church such as the ZCC, the eucharist, now an ecumenical sacrament—without losing sight of the soteriological implications for humans—culminates in another form of divinely and ecclesiologically inspired mission, namely earth-care. In other words the church, as a united force, is called to accomplish a neglected part of its missionary task through a broadened perception of the gospel as salvation for all creation! Whereas the ZCC campaign described above leads to individual change, spiritual growth, and church expansion, the AAEC aims at recruiting churches to expand Christ's earthkeeping mission. The ministry of earth healing itself, it is realised, has its own salutary dynamic of facilitating the spiritual change and growth of individual tree planters. Whereas most member churches of the AAEC conduct several paschal celebrations annually, over and above their tree-planting eucharists, it should be noted that the two strands of ecclesio-missiological action triggered by this sacrament complement and enrich rather than exclude or replace each other. Both human and cosmic salvation is at stake!

Probably the single most significant difference between the ZCC and the AAEC missionary eucharists is the emergence in the AAEC context of a whole new generation of iconic leaders. Whereas Bishop Mutendi mirrored Christ by sending his followers to preach, teach, convert, and baptise, the AAEC icons add yet another face or type of presence to the incarnate Christ: that of healer, saviour, or liberator of all the earth. Instead of a single leader embodying the presence of the Messiah in African rural society by way of mediating rain and good crops for peasants, faith-healing, education, and sociopolitical involvement, all concentrated in or emanating from a single holy city, the focus is broadened: it now encompasses a whole group of icons, united and moving out from their respective Jerusalems, Moriahs, and holy cities to establish the grace and salvation implicit in Christ's presence in the creator's neglected and abused 'garden,' thus declaring the entire *oikos* God's holy city. Through these iconic leaders Christ reveals a disturbing truth in the African context, namely that all agro-economic progress is meaningless unless it is accompanied by a message of environmental sanctification, of nature's restoration, of an ecological economy which, under the reign of Christ, consciously strikes a balance between exploitive agricultural advancement and altruistic restoration. This is the true purpose of an expanded missionary message proclaimed by the new breed of iconic leaders as they respond to their messianic calling.

Aware of their limitations and the relative sense in which they can be the saviours or healers of creation (Duchrow and Liedke 1987), all the AAEC's iconic leaders—bishops, prophets, and women leaders—belong to peasant society, rely on the land for sustenance, and therefore are ideally placed to demonstrate convincingly their own and their churches' solidarity with nature. Their identification with Christ's lordship is reminiscent of the Old Testament prophets who related Israel's salvation to the history of their holy land. Just as Amos prophesied the fall of the kingdom of Judah because of Israel's weakening faith, over-exploitation of the land, and disregard of the poor, so the iconic prophets are increasingly attributing wanton destruction of the earth and the related droughts, floods, famine, and the like to human hubris and defiance of the universal reign of Christ. Just as Hosea warned against the loss of the covenant and the land (Hs 2:3; Carmody 1983:87) by using environmental and fertility images, so the AAEC icons are relating environmental instability, diminishing crops, and the accompanying threat to quality of life to the ecological sins of humans, spiritual stagnation, and the church's insensitivity to the cosmic implications of Christ's headship. Hence, as in Old Testament times, salvation, peace, and wellbeing correlate with land husbandry and agricultural efficiency.

Carmody (1983:88) rightly maintains:

> . . . The land was too central to the covenantal promise not to reflect Israel's overall fortunes in faith. Nonetheless, we note that neither the historians nor the prophets made much of the land or nature as a positive creation in its own right. By and large their biblical perspective was ethno-centric. The land was a wonderful gift from God, and so should have been used well, but the land had few rights over against its human stewards . . . the biblical authors were not positioned to see that abuse of the land struck at the heart of a creation larger in its purpose than Israel's prosperity.

In this respect the AAEC represents a remarkable breakthrough. Although pragmatic motives are noticeable in the importance assigned to human progress and prosperity deriving from a restored environment, the earthkeeping icons' emphasis on altruistic stewardship, for the sake of God's kingdom and for the salvation of all of creation in its own right, is unquestionable.

Who, then, are the icons in the AAEC context? I mention only a few. Both Bishops Farawo and Wapendama are living examples of church leaders who have accepted the earthkeeping lordship of Christ as the condition for an alternative life style. Consequently, they have changed and remodelled their church head-quarters to become earth-healing institutions. To the extent that they devote their lives to an environmental ministry, which includes the mobilisation of their church communities and of schools in tree-planting ventures, they epitomise the Christ figure's concern for all creation and establish a vivid understanding in peasant society of a truth which has long remained hidden in African Christianity, namely that in Christ 'all things hold together' (Col 1:15f).

Raviro Mutonga of the Women's Desk and Farai Mafanyana, a ZIRRCON research worker, in their turn represent a theology of abundance and compassion. At ceremonies their regular use of the slogan: '*Zvose, Zvose, Women's Desk!*' (Everything, Everything, Women's Desk!) illustrates their conviction that Christ's lordship implies a comprehensive ministry, encompassing all of life. The Women's Desk they are involved in combines socioeconomic upliftment of people with earth-healing action. Their own personal liberation, in the form of social status and influence, is expressed not so much in abrasive leadership as in dedicated service. This is evident at ceremonies when they prepare food together with the local women, assist at all levels of ceremonial procedure, notably in song and dance, and generally show a compassionate concern for humans and the environment from a position of devout Christian discipleship. In their support of female initiatives in community development and ecological programmes they live a message of opportunity and wellbeing for all women. Add to this their spontaneous promotion of networking between traditionalist and Christian Women's Desks, and it is apparent that their vocation represents the antithesis of gender and religious discrimination. Their willingness to serve both people and the environment with unselfish care and joy indicates an understanding and acceptance of Christ's lordship manifested in servanthood and loving humility. In their understanding Christ requires a comprehensive mission of compassionate outreach, unfettered by a strictly defined mission policy.

Three of the movement's most influential iconic leaders operate from ZIR-RCON's administrative centre. First, Bishop Reuben Marinda, the former 'scribe' of the movement, is known in the ritual context as *Mutiusinazita* ('the tree without a name'). This nickname was deliberately chosen as a reminder that our preoccupation with *chimurenga* names could lead to such emphasis on individual performance and honour that Christ himself, the Lord and guardian of creation, would be eclipsed in our earthkeeping worship. To further counteract any such tendency Bishop Marinda built a strong christological focus into the liturgy of our tree-planting eucharist. He also elaborates on Christ's role as saviour earthkeeper in all his sermons.

Second, Rev. Solomon Zvanaka's nickname in the green struggle is *Muzambiringa* (the vine), a name aptly chosen as a reminder of ecumenical unity in Christ the vine (Jn 15). More than any other leader in the movement, Rev. Zvanaka promotes a spirit of reconciliation and positive cooperation in a religiously pluriform situation. Burdened with heavy responsibility as my successor to the ZIRRCON directorship, Zvanaka remains an unruffled and fair negotiator and peacemaker in any disputes or conflict within the movement. In a very demanding position the man's wise, irenic spirit reflects the image of Christ the vine providing life and sustenance for his disciples, the shoots. But Zvanaka's ecumenical vision stretches beyond unity among AICs. To him the shoots of the vine, at least in the earthkeeping context, represent all people. In both attitude and teaching he at all times promotes close ties between AZTREC and the AAEC, traditionalists and Christians. The ZIRRCON director's theological stance is illustrated by the following summons to concerted action in a sermon at a tree-planting eucharist at Bishop Mupure's village in February 1994:

> The bishops, ministers, and dignitaries of the church are not only called to preach and convert people. They also have a great responsibility for guarding creation, for without trees there can be no human life. We recognise differences in religious persuasion, as we know full well that those of the traditional faith are not with us during our Sunday services. The spirit-mediums, likewise, have their own ceremonies which the bishops [i.e., church people] do not attend. *But when we plant trees it does not matter who attends.*
>
> Do we say the oxygen of this or that tree goes to a bishop or a spirit-medium? Certainly not! Whoever you are, you simply breathe the fresh air produced by that particular tree . . .
>
> Remember the saying: '*Rimwe . . . rimwe, harikombi chinhu.*' (A single endeavour does not achieve anything). Therefore this is not a task for a solitary individual or for the church alone, but for many, for all of us! We unite our efforts: the women, the nursery keepers, the chiefs, the churches, each of us doing his or her duty. Once the task is completed you of the churches can then rest, go to heaven, knowing you have fulfilled your task of guarding creation. And you *vanhu venyika* [literally 'people of the earth,' traditionalists] will be seen as proper descendants of those ancestors who have left you the task of keeping the land.

For a Spirit-type leader, fully aware of Zionist and Apostolic leaders' exclusivist if not judgmental attitudes to traditional religion, this is a bold statement. It was made in the realisation that, however important Christian identity and witness remain in Christian discipleship, Christ's lordship mysteriously levels human religious divisions, shattering the presumption and self-righteousness inherent in the distancing of the so-called elect from fellow human beings. In a perception of God's kingdom which embraces all creation environmental concern in a sense acts as a great equaliser of all human beings.

In the third place, I include myself in this category of leadership because of the role in which the AAEC has cast me. During the past few years (1992–1997) the AIC leaders have insisted that the nickname *Muchakata* (Daneel 1998:206) refers to my 'traditionalist' identity and that AZTREC should continue using it, but that in the AAEC context I should be called Bishop Moses. Somewhat embarrassed by this name, I have so far tended to joke about it at ceremonies, as I make no pretence of being a Moses figure. Nevertheless it has become common practice for me to don a bishop's robe at AAEC tree-planting eucharists and to be addressed or referred to in sermons as Bishop Moses. Despite my own misgivings about the negative implications for the movement if I were to become a patriarchal cult figure, it is understandable that after thirty-five years of close association with the AICs some people will be inclined to single out the liberationist impact of my work. The AIC movements I have founded and helped to build did in fact bring a degree of liberation from erstwhile ecclesiastic isolation, lack of theological training, lack of community development opportunities and non-involvement in environmental reform.

It is from this position that I tend at afforestation rituals to speak about Christ the earthkeeper, the ultimate guardian of the land who, as creator and ancestor, fulfils and expands the ancestral guardianship of the holy groves and the land generally, which Africa has known all along. With reference to Matthew 28:18,19 I emphasise Christ's reign as a form of empowerment which keeps vitalising and mandating the church's missionary task through the ages. As humans already living in God's kingdom, we are freed to proclaim and spread a gospel which focuses on conversion and church planting, but which is not complete if this process of Christian discipleship does not consciously reach out and embrace the full richness of the earth. In other words, I attempt not to dilute the evangelical thrust of the church's outreach but to liberate it from its overly spiritualised, pietistic insulation and to widen the perception of Christian mission through an inculturated, missionary conception of earth-care. Texts like Colossians 1:17 and Ephesians 1:10 are brought to bear on this broadened interpretation of the church's mission, an interpretation which always acquires immediacy and urgency because of the signs of environmental abuse and degradation where our ceremonies are held. In qualifying the church's mission, the interwovenness of witness and unity on the basis of such seminal texts as John 17:21,23 is frequently mentioned as a reminder of the biblical basis for the existence of the AAEC. And insofar as human endeavour features prominently in the church's holistic mission, texts like Isaiah 41:19,20 ('I'll set in the desert the cypress, the plane and the pine together; that man may see and know . . . that the hand of the Lord has done this') serve as warnings against the pitfalls of human hubris in what essentially remains *missio dei*.

This picture of AAEC christology and its bearing on ecclesiology remains somewhat fragmentary. However, pinpointing some characteristic features of iconic leaders' individual contributions provides some questions and clues for future theological reflection. How, for instance, can the image of Christ as the liberator of women through their ecological activities, as an expression of a theology of abundance, opportunity, and compassion, be given greater substance in the church's drive to help establish justice in this world? What are the prospects of developing the ecological care-taking function of the church as an inherited mission within the framework of African inheritance and related kinship obligations? How does the biblical lordship of Christ, in our context of unity and fellowship between traditionalist and Christian earthkeepers, inform a praxis-oriented theology of religions? Is our emphasis on ecumenism and interfaith unity in the green struggle moving in the direction of assumed religious universalism and relativism at the expense of the uniqueness and 'offensive' (*skandalon*) witness character of the Christian message? Are the roles of those Christians who somehow cross the divide as part-participants, part-observers at traditionalist rituals justified on account of what Rahner would call 'anonymous Christianity,' an unwitting acceptance of Christ's lordship which extends well beyond the boundaries of the visible church?

What both the ZCC tradition and the AAEC tree-planting eucharist convincingly demonstrate is that to the AICs the sacrament of holy communion is the key to constant renewal of missionary awareness and inspiration of the church's outreach to the world. In a sense the AAEC's tree-planting eucharist is the earthkeeping church's mission. This crossing of frontiers between humans and the rest of creation is the most meaningful ritual expression of acceptance of Christ the earthkeeper's lordship. At present this mission takes ecological shape mainly in tree planting and the protection of water resources. It is bound to expand further into the creation of wildlife sanctuaries and related activities. Can all this be theologically validated as a legitimate ministry of the church? And if so, does the image of Christ the earthkeeper not only affirm the development of a new environmental ethic but also require the church to incorporate in its mission an ecologically legislative and disciplinary function, as some AIC leaders are requesting? In the previous chapter I cited Bishop Nhongo and his son's convictions that the church as the keeper of creation should introduce strict environmental laws and the means of exercising discipline accordingly, an ecclesiastic function which assumes that Christ as head of the church is, amongst other things, environmental law-giver and judge. Seeking to express and plumb the implications of Christ's law of love for all the earth in human society promises to be an exciting, if daunting, undertaking.

THE SUFFERING CHRIST

African theologians in South Africa have understandably related their interpretation of the suffering Christ to the sociopolitical dilemma of their country during the apartheid era. The central theme in both Setiloane's poem 'I Am an African' (Setiloane 1976:128–131), and Buthelezi's article 'Daring to Live for Christ' (Buthelezi 1976:176–180) is black South Africans' identification with Christ on the cross from their own existential experience of oppression and dehumanisation. Setiloane depicts the irresistible attraction of the suffering figure on the cross:

> And yet for us it is when He is on the Cross
> This Jesus of Nazareth, with holed hands and open side,
> like a beast of sacrifice:
> When He is stripped naked like us,
> Browned and sweating water and blood in the heat of the sun
> Yet silent
> That we cannot resist Him.

Setiloane's poem is embedded in the African context: a proud affirmation of the black self, aware of a close bond with the ancestors. By directly identifying Yahweh of the Bible with such African deities as Umvelingqangi, Unkulunkulu, Modimo, and others, he is introduced into the world of African religion as the great God in whose presence the ancestors dwell, mediating between the living and God. At this point it seems as if Yahweh is assimilated into the God of Africa to the extent that he cedes his Old Testament role of interacting directly with humanity to the mediating ancestors, the 'little gods, bearing up the prayers and supplications' (Setiloane 1976:129).

Even so, the traditional concept of God transcends and transforms this indigenised, somewhat attenuated African God. The cleansing blood of the suffering, dying, sacrificed Christ, the son of Yahweh, Modimo, and Unkulunkulu, breaks down the barriers of skin colour, race, and tribe, the confines of ancient Israel and of African tribes:

> His blood cleanses
> not only us,
> not only the tribe
> But all, all mankind:
> Black and White and Brown and Red
> All mankind.

Thus, while Setiloane clings to the traditional portrayal of the God of Africa by identifying him with Yahweh, the breakthrough from a locally confined tribe to a universal concept of 'all mankind' in the atoning death of Christ introduces a completely new dimension—the 'totally other'—which by implication also transforms the old conception of Modimo, Unkulunkulu, and Umvelingqangi (Setiloane 1975:24–38). Setiloane admits that because of blacks' experience of slavery, colonialism, and exploitation, some black Christians are calling for a rejection of the pale white God and the worship of a 'God as black as black as we!' (Setiloane 1975:37). Despite this, he believes that the majority of black Christians still consider God to be one: 'He gathers into one herd friend and foe, exploiter and exploited, oppressor and oppressed, apartheid-ist and those he sets "apart"' (Setiloane 1975:37). This poignantly expresses the universal dimension and the essential liberation (salvation) effected by the suffering Christ: it is valid for all people, oppressor and oppressed.

In 'Daring to Live for Christ' Manas Buthelezi (1976) refers to the false dichotomy between *human life* and *Christian life*, which led to blind spots in the pre-1994 South African situation. It allowed some Christians to call for an encounter at the foot of Calvary without realising that this meant that Christian human beings must meet at the foot of Table Mountain to make laws for the body which is the temple of the Holy Spirit. To the extent that Christian behaviour ceases to float in a vacuum and becomes incarnated in social, economic, and political structures, Christian life becomes an ordinary, everyday human phenomenon:

To dare to live for Christ means to have a Christian impact on these structures. It is a daring act because it involves the risk of suffering just as Christ
suffered as he made concrete his love for humanity (Buthelezi 1976:178).

Buthelezi distinguishes between 'oppressive suffering' and 'redemptive suffering.' The former stifles all initiative to a point where suffering becomes fatalistic,
a way of life that destroys God's purpose for the victim. As an example Buthelezi
cites the inadequate educational facilities in the old South Africa (a situation
which is likely to continue for some time even in the new post-1994 political dispensation), which create a culture of ignorance that holds the victims in its oppressive grip. By contrast there is redemptive suffering, modelled on Christ,
which is not an end in itself and which issues in love for the other so that the other
may be freed. This is self-sacrificing suffering which relinquishes personal security and interest for the sake of the other. Articulation of personal suffering and
that of others is the beginning of the redemptive phase of suffering. Buthelezi
(1976:180) concludes as follows:

> At this moment in South African history the suffering of black people is be-
> coming redemptive. The black people are now regarding their suffering as a
> step towards liberation instead of a pool of fate and self-pity. Black con-
> sciousness is an instance of how the black people have transmuted their
> present suffering into the medium of liberation towards self-esteem. This is
> redemptive suffering.

Despite Buthelezi's reminder that human redemptive suffering should be modelled on Christ's suffering and his emphasis on the sacrificial motive for love, he
appears to ascribe an inherently self-determined quality to blacks' suffering
which suggests personal merit and is therefore theologically suspect. Can human
suffering be redemptive? It seems to me that human suffering, insofar as it is consciously *identified* with the suffering of Christ, can only take on a character of
witnessing to the saving and liberating power of Christ. Christ alone can suffer redemptively, and human suffering is only 'redemptive' when fully identified with
the source and author of redemption.

Other black South African theologians have also placed the image of the suffering Christ in the context of their people's sociopolitical plight and need for liberation. Hence Bonganjalo Goba's (1980:27) assertion: 'Christ opens the path of
liberation as he shares our common humanity and with God in his forsakenness
suffers with us as the one who is crucified.' Siqgibo Dwane urges a 'detheologis-
ing' of the Christian message so that the person of Christ, identified in Western
society with the middle and upper classes, can emerge in its full humanity as one
of the poor and humble. This means 'to discover the man who died on a city dump
outside Jerusalem' (Dwane 1977:8–9).

AAEC theology adds a new dimension to this focus of South African theologians on the cross of Christ in humanly oppressive socioeconomic and political circumstances. Christ's suffering relates not only to the plight of humanity but to that

of all creation. The tree-planting eucharist illustrates this point in several ways. First, the symbolism of earthkeepers partaking of Christ's blood and body while holding seedlings to be planted as part of the sacrament is a powerful statement that Christ's cross has relevance for all the earth. In this symbolism Christ's suffering and death connote a *new message of hope*. Death is not the end of the line. In Africa it is a communal event which does not negate individual self-expression or sever ties between deceased and living. Christ's death holds the promise of new life. In the tree-planting eucharist the perception of community is widened to encompass all the denizens of the earth: humans, all living creatures, all forms of vegetation, trees, grass, shrubs, etc. The seedling in the earthkeeper's hands at the communion table and the seedling addressed as brother or sister are a recognition of the entire earth community as partakers or recipients of holy communion, a way of extending the hope of reconciliation and new life, emanating from the cross, to all creation.

In a sense the tree-planter's eucharist gives expression in the widest sense of the word to an African theology of the cross as proposed by Kwesi Dickson (1984:185–199). In an attempt to overcome the negative and pessimistic features associated with Christ's death on the cross in Western theology, Dickson proposes an approach more compatible with African perceptions of death. The cross, he says, should be presented in 'glorious affirmation of it as that which is the *basis of Christian hope*' in that it 'demonstrates human degradation and evil, but it also *demonstrates triumph*' (quoted by Nyamiti, in Schreiter 1991:8). In the eucharist believers share both the death of Christ on the cross and life with one another. The seedling going into the soil expresses human sharing of life with each other and the denizens, animate or inanimate, of all the earth, not in naive triumphalism but in a humble act of proclaiming the good news of the cross, which at no point loses sight of resurrection and salvation.

Second, the liturgy of the tree-planting eucharist relates Christ's body and blood directly to all creation (Appendix 3, pages 305–6). Christ's sacrificial surrender, according to Bishop Marinda, has nothing to do with fatalistic helplessness. His liturgy portrays Christ's expulsion of the merchants from the temple in Jerusalem as a deliberate show of strength 'to save the animals and the birds from the cruel fate [of sacrificial offering] that awaited them.' This demonstration of power and authority is integral to the crucifixion event, a prophecy of the kingship which is to come about after Christ's resurrection as the foundation of mission to, and deliverance of, the whole world.

In the third place, the tree-planting eucharist provides the context for considering the twofold nature of the body of Christ as church and as creation: the body of believers sacramentally mobilised for holistic mission, and the cosmic body of the saviour-earthkeeper present in creation. It is this latter image, taken from the AAEC's core text (Col 1:17, 'In Christ all things hold together'), which adds a new dimension to the understanding of the suffering Christ. In ceremonies which repeatedly refer to the abuse of nature and its restoration at the behest of an ever-present earthkeeper, Christ emerges and is sensed, by preachers and listeners alike, as the wounded healer, the one who feels and is saddened by the destruction of his own body, creation.

Discussions with some of the AAEC's leading figures about the suffering body of Christ within the earth and in relation to tree planting indicate that this is a matter of growing consensus and not just the pet subject of a few preachers, including myself. Said Rev. Tawoneichi: 'Our destruction of nature is an offence against the body of Christ [which] suffers as a result. The random felling of trees hurts the body of Christ. The church has to heal this wounded body . . . [That Christ's body is part of the earth] follows from the biblical creation story, because Christ's spirit hovered over the waters.' And Bishop Mupure responded: 'Yes, the earth is Christ's body. It is his dwelling place which holds his footprints. It is part of him and everybody relies on it, whether they are Christians or not. Now that Mwari is withholding rain because of people's abuse of this body you can observe their dependence. Everybody, believers and unbelievers alike, is looking at the heavens, seeking help. They say: "Oh God, what have we done?"'

These remarks reveal close identification of Christ with a suffering earth. Christ himself suffers because, as Mwari's co-creator, his spirit once hovered over the primordial mass of waters, as a result of which he feels the destruction of his body, the earth. Yet as a person he also dwells in creation where his footprints are symbols of intimate interaction with the earth community, and he is grieved by all forms of desecration of his wonderful world. When the rains fall because of God's anger and/or Christ's suffering, human beings are overcome by their guilt of earth-destruction and start seeking means of repair. Hence being in Christ as individual parts of the body of believers means sharing in his suffering. In the AAEC such suffering ceases to be fatalistic acceptance of the earth's demise, and in the planting of trees it proclaims hope of renewal. It witnesses to the redemptive suffering of Christ which is liberating creation from oppressive exploitation.

The tree-planting eucharist highlights the bond between the suffering earth-keeper and his fellow earthkeepers. In taking the sacrament, a legion of Christ's co-workers share the earth's wounded state and show their willingness to transform that burden into dedicated environmental action as a message of redemption. That is the upshot of the communicants' partaking of the crucified body of Christ as members of the church and in the communion of his cosmic body, the wonderful yet broken earth.

Inasmuch as the tree-planting eucharist strengthens the earthkeepers' identification with the wounded healer and their resolve to wage war against the forces of environmental destruction, the image of a suffering Christ is inevitably also reflected in the lives of the movement's iconic leaders. It has been pointed out that engagement in the green struggle sometimes takes a heavy toll. Here I merely mention the late Leonard Gono, the movement's field operations manager, who exemplified in a powerful if unpretentious manner the presence and acute agony of Christ the suffering earthkeeper in the context of our struggle (Daneel 1998:204, 259). Fired by a vision from beyond and with a great love for trees, wildlife, and rivers, Leonard in the space of a few years spent himself in a cause where the need of the earth was always greater than his own. As *Mabvamaropa* (literally 'which brings forth blood,' the kiaat tree) he established, organised, and maintained nurseries; mobilised entire communities to plant and nurture trees in new woodlots; gave direction to earthkeeping planning, policies, and project implementation; and inspired both traditionalist and Christian earthkeepers by example. Leonard Gono had his fair share of ordinary human failings but these never interfered with his environmental mission. To us he was the epitome of the earthy missionary, his soul attuned to creation and its maker. He rarely spoke about Christ, but he drove himself uncomplainingly in testimony to the one who is suffering in the barren earth. He left us a legacy of the meaning of the earthkeeper's mission in Africa, a legacy not recorded in books but living on in the hearts and activities of thousands who know the agony of withering crops under a scorching sky and who find promise and hope in a greening countryside.

CHRIST IN KINSHIP

One of the commonest analogies which African theologians draw between the African religious world and the dispensation of Christ is that of his humanity in relation to the traditional kinship structure. Pobee—who outlines an African christology against the background of the West African Akan tribe—states that, in contrast to Descartes's *cogito ergo sum*, the Akan maintain a position of *cognatus ergo sum*—'I belong through kinship therefore I am.' In other words, among the Akan one becomes fully human by belonging to society. The goal and sense of existence is determined by belonging to a family, clan, and tribe. 'Since belonging to a kinship group is a mark of a man,' says Pobee (1979:88), 'our attempt at constructing an African christology would emphasise the kinship of Jesus.' Jesus' membership of a family underlines the fact that fullness of life consists largely in community, in breaking down individual isolation. To the Akan it is a pain and a curse to be alone. 'The fullness of a man's humanity is underscored by the relationships he has, a point which is well made by the extended family system in Africa' (Pobee 1979:89). To the Akan Jesus' circumcision illustrates this bond with a kinship group, and his baptism is a rite of solidarity with the rest of humankind.

Mbiti points out that in African society one is not fully human until one has been officially incorporated into the community by the rites of passage. Against this background the African is particularly interested in the birth, baptism, and death of Jesus, which make him a complete person via the necessary rites of passage (Mbiti 1968:56). With regard to the cross, he says that Africans do not think primarily of the atonement (not that they deny the salvific significance of the cross) but see it as symbolising Jesus's complete humanity (Mbiti 1968:57). Mbiti also shows how *kinship* dominates all of traditional African life. It operates vertically by uniting the living with the dead, and horizontally by declaring the individual in his village and neighbourhood a relative of every other person. In such a context an individual's self-awareness is experienced only in terms of community and tribal solidarity. Mbiti then suggests that the church, as the body of Christ, can transform this traditional self-awareness into ecclesiastic solidarity rooted in Christ. A black Christian experiences the new community by saying: 'I exist because the body of Christ exists.' 'At the individual level,' says Mbiti, 'this is what the *new kinship in Christ* should mean: a discovery of one's true being as hidden in the *Man par excellence*, and a discovery of one's existence as externalised in the Body of Christ' (Mbiti 1968:62). Mbiti quite rightly infers that it is by discovering kinship in Christ that the church in Africa can have a meaningful and deep impact on life.

It is true to say that to a large extent the AICs had already in their own right—before the formation of the AAEC—discovered what the new community, the new kinship in Christ, signifies in their own diverse contexts. It is equally true that within the framework of AAEC activities this unfathomable yet very real kinship in Christ is acquiring ever wider and more enriching connotations. By perceiving Christ as earthkeeper, the new family or tribe—the extended family of churches who accept earthkeeping kinship and give expression to it by constantly proclaiming the unity of the shoots (churches) in Christ, the vine—receives a new leitmotif: a ministry of earth-care.

In the extended family of earthkeepers Christ is portrayed by some of our green bishops as an elder brother. Said Bishop Farawo: 'Christ is our *mukoma* (elder brother). He is happy when we plant trees, because it shows that we are his family and that we care for all of his creation. Christ is particularly happy if we preach the gospel of tree planting.' The image of Christ as *mukoma* in Shona society is apt, in that the elder brother has authority over his younger siblings and is therefore in a position to determine the direction of the family's activities. As name bearer of the family head the elder brother inherits, at his father's death, ritual responsibility for the family. In the ritual context he then acts as the deceased family head. Applied to Christ, the Shona analogy of relations between elder brother, father, and family is quite striking. This analogy is fulfilled and transformed in its biblical qualification. As Penoukou (in Schreiter 1991:45) puts it:

What Christ has in common with God the Father, he expresses in terms of *communion of being* but in a *relation of filiation*: 'That they may be one, as you, Father, are in me and I in you' (John 17:11, 21). Furthermore, what Christ has in common with the human being is also expressed in terms of *communion of being*, but in a relation of *union of siblingship*: 'That they too may be one in us . . . as we are one, I in them as you in me . . .' (John 17:21–23). And: 'Whoever does the will of my Father is a brother to me . . .' (Mark 3:32–35) . . . It is this communion which is experienced and confirmed in the sacraments.

Where the 'elder brother' is recognised as keeper of the earth, the union in siblingship is manifest in the new family. As siblings, the member churches of the AAEC accept new ecological codes of conduct. These are based, first of all, on identification with the destructive sins of the first Adam, evidenced in the AAEC's ecological confessions which form part of the tree-planting eucharist; and, secondly, on a comprehensive response to the second Adam, Christ, who effects the undoing of the first Adam's disobedience—in this instance by involving his siblings in the liberation of creation. We have already described how this family concern promotes a new understanding of the church and how it proliferates in a wide range of earthkeeping activities, including the development of a green ethic. Thus the AAEC's earthkeeping ministry signals understanding of and identification with the comprehensive nature of Christ the Earthkeeper's kingdom and care. In the words of C. de Witt (1991:112):

> The reach of Christ's work extends everywhere (Eph 1:19–23; Col 1:15–20). The work of the last Adam, Jesus Christ, is as broad as the reach of the damage wrought by the first Adam. The work of Christ impacts all human relationships—those with God, with others, and with the cosmos . . . redemption is our calling to all of them, and not one to the exclusion of others.

Here we see a unique feature of the AAEC: the establishment of an extended family of earthkeepers, whose activities in siblingship recognise and affirm particularly the ecclesiastically much neglected dimension of the elder brother's redemptive work on behalf of the cosmos. In networking across the boundaries of ecclesiastic diversity, the will to establish a just order in all of society, especially on behalf of inanimate members of the kin group (trees, grass, birds, animals, water), is apparent. The communal will in the new family to erect convincing signposts of Christ's social justice for all humankind and eco-justice for mother earth emerges daily in the ZIRRCON team's search, through Bible study and prayer, for the 'elder brother's' green guidance and strategy. In this endeavour the boundaries of gender, class, authority, and socioeconomic privilege between team members pale significantly . . . so that all the earth, in our small corner of the world, may live and breathe.

In African society, as Mbiti has indicated, kinship inevitably links the living and the dead. Without the ancestors the African kin group is incomplete! Hence the image of Christ as a kinsman necessarily raises the question of his relationship with the living dead, the *midzimu* (ancestors), who in all Shona belief systems—both traditional and Christian—keep influencing the lives of their living relatives. On the whole the Shona AICs, and the Spirit-type churches in particular, have refrained from calling Jesus a *mudzimu*, probably because they reject ancestral demands for veneration as contrary to the Christian message. In the AAEC context church leaders may be even more hesitant to portray Christ as an ancestor because of their awareness that many of their traditionalist counterparts in AZTREC tend to view Christ merely as a white *mhondoro* (tribal spirit), equal in standing to such national hero-spirits as Chaminuka. To my knowledge only the Apostles of Johane Maranke use the term *mudzimu* with reference to the Christian Godhead. They refer to the Holy Spirit as *Mudzimu Unoyera* (literally 'holy ancestral spirit'), but the revelations of the Holy Spirit in their church are so starkly opposed to traditional ancestral demands that the name causes little if any conceptual confusion in the Apostles' understanding of the Spirit's Christian nature and work.

Nevertheless, several African theologians have depicted Christ as ancestor in their attempts to develop a contextualised christology. Nthamburi (in Schreiter

1991:67) discusses Pobee's (1979) attempt in this regard. 'Pobee,' he says, 'maintains that Jesus has a heavy *Kra* (Akan, 'soul') which links him to God. The superiority of the ancestorship of Christ is demonstrated by the fact that since Christ has authority over all cosmic powers he has authority over other ancestors as well.' According to Ambrose Moyo (1983:97) the Shona traditionally referred to God as *Mudzimu Mukuru* (great ancestor). Jesus, being his direct offspring, is therefore *Mudzimu*, with powers of intercession. As the 'heavenly one' Jesus is also the 'supreme universal ancestral spirit' who links all of humankind (Nthamburi, in Schreiter 1991:67). Nyamiti, again, emphasises the importance of death in the making of an ancestor: 'Through his death, therefore, Christ becomes our brother-ancestor in fullness. By being linked with Adam, Christ's ancestorship acquires a transcendental quality since he is able to transcend family, clan, tribal, and racial limitations in a way that our own ancestors cannot' (Nthamburi, in Schreiter 1991:67, with reference to Nyamiti 1984).

Although the AAEC earthkeepers refrain from calling Christ an ancestor, the tendency to proclaim his lordship over all creation and to envisage him as the controller of all cosmic and life-giving forces strengthens the perception of an earthkeeper who, as part of the human family, necessarily relates to the ancestral world as well. And the analogy to this interrelationship which immediately comes to mind is that of Christ as the universal *muridzi venyika* (guardian of the land). In a number of tree-planting sermons I have myself compared Christ's earth-care with the Shona tribal guardian ancestors' concern for the environment. The theological assumption in this portrayal is that through the ages the traditional guardian ancestors have, by virtue of their closeness to Mwari the creator, sensed and accepted their responsibility for the land under their political jurisdiction. Thus they were prototypes prefiguring Christianity among the Shona. Christ's role as *muridzi venyika*, therefore, both fulfils and transforms this ancient guardianship. Through his Spirit, Christ, the earthkeeping *muridzi*, somehow inspires and holds sway over generations of Shona *varidzi*. Through them he appeals to all their living descendants of whatever religious persuasion to share and extend their responsibility for the earth. As Pobee would say, Christ shares ancestorhood with the living dead on account of his *Kra* (soul) linking him with God. However, he also transcends the regional and tribal confinement of the African senior ancestors by linking the local Shona environment and kin group with the universal cosmos and the universal family of humankind (as inferred by Moyo and Nyamiti). The same theological extension to an increasingly continental and global perspective is, of course, also evident in AAEC praxis in the form of widening ecumenical horizons and financial and moral support from the Christian earthkeeping community worldwide.

The need for a well-developed christology which clarifies Christ's relationship with the ancestors is evident, particularly in those tree-planting ceremonies which are attended by large contingents of both traditionalists and Christians. By way of example, here are a few excerpts of speeches delivered at the AZTREC ceremony in Chief Chivi's district on 27 August 1993. Following Bishop Chimhangwa's sermon, which included a plea for environmental stewardship on the basis of the garden of Eden story (Gn 2), a traditionalist, Muzenda, responded as follows:

We do not forget your message, Bishop Chimhangwa. When *sekuru* Chaminuka [a spirit-medium] knelt over there, it was in honour of all our ancestors. He said: 'You, our forefathers, are ahead of us. So talk to those you find there [in the world of the dead], those we do not know. Talk also to Mwari.' We surely do not forget Mwari. The ancestors, if they are determined, will emerge in the life of Mwari.

King Solomon asked only one thing from God, namely wisdom to rule Israel well. As chiefs we need the same wisdom. For things were complicated by these different religions all worshipping Mwari. If we want to succeed, let us worship Mwari. But right now, let us first call on spirit-medium Chaminuka to address us.

As spirit-medium Chaminuka rose to his feet the people cheered, saying: 'Forward with one family in Zimbabwe!' Chaminuka then proceeded to speak:

Down with hatred! Forward with tree planting! Forward with the protection of trees! Down with tree felling! . . . *We are united here like one big Shumba family*. When you think of it, to be united is not such a difficult thing, but if you refuse to think it through you will not cooperate with each other.

When the comrades [freedom fighters] were in the bush they cooperated because of one purpose and one family. They were all *the children of one mother*. But nowadays they compare the sizes of their houses [are diverted by individualistic ambitions of luxury and improved lifestyles]. The decisive issue [for united action] is the soil [i.e., the ancestors identified with the soil]. If the soil refuses, you have gathered here for no purpose whatsoever. In your union here today you fulfil the laws of the soil. For this occasion the *mutezo* [believer] who has come here is not the child of this father or that mother, or this church or that church but is simply of the forefathers, a descendant of the land. The driving force for this event is the soil [*vhu*] . . . the council of [deceased] elders is right here. All the *madziteteguru* [senior ancestors] are congregated here. So you who are here are fulfilling the laws of those who have gone before, those who trod this earth. We are all of one heart!

We thank all the elders who have come here to Gwenyaya. You strengthen this ward of Nyanyingwe, which is situated in the chiefdom of Chief Chivi. It is Chief Chivi who has called *sekuru* Chaminuka [the Shona hero-spirit] to raise this matter. We of the soil [at this point the medium identifies with and talks as Chaminuka] only want love, that which inspires the youth when they observe tomorrow that our love has clothed the land. *In this we follow our forebears whose task was to build the family of humankind, to live in harmony.*

You must cooperate with Gwenyaya and with the grandmothers [older women] here, as well as the grandmothers where you all come from. Let us ululate in honour of this land so that *all of Zimbabwe can be one*, from those who worship according to the books [*vanonanata mumabhuku*] to those who worship according to the soil and the snuff horns [*muvhu nezvibako*]! In these laws of earthkeeping Zimbabwe unites. *Sekuru* [Chaminuka] affirms all this.

After much ululation the song '*Chaminuka ndiMambo*' (Chaminuka Is King) was sung.

Towards the end of the ceremony medium Chaminuka once more addressed the crowd: 'We thank you for gathering the people of the lineage of the vaMhari [dominant tribal group in Chivi district] to plant trees. The soil [ancestors] will *unfasten the heavens* so that the rain will sprinkle the trees and ripen the fruit of tomorrow . . . Chief Chivi, this work is of great magnitude. *It is the work of salvation* [*ruponeso*].'

The strength of the traditional worldview and faith in the ancestors is overwhelmingly evident in these speeches. Muzenda pays tribute to a Zionist bishop's sermon and acknowledges the connection between the ancestors and Mwari. He even complains about the confusion caused by different religions worshipping Mwari and calls for increased ardour in the worship of this divinity. But it is quite evident that for the present occasion the important matters are the soil, the ancestors. This is clearly borne out by spirit-medium Chaminuka's speech. Unity of purpose and action in the environmental struggle, in the whole nation of Zimbabwe and in the earlier struggle for political independence, emanates entirely from the soil, the ancestors. Moreover, the Shona hero-ancestor, Chaminuka, is considered to be present at the ceremony in the living person of the medium. Consequently those attending the ceremony and engaged in tree planting are seen as obeying and fulfilling the laws of the ancestors. The ancestors get credit for building the family of humankind and it is implied that they also instil religious unity by bringing together the worshippers who read books (Christians) and those who venerate the soil with sacrificial snuff (traditionalists). It seems that even the important work of environmental 'salvation,' to which Chief Chivi referred, is somehow attributable to the ancestors.

When one considers the centrality of the ancestors in this ceremony, some cardinal reasons that the AAEC requires a clear-cut and convincing christology in relation to the spirit world are the following. First, some of the claims made by traditionalists conflict with AIC convictions. Tree planting in a pluriform religious context does not mean that everybody present is intentionally complying with ancestral directives, as Chaminuka implied. It could become quite confusing to well-intentioned AIC members, who are urged to fight the war of the trees in concert with traditionalists, if they lack a strong, clear-cut christology in the face of this kind of assertiveness about the ancestors. Christian participants could well feel that the witness-character of their faith should be repressed in these circumstances for the sake of ecumenical unity. It should be made clear that religious tolerance and ecumenical interaction do not exclude Christian witness. And the AAEC should give clear guidance about the meaning of Christ's lordship and his role as supreme earthkeeper amongst the Shona *midzimu*, the guardians of the land in particular. Christ's cross and resurrection need to be made manifest in the domain of the soil.

Second, there are many points of contact in the presentation given above which could be fruitful for a contextualised christology. References to love and harmony in family life, religious interaction, and unity, as well as environmental salvation reflect interaction between Christian and traditionalist values. These notions can be spelled out in greater detail if the soteriological nature of the *descensio Christi* can be convincingly applied in this context. For instance, the chief's interpretation of salvation probably relates to Chaminuka's claim that the ancestors 'unfasten the heavens' for the life-giving rain to fall. This interpretation could be the starting point for a more comprehensive teaching of salvation (*ruponeso*)—applied to both the human family and the cosmos—in Christ's communication with the ancestors.

Third, the numerous references to the importance of kinship and a united family as basic to success in the environmental struggle further illustrate the appropriateness of our theme of 'Christ in kinship,' if Christ's incarnation is to achieve real meaning in the African setting. Due to Chaminuka's seniority as a national ancestor in the 'family of Zimbabwe,' and his prominence in the spirit war council concerned with all forms of liberation struggle in the country, the universal position of Christ as Chaminuka's 'elder brother' and as chief 'councillor' relating to Mwari on all matters of salvation and liberation throughout Zimbabwe and all creation, requires explanation in AAEC circles—at least, if biblical criteria are to remain definitive in the development of a contextual christology.

An ancestor-oriented christology would be incomplete if it does not include the subject of the communion of saints, the *communio sanctorum*. Taylor (1963:166) writes that 'when the gaze of the living and the dead is focused on Christ they have less compulsive need for each other.' But need is not the only basis for relationships, and since Christ, the second Adam, promotes the corporateness of the community as a whole, Taylor believes that the time has come for the church to give the doctrine of the communion of saints the prominence that Africa wants to assign to it.

How does the *communio sanctorum* relate to the member churches of the AAEC, the majority of whom radically reject the claims of ancestors and ongoing dependence on ancestral protection? The answer to this question revolves around the fact that the churches in question have replaced virtually all ancestral rites with adapted, imaginatively Christianised ceremonies which effectively accommodate traditional needs for communion between the living and the dead. A striking example is the replacement of the key rite, the *kugadzira* (when a deceased person is elevated to the status of ancestorhood), with the *runyaradzo* (consolation ceremony).

In the latter ceremony, instead of bringing the deceased home and inducting him or her into the realm of *midzimu*, the late believer is 'accompanied' (*kuperekedza*) to heaven and more or less presented to the Lord by the church (Daneel 1974:131).

In the *runyaradzo* context an earthkeeper's *communio sanctorum* makes sense. The AAEC has admittedly not paid much attention to this subject, possibly be-

cause there is as yet no consensus on a convincing christology relating specifically to the ancestral world. In addition, the movement is still too young for commemoration of its pioneer leaders to have become a direct concern. However,
once a number of leading earthkeepers have passed the divide between the living
and the dead, yet another tradition in AIC ritual life is bound to be established.
For *runyaradzo* ceremonies on behalf of deceased earthkeepers will no doubt entail lengthy narratives of their contributions as tree planters, nursery keepers, in-
structors, and mobilisers of the people. Their exemplary lives, even their failings,
will highlight the relationship they had, and continue to have, with Christ the
earthkeeper, their elder brother, fellow ancestor, healer of creation, and saviour. I
anticipate that only during this phase of development will the inspirational impact
of the Christian dead on the still living family of earthkeepers become existentially manifest. Only then can one expect a more comprehensive and definitive
christology of the soil (ancestors) to take shape. For in the AICs it is only from the
ritual enactment of experience that new tenets of theology are born.

CHRIST THE HEALER

The traditional healer, the *nganga*, has provided the primary paradigm for an indigenous christology since the inception of African Christianity. Setiloane
(1979:64) believes that an authentic African christology should be sought in the
healing practices of the *bongaka*. Pobee, again, considers the parallel between the
Akan healer and Jesus a suitable illustration of the divinity, and especially the
power and authority, of Christ. The similarity is that both are 'ensouled' by God
during the process of healing. According to Pobee (1979:93) the difference, however, would lie in the intensity of such ensouling by God: 'Jesus was in a perpetual state of holiness, perpetually ensouled by God, so much so that the divine
power was like a continuously flowing electric power in him, unlike the traditional healer, who has the occasional experience of it.'

Buana Kibongi (1969:52–54) gives the following description of the *nganga*'s
relationship with the Christian church in Congo:

> For good or ill, Christianity has not always escaped the heritage of *nganga*.
> The Christian missionary drew part of his authority, without knowing it,
> from the psychological state which *nganga* had created. The missionary
> was called *nganga Nzambi* (God's priest), as distinct from *nganga nunkisi*
> (the fetish priest). It goes without saying that the missionary benefited from
> the respect which was formerly due to the *nganga vankisi* . . . The Con-
> golese priest or minister is also called *nganga Nzambi*. He profits from the
> situation created by *nganga* and the missionary. *Nganga* has not only as-
> sured to some extent the social status of Church workers; he has also left
> them the legacy of religious and conceptual moral tools: it is undoubtedly
> *nganga* who created words such as *Nzambi* (God), *munuka* (to define one-
> self; hence *masumu*, sin) . . . *Nganga*'s work partly enabled the Bible to be
> translated into Congolese languages. The Christian preacher consciously or

unconsciously uses part of the vocabulary left by *nganga*. This is where Congolese priesthood confronts Biblical revelation.

Kibongi also shows that the Congolese *nganga* was never a mediator between *muntu* (humans) and *Nzambi* (God), but only between human beings and the departed spirits. The *nganga's* activities evoked the concepts of liberation and redemption: '*Nganga* is certainly the saviour or the liberator of *Muntu*' (Kibongi 1969:54). Buana Kibongi evidently regards the *nganga* as the precursor of the priest and the minister—not only as a healer but especially as a religious leader. After all, the *nganga* is Christ's precursor in Africa: he, as the new *nganga*, is the fulfilment of the traditional one. '*Ngangas* willed to save man, but did not succeed in doing so; Christ did so fully once for all. Christ has therefore accomplished the work of *Nganga*' (Kibongi 1969:55).

The prophetic Independent Churches illustrate the paradigm of Christ as the 'healing *nganga*' more vividly than any other churches in Africa. In this respect they are making a decided contribution to an African christology, one which African theologians would be well advised to note. In the Shona prophetic movements the prophetic healers naturally see their faith-healing activities as a substitute for, and in opposition to, traditional *nganga* practices (Daneel 1974:186f). Nonetheless, their diagnostic and therapeutic work—the focal point of these movements and certainly their most dynamic recruiting technique—is largely based on the ideas and techniques of the *nganga*. The chief similarity is that the prophet, like the *nganga*, ascribes disease, misfortune, or lack of success to spirits, evil powers, magic, and the like. However, the prophets explicitly state that their extraperception comes from the Holy Spirit and not from the divinatory means used by the *nganga*. The prophets insist that the spirits in question have no legitimate claim on the beleaguered patient. Therapy therefore does not consist in traditional sacrificial rites or the use of medicine, but in the exorcism of threatening spirits and symbolic actions representing the healing power of the Christian God. In their dealings with patients prophets emphasise mainly the work of the Holy Spirit. This does not mean that there is no christology, but rather that it is presupposed as the basis of all healing practices. In fact the prophets themselves personify the liberating and healing ministry of Christ. In them the *nganga* tradition is partly continued, even fulfilled, but it is also radically Christianised.

Through the activities of the AAEC the Shona prophetic movements are widening their perceptions and ministry of healing. Instead of being presupposed in the prophets' Spirit-filled outreach to afflicted humanity, Christ now emerges more decisively than before as the healer of all creation, as the one who deals consistently with both human and environmental illness. This is manifest in the AAEC's tree-planting eucharists which, in contrast to AZTREC's *mafukidzanyika* (earth-clothing) events, are called *maporesanyika* (earth-healing) ceremonies. The name places the main emphasis on healing. '*Maporesanyika* ceremonies,' says Rev. Solomon Zvanaka (In ZIRRCON Annual Report 1994:10), 'combine with the eucharist, where Christians experience the newness of life in a novel way, where relationships are expressed, between God and man, and between man and all of creation. There is new theologising where celebrants express new perceptions of sins, salvation, and reconciliation, the lordship of Christ and the unity of creation. Relevant biblical texts are read and interpreted to the people. What a novelty! What an impetus that drives people to exercise Christian stewardship over the earth!' Zvanaka here captures something of the breadth and richness of the ritual context in which Christ emerges as *healer* and *saviour*.

Keen group awareness of Christ's presence as healer marks most *maporesanyika* ceremonies. Bishop Wapendama's sermons illustrate the common interpretation of AAEC earthkeeping as Christ's work, an extension of Christ's healing mission. Other sermons confirm this trend. At Bishop Marinda's *maporesanyika* ceremony in 1993, Rev. Machingura combined the themes of sacrament and healing as follows:

> They [our friends from ZIRRCON] came here today because of the presence of Jesus Christ. This is a holy occasion, our *Paseka*, ordained by Jesus Christ, who gathered his disciples for the use of the sacrament . . .
>
> In 1 Corinthians 5 Paul says that we are the temple of God and therefore should become holy people. It must be seen that Jesus is drinking his cup (*mukombe:* gourd) among us. That is our covenant with him. We must make sure that there is nothing which prevents us from meeting the blood of Christ. Drive out the wicked among you (1 Cor 5:13)! You believers, do not allow Christ's blood to be polluted. Remove the evildoers! I have told you: remove the *varoyi* (wizards)! Will we look at one of the big trees and think of felling it? NO! Even if you are inquisitive, leave it as it is!
>
> We are all sinners. We have to confess fully so that we can be cleansed. We confess because of the blood of Jesus Christ. His blood is *mushonga* (medicine) inside the body of a human being. Jesus's blood therefore has great *simba* (power) to heal.
>
> In the past there were no hospitals. People ate fruit: *nhunguru, matunduru, mishuku* . . . sweet and sour fruit. The fruit itself contained Mwari's medicine and was adequate to keep people healthy. Likewise, if we follow Christ's directives today in our paschal celebrations, he will protect and keep us.

As is characteristic in the AICs, cleansing or purification of the communicants receives great attention in this sermon. The occasion is holy and therefore participants must prepare themselves to be worthy of communion with the body and blood of Christ. Significantly, the wicked who should be excluded from sacramental participation are not only the moral transgressors, but specifically also the wizards who destroy nature through wanton tree felling. The implication is that Christ's blood—that is, his person—addresses, cleanses, and heals both people in the conventional sense and creation, through the body of sacramentally united earthkeepers. In the eucharist Christ features quite dramatically as healer in that his blood is perceived as medicine or 'life force' in the bodies of the celebrants— perhaps a combination of African symbolism, residual beliefs in the *nganga's* magical healing praxis, and an indigenised version of Roman Catholic transubstantiation as regards the elements of the sacraments? Whatever the answer to this question, the preacher introduces the 'medicinal presence' of Christ in the communicants in the context of Mwari's natural provision for human healing in nature, a further indication of the interconnectedness of ecological wholeness and a healing christology.

Insofar as the Shona Spirit-type churches consider Christ's salvific work to be integral to healing, the preacher cited above is actually expressing, at the African grassroots, christological convictions very similar to those propounded by Shorter (1985:51–58), albeit less systematised. All healing, he contends, is directed to eternal life and wholeness: 'In the church this is realized through the sacraments, especially the Eucharist, which is the renewal of the mystery of Christ's cross and resurrection.' The sacraments are the works of the divine Spirit, whom Shorter calls 'medicine of life,' since it continues Christ's healing mission (in Schreiter 1991:10).

The christological significance of the AAEC's tree-planting eucharist lies in its ritualised blending of the wide-ranging tenets of Christ's healing ministry. Observations by commoners participating in the *maporesanyika* ceremonies reflect a growing awareness of the comprehensive nature of this ministry; thus illustrating its conscientising impact. Said one of the villagers in a *maporesanyika* speech: 'The protection of trees is a holy matter. The land is barren. The blanket of vegetation which should cover it has been torn away. In its nakedness the land is ill. We, too, the people of Mupakwa, are ill. *We have come to be healed, together with the land.* In Jesus' time you only needed to touch his garment to be healed. In clothing the land with trees we, too, are being healed.'

These words show a simple yet profound understanding that Christ came to heal the sickness of the entire world. Human and environmental illness are interlinked and the earthkeepers' care for the environment is part of the therapy for their own malady. Once again the AAEC's ritualised earthkeeping experience, verbalised by an unsophisticated peasant, corroborates Shorter's observation about an African healing christology when he says that 'healing becomes a possibility to establish and maintain harmony with the natural environment. Environmental wholeness is fundamental to human well-being' (in Schreiter 1991:10). Indeed, the villager quoted above realised that the disruption of nature's equilibrium was also distorting and threatening human life. Both shared a need for healing and salvation. Both were present at the tree-planting eucharist to seek and share in the deliverance wrought by the 'wounded healer' of Nazareth. For this AAEC earthkeeper healing and well-being lie in restoring harmony in creation, a function which requires sacrifice on the part of Christ's present-day fellow wounded healers.

Finally we consider the healing christology implicit in the various phases of the tree-planting eucharist.

HEALING AND CLEANSING

In anticipation of Christ's healing presence in the sacrament, the communicants prepare themselves by publicly confessing their moral and ecological sins. The cleansing and spiritual self-renewal are necessary if Christ is to be 'seen' breaking the bread and drinking the cup of wine in the midst of his present-day disciples. Destructive attitudes of communicants, it is believed, should be prevented from polluting Christ's blood, which heals the communicants and enables them to fulfil their own environmental healing task. So Christ is already actively present in the cleansing of communicants prior to the actual taking of the sacramental elements, confronting through his Spirit the unrepentant wizards who spoil the earth.

Here, too, the healing effected by Christ differs from that of the *nganga*. The prophets in charge of confessions do not as a rule impose ostracism on an exposed *muroyi venyika* (wizard of the earth), as the *nganga* would have recommended. Prophetic disapproval is expressed in public exposure of the wizard and, in the event of an unrepentant spirit, exclusion from the eucharist. But the prophet leaves the door of reconciliation open by keeping the *muroyi* in the church community. Hence there is still a prospect of Christ's forgiveness and healing (enacted in the *muroyi*'s eventual change of heart), reinstatement in the community of believing earthkeepers, and full participation in *maporesanyika* ceremonies. Strict as the conditions for confession and cleansing may be, Christ emerges at this juncture as a forgiving healer, whose mercy entreats wizards to change their ways from environmental destruction to earth-care. Healing thus entails reconciliation and harmony between humans and all creatures; it seeks to establish respect for life and mercifully defers final judgment of the as-yet heartless exploiters of creation.

HEALING AND PROCLAMATION

In eucharistic sermons Christ emerges, as was shown above, as the Lord of creation who mandates his church to conduct an extended mission, which includes spreading environmental good news; as the earthkeeper who suffers because of the destruction of creation; and so forth. In all these images, however, Christ remains essentially the healer/saviour who fulfils the Old Testament prophecies of Isaiah 40–43, in that he brings life—water, trees and wildlife—to the wastelands. Through ZIRRCON's iconic leaders he provides the means for restoring and holding together (Col 1:17) the things of nature which are falling apart. The presence of numerous prophetic healers, moreover, who are living representatives of Christ's New Testament healing ministry, rekindles hope of harmony and wholeness in a better future. And the repeated messages about Christ's body and blood as 'medicine' for his disciples inspire commitment, in renewed health and vigour, to an otherwise all but impossible, daunting task of earth healing.

HEALING THROUGH SACRAMENTAL EMPOWERMENT

The earthkeeper's holding a tree seedling while partaking of the bread and wine symbolises identification with and dependence on the healing powers of Christ. The queues of communicants from many and diverse denominations become a united army of healers at the communion table. In the sacrament their divisions are overcome as their union in the body of the great healer empowers them for their environmentally therapeutic task. As if touching the garment of the historical Christ, the communicants themselves are being healed in Christ, and their healing motive or task—both for the 'soil' and for humans—is somehow divinely affirmed. Hope is rekindled in the ranks of the earthkeepers, and they draw encouragement from the cleansing, 'medicinal' blood of Christ. Knowledge of the universality of Christ's healing powers also makes the communicants aware of the global dimension of their regionally expressed service of stewardship.

HEALING THE SOIL

Through the procession of communicants going into the new woodlot to plant their seedlings, Christ the wounded earthkeeper addresses the eroded soil. It is he who, in the tree planters' dialogue with nature, implores the seedlings to grow strong roots to prevent further soil erosion by water and wind. It is his healing hands which plant the seedlings in the soil, and with them the promise of protection and a new cycle of life. Some tree planters, on the other hand, consider the act of planting to be healing the soil, the abused cosmic body of Christ. Thus they witness to their union in the body of Christ, which has just been sacramentally affirmed, and their responsibility for it.

There is also a spiritual dimension to Christ's healing of the soil. For the duration of *maporesanyika* ceremonies at least, concern for the traditional spirit provinces of the guardian ancestors and the old conflicts and rivalries associated with past conquests of the land are pushed into the background. The presence and participation of chiefs, headmen, and a wide range of AIC members—all of them from the surrounding territories and all of them representing different, often inimical histories, myths, and ancestral bonds with the soil—are conducive to mutuality and reconciliation rather than rivalry. It is at this juncture that the AICs involved in the ceremony could ritually develop this interaction between Christ and the *varidzi venyika* by intimating that the former's lordship over all creation breaks down territorial divisions and mobilises spirit unity in the interest of concerted action for environmental restoration.

HEALING HUMAN BEINGS

Finally, as the tired tree planters return to the meeting place where the sacrament was administered, the healing cycle comes full circle. Women with sick children, elderly people with ailments, young people with problems—all the *maporesanyika* fighters who seek help—flock to where the prophetic healers are getting ready to tend to the needy. Once again the drums of Zion, of the AAEC, can be heard beating rhythmically; rattles are shaken and the women start swaying in song and dance. The healers shake and speak in tongues to confirm the presence of the Holy Spirit. The spirit of Christ the healer moves in our midst. The late afternoon sun rays beaming through the flimsy leaves of seedlings in the new woodlot and in the expectant eyes of afflicted people tell their own story: *Christ's healing of the land and his healing of people join hands, are one!*

I stand among the healers, praying and laying on hands, sprinkling people with holy water, blessing newly filled bottles of water, healing and being healed. I have never claimed any healing vocation or powers, but I participate nevertheless, having learnt about diagnosis of illness in terms of African worldviews and about the value of the AIC symbols of Christ's healing and protective power. I am no longer surprised at hearing patients answer affirmatively when I ask questions about vengeful spirits, spoilt relations, or *uroyi* (wizardry). Feeling the straining body in a state of possession or the heat of witchcraft medicine in a victim's system no longer disturbs me. Every time I am thus engaged the nagging questions of my rational mind recede and I find quiet and peace in the doing. Indeed, as the villager above observed: '*We have come to be healed, together with the land.*'

In front of us is a sea of black heads, faces with hopeful eyes, eyes full of pain, fear, rejection, or joy. Hands, black and white, are laid on those heads in prayer, conveying a message of reconciliation and wholeness. They are the hands of icons, illuminating the presence, empathy, love of Jesus. They are wounded hands, suffering hands, still dusty from planting seedlings in the soil. In the dying sun they are the reassuring hands of the Lord himself, holding a promise of new life, resurrection . . . where all evil ceases.

Cécé Kolié (1991:141–142), after surveying the emerging christologies in the Roman Catholic and established mission churches in Africa, concludes that Christ the healer does not function convincingly in the existential reality of individual believers. This, he claims, is because the established churches are still foreign to the fundamental problematics of black people. 'Our liturgies,' he maintains, 'do not celebrate human beings fighting disease, or struggling so hard to get up on their feet, or striving to be free.' Consequently, he states, 'to give Christ the face of the healer in Africa (even though this was his principal activity in Israel) will not be feasible until the manifold gifts of healing possessed by all of our Christian communities have begun to manifest themselves.'

Kolié's criticism correctly identifies a serious limitation in Western-oriented Christianity in Africa. To many believers the face of Christ remains alien and masked when it comes to their existential problems. However, the AAEC's blending of a ministry of human and environmental healing clearly shows that both in liturgy and individual experience the healing features of Christ are being unmasked and revealed. The 'manifold gifts of healing' are emerging forcefully and understandably in the African context where Christ meets his fellow wounded healers. He does so in the prophetic diagnosis of all ills, cleansing confessionals, tree-planting hands, exorcising hands . . . all to the rhythm of dancing feet in which the inner struggle for life, dignity, and wholeness is fierce and relentless.

CHAPTER 11

Toward an African Theology
of the Environment 3

The Holy Spirit in Creation

According to Moltmann (1985:9) the trinitarian interpretation of creation in theological tradition has tended to emphasise God the Father as creator, in contradistinction to his creation, in a monotheistic way. Consequently attempts were made to develop a specifically christological doctrine of creation. Moltmann, however, deliberately chooses to focus on the third person of the trinity: creation in the Spirit. He argues that all divine activity is pneumatic in its manifestation. It is always the Spirit who brings the activity of the Son to its goal. Everything that exists does so through the inflow of the cosmic Spirit's energy and potency. 'This means,' says Moltmann, 'that we have to understand every created reality in terms of energy, grasping it as the realized potentiality of the divine Spirit.'

Moltmann (1985:11–12) notes a similar interpretation in Calvin's work. To Calvin the Holy Spirit, the 'giver of life' of the Nicene Creed, is the fountain of life (*fons vitae*). Just as the Holy Spirit is poured out on all created beings, so Calvin's 'fountain of life' is present in everything that exists and lives:

> If the Holy Spirit is 'poured out' on the whole creation, then he creates the community of all created things with God and with each other, making it that fellowship of creation in which all created things communicate with one another and with God, each in its own way. The existence, the life, the warp and the weft of interrelationships subsist in the Spirit. 'In Him we live and move and have our being' (Acts 17:28).

The cosmic Spirit referred to by Moltmann and Calvin has no relation to Stoic pantheist notions. It remains God's Spirit acting in this world in the differentiated modes of *creating, preserving, renewing, and consummating* life. In view of this I fully agree with Moltmann's (1985:112) basic assertion:

> Creation in the Spirit is the theological concept which corresponds best to the ecological doctrine of creation which we are looking for and need today. With this concept we are cutting loose the theological doctrine of creation from the age of subjectivity and the mechanistic domination of the world, and are leading it in the direction in which we have to look for the future of an ecological world-community . . .

Faced with . . . [the progressive destruction of nature and the pile-up of nuclear armaments] we have only one realistic alternative to universal annihilation: the non-violent, peaceful, ecological world-wide community in solidarity.

Moltmann introduces several distinctions to explain the position in creation that he assigns to the Spirit. We shall not dwell on these, but merely note that an integral part of his view is that of God's immanence in creation. He also refers to the interpenetration (*perichoresis*) of the trinity—the social doctrine of the mutual indwelling of Father, Son, and Holy Spirit. In this interactive principle (God in the world and the world in God; heaven and earth in the kingdom of God; soul and body united in the life-giving Spirit into a human whole; etc.) there is no such thing as a solitary life. All living things, each in its own distinctive way, live in, with, from, and for one another. This trinitarian interpenetration—which shows a distinct parallel with African religious holism in which nothing is solitary or self-existing—is the key to Moltmann's envisaged ecological doctrine of creation. Inasmuch as the cosmic spirit is also the organising principle of human consciousness, it is important to remember that through the Spirit we are bound together with other people socially and culturally (an interlocking association which can be described as the common spirit of humanity) and that

through the Spirit we are bound together with the natural environment. This association is a system comprising human beings and nature. *We might describe it as a spiritual ecosystem.* Through the Spirit, human societies as part-systems are bound up with the ecosystem 'earth' (*Gaia*) . . . So human beings are participants and subsystems of the cosmic life-system, and of the divine Spirit that lives in it (Moltmann 1985:18) (my italics).

Why this lengthy discourse on Moltmann's views? I include it because I subscribe to the main tenets of his ecological doctrine and because of its relevance to the AICs. Moltmann's idiom may be alien and the context of his appeal may be mainly the academic West and the threat of modern industrialisation to our planet. He observes, however, that our only realistic alternative to annihilation lies in the solidarity of a worldwide ecological community. This is where, for Africa, traditionalist ecological concerns and the enacted theology of the AICs enter into it. The latter's vision of creation in the Spirit can help to mobilise and inspire the desperately needed ecological mass movement. Besides, Moltmann's views on the cosmic spirit in creation poignantly express a central concern of AICs of the prophetic type.

THE HOLY SPIRIT AS THE 'FOUNTAIN OF LIFE'

In some respects the AIC prophets of Africa probably understand and experience the life-giving power of the outpoured Spirit better than either Calvin or Moltmann. Their knowledge is shaped by their non-Christian forefathers, who sensed as well as any Old Testament sage that the *mweya* (spirit) imparted by God the *musiki* (creator) was the source of all life. This intuition ultimately blossomed into an all-pervading testimony to the life-giving power of the *Mweya Mutsvene* (Holy Spirit) in the Spirit-type churches, especially in their healing colonies.

Observe, for instance, a Zionist 'maternity clinic' in which the ritual and worship revolve entirely around new human lives. The expectant mothers wear holy cords around their bodies to ward off the attack of evil powers such as witches. Special prayer meetings and dances invoke the presence of a protective Holy Spirit. In the early morning the prophetesses prepare holy water and take all the newborn babies outside into the rays of the morning sun where they are stripped naked and sprinkled liberally with the life-preserving water of the Spirit.

Witness, too, the healing ceremonies of the sick, where the Holy Spirit's power is symbolised by smoke to repel harmful spirits. There are hours of sympathetic pastoral counselling between prophet and patient; laying on of hands, touch of the leader's holy staff, sprinkling of holy water and the use of a host of symbolic objects to cure or preserve life. In a sense, too, the blessing of the seed for the crops and the pegging of maize fields with prophetically blessed stakes symbolise the healing and protective power of the Holy Spirit over inanimate things.

All these symbols testify to the outpouring of the Spirit, the fountain of life in creation. It is a chorus of supplication. It takes place in the midst of suffering. But in the final analysis it is a massive celebration of faith to honour the only true source of life, the Holy Spirit.

This massive testimony to the Spirit's life-giving powers undoubtedly shows certain flaws. To some participants the holy cord or water which is believed to ward off evil forces is little more than, or equivalent to, a traditional amulet. The cord may be seen as a power in itself, without faith in the triune God playing a significant role. Here the magical belief system still holds sway. In this respect Beyerhaus (1969:75) and Oosthuizen (1968:119–142) have indicated a misinterpretation of the work of the Holy Spirit in the AICs. In my experience among the Shona, however, such misinterpretations are the exception rather than the rule. They resemble our own Western Christian misconceptions when we seek merit rather than evidence of grace in the good works we perform, or when we try to manipulate God to favour us by producing yet another 'truthful' theological statement, even if born of a loveless heart.

Most AIC prophets experience the Holy Spirit as the indwelling Spirit of God, whom they do not control or manipulate. Interviews with prophetic church dignitaries show that the initiative for inspiration or revelation through the Holy Spirit is ascribed overwhelmingly to God and not to any human being. Prophets often declare that they only receive guidance from the Holy Spirit after fasting, Bible study, prayer, and seclusion. They also readily acknowledge that these actions are not causal or manipulative, but that the Holy Spirit retains the initiative. Few prophets claim that they can 'give' the fullness of the Spirit to a lay member of the church. It remains an *act of faith*. In addition, the spiritual state of the recipient and the ultimate will of God determine whether there will be new life, preservation of life, healing, or special gifts such as prophecy and speaking in tongues (Daneel 1987:262).

In the Spirit-type churches the *fons vitae* flows freely, uninhibited by written dogma. Here no one speaks about 'trinitarian perichoresis.' It simply exists: God *in* the world, and the world in God. In the AIC prophetic community there is no such thing as a *solitary* life, unless of course the presence of a *muroyi* (wizard) necessitates cleansing, sanctification, and reconciliation. Through this holistic interpenetration of God, people, and things, where the fountain of life is manifest in unquestioned action, the Spirit has prepared fertile soil for an ecological theology.

The AAEC bears testimony to this. The reflections of leading figures about the origins of their movement show an awareness of the pneumatic action of God both in and since the creation of the universe. Consider the following statements:

> *Bishop Farawo:* The Holy Spirit is the founder of this movement, because he first of all created Adam and Eve and gave them the task of keeping the trees and the animals. Today the AAEC is there to continue this tradition, this task of keeping all created things.

> *Bishop Machokoto:* Without the inspiration of the Holy Spirit the thoughts for this tree-planting task would not have arisen. Bishop Moses's (Daneel's) conviction to unite the churches in earthkeeping endeavour therefore came from the Holy Spirit.

> *Bishop Mupure:* God's Word revealed quite clearly today that our relation to the environment and our survival are totally interlinked. The Word feeds us with the message of the Spirit. *Heaven starts here!* It pleases the Holy Spirit if we sort out matters of the earth right here and now! This task of healing the land gives us a good chance of entering heaven.

The word of God remains the criterion for assessing Spirit-filled activity, despite varied and often conflicting interpretations of the Bible in AIC circles. Bishop Mupure does not doubt that the Spirit urges earthkeeping and that such activity has a direct bearing on entering heaven. Heaven starts now, if the Spirit's call to heal the land is heeded. One could question the notion of human merit which appears to be conditional for salvation, as opposed to God's free grace. But the Spirit's presence nevertheless seems to focus and telescope the time of salvation: the origins of life in the past, the nurture of new life here and now, and the assumed prospect of eternal life in heaven, rooted in the present yet reaching out to the future. In the balance between axe and hoe a new dispensation takes shape. Holistically, in the Spirit of creation, the life of trees and the life of humans (current and/or eternal) interrelate, become one. For, as the AAEC earthkeepers believe, wherever the Holy Spirit takes hold of people and their environment, new life starts.

THE HOLY SPIRIT AS 'HEALER OF THE LAND'

On the whole the AIC prophets do not refer to the Holy Spirit as *murapi venyika*, (Healer of the Land) even though the Spirit is central to all their healing activities.

This reflects the tendency in these churches, established prior to their AAEC involvement, to conceive of the life-giving Spirit first and foremost as the healer of humankind. Yet we have noticed that in the tree-planting eucharist healing of people and healing of the land blend into a single totality, as do the functions of Jesus Christ and the Holy Spirit. The assumed and professed interpenetration of Son and Spirit is evident in the comprehensive *maporesanyika* healing described in the previous chapter. Ritually christology and pneumatology become one as Africans enact the conviction that 'the Spirit always brings the activity of the Son to its goal' (Moltmann). In the promptings of the Spirit, Christ the king (*mambo*), guardian (*muridzi*), saviour (*muponesi*), and healer (*murapi*) of all creation keeps entering life here and now as an incarnate being.

Having said this, it would be repetitive to reconsider all the pneumatic features of healing already mentioned in the previous chapter. Nevertheless, the role of the Holy Spirit as life-giver and healer is so prominent in all the Zionist and Apostolic churches (the vast majority in the AAEC) that some observations about their sacraments in relation to the development of a 'green pneumatology' are called for.

In the AIC's pentecostal tradition the Holy Spirit features pre-eminently as purifier and healer of people in the build-up to both baptism and the eucharist. Prior to the baptism of novices the sermons of church leaders focus increasingly on their experiences of healing through the Spirit. The entire congregation is transformed into a body of witnesses to healing, and the group of believers receiving the baptisands on the far side of 'Jordan' stand there as disciples of Christ, healed of sin, brokenness, isolation from meaningful communion, illness, and a host of human problems.

Then, when the baptiser enters Jordan, he actually blesses the water by diving into it with a loud splash, or stirring it repeatedly with his holy staff and/or cord. In a sense he or she is transmitting the life-giving force of the Holy Spirit to the water, so that it literally cleanses the baptisands of sin and pollution, totally renewing and healing them. Baptism is therefore also a healing ceremony! During the ceremony many members of the congregation will enter Jordan to drink the Spirit-filled water to obtain healing or add meaning to their lives.

At first I was inclined to interpret this feature mainly as a relic of the traditional magical philosophy—in other words, an attempt by people to lay hold of whatever life force or power could aid them. This may be true of some believers. The question that arises, however, is whether the practice does not present a golden opportunity to widen the interpretation of baptism. Can it not be said that the Spirit's presence in Jordan is a sign of God's creation being redemptively healed? Can we not say that the Holy Spirit manifest him/herself at Jordan as the healer of the land? This would obviously include the converts, who are healed and changed by moving into the body of Christ. But the Jordan river and its often barren environment are likewise changed and taken, symbolically, into the body of Christ the king, so that his redemption is sacramentally proclaimed over the whole of creation.

In that case the drinking of Jordan water symbolises not just the person's healing or salvation, but his or her participation in cosmic healing. The focus shifts from private and personal benefit by the Holy Spirit's healing powers to a statement of human solidarity with all creation and an affirmation of new commitment, through individual conversion, to the healing and restoration of nature. What happens, then, in the sacramental context is that human beings' knowledge about creation through domination is replaced by knowledge gained through communication between them and nature. In a sense one could call it a *baptismal naturalisation of the human being* (Altner, in Moltmann 1985:50): 'It assumes that, fundamentally speaking, the human being does not confront nature: he himself is nothing other than one of nature's products.'

The image of the Holy Spirit as *murapi venyika* is thrown into even sharper relief in the paschal celebration leading up to the eucharist. First, there is the 'seed conference' (*ungano yembeu*), an integral part of *Paseka* which, as we have seen in the case of the ZCC, replaces the traditional rain requests at the Matopo oracular shrines. Here the concept of an immanent creator as *muridzi* (guardian) is fused with that of the Spirit as *murapi* (healer). For when drought and pests threaten, the seasons and crops that are guarded are also healed to bear a life-sustaining harvest. Second, there is the need for confessing ecological sins. Here, too, it is the Spirit who heals by laying bare those abuses and violence against nature which obstruct its redemption and life-sustaining fertility. This theme will be considered in the next subsection. Third, it should be noted that, as when the Jordan water is drunk by believers for its medicinal value, the elements of bread and wine have the same extended or post-symbolic significance to many participants. Mothers with sick babies, for instance, take extra pieces of sacramental bread home for their stricken little ones. We have also noted how at tree-planting eucharists some preachers emphasise the life-giving and/or medicinal value of the bread and wine in the bloodstream of the communicant, the implication being a Spirit-empowered and committed earthkeeping vocation. In the fourth place, the Spirit's healing potency is symbolically transferred to the new woodlot prior to tree planting by sprinkling holy water and pouring holy oil over the area to be restored. In such symbolic action, repeated in numerous variations, the Spirit is seen to overpower the destroyer of creation and to establish the new dispensation of God's kingdom.

To sacramental purists the 'magical-pneumatic' dimension in the ecologically inclusive baptism and eucharist may sound blasphemous. But is this not just another indication that the healing *charis* of Christ's sacrament, combined with the unfathomable movement of the Spirit, mysteriously extends far beyond our theories and conceptions? And does this not mean that we can celebrate the eucharist in a manner which emphasises our corporate identity with nature in Christ, making us as dependent on the Holy Spirit's healing activity as all other natural beings? In these contextualised sacraments of Africa, whether interpreted magically or symbolically, we earthkeepers declare ourselves, under the kingship of our elder brother Christ, his fellow guardians of creation. Likewise, in the therapeutic sweep of the Holy Spirit over all the world we are fellow healers without pretending that we ourselves are the saviours of creation.

THE HOLY SPIRIT VERSUS THE DESTROYER

The basic theme in all African prophetic healing is the struggle between light and darkness, between the almighty Holy Spirit and the evil perpetrated by Satan. Throughout this ministry there are continuous interaction and confrontation between African traditional cosmology and contextualised Christianity. Prophetic diagnosis, attributed to the revelatory presence of the Spirit, invariably identifies afflicting ancestral or alien spirits with demonic powers. Wizardry (*uroyi*) in particular is considered to be the embodiment of evil, Satan himself, who epitomises the destruction of life. Whether diagnosed as demons or *uroyi*, the destructive forces considered to be the cause of any tragedy or malady are driven off through exorcism in the name of the triune Christian deity. In addition a host of symbolic rituals are performed to fortify and protect the threatened party against future demonic attacks. Hence, in a broken world, the lordship of Christ is repeatedly enacted in what is believed to be and experienced as the Holy Spirit's vanquishment and subjugation of the destroyer. The main features of this struggle in the spirit world as it relates to earthkeeping are discussed in the following sections.

EMERGING AWARENESS OF ECOLOGICAL SINFULNESS

The growing consensus about the near-unpardonable evil of environmental destruction stems from ZIRRCON's conscientisation programmes via workshops, conferences, and executive meetings. But above all, the special focus on ecological sins in *maporesanyika* sermons and in the confession ceremony prior to tree planting highlights the presence of the Spirit in the ranks of the earthkeepers. The Holy Spirit, the originator of the movement, is regarded as the primary conscientising agent responsible for the growing awareness of human guilt in the deterioration of nature. Even if this is not always mentioned in sermons, most preachers, if asked, will unhesitatingly attribute the gist of their message to the inspiration of the Spirit. Couched in the idiom of fighting *uroyi*—evil in its vilest and most ruthless form—the struggle between the Spirit and the destroyer is drawn palpably into the existential world of the congregated earthkeepers. The following excerpt from a sermon by Zionist Bishop Mutikizizi (at Bishop Mupure's ceremony; Zaka, February 1994) illustrates this point clearly.

> There is a type of wizardry which destroys the land. It is the wizardry of deforestation. It is a terrible *uroyi*, more destructive than the evil of those who rise at night to hurt people. Some people just fell all the trees to burn bricks or sell firewood and then, to make matters worse, they squander the money on liquor. These people have no insight into the destructive effects of their deeds. They refuse to see! Such is the wizardry of land destruction. This violates the responsibility God gave people when he created the earth. Environmental wizardry (*uroyi hwenyika*) is a grave sin because it denies the custodianship over creation which Mwari requires of human beings.

Zionist Bishop Marinda said the following at a ceremony at Gutu, in March 1993:

> All of us must confess our sins as we pass under the scrutiny of the Holy
> Spirit at the gates [consisting of pairs of prophets]. In this way the *sins of
> tree felling* will be revealed. They kill the land, because where the sledges
> strip the land the gullies start forming. Consequently people have little land
> left to cultivate and there is no grazing for their cattle. *I have never seen
> such wizards!* This differs from the witchcraft which kills an individual at
> home, for it wipes out an entire tribe [*rudzi*]. This environmental *uroyi* de-
> stroys everybody. So we queue for confession to be searched by the Spirit.
> Whoever gets caught out gets caught out. The prophets are here. Stand at
> the gates, you prophets! Stand at the gates! Reveal to us the wizards who
> still pull their sledges.

The disquiet of all these preachers about the *wrong relationship* between humans and their environment is very evident. Their call to all participants to confess their rebellion against God through mindless destruction of the ecosystems
which sustain life reveal an awareness of the holistic nature of sin as depicted in
the Bible, in that it 'not only distorts inter-human relations and human-divine relations, it also affects the life-sustaining harmony between human beings and the
Earth' (McDonagh 1985:125). Here the critical consciousness of African peasant
society voices insight similar to that of the Western theologian Emil Brunner, who
notes that estrangement between humans and creatures coincides with human
withdrawal from God:

> The more man distinguishes himself from the rest of creation, the more he
> becomes conscious of himself as the subject, as an 'I' to whom the world is
> an object, the more does he tend to confuse himself with God, to confuse
> his spirit with the spirit of God, and to regard his reason as Divine Reason
> (in McDonagh 1985:125).

What the AAEC earthkeepers are in fact saying is that humans in the local setting arrogantly set themselves up as God in false dominion over the earth, in opposition to God's intentions for creation. Like Lucifer or Satan, they become
earth destroyers. In their exploitation of the earth, hubris prevents them from seeing and admitting the life-destroying implications of their actions.

An intriguing aspect of the AAEC perception of ecological sin is that there is
no attempt to avoid communal guilt by setting up Satan or evil as a kind of objective force outside humankind, the real source of destruction which exonerates humans from guilt. Instead, the overriding concern with environmental wizardry reflects recognition of a serious flaw in humans, in their relations to both the
creator, the life-giving Spirit, and creation.

Those who abuse their freedom in African rural peasant society are people
who disregard the land husbandry laws—both the old *marambatemwa* restrictions of the forefathers and modern agro-forestry requirements for sustainable

agricultural produce. Unrestricted tree felling and practices promoting soil erosion diminish both arable land and pasturage. Ultimately all of society suffers: the human exploiters who continue sinning against the life-giving Spirit despite the obviously dwindling resources, together with the responsible caretakers of the land and the voiceless denizens of the earth, the animals, birds, grass, and trees.

Does the characterisation of the abuse of human freedom in terms of *uroyi* not distort the perception of ecological sinfulness? Does it not reintroduce the traditional practice of branding one or a few individuals scapegoats for causing inexplicable deaths or social ills? And is the fate of environmental wizards not the same as that of the *varoyi* of old—stigmatisation, ostracism, even death?

There is a real danger that the more arrogant tree fellers, grass burners, and sledge owners will be stigmatised and identified with the destroyer of life more readily than 'minor' sinners, who may confess to some environmental abuse but conveniently forget that they contribute equally to overpopulation and other less commonly mentioned 'sins' which are also earth-destructive. Pharisaic bigotry, it seems, is not necessarily absent from the AAEC's concern with environmental *uroyi*. Nevertheless, there are two clear trends indicating that we are not dealing with direct assimilation of an ancient practice with all its negative implications. First, the AAEC preachers' intention when identifying environmental destruction with *uroyi* is to drive home in the collective mind of the audience the tremendous seriousness of the issues at stake. *Uroyi* is evil and heartless. It creates the heat of destruction and spells death, without mercy or compromise. It is the ultimate in exploitation, the antithesis of life-giving forgiveness and redemption; hence, sin against God and creation which cannot be countenanced. Second, the sermons quoted above tend not merely to accuse others as *varoyi* but to identify with them, to detect the evil of destructive exploitation in oneself, in our ranks. Thus communal guilt is established, the shadow-side of each and every participant.

PNEUMATIC EXPULSION OF EVIL

Maporesanyika sermons reflect more than just awareness of ecological sinfulness. Implicit, too, is a summons to admit common guilt of earth destruction. Such admissions or confessions can only be elicited from individual communicants through the powerful work of the Holy Spirit, manifested in prophetic activity. Thus the preachers also propagate their convictions about the revelatory and protective role of the Holy Spirit via earthkeeping prophets. Said Zionist Rev. Chamakaita at Bishop Marinda's ceremony:

Did Jehovah not make use of his *svikiro* (spirit-medium), the prophet Isaiah? And are our prophets here not speaking as the mouthpieces of Jehovah, of Mweya Mutsvene? Our prophets reveal our sins of killing the land. They act as protectors! Thus, if any of you should come here and fell the trees in this woodlot, the *ngozi* (vengeful spirit) you'll provoke will finish off all your kinsfolk. Then our prophets will no longer prophesy on your behalf. They will refuse because you have felled their friends . . .

The earthkeeping prophet's ministry highlights the relentless combat between Holy Spirit and destroyer. As the people file through the 'gates' to celebrate the eucharist, the intensity of the prophet's emotive glossolalia and body tremors reveals the Spirit's disapproval of the evil which they have perpetrated against creation. Attitudes of arrogance or unconcern for God's creation especially provoke prophetic disapproval, evinced in displays of vehement emotion. These near-frenzied outbursts indicate that grievous sins have been committed against the life-giving Spirit. As in all African healing ceremonies, identification of the cause of the malady is of the utmost importance. Thus the Spirit reveals to the prophet the unconfessed and still hidden sins of each communicant, preventing the mass confession from deteriorating into a generalised, face-saving exercise. When tempers flare and people remonstrate with the prophets, this is considered evidence of the destroyer's resistance. It is in the detection of specific environmental evils committed by each individual and the public admission of guilt that the Holy Spirit's victory over the destroyer is convincingly demonstrated. Such confession, elicited by the Spirit-filled prophet and willingly submitted to by the communicant, represents a kind of purificatory exorcism, a renouncement or expulsion of environmental wizardry.

The sins confessed are numerous: from unwise use of the destructive axe, riverbank cultivation, use of sledges, excessive consumption of firewood, grass burning, neglect of contour ridges, and over-cultivation; to pollution of water resources, over-fishing, hunting rare game species, hunting out of season, hunting in out-of-bounds areas such as the *marambatemwa* or game sanctuaries, and so forth. Still known by the nickname *Mafuranhunzi* (literally 'the one who shoots the fly,' sharpshooter), I often get tripped up by the prophets for my hunting sins in earlier life. In addition I confess to the sin of air pollution through endless use of a vehicle over many years. Maybe through these confessions the Spirit is also pointing to something else—the unequal distribution of means, resources, and privileges in Africa, the gap between rich and poor. Taking a vehicle for granted as a privileged white African while working among the poorest of the poor is certainly as bad a form of wizardry as snaring the few remaining rock-rabbits—the sentinels of the ancestors—in the protected zone of a holy grove.

To the serious earthkeeper spiritual cleansing ensues after the Holy Spirit's expulsion of evil in the process of confession. This process is characterised not only by the prophets' emotional outbursts but also by a mixture of gravity and laughter, since sins are sometimes confessed in highly original ways, or a prophet may use swear words learnt from a white farmer to rebuke an earth-destroying demon. Humour in such instances seldom reflects irreverence. It is rather a lightness of comic relief in an atmosphere heavily charged with divine significance. In the spontaneous bursts of laughter one feels that God is smiling at the antics of his people.

In traditional rituals to exorcise *uroyi* spirits from their hosts the latter have to physically distance themselves from the destructive agent by leading a black goat off into the bush and leaving it there, or by destroying witchcraft medicines on the bank of a river and then swimming across, away from evil. In the Spirit-type AICs *uroyi* exorcisms also include public burning of all medicines and symbolic objects associated with wizardry, such as witch familiars. In the AAEC's battle against environmental evil the prophets have not yet insisted on the burning of destructive axes, sledges or the bows and arrows of poachers. Yet the expulsion of evil through Spirit-induced confession culminates in the communicant picking up of a seedling and moving to the sacramental table for communion in the body of Christ. This act affirms the individual's rejection of earth destruction and signifies a deliberate choice for life itself, acceptance of the Spirit's life-giving directives. Together with the prophets, the communicants now demonstrate their bondedness and friendship with the trees, their acceptance of the responsibility of tree protection.

The actual tree planting subsequent to holy communion puts the seal on the choice for life and light as opposed to death and darkness. Once again the Holy Spirit's liberating power is evinced in a bishop sprinkling holy water and soil in the new woodlot to rid the land of any contamination. The final act of addressing the trees as brothers and sisters as they are being planted epitomises the message of salvation to all creation. The *ngozi* (vengeful spirit) of the neglected soil is appeased by the *mutumbu* payment of trees, and the *muroyi*'s attitude of ruthless exploitation is replaced by genuine service and stewardship. The good news is that the Spirit of life overcomes the destroyer.

THEOLOGICALLY EVALUATING EXORCISM IN AFRICA

When assessing the Spirit-based ministry of exorcism in the church of Africa, a distinction can be made between those church leaders and academic observers who either practise or theoretically support such a ministry, and those who oppose it or are highly critical of its seemingly negative implications. The former (e.g., Ingenoza 1985:179; Hebga, in Lagerwerf 1985:67; Milingo 1984:103; Taylor 1963:211; Daneel 1974:343–347) emphasise the liberating value of a ministry which appears to confront the existential needs and fears of people in a ritually understandable and therefore psychologically and religiously satisfying manner. The latter, whose views I outline below, are sceptical of the long-term impact of a practice which is considered counterproductive, in that it reinforces the traditional cosmology and therefore enslaves people to the world of demons, wizardry beliefs and fears without providing a realistic Christian solution. The obvious question is: does the AAEC prophets' concern with environmental *uroyi* fall into this trap?

Shorter's (1985:95) reservations about exorcism as a pastoral tool in the church of Africa are closely linked with his views on the destructive impact of witchcraft theory and practice on African society:

> Witchcraft is a kind of penumbra of human wickedness, an inborn preternatural power to harm and kill enjoyed for its own sake. To see all the misfortune, especially the more dramatic disasters, as traceable to human causes is intellectually satisfying. It also creates an illusion of control over evil forces, but ultimately it is not credible . . . It entails unjust judgements.

Shorter (1985:96) is particularly concerned about the illusory control over evil, the injustice of witchcraft accusations and the witch-finder's pretence of finally judging the witch. Witchcraft accusation, in his view, is a form of self-salvation or self-justification, a mechanism for evading personal responsibility for misfortune and sinful acts, at the expense of whoever is branded the common enemy of the community. Witch-finders usurp the position of God by acting as both judges and executioners. Their accusations destroy the social personality of the accused. By implication all witchcraft-eradication movements, through their very inclusion of witch-finding and accusation practices, only strengthen people's fear of witches and their acceptance of the underlying theory. They provide no viable solution or true liberation from an oppressive belief system.

Exorcism, in its popularised form in the church of Africa, can include traditional aspects of witch-finding and accusations and may lead to indiscriminate attribution of misfortunes to evil forces, and hence to intensified exorcism procedures. Consequently it can lead to horrors similar to the European witch hunts. Shorter's misgivings on this score are therefore understandable. He reminds us that although Christ practised exorcism in the case of epileptics, he did not attribute every affliction to diabolic possession. Likewise, it would be wrong for the priest-exorcist to try and win over fellow believers to his views of demon possession—a terrible prospect, considering the historical background of European demonology. Instead, Shorter (in Lagerwerf 1987:58) feels that the church should develop a more original and enduring ministry:

> We should discourage interest in the spectacle of exorcism and dissociated personality in the normal context of healing and prayer over the sick. For the Christian African the world must be alive in a new sense, not with the self-orientated, depersonalizing theories of African tradition, but with the knowledge that 'the world is charged with the grandeur of God' and that all natural human realities are communications of divine love and salvation in Jesus Christ.

Without totally rejecting exorcism, Shorter suggests that the solution to wizardry should be sought in alternative measures: first, refusal to enter into discussion about the objectivity of wizardry beliefs; second, conscious relinquishment of the dualistic philosophy underlying wizardry beliefs; and third, transformation of the social world through socioeconomic development and Christian community building—that is, the creation of a setting which will dispel wizardry-related fears.

David Bosch distinguishes between two different approaches to the combating of wizardry. The first essentially accepts the African traditional interpretive framework, while the second insists on changing this framework, in other words, on switching to a new paradigm. Like Shorter and Singleton (1980:23), Bosch (1987:52–60) opts for the second approach. He also refers to Andrew Walls's (1982:97–99) distinction: the first approach is based on the indigenisation principle, in which the Christian faith is incarnated in a particular culture; the second rests on the pilgrim principle, through which God in Christ transforms culture. Of course, one might ask whether these principles should be interpreted as mutually exclusive. Incarnation as envisaged by the indigenisation principle in fact includes Christ's transformation of culture. In practice at least, indigenisation seldom involves a straight-forward and passive adaptation of the Christian faith to the indigenous culture. It seems to me, therefore, that we have here two principles displaying different emphases rather than an absolute antithesis.

This point is not sufficiently recognised in the categorical theoretical distinctions between the two. Bosch, for instance, classifies both the confession of witchcraft practices (described with reference to the *Shinga Postora* movement, Daneel 1974:267f) and exorcism (mainly with reference to Milingo's ministry) as belonging to the first approach. Thus the impression is created that these practices merely accept and strengthen the traditional cosmology and make no real contribution to a final solution, a paradigm shift. What is not sufficiently considered is the possibility that exorcism—and not only Milingo's kind of exorcism along European demonological lines, but also the AIC ministry—may change the traditional worldview; that exorcism in its varied manifestations in Africa may be instrumental in bringing about a paradigm shift.

What, according to Bosch, are the requirements for a paradigm shift? Firstly, Christians should help their community rid itself of the scapegoat theory by invoking the message of Christ, the one true 'scapegoat' who carried away the sins of this world once and for all. Secondly, Christian teaching should emphasise the co-responsibility of all individuals for what goes wrong in society, lest the tendency to blame a wizard for misfortune encourages a superficial understanding of conversion. Thirdly, a new understanding of human suffering should be fostered in order to change the philosophy which links suffering with evil and consequently imputes the practice of wizardry to the misdeeds of others. Fourth, a fundamental change in attitude towards magic is required. Healing, reconciliation and mutual service should replace the tracing and elimination of alleged human causes of misfortune. Fifth, the Christian message should be proclaimed to the effect that evil has no future. The future lies with God. Satan and all manifestations of evil can therefore only be seen as conquered in advance by God. In this respect Bosch (1987:58–59) indicates that the church in Africa has not always managed to communicate the message of an ever-present God. The more remote God appears to be, the greater the need for magic to counteract the destructive forces of evil.

Although I agree with these requirements for a paradigm shift, the question remains how one is to convey this message effectively to a society which still by and large applies the scapegoat theory, where the belief in magic is still rife and where one is constantly confronted with outcasts, misfits and marginal figures— those already accused and stigmatised, in search of a cure or a lasting solution. What do you do with the afflicted members of families who for many generations have had a tradition of inherited wizardry? When such individuals fall ill and have dreams which are interpreted by society as call-dreams to perpetrate wizardry, they are at once stigmatised in their neighbourhood. In their appeal to the church for a solution, do we avoid talking about the objective reality of wizardry as it features in their lives for fear of giving credence to such beliefs, as Shorter would have it? Or do we confront those beliefs with the message of the one Scapegoat, Christ, and exorcise the invading spirits as part of the solution to a tradition-based problem, despite the risk of misinterpretation in certain quarters?

As regards the prophetic exorcist activities of the AICs, I have pointed out that to many adherents of the Spirit-type churches exorcism symbolises the liberating and protective function of the church, the victory of the Holy Spirit over Satan. The built-in safeguards against possible misinterpretation of this ministry were described as follows:

> The ritual context within which exorcism takes place is quite different from that within which the *nganga* (the traditional 'doctor' or 'exorcist') operates. Here we have a group of people professing to be Christians who dance and sing Christian songs in the expectation of a manifestation of the Christian God's delivering power. The act of driving out the inhabiting and unwanted spirit is usually performed in the name of the triune Christian God, with special emphasis on the presence of the Holy Spirit evinced in emotionalism and speaking-in-tongues. Prophets generally recognise that the act of expulsion does not imply a self-willed manipulation of divine power and that God himself is the final authority who decides whether their dramatised and symbolic action will be successful. Some of them admit failure, often with reference to God who willed otherwise. Then there is also the accompanying pastoral care and the insistence of prophets that afflicted persons themselves should pray perseveringly to be rid of troubling spirits. Thus we have a group-integrated technique with interaction between participant congregation, exorcising prophet and praying patient—all of them in action before and depending on the great Deliverer of evil powers. This is a far cry from manipulative magic, had such ministry evolved from a non-transformatory application of the *indigenisation principle* (Daneel 1974:342).

Because of these decidedly positive features of a contextualised pneumatology integral to prophetic exorcism, as well as a continual need for pastoral care in the face of the high incidence of spirit possession observed among the Shona, I support J. V. Taylor's (1963:211) call for 'the development of some properly safeguarded ministry of exorcism' in the church of Africa.

In the field of wizardry I have pointed out weaknesses of the prophetic ministry of medicine-finding, wizard-detection, and the exorcism of *uroyi* spirits. Some prophets, for instance, concentrate on the recruitment value of these services to such an extent that they neglect pastoral care of their flock. Others exploit the fears of people who feel threatened by the powers of wizardry. In some cases the discrimination and stigmatisation caused by exposure of potential or practising witches override the Christian spirit of love and sympathetic understanding, with detrimental effects for the social status particularly of the women concerned.

It was felt, however, that the positive features of the prophetic campaign against wizardry practices preponderate, in that the message of God's protection and liberation is convincingly carried into a realm frequently dominated by stark terror. The Christian message of reconciliation, moreover, conveyed to the wizards—the outcasts and misfits of society—in a manner which provides, through the church, new hope of social rehabilitation. This is in direct opposition to traditional belief: once a wizard always a wizard—which assumes the incontrovertibly evil nature of whoever is branded a witch or sorcerer in African society (Daneel 1974:343–347).

If we finally evaluate the significance of the AAEC's concern with environmental wizardry with due regard to Shorter's and Bosch's reservations about witchcraft beliefs and accusations and their insistence on a paradigm shift, the following observations appear relevant.

First, the AAEC prophets do not deliberately avoid discussing the objectivity of witchcraft beliefs, nor do they refute the dualistic cosmology underlying wizardry beliefs (Shorter). Most of them adhere to a culture and cosmology which experience wizardry as an existential reality, an evil to be dealt with from within Christianity. In this respect they represent the indigenisation principle (Bosch, Walls) but not in a manner that excludes Christian transformation.

Second, the earthkeeping prophets do in fact transform the social world through a type of Christian community building (Shorter), which provides reconciliation for the stigmatised wizard in the midst of a body of believers who know about understanding and forgiveness. In addition, accusations of earth destruction are followed by an entirely new and innovative ritual in which exorcism means an opportunity for the guilty to engage meaningfully in earth-care, the antithesis of *uroyi* against the soil. Hence, the indigenisation principle is augmented with the pilgrim principle, for it is through the power of the Holy Spirit, illuminating the lordship of Christ the saviour and earthkeeper, that the hold of self-seeking *uroyi* is broken.

Third, prophetic detection of environmental *uroyi* during the public confession of sins is not accompanied by an 'illusion of control over evil' (Shorter). The prophets know only too well that human sinfulness and greed will persist in this existence, that they will continue detecting ecological sins at *maporesanyika* ceremonies. This does not detract, however, from their proclamation of the message that 'evil has no future, the future lies with God' (Bosch).

Fourth, in the context of tree planting, *uroyi* accusations take the form of prophetic detection of a common evil rather than putting all the blame on one or a couple of scapegoats. Thus *uroyi* beliefs become a platform for convincingly proclaiming the seriousness of environmental offences without the 'witch-finders' professing to pass final judgment on ecological wizards or of establishing a form of self-salvation (Shorter). Instead of creating a convenient escape from personal guilt and environmental sinfulness, both preachers and prophets tend to identify with the *uroyi*, thereby teaching co-responsibility of all individuals (Bosch) for the abuse of God's earth and arriving at a more biblical view of sin than traditional witchcraft allegations allowed.

Fifth, Bosch's requirements for a paradigm shift in terms of a new understanding of human suffering (as not necessarily linked to evil perpetrated by humans) and a breakthrough in attitudes to magic, are not entirely fulfilled in the AAEC. Yet by affirming the cross and salvific blood of Christ and accepting common guilt for earth destruction, the scapegoat theory appears to be effectively overcome. The communal 'exorcism' of evil through confession and tree planting in itself signifies transformation of the old belief system and rituals, as well as the beginnings of a paradigm shift.

Sixth, the work of the Holy Spirit is focal in the struggle against environmental evil. Does the African magical mind-set in this instance lead to a distorted pneumatology in the AICs, as some observers have suggested? Martin (1964:161) is a case in point:

In prophetic and messianic movements the prophets and messiahs 'possess the Spirit' like an impersonal power, they get hold of it in their own way, and the 'Spirit' must give utterance in a visible and audible way (glossolaly, trembling, leaps), and not in the hidden manner of the new life in Christ which is the fruit of the Spirit (Gal 5:22f). In the same way as the black messiah must be visible here and now and deliver from suffering, so the Spirit must manifest its power in visible and audible phenomena.

With reference to the Ngunza-Khaki Church, Oosthuizen (1968:124, 133) states:

The Spirit has here become the monopoly of the leader . . . One of the main tasks of the prophets in this movement is to 'give' the Spirit to its members. Just as in animism the spirit is invoked by those entrusted with the task; the spirit is 'given' by man's initiative and not by God's. The central doctrine of the Holy Spirit is obscured and distorted here beyond recognition. The position of the doctrine of the Holy Spirit in a Church indicates whether that Church is standing or falling. In a utilistic religion, such as that of the nativistic movements, 'the Spirit' is at man's disposal.

As the Shona Zionists and Apostles (the majority in the AAEC) belong to the group of movements generally characterised by Oosthuizen as nativistic and by Martin as prophetic, these criticisms also apply to the Shona Spirit-type churches. If so, I would like to point out, as stated above, that there are quite a number of built-in safeguards in AIC prophetic praxis which invalidate or counterbalance charges of an impersonal force, and therefore a false pneumatology. Terms like 'possess,' 'at the disposal of,' and 'giving the Spirit to others' are quite misleading and cannot generally be applied to the pneumatology of the Shona Independent Churches. Despite inconsistencies in their understanding of the nature and work of the Holy Spirit, many prophets have gained sufficient insight into the work of the Holy Spirit, according to biblical norms, to be aware of the danger of misinterpretation.

Judging by the scriptural references to the presence and work of the triune God—particularly the role of Christ as healer and saviour—in *maporesanyika* ceremonies, it appears that the manifestations of the Holy Spirit in the AAEC have definite, healthy Christian connotations, as opposed to animistic and magical ones. The dangers are unmistakable in view of limitations in AIC pneumatology. Yet the Spirit is believed to be the agent casting out environmental evil, sensitising the conscience of all human beings as stewards of the earth, and mobilising the mass action of earthkeeping which originates from Scripture. Does it really matter that our Independent Churches lack formal doctrines? Do any of us Christians fully comprehend the work of the Holy Spirit? Maybe it is better to feel inspired by the Spirit and engage in earth-healing praxis than to formulate a perfect pneumatology and shout the odds from the sidelines while passively allowing the environment to deteriorate. The Holy Spirit moves where it wills!

CHAPTER 12

Current Developments and Future Challenges for ZIRRCON

EXPANDING ORGANISATION AND ENVIRONMENTAL OBJECTIVES

Over the years ZIRRCON has developed from the loosely knit movement described in part 1 (see also Daneel 1998) to a stable institution with its headquarters and administrative centre in Masvingo town and its grassroots constituency spread widely throughout Masvingo province and some adjacent provinces. Its environmental vision and activities have expanded, partly as a result of developmental projects, youth work, and women's clubs, and partly by linking environmental endeavour with income-generating projects. Having focused thus far on the ritualisation of earthkeeping and the concomitant theological developments, I shall now outline ZIRRCON's institutionalisation and expanding objectives.

INSTITUTIONALISATION AND SPECIALISED ACTIVITIES

Organisation and Leadership

ZIRRCON's basic team of about fifteen officers operates from the administrative headquarters in Masvingo town. They are supported by some thirty nursery keepers stationed at nurseries located in the various districts of Masvingo Province. Thus the movement has a nucleus of more than forty salaried employees. The main organs through which it operates are AZTREC (the majority of chiefs, headmen, and spirit-mediums in Masvingo Province), the AAEC (150 affiliated AICs with an estimated total membership of two million people), the Women's Desk (eighty women's clubs), and some thirty youth clubs at rural and urban schools.

One of the most important changes in ZIRRCON's leadership hierarchy in the course of 1994 was the election of Rev. Solomon Zvanaka to succeed me as director. This was necessary, partly because I could not do justice to all the responsibilities of the directorship on top of my academic duties at the University of South Africa, and partly because I believe—on the basis of missiological principles of church planting—that a black African movement of this nature should become self-supporting, self-propagating, self-governing, and should generate its own theology while still accommodating a privileged white African participant. The fact that Rev. Zvanaka was elected unanimously by the ZIRRCON executive—which includes AZTREC and AAEC representatives—indicates the status and respect he had already gained among his colleagues at that time.

The change in leadership does not mean that I have withdrawn from the movement. On the contrary! Now that I am relieved of administrative duties I am in a position to pay more attention to other aspects of our work. Having established the initial ties with donor agencies as founder of the movement and chief fundraiser, I hope to continue for some time to chair ZIRRCON Trust, the board of trustees. This will enable me to explore new sources of sponsorship for ZIRRCON and to support the director in consolidating the existing system of financial control and accounting.

Departmental Development

ZIRRCON's original headquarters was my house in Masvingo town, where executive meetings and consultations with key figures in the movement are still held. Recently constructed outbuildings provide office space for research workers and contain a veritable archive of field research data which I have collected over the past thirty years. The combination of my library and ZIRRCON's research centre should provide a resource base for AIC theologians interested in studying and developing the theologies and general concerns of their churches.

But the administrative demands of our growing movement far exceed the space I can provide. Hence ZIRRCON has recently purchased a house in the centre of town to provide office space for its expanding departments and desks. Several additional offices will be constructed behind the main house to meet the growing need for space. Ideally, if funds can be raised, a new centre with administrative, library, teaching, conference, and accommodation facilities should be erected.

There are no rigid distinctions between ZIRRCON's departments and desks, and several staff members serve in more than one of these bodies. The working situation, therefore, is fairly fluid without watertight compartmentalisation. However, the general perception of our departments is that they have a greater degree of professionalism because of their qualified members, in the Western sense, than the desks, the latter dealing more directly and regularly with grassroots communities in the field. For instance, the administrative department, via the director and bookkeeper/secretary, takes care of funding, salaries, auditing, and reporting; the research department, under my jurisdiction, creates databases and produces reports and publications based on empirical research; and the training department produces literature for workshops, etc. All these functions are performed or overseen by staff members with the necessary expertise. By contrast, the desk coordinators spend much of their time in the field, initiating and facilitating projects in their respective grassroots constituencies. Here they develop another kind of expertise, derived from field training and growing experience of the activities and needs of rural society. Such experience keeps ZIRRCON headquarters, particularly the more office-bound staff, in touch with rural developments. It permits, for instance, realistic fund-raising drives which increasingly become a joint venture between representatives of administration, departments, and desks.

ZIRRCON's research department has always played a pivotal role in the movement. In fact, the earthkeeping movement grew out of the network of contacts established in the course of my study of the spirituality of *chimurenga*, the liberation struggle. Prominent earthkeepers such as the late Leonard Gono,

Bishop Marinda, and Rev. Zvanaka were all empirical research assistants at one time or another. These close links between researchers and peasant society forged earlier on have facilitated the building of a grassroots organisation.

Through the research department I have been able to further and supervise several academic field studies for degree purposes.[1] Although ZIRRCON is not officially affiliated to any university, the kind of inter-university research service it renders is highlighted by my own participation in conferences and seminars at various universities in Southern Africa and abroad. ZIRRCON's field assistants have enabled me to consistently monitor religio-ecological developments in our movement, as a result of which quite a lot of praxis-related insight was gained and developed into articles for academic journals. This study of African earthkeepers benefits directly from research assistants' regular interviews at both traditional and Christian ecological ceremonies, which are tape-recorded and transcribed.

ZIRRCON's research department also promotes the development of a local AIC theology. Both Rev. Zvanaka and Bishop Marinda were engaged in a major research project called 'African Initiatives in Christian Mission,' sponsored by The Pew Charitable Trusts in Philadelphia, and aimed at producing a comprehensive series on the roles of African Christians in the propagation, growth, and interpretation of Christianity in Africa.

ZIRRCON's academic goals lead to international exposure at university conferences, lectures, and seminars, as well as regular publications on its activities. Its eco-theological goals promote the monitoring of innovations in this field and the development of a written local AIC theology which should eventually enrich more sophisticated, Western-style African theologies. And its praxis-oriented environmental goals facilitate operational planning, training, and implementation of its conservationist projects.

All ZIRRCON's afforestation activities, and its tree-planting ceremonies in particular, involve conscientisation and mobilisation to transform the attitudes and behaviour of grassroots communities towards the environment. The training department, formerly the responsibility of Bishop Marinda, promotes ecological awareness building by way of workshops or seminars. This is a form of non-certificated environmental education aimed at imparting the requisite skills to enable communities to identify, analyse, and solve their own problems. The starting point is to make communities fully aware of their environmental situation; the extent of the crisis (deforestation, wind and water erosion, gully formation, water pollution, siltation of river beds and dams, dwindling wildlife resources, etc.); the causes (unfair land distribution, over-exploitation of natural resources, random bush clearing, poor land husbandry, etc.); and then teach skills to resolve the crisis.

The first two training manuals, which Bishop Marinda wrote in the vernacular, target mainly the AICs and reflect ZIRRCON's religio-ecological interactive emphasis. In his newly published *Theology of the Environment* Marinda combines his own interpretation, in Zionist perspective, of biblical injunctions for earthcare with an exposition of AAEC innovations in environmental liturgies and ethics. His second work, *A Theology of Development*, analyses and assesses environmental exploitation in relation to so-called socioeconomic progress, as well as the implications for grassroots society.

In workshops the teaching blends eco-theological insight with practical instruction, such as the planting of various tree varieties for commercial, fuelwood, carpentry, and other purposes, the use of *vetiver* grass as a substitute for contour ridges and for gully reclamation, and so forth. Workshops tend to integrate ZIRRCON's liberationist ideologies and mobilisation strategies with the environmental practicalities propagated by the departments of Forestry, Natural Resources, Parks and Wildlife, and Agritex. Representatives of these bodies participate in workshops, so that ecological experts encounter traditionalist and Christian commitment. Workshops sometimes differentiate between and at other times combine AZTREC and the AAEC. Thus they also help to promote solidarity between chiefs and church leaders in the war of the trees. The two groups participate together enthusiastically and are themselves increasingly emphasising their unity of purpose and earthkeeping commitment at all levels. Once the women's clubs become more active in environmental education, as requested and planned, a broad spectrum of rural African society will receive regular instruction.

ZIRRCON's ecological department is in charge of the main thrust of the entire movement, namely earthkeeping, so far primarily by way of afforestation programmes. In a sense, therefore, the ecological department encompasses the whole of ZIRRCON, since all its activities—from funding and administration to research, training, and religious innovation—basically focus on healing and conserving the earth. Everybody works towards this end: researchers monitoring the survival rate of trees; liaison officers recruiting chiefs for AZTREC or new member churches for the AAEC to extend the green army; the coordinator of the Women's Desk teaching nature conservation to women as part of their income-generating projects; temporary workers from abroad involved in nursery keeping, nursery expansion, and the cultivation of new tree species; the executive director and senior consultant planning new fund-raising strategies, drafting budgets, and promoting public relations or media exposure.

Women's, Youth, and Development Desks

Women's Desk
Appreciative of the significant role which women were playing as earthkeepers and aware that they constitute the majority of participants at virtually all earth-keeping ceremonies (up to 80 percent of all adult AIC members are women!), the ZIRRCON executive—in consultation with leading women in African society—decided to promote their cause, not only in earth healing but also with a view to improving their general socioeconomic status. In September 1993 ZIRRCON's Women's Desk was officially established. Raviro Mutonga, former research assistant, was appointed as its coordinator. As with AZTREC and the AAEC, a constitution was drafted for the WD, an executive committee was put in charge of its programmes, and regular annual general conferences are held.

Under the able leadership of Ms. Mutonga and a number of enterprising women leaders some forty women's clubs were formed in the course of 1994. By the end of 1997 more than seventy clubs had officially registered with the WD and the numbers keep escalating, despite the fact that the facility ZIRRCON offers can barely cope with the needs and drive of its current members. On average a women's club consists of thirty to forty members. Affiliation is less strictly determined by religious identity than in the case of AZTREC and the AAEC. Nevertheless, a kind of natural ecumenism emerges in some clubs where *Ruwadzano* (Mothers' Union) leaders from one or several churches—either AIC or mainline mission or a combination of both—decide on the religious nature of ecological ceremonies. In clubs where the wives of kraalheads or headmen play a prominent role, traditionalist *mafukidzanyika* (earth-clothing) ceremonies are held, with ritual offerings of beer and ancestral addresses.

As ecological performance is a condition for any club to receive financial aid from the WD, a considerable amount of work has been generated in this field since the inception of the new desk. During the first two years several full-fledged and satellite nurseries were established; twenty-two woodlots were developed and, because of the pride the women take in their aftercare, they generally have a far higher survival rate of trees than ZIRRCON has achieved so far. In addition to stepping up the war of the trees by setting an example and taking on challenges themselves, the women's clubs have taken the initiative in approaching schools and activating school communities to engage in new environmental ventures. Having composed their own slogans and songs, the women also emerged as an increasingly well organised component at AZTREC and the AAEC tree-planting ceremonies. Their slogan '*Zvose, zvose, Women's Desk!*' (All! All! Women's Desk) not only suggests that united action will produce abundance but that where there is a will, anything and everything is possible.

Far from signalling wishful thinking, these slogans reflect actual accomplishment in a variety of self-help income-generating projects. To date quite a number of sewing, bakery, soap-making, gardening, poultry-keeping, goat-keeping, bee-keeping, and nursery (or satellite nursery) projects have been launched by various clubs. Significantly, these clubs have raised considerable sums of money themselves to initiate or forge ahead with their own projects, independent of outside support. Funds for larger projects will, of course, be raised in the future. In cooperation with the ZIRRCON executive, Ms. Mutonga has completed several project funding applications for the consideration of Plan International, the German Development Service, the Japanese Embassy, and other donor agencies. But the women are setting a trend of independent endeavour, inspiring ZIRRCON generally to strive for greater self-support than in the past.

In its conscientisation programme the WD collaborates with the training department through joint workshops for both genders. Ms. Mutonga also conducts regional workshops, in which clubs in particular districts participate. She has been focusing on subjects like development and women's leadership, institution building, environmental rehabilitation, and income-generating activities such as poultry, bee-keeping, and clothing manufacture.

In the emergent histories of individual women's clubs lie the measure of their societal impact and success. I mention one example in passing. Ms. Gwamure of Chivi district, during a severe drought, formed the *Nzara imhandu* (Hunger is the

Enemy) committee to help women contend with the serious problem of dwindling food resources. She insisted that members contribute their own money to establish the *Takabatana* ('We are united') bakery. Simultaneously she encouraged her club friends to start their own nursery, where they cultivated 5,000 seedlings to start with. From the proceeds of both nursery and bakery the club members managed to supply their families with food and to expand their club work. Subsequently Ms. Gwamure introduced ZIRRCON's activities to the Zunga school. As a result, pupils and teachers, together with the women's club, embarked on tree planting and related conservationist work. This escalated as surrounding village communities started planting orchards and small woodlots with seedlings purchased from the women's club. Thus Ms. Gwamure's inspired leadership, supported by ZIRRCON, has launched a new cycle of environmental rehabilitation in her own locality, as well as providing a mechanism for women to cope with poverty and famine.

Youth Desk
Over the years ZIRRCON has consistently striven to relate to school communities and activate them to engage in earthkeeping. Schools have been supplied with seedlings to plant their own orchards and/or woodlots; some have been assisted to establish their own nurseries; interschool competitions have been held in the field of progressive conservationist work; school children collect seeds for ZIRRCON's nurseries; and they usually take an active part in ZIRRCON's traditionalist *mafukidzanyika* and Christian *maporesanyika* ceremonies, providing conscientising entertainment in the form of choir singing, recitals of poetry, theatrical presentations, and the like, all on green themes and produced by the pupils themselves.

In recent years thirty youth clubs have been formed at schools in the vicinity of Masvingo town. Two ZIRRCON youth officers stay in regular touch with the teachers and students involved in each club. The youth clubs have developed their own satellite nurseries and planted trees in indigenous and eucalyptus woodlots and/or orchards at their schools. Nature study and tree-identification programs have been introduced. In addition, visits to game parks are undertaken to familiarize students with a wide variety of game species, most of which they have never seen in the communal lands where they grew up.

Development Desk
Since the inception of ZIRRCON and its sister organisations, the chiefs and bishops have requested support for income-generating development projects to improve their standard of living. They associate me, the founder of the *Fambidzano* ecumenical movement, with the community development, sewing, clothing manufacture, carpentry, agricultural, water development, and other schemes for AICs which I supervised and raised funds for in the past (Daneel 1989). Having seen the detrimental impact of *Fambidzano*'s development work on its originally focal theological training programme, I was aware of the risk of being distracted from ZIRRCON's basic environmental drive. Consequently I tended to resist this trend, although I understood and sympathised with the economic hardships many of the AZTREC and AAEC

members were enduring. For nearly a decade I kept insisting that environmental rehabilitation was, first and foremost, our overriding concern and I confined ZIRRCON fund-raising to this task. In addition, it was always clearly stipulated that a convincing record of solid involvement in ZIRRCON's war of the trees would be a condition for development aid once we had created the institutional framework to provide it. In other words, ZIRRCON was not prepared to introduce economic development programmes independently of earthkeeping as an end in itself.

The Women's Desk has turned out to be a trend setter in this respect. In the affiliated clubs ecology and commercial enterprise clearly interrelate on the lines indicated above. Now that this example has been set and the ecological identity of the movement has been safely and solidly established over nearly a decade, the creation of a development desk appears appropriate. For some time, Mr. Mabhena—formerly employed as senior development officer at *Fambidzano*—was appointed by ZIRRCON for a trial period to establish the envisaged desk. His mandate included the identification of AZTREC and AAEC development projects, conducting feasibility studies on site, writing up project proposals and, together with our managing director, engaging in fund-raising. It was agreed that Mabhena's success in this last task would determine the viability of the development desk and the continuity of his own salary.

ENVIRONMENTAL CONCERNS

Reforestation

The hub of ZIRRCON's war of the trees has all along has been its ten nurseries: Nemanwa, Chivi, Mtirikwe, Nyika, Nyajena, Chinyabako, Muuyu, Muchakata, Nyamakondo, and Zimuto (the last two being WD projects). Despite the black frost which wiped out hundreds of thousands of seedlings in our nurseries in the course of 1994 and 1995, more than three million tree seedlings have been successfully cultivated and distributed for planting over the past nine years. Each nursery, run by two regular nursery keepers and occasional casual labour, aims at cultivating at least 50,000 seedlings annually; some of them achieve a total of up to 70,000 seedlings when seed collection, water supply, and other conditions are favourable. New nurseries are being developed in Gutu, Mwenezi, and Chiredzi districts so as to cover the whole of Masvingo Province. Within the next few years we hope to run some twenty nurseries. A much-discussed goal in the war of the trees is to cultivate a minimum of one million tree seedlings annually. We will need to produce even larger numbers if we want to actually plant a million trees each year. Experience has taught us that some indigenous species like red mahogany need to stay in the nurseries for two or more years to secure reasonable survival rates in woodlots. In other words, there is a discrepancy between the number of seedlings cultivated and the trees planted in any particular year.

ZIRRCON has planted some six million trees in well over 3,000 woodlots spread throughout Masvingo Province, as well as in the provinces of Manicaland and Matabeleland where there are respectively ten and twenty member churches of the AAEC. There is no accurate count of woodlots at this stage, since nursery keepers have not kept records of orchards and small woodlots comprising only a cluster of blue gum or indigenous trees belonging to individuals or families. Even some of the larger woodlots planted during the late 1980s were not recorded, a situation which will hopefully be remedied by our monitoring team. It is unlikely that we will be able to keep track of all the small orchards and individual wood-lots consisting of ten to one hundred trees from our nurseries, but eventually all the larger woodlots containing several hundred or a few thousand trees should be accounted for. To my knowledge, the largest ZIRRCON woodlot, in the Gutu communal lands, contains 8,000 trees. The unavailability of large tracts of land in the communal lands and the problems which are bound to arise over maintenance and ownership have deterred us from seriously considering the establishment of large plantations.

ZIRRCON woodlots are owned either by individuals together with members of their extended households, or by larger communities such as the inhabitants of one or a cluster of villages (usually under the leadership of a chief, headman, spirit-medium, or a prominent traditionalist, if the tree planting was initiated by AZTREC); a congregation or church (AAEC); a school; or a women's club. In most cases ownership is collective. Special committees are sometimes appointed by the group concerned to undertake aftercare such as watering trees and pest control, maintaining fences, and preventing tree felling when the trees mature. In areas where goats or cattle are a threat, committee members are known to have drawn up a rota to ensure round-the-clock protection of the woodlot. Some tradi-tionalist male elders engaged in night duty claim to rely on the guidance and pro-tective powers of the guardian ancestors of their region. Representatives of col-laborating agencies such as the departments of Forestry, Agritex, and Natural Resources pay the owners of woodlots field visits to help them with post-planting care and other technical advice.

Collective ownership normally makes for fair play and equal distribution within the community when blue gum woodlots are harvested for building and carpentry materials or for commercial purposes. ZIRRCON's executive acts mainly in an advisory capacity concerning the use of trees from its nurseries. It will most likely involve itself directly in the use of woodlot trees only in cases of obvious environmental abuse or unfair commercial exploitation by individuals at the expense of the community.

Survival rates of trees have always caused ZIRRCON headaches. On the whole, blue gum trees have a survival rate of 80 to 90 per cent even during droughts. Yet we have deliberately held back on blue gum production to keep it to an estimated 20 per cent of our total nursery yield, since blue gums are known to have a negative impact on underground water resources. Besides, the concern about dwindling forests of indigenous trees, coupled with ZIRRCON's reli-giously inspired motivation to restore something of the old order in nature, caused a conscious preference for the cultivation of indigenous trees. This choice, how-ever, entails numerous problems because indigenous trees either are slow growers or require special conditions (soil types, altitude, frost or heat, state of seedlings in terms of the size of stems, taproot development, etc.) to achieve a reasonable survival rate.

It was possible, for example, to successfully cultivate such species as the *msasa* and *mutondo* acacia, *mudziavashe* ('toilet paper tree,' for firewood), *mukamba* (red mahogany), *mukurumbira* (kiaat), and virtually all types of wild fruit trees in our nurseries. Yet the results of planting these trees in woodlots or existing forests proved much less predictable and the survival rate much lower than was the case with blue gum, tipuana tip, leucaena, and other exotic species. Part of the problem has always been that we have to proceed by way of trial and error as there are relatively few experts in the growing of indigenous trees in the country, even in the Forestry Commission. It was found, for instance, that *msasa* and *mutondo* stood little chance of survival if planted in the open, however favourable the soil and water conditions. Apparently these seedlings stand a better chance of maturing when planted on the fringes of existing *msasa* and *mutondo* forests. But even this hypothesis has not yet been fully proved by our tree planters. The *mubvumira* (wild seringa) grows well in woodlots but has hardly any commercial value. In deference to the ancestors, traditionalists nevertheless take pride in caring for these trees. The *mudziavashe* presents its own mystery. Since it is easy to cultivate in nurseries, we initially planted hundreds of these trees in several woodlots in varying conditions and took special care to water them. Yet the survival rate of this tree, highly rated as excellent firewood, was so poor that we stopped cultivating it in our nurseries. We found the *mukamba* (red mahogany) an excellent, if slow, grower. Yet it is so vulnerable to frost that it is preferable to plant this species, like the mopane tree, in the lowveld and not in the higher regions surrounding Masvingo. Both red mahogany and kiaat are slow growers but, being the country's finest hardwood, they have increasing commercial value. It is therefore gratifying to see village elders plant them as an investment for coming generations.

Wildlife

Elsewhere I have discussed the prospect of ZIRRCON converting some of the existing holy groves (*marambatemwa*) in the communal lands into game sanctuaries (Daneel 1998:219–224). I argued that, in view of the traditional religious sanction underlying all customary conservation laws and the continuing significance of holy groves as geographical symbols of abundant wildlife which these laws were designed to preserve, the *marambatemwa* provide ideal launching pads for the reintroduction of game in the communal lands. The scheme has great appeal for tribal elders, as discussions out in the communal lands during feasibility studies and at annual general conferences have disclosed. These game sanctuaries will differ from commercial game farms in that less land is available, implying smaller game populations. Yet through the empowerment of traditional elders and rural council members via the initiating agency, ZIRRCON, such a game restocking exercise will be an essentially African community enterprise, based on reconsideration, adaptation, and implementation of traditional conservationist codes. It is conceivable, for instance, that anti-poaching and anti-snaring measures could be effectively applied in sacred game sanctuaries because of the persistent belief in the mystical protection of the ancestors. The chiefs and mediums of AZTREC are bound to declare imported game the 'property' of the *midzimu*. If initial experiments with small game such as rabbits, steenbok, duiker, reedbuck, and impala prove successful, one could consider the reintroduction of threatened species such as pangolin and klipspringer. The latter is a small buck which should thrive in the mountainous terrain of holy groves, especially Mount Rasa (see Daneel 1998:224). One could also consider introducing bird species like guineafowl, pheasant, duck and geese, which in some areas are becoming increasingly rare. Controlled bird hunting by tribespeople in the immediate vicinity of game sanctuaries will enable them to benefit directly from ZIRRCON's wildlife projects and give new flocks of birds a chance to establish themselves and breed regularly in protected zones.

In recent years ZIRRCON engaged in the planning of two major conservancy schemes: a part of 1,000 acres in Gutu South, situated in the Mupata gravite hills and called *Ngururu* ('Klipspringer') Game Sanctuary, and Masvingo East Game Conservancy, encompassing some fifteen commercial farms, some of which border the Kyle National Game Park. The former project aims at preserving small game, especially klipspringer, in an area ideally suited for them. Local communities and members of Gutu's district council will share responsibility with ZIRRCON for the implementation of this venture. The latter project aims at the conservation of plains' game and bird life as a basis for eco-tourism: photographic, game-viewing, bird-watching, and fishing safaris. During numerous meetings at my house in Masvingo town, black, white, and Indian farmers agreed to collaborate in this conservancy as a reconciliatory undertaking. Unfortunately the farm invasions of the year 2000, accompanied by economic and political destabilization, caused ZIRRCON to place its entire Wildlife program on hold.

Water Resources

ZIRRCON has not yet launched into concerted action in the field of water resources to the same extent that it has done in afforestation. Nevertheless the importance of water as the substance of life, and hence of good rains as a prerequisite for successful tree planting, has made rural people at both *mafukidzanyika* and *maporesanyika* ceremonies more aware of the actual state of the water resources they depend on in their immediate vicinity and the vital need to protect these resources. AZTREC's annual pilgrimage to the oracular shrine at Matonjeni has also served to motivate chiefs and mediums to take greater responsibility in this regard back in their home districts. Consequently these tribal elders are increasingly introducing control systems to combat riverbank cultivation, while the mediums police the remaining fountains, pools, and rivulets, still considered to be inhabited by the environment-friendly *njuzu* spirits, to stop pollution. These activities reflect an emerging ethic which stigmatises water pollution, like wanton tree felling, as a form of wizardry (*uroyi*), punishable by fines or withdrawal of land-holding rights. Such accusations—similar to those directed against collaborators with the Rhodesian administration during *chimurenga*—are a sure sign that the traditional custodians of the land are existentially committed to the green struggle.

ZIRRCON's other awareness-building activities relating to water include teaching (by both the training department and Women's Desk) on subjects such as the causes of river and dam siltation, water pollution, water conservation, use of underground water resources, and possible causes of changing weather patterns, as well as the provision of seedlings and grass for gully reclamation and new water schemes. I have, moreover, made several proposals, both orally and in writing, for future water projects.

ASSESSING ZIRRCON'S RELIGIO-ENVIRONMENTAL CONTRIBUTION

Compared to the immensity of environmental problems facing humankind all over the world, ZIRRCON's contribution is but a drop in the ocean. Even if it achieves its current goals of planting one million trees annually, reclaiming numerous gullies, establishing a few wildlife sanctuaries in the communal lands, and successfully protecting some water resources, it will still have done relatively little about the situation in Africa. One should, therefore, be careful not to overrate ZIRRCON's achievements.

However, in the local perspective of rural Masvingo Province, where there was hardly any earthkeeping endeavour prior to the formation of ZIRRCON, its impact has been dramatic. Through institutionalisation ZIRRCON has become a relatively stable organisation which has actually managed to activate and empower grassroots participation in environmental reform. The scale of this participation, its persistence, and the wide range of opportunities created under the umbrella of earthkeeping are unprecedented in our part of the world. It is no mean achievement for an institution to fire the imagination of scores of chiefs, headmen, and mediums and, having empowered them, to take part in their earthkeeping activities over more than a decade. There is also the accomplishment of ecumenically uniting a large number of African Independent Churches and participating in that union, constructed around a new ecological ethic and theology in the face of many humanly understandable pitfalls of ambition, opposition, and possible defections. All that has been achieved despite shoestring budgets, desperate financial straits and uncertainty which hit ZIRRCON staff from time to time. To some extent these were teething problems, for ZIRRCON's sponsorship has stabilised and improved over the years. The point is that it needed the courage and commitment of all ZIRRCON's members to persevere during periods of adversity. Its survival and tenacious sense of purpose under adverse conditions are the measure of ZIRRCON's significance.

ZIRRCON did manage to place environmental concerns fairly and squarely in the liberationist tradition of peasant society. In declaring a war of trees the sentiments and unifying forces of *chimurenga* were resuscitated to give special historical meaning to the struggle of further liberating the agriculturally overtaxed, tired soil. Propagating earth healing by paying tribute to the old heroes who fought white rule and simultaneously creating opportunities for new heroic exploits in the post-Independence struggle largely explains the fascination and staying power of ZIRRCON's cadres of green fighters. There are, no doubt, some pragmatic and exploitive motives in the ranks of ZIRRCON earthkeepers. After all, who in peasant society would not like to capitalise on the availability of fire-wood or building and carpentry materials in accessible woodlots? But it takes much more than mere pragmatism for the same people to persist with afforesta-tion year after year, despite black frost wiping out their seedlings, entire woodlots being ravaged by livestock desperate for grazing, and any number of obstacles. Our movement has indeed applied cool-headed agroeconomic reasoning in wag-ing its war of afforestation. But its long-term durability and success lie in har-nessing the people's love of the land and their willingness to sacrifice and suffer so as to restore what essentially spells home to them.

Psychologically, I consider ZIRRCON's major breakthrough so far to be the switch of rural peasants' attitudes from fatalism and lethargy to new hope and conviction that something can be done to stem the destructive tide of environ-mental deterioration. By motivating and empowering people to implement their own conservationist projects, ZIRRCON has enabled large numbers of peasant families in the communal lands to get a new grip on their destiny and to build a movement of which they can be proud. Through large-scale mobilisation and the creation of regular rallying points where earthkeepers can meet and plan together it is instilling a sense of unity, dignity, strength, and competition in the struggle against the common enemy of earth destruction. Constant reminders at meetings and earthkeeping events that the struggle has just begun are effective deterrents against complacency.

Despite the limited scale of ZIRRCON's earthkeeping contribution and its rela-tive lack of Western ecological expertise, it has managed to strike a healthy balance between instructive conscientisation and earth-healing action. Far from satisfying itself with rousing meetings, conferences, and workshops—valuable and indispen-sable as these may be—the movement went into concerted action from its incep-tion. Thus it has created its own very real myth, embodied in nurseries and wood-lots, on which to build and which in itself provides the example and motivation for continued earth-healing action. ZIRRCON's durability and future growth hinge to a large extent on this combination of convincing action and inspired teaching.

To try and separate ZIRRCON's environmental work from the religio-cultural mould in which all its activities are cast would be to misunderstand the entire movement. The one cannot be assessed without the other. AZTREC and the AAEC have been vehicles of contextualisation, shaping the idiom in which earth-keeping concern is couched. Have these two arms of ZIRRCON really succeeded in setting rural environmental endeavour on a new course, or have they merely de-vised ephemeral gimmicks to attract the masses, the *povo*?

The Traditional Dimension

AZTREC's revitalisation of traditional religion in its quest for responsible earth-care was assessed above. But in view of the close ecumenical cooperation be-tween this movement and the AAEC in the war of the trees, the parallel ritual and conceptual developments in both, and the broad overview attempted in this chap-ter, AZTREC's achievements are outlined here as well.

Significantly, neither of ZIRRCON's religiously inspired green armies has adopted a conquest mentality in regard to the other. Despite minor frictions over project implementation, retention of religious identity and mutual respect have always been the rule. Shared ecological commitment and willingness to seek new ways of jointly combating a common enemy have led to meaningful interfaith exchange and parallel internal innovation in each group, notably the traditionalist earth-clothing (*mafukidzanyika*) and the Christian earth-healing (*maporesanyika*) ceremonies. In both instances communion with the spirit world and/or divinity strengthens spiritual, communal, and ecological resolve.

The most outstanding feature of AZTREC's work is the ability of the traditional custodians of the land to appropriate and revitalise Africa's age-old religio-ecological values in a modern programme of environmental reform. AZTREC has demonstrated convincingly that where the authority of the traditional leaders, the chiefs and the mediums, is still relatively intact they are capable, once motivated and empowered, of mobilising rural society in large-scale environmental programmes. Appropriation and revitalisation of traditional values amount to much more than mere reversion to or revival of an old religious and cultural order. As a result of AZTREC's ecological engagement the spirit guardians of the land are now conceived of as insisting not only on customary ecological laws to preserve the holy groves, but also on a much more aggressive and geographically extensive process of healing and clothing the barren land through reafforestation and related programmes.

How does this traditionalist appropriation of the old religious order, the building on old foundations, introduce innovative change? I mention a few of the most significant examples. First, the *mafukidzanyika* tree-planting ceremonies resemble traditional *mukwerere* rain rituals in their invocation of the guardian ancestors of the land. Yet ancestral demands have changed considerably in that the right-mindedness required for their mediation of abundant rains and good crops involves more than just respect and veneration symbolised by libations and ritual addresses. In the new ritual context the senior ancestors in fact require the living earthkeepers to create the conditions for good rainy seasons, namely ample vegetation, through reafforestation. This is entirely different from the traditional requirement of merely conserving the abundance which nature itself could keep regenerating before overpopulation, land pressure, and deforestation got out of hand. The viability and environmental success of AZTREC lies in 'modernising' this ancestral sanction in an earthkeeping praxis which in some respects transcends traditional conservationist customs without alienating people from their roots.

Second, even the spirit world appears to be regrouping in AZTREC's rendition of the war of the trees. As in the war years, the senior guardian ancestors of chiefdoms and districts are collaborating in the spirit war council (*dare rechimurenga*) presided over by Mwari. This is evident in the geographically more comprehensive representation of spirit hierarchies at tree-planting ceremonies. The involvement of Mwari, the oracular deity, particularly underscores this trend. AZTREC visits to Matonjeni strengthen our traditionalist constituency's awareness that their struggle has national, even universal, implications.

Here too, as in the AICs, the creator God draws close as an insider. His/her immanent presence in nature is emphasised. The dimension of an elite of cult officials mediating on behalf of the entire population and the perception of the traditional Mwari as *Wokumusoro*, the remote one in the skies, are transcended through regular visitations by tree planters—commoners rather than privileged cult messengers (*vanyai*)—who draw Mwari into the fray of afforestation.

In the third place, traditional perceptions of evil are imaginatively applied to environmental destruction in an indigenous ethos aimed at ecological repair. The will of traditional authorities in AZTREC to take drastic measures against environmental trespassers—as also happens in the AAEC—surfaces in the stigmatising of such offenders as *varoyi venyika* ('wizards of the land'). Customary law has always allowed for punishment of *varoyi* because of the threat they pose to the wellbeing of people and thus of society. Branding wanton tree fellers and cultivators of riverbanks *varoyi* is creating a situation in which transgressors of the emerging green ethos can be effectively disciplined.

AZTREC's traditionalist model of earthkeeping is certainly worth considering for the development of inculturated environmental strategies elsewhere in Africa. It enables traditional authorities to harness African cosmologies and worldviews for lasting ecological action. In terms of mobilising grassroots communities in afforestation programmes, AZTREC has achieved what the Forestry Commission of Zimbabwe, by its own admission, has not been able to do, despite its greater financial stability, salaried staff, and other resources. In my view AZTREC convincingly illustrates that the institution of chieftainship, including spirit-mediumship, is capable of orchestrating comprehensive environmental reform in Africa. For the chiefs and mediums to contribute their own ecological creativity, they need a platform, organisationally and financially independent of government and environmental institutions.

The Christian Dimension

In the formation and expansion of the AAEC the AICs have amply demonstrated their commitment to ecumenical interaction, their willingness to form a united front so as to give clout to their earthkeeping mission. The ecclesiastic union existing today reflects a communal understanding that unity in Christ is not an end in itself but acquires meaning and purpose when it manifests in specific witness to the world (Jn 17:21, 23)—in this instance that Christ's salvific work includes the liberation and wellbeing of *all* creation. Christian unity becomes meaningful in the AAEC where service is rendered to fellow human beings and to the environment, where members of many churches sense that when they act together as co-workers of God the creator, Christ the saviour and earthkeeper, and the Holy Spirit, the source of life and architect of all earth-healing activity, the boundaries of church-ism are transcended. Ecumenism is evident in joint confessions of ecological abuse, in prophets of different churches prophesying in the Spirit on behalf of one creation, in healing hands of all denominations placing new life and hope in the soil of the one creator, in dancing feet below billowing garments in the colours of diverse church orders obeying one rhythm of celebration in the Lord.

That is when denominationalism, that 'scandal to the world and a sin before God' (Messer 1992:23), is overcome.

In the planning stage AAEC ecumenism may have been intended as ecclesiastic unity for the sake of earthkeeping. In practice, however, the process is two-way. AIC unity indeed facilitates wide-reaching and effective afforestation, but earthkeeping programmes in the field in their turn feed and reinforce AIC ecumenism and spirituality. To the extent that earthkeeping in nurseries and woodlots requires sustained commitment—often across boundaries of religious differentiation—there is a constant challenge to unity of purpose and action, one which goes way beyond the more fashionable, and probably more easily achieved, religious unity at occasional ceremonies. In the earthkeeping process of communal living—*in* the nurseries, *in* the woodlots, *in* the ZIRRCON offices, *in* conference halls, etc.—new and exacting patterns of day-to-day interaction emerge. In such interaction the role players, representing both religious pluriformity and unity, become icons of a twofold ecumenism within the green struggle: that between Christian churches and, more broadly, between all participant religions, Christian and non-Christian.

As an ecumenical body the AAEC is distinguished by three remarkable achievements. First, it empowers its member churches to develop an earthkeeping ministry, with practical implications both for environmental reform and for theological growth. Second, the AAEC as an institution which stimulates regular and intensive interaction breaks through the kind of isolation which some of these churches experience as a result of their geographic remoteness from the country's highways and their limited financial resources. In this respect the AAEC follows and augments the AIC ecumenical tradition already established by *Fambidzano*. Third, the existence of the AAEC as the Christian counterpart of AZTREC provides a valuable platform for interfaith dialogue. Despite a degree of understandable conflict between AIC prophets and traditionalist spirit-mediums, the bishops through their earthkeeping institution have formed close ties with many of the AZTREC chiefs. They have found that the latter, many of whom are Christians as well as active ex officio traditionalists, contribute to the removal of religious bias and the promotion of tolerance whenever the green struggle requires interreligious planning and/or action. At tree-planting ceremonies in particular, where contingents of AIC and traditional leaders interact, friendships, acceptance, and respect for each other's dignity and convictions are established. Hence it is *in* the green struggle, in striving and working for a common cause, that spontaneous dialogue about God, the ancestors, church life, and the earth takes place. This is the more remarkable because of the fairly rigid and doctrinaire orientation of Zionists and Apostles—the vast majority in AAEC circles—towards traditional beliefs and rituals. In a prophetic tradition which brands ancestors 'demons' and forbids any form of participation in traditional rituals, religious interaction is invariably characterised by radical confrontation and deliberate transformation of the old in the context of the church, rather than by reconciliatory and constructive dialogue. This tradition obviously prevails to a large extent, but in the AAEC's earthkeeping context it acquires a humane face, becomes more tolerant and sheds much of the judgmentalism which so often bedevils interfaith relations and attitudes.

Not only are the ecumenically interconnected AICs a green force to be reckoned with; individually, too, as grassroots organisations with considerable influence in African society, they are proving to be effective vehicles of earthkeeping. One of the main reasons for this is their composition. On the whole their membership comprises rural peasant families whose very existence hinges on subsistence farming and, therefore, on an agriculturally healthy environment. So when the church itself actively empowers afforestation and related conservationist projects, its constituency, by virtue of its nature and existential need, is bound to respond positively. In addition, the holistic, seamless theology of the AICs—less fettered by ages of doctrinal history than their counterparts in the West—is forged in the hard school of nature, agricultural praxis and survival in the face of changing seasons. This dialectic between biblical text and church praxis lends itself to the kind of innovation and improvisation required for the introduction of earthcare in worship and sacrament. Such integration inspires hope of institutional continuity of this ministry beyond the lifespan of present-day iconic church leaders. This, to my mind, is the major and, I trust, lasting contribution of the AAEC—not only to the environment of Zimbabwe but also by way of a challenge to world Christianity.

What is the core of the AAEC's eco-theology, the salient features of a green experience which could arrest the attention of other members of the Christian family worldwide? The richness and diversity apparent in earlier chapters preclude straightforward answers to this question. Nonetheless, even at the risk of caricaturing or being one-sided, I highlight a few noteworthy themes.

Earthkeeping has undoubtedly broadened the AIC perception of the nature of the Christian church and its mission in this world. The notion of the church as a healing institution was already well developed in the Spirit-type churches prior to the advent of the AAEC. This made it possible to extend the image of the church to that of keeper of creation and environmental hospital once the new ministry started taking shape. Salvation, which in the black Zion Cities and Jerusalems already had a strong this-worldly emphasis, now broadened its predominantly human orientation—Christ's death and resurrection on behalf of a wayward human race—to include all of creation. Conversion and discipleship, it was realised, could not be restricted to change and wellbeing for individuals and communities if the *missio dei* was to be fulfilled in this existence. All the earth had to be included in the good news and the change it brings if the new dispensation of God's kingdom, the new heaven and earth, is to take shape and make sense here and now. Conversion and spiritual growth, it now appeared, are interwoven with and not separate from earthkeeping, the latter being integral to God and his church's mission to this world. The earthy dimension to the church and its missionary mandate in no way lessens the challenge of individual spiritual growth, scriptural knowledge, and the sanctity of life. On the contrary, it interacts with and enriches these personal and interpersonal concerns.

In discovering its earthkeeping mission and ministry the church has experienced a phase of renewal. Placed squarely in the *chimurenga* tradition through the direct link between the liberation of both politically and ecologically lost lands, it has become more visible, especially in rural society. Christ appears to have been rediscovered as saviour-healer and as earthkeeper par excellence. *His* new laws of love and freedom, justice and peace are reinterpreted as applying to the entire created community—humans, animals, birds, plants, all animate and inanimate beings. These laws permeate the very being of his church. Hence the church assumes both responsibility for an emerging environmental ethic and custodianship of the earth.

Although this extended and enriched image of the Christian church may not be fully evident to all the AAEC earthkeepers involved in the green struggle, the symbols of change and growth are there for all to see. The AIC leaders are the green icons, whose headquarters and schedules indicate ecological commitment, whose newly improvised sacraments and liturgies proclaim an earthbound spirituality. The ecclesiastic instruments of afforestation, the industrious nurseries and budding woodlots, reflect obedience to an age-old yet previously neglected divine commission, and a growing common will to practise earth custodianship and help enforce its laws in a way that will make a difference. To the Christian community the church now provides the religious incentive for, and legitimation of, the green struggle. In an ongoing dialectic, the green struggle in its turn informs and stimulates the church's internal growth and external missionary outreach. Hence, the process of contextualising Christianity, originally set in motion by the AICs as they emancipated themselves from Western missionary tutelage, acquires new impetus and concrete meaning as it starts to address more seriously the immediate needs of peasant society within the confines of its environment.

In the development of its image as an earthkeeping institution the church has become the vehicle of what I have called an 'existential people's theology'—expressed mainly in imaginative earth-oriented ritual, song, and dance but also, increasingly, in written reflection as the need grows for local instruction and self-interpretation in relation to global Christianity. Judged in terms of Henry Venn's three-selves principle, the AICs—which, since their inception, have, in part unwittingly, been self-governing, self-propagating, and self-supporting institutions—have now added a 'fourth self' principle more consciously than before: that of self-theologising (Messer 1992). Significantly, local theologising suggests that the war of the trees is not just a passing fad but a penetrative ministry and soul-searching experience, reaching into the inner recesses of human conscience where neglect and abuse of God's creation have long festered as one of the most serious signs of humankind's rebellion against, even betrayal of, the creator. By imposing the embarrassment of publicly confessing ecological sins and doing penance through sacrificial planting of trees, the AIC's environmental theology unmasks hidden guilt and qualifies its religiously driven earthkeeping as an inescapable way of life, the objective of which is to overcome the 'wizardry of the earth' and restore harmony and hope to creation.

I have outlined how the AIC's grassroots theology 'defines' the creator God as insider and the traits characterising its christology and pneumatology in the dialectic between scriptural texts and earth-care, between AIC prophetic tradition and the customs associated with traditional rituals and ecology. Because of the AIC leadership's lack of scholarship one cannot expect their theology to be fully informed by in-depth scriptural studies. Nevertheless, as I have indicated, certain biblical texts and truths have been discerned and, through constant proclamation and consideration in a group context, are starting to function as signposts of the green passage which the movement is prepared to follow. In the AAEC movement as such the conviction predominates that scriptural norms and the guidance of the Holy Spirit sanction and inform its beliefs and programmed activity. Hence, despite considerable freedom and variation in religious expression and spontaneity in liturgical improvisation from one tree-planting ceremony to the next, the basic convictions discernible in group consciousness reveal a remarkable consistency. This has made possible the kind of theological distinctions and generalisations that I have made in the previous three chapters.

Thus there is no question in AAEC circles about the immanence and presence of Mwari the creator, both as an inherent force in nature and as a personal being with anthropomorphic attributes who communicates with human beings. Neither is there any doubt about Mwari being the prime mover, the one who activates, inspires, and empowers all earthkeeping endeavour, or about the realisation that God's call to such a ministry leads not only to some legitimate satisfaction at a service rendered but also to the hurt of suffering with God in an abused and partially destroyed creation. The perception, too, of a Christ figure who brings atonement to all the world is unmistakable. He is the earthkeeper who, through his church, extends his healing mission to mend and bring wholeness to the entire cosmos. He relates to Africa's ancestors as an elder brother who, in human dignity and humility as well as in divine sovereignty, appropriates and fulfils the age-old task of guardianship of the land.

Equally strong and uncompromising is the belief in the Holy Spirit who is the source of all life and who inspires and calls all human beings to conversion which, by its very nature, encompasses the vocation of earthkeeping. The Spirit is the one who confronts and combats the earth-destroyer. The Spirit writes the daily script of the strategy adopted in the green struggle. And the Spirit exposes, through the army of prophet-guardians,the perpetrators of *uroyi hwenyika*, so that evil may be expelled and all the relationships of the earth community be reconciled anew.

These, then, are the main traits of the AAEC's earthkeepers' understanding of divinity, the main traits of a theology informing environmental reform while simultaneously being moulded by the green struggle itself. When all the strands of motivation, belief, and action are woven together a powerful statement takes shape—a clarion call to Africa and the world to heed the divine charge to care for the earth.

WIDENING PRACTICAL, CONCEPTUAL, AND SPIRITUAL HORIZONS

There is growing awareness of the global environmental crisis in world Christianity today. An expanding body of eco-theological literature, examples of which have been quoted in this study, confronts us with the urgent need for environmental stewardship. Significant church or church-related developments, such as the World Council of Churches' JPIC (Justice, Peace, and the Integrity of Creation) programmes, the Reformed initiative at the Au Sable Institute, church participation in the Rio Earth Summit and Orbis Books' introduction of a new series of publications entitled Ecology and Justice (Burrows 1995:173) all point to a growing will within the Christian church to face up to environmental issues consistently and realistically. Yet despite these positive signs one cannot deny that on the whole the Christian church as a community has been slow to respond to the environmental crisis by means of prophetic witness and telling action.

It is against this background that ZIRRCON's prophetic ministry of earthkeeping should be evaluated. The new vision and environmental missionary activity in the ranks of the AAEC—largely in spontaneous and spiritually informed response to local conditions, without much exposure to modern eco-theological literature—present a challenge to the world church. This is not because the AICs involved at any point intended their earthkeeping ministry to counteract or correct the limitations of Christian churches elsewhere, but because their earthkeeping unfolds as an authentic act of faith. It is a conscious response to the movement of the life-giving Spirit, and manifests itself in a culturally relevant form. The appeal and inspiration of the AAEC lie in its humble environmental creativity and in a 'prophetic liberation of the imagination' which sets it on an exciting, unprecedented course of Christian mission in earth stewardship. As in all new Christian missionary ventures, activity entails widening horizons, both visionary and geographical. This will be the focus of our concluding chapter.

INTERNAL GROWTH

Eco-Spirituality

In my description of the AAEC's environmental ministry I have used terms such as 'commitment,' 'dedication,' 'determination,' 'bondedness,' and 'care.' All these terms refer to participant earthkeepers' changing attitudes towards each other, God and the earth. At the core of this phenomenon lies conversion—a change of heart, more in the sense of a gradually developing relationship with nature through ritual communion and deepening respect for God's creation born of nurturing it, than the radical, abrupt change that sometimes characterises the initial act of turning to Christ and the Christian church. Difficult as it is to gauge the extent of attitudinal change in a broad movement, I think it is fair to say that conversion to earth stewardship, as observed in ZIRRCON, is basically a move from exploitive, *eros*-type love to biblically informed and Spirit-inspired *agape* love for nature.

To clarify this statement we need to look at Susan Bratton's paper entitled 'Loving Nature: Eros or Agape?' (1992). Citing Old Testament texts such as Hosea 1:18 (which illustrates that a divine covenant between God and Israel includes creation as a participating and benefiting party) and New Testament texts like John 3:16 ('For God so loved the world [*kosmos*] . . .'), John 1:10 ('He [Christ] was in the world [*kosmos*] . . .') and Romans 8:19–21 (which distinguishes between the material world and humankind without, however, restricting Christ's redemption to the latter), Bratton argues that God's love for nature is not 'second-hand' but has the same form and characteristics as God's love for human beings. Because agape love is self-giving, it is preferable to eros when it comes to relationships with the environment. Eros, being the physical form of human love, has severe limitations because it 'has been modified by separation from God, competition, and shortage—its tendency to desire and possess denies the flow of God's providence and blessing.' Consequently 'eros has always been a limited form of love, inviting finite beings who must of necessity draw some of their sustenance . . . from each other' (Bratton 1992:12). Agape, being Love given from beyond humanity, is capable of transforming human-need eros and aesthetic eros, delivering these forms of 'love' from acquisitiveness and self-orientation (Bratton 1992:13).

In her discussion of agape as a 'value-creating principle,' Bratton (1992:15) says 'this characteristic implies that it is God's love directed toward nature in blessing, covenant, and other forms that gives nature worth. Because agape love for nature must come from God, humans who purposefully ignore or avoid divine influence cannot perceive nature as truly valuable.'

As the 'initiator of fellowship with God,' agape defines meaningful relations between humans, God, and nature. Bratton (1992:15) writes:

Without agape human love for nature will always be dominated by unrestrained eros, and will always be distorted by extreme self-interest and material valuation (which results in acquisitiveness). Not only can agape transform eros, but it can also provide an eschatological vision of nature, quite independent of our day-to-day needs. If agape is characterised by divine fellowship, it brings humans and creation together (and considers the needs of both simultaneously).

Some outstanding features of Christian agape love for nature, as described by Bratton, are: a shift from dominion as 'taking control over' towards 'taking loving responsibility for' nature; the pursuit of Christian virtues such as simplicity, compassion and humility which—as in the case of Francis of Assisi— can lead to a comprehensive ministry in nature, one which includes even the most elementary forms of life; the replacement of human will with divine insight, which includes attention to the values expressed in Christ's teaching and the concerns of God's kingdom; the will to be self-giving to the point of sacrifice and suffering; and interaction with nature in the knowledge that God's love and grace can be received through nature in common expectation of God's kingdom of peace.

The distinction between eros and agape love for nature, based on the interpretation of biblical texts, Platonic philosophy and/or Western theology, does not feature explicitly in AZTREC and AAEC speeches or sermons. The Shona word for love (*rudo*) is seldom used to describe the relationship between humans and nature. Nevertheless, the common qualification of earthkeeping endeavour as '*kuchengetedza zvisikwa zva Mwari*' (to care for or protect God's creation) reveals an altruistic self-sacrificing attitude towards nature, implying a spiritually inspired love or care similar to that described by Bratton. The radical distinction

between *varoyi venyika* (wizards of the earth), who exploit the earth without concern for the future, and earthkeepers, who attempt to clothe and heal the earth,
suggests awareness of the eros-agape conflict in the human psyche, and implies
that individual and ritual development will be from an exploitive eros orientation
to a caring agape attitude which benefits both nature and fellow human beings.
Admittedly the green struggle itself is imperfect, with occasional cross-currents
of self-serving individualism as opposed to sacrificial service. Yet the dominant
trend discernible in a deepening eco-spirituality is one of growth, as signposts of
hope and love for all creation are joyfully erected along the consciously chosen
path of earthkeeping. This observation needs to be substantiated with some telling
illustrations from our AAEC experience.

Before doing so, however, it should be noted that a similar development towards an agape relation with nature is also apparent in the traditionalist eco-
spirituality of AZTREC. Although one cannot discount Christian influence in
this association, intense interaction with the guardian ancestors at *mafukidzanyika* earth-clothing ceremonies and the direct involvement of the oracular deity at Matonjeni undoubtedly foster greater care for the environment
and a more personal identification with the plight of nature in traditionalist circles. This is evident in the full-time involvement of AZTREC spirit-mediums
with land issues and their willingness to risk hardship and suffering incurred
by prophetic criticism of land ownership and land distribution as administered
by the ruling African elite. There are also the chiefs' intensified efforts to re-
vive the customary conservation laws on holy groves, to curb riverbank cultivation in their chiefdoms, and their 'love affair' with trees. All this is revealed
in changed lifestyles as new patterns of eco-spirituality take shape. Hence the
traditional holistic worldview, which tends to become obscured in the struggle
for survival in an agro-economic situation of depleted land resources, resur-
faces and is rejuvenated by intensified communication between the living and
the living dead on behalf of abused members of the earth community who
reach out silently for care and justice. In a Christian perspective I am inclined
to attribute this development in traditional religion to the flowering of the inclusive grace and general revelation of the universal God, which have been op-
erative in African traditional religions through the ages. It parallels the development from eros exploitation to an agape relationship with nature observed in
AIC circles.

As for the AAEC, the following aspects of eco-spirituality illustrate the shift to
agape concern for nature.
• The conceptualisation of God in the AAEC's emerging environmental theology
  reveals the realisation that authentic *earthkeeping is a divine initiative*. The new
  agape relationship with nature stems from the pervasive presence and the summons of Mwari the creator that his people should engage in responsible earth
  stewardship. It is rooted in Christ's sacrificial death and resurrection for the entire cosmos which, among other things, answers the call of the guardian ancestors to heal the barren land. Agape attitudes are also inspired by the Holy Spirit,
  who reveals the sinfulness of people's overexploitation of nature as a condition

for genuine ecological conversion. All this surfaces in the sermons, discussions, and actions of the fighters in the war of the trees. Such awareness evokes humility, which expresses itself in opposition to the triumphalist certitude of human dominion over nature. Instead, it proclaims the interwovenness of humans and nature in the presence of God, causing earthkeepers spontaneously to declare their union with the trees on whom they rely for the breath of life itself. Trees as the 'property' of a jealous God also acquire intrinsic value. They are to be respected as beings and equals who are given a voice in the AAEC's tree-planting liturgy. Thus trees—trees spoken to, trees protected, trees nurtured and treasured—symbolise our freedom fighters' changing attitudes to creation.

- The *individual lives* of fighting cadres in our green resistance movement, key figures and villagers alike, attest an all-absorbing spirituality which informs and directs their new-found, diverse vocations. Mention was made of iconic leaders, most of whom have taken up earth healing as a life task. Self-interest is bound to play some role in the case of salaried workers. Yet several of our best paid staff are in a position to choose other, and in some cases more lucrative, careers. Apparently the call to mission, based on growing concern for God's creation, imposes a decisive mystical constraint on their lives, somehow overriding other considerations. Then there are the unsalaried church leaders and many of their followers who spend much of their time tending seedlings, nurturing trees, travelling on earthkeeping errands, attending meetings for days on end with little or no prospect of remuneration. Add to this long and exhausting weekends of tree-planting ceremonies which tax the energies of all concerned, and the stamina and enthusiasm of key figures at the centre of events, who are seldom absent, and one must conclude that only passion and sacrificial love from beyond can trigger and sustain such activity, such lives.

- The *incorporation of nature into church rituals* affirms the common will of believers to draw all the members of the earth community—animate and inanimate—into the circle of worship of Mwari and caring for each other. The tree-planting eucharist is an obvious case in point. It not only constitutes a new dimension of missionary outreach but declares publicly that the representatives of nature, the trees, have the value and status that God attributes to them, that they are worthy of love and care. Unlike the ZCC missionary strategy where the eucharist is the springboard of missionary mobilisation within the church, the AAEC tree-planting eucharist is a witness event in its own right, a vehicle of mission proclaiming the good news to all creation. Not that the classic missionary command in Matthew 28:19 is eclipsed by ecological endeavour, allowing it to supersede the call for repentance, conversion, human salvation, and church formation—these remain the essential missionary dynamics of all prophetic AICs. But the missionary mandate here is derived from the healing ministry of Christ, related to the believer's stewardship of all creation as required by Mwari in the creation story of Genesis, and highlighted repeatedly with reference to Christ's involvement in creation (Col 1:17). What Christ literally holds together in this eucharist is the healing and wholeness of both nature and people. His blood was spilt to atone for all creation. The celebrating earthkeepers recognise this by allowing the empowering blessing of the sacrament to translate into an act of earth healing. They then kneel down in recognition of the human need for healing. The sacrament thus conveys a powerful message of Mwari/Christ's love for the entire cosmos and of human attempts to give expression to the implications for themselves and their environment.

- Patriarchy often characterises AIC leadership. This is attributable to the influence of male authoritarianism in patrilineal kinship, the 'inheritance' of church leadership by the eldest son of a deceased bishop and the fascination of AIC bishops with some of the Old Testament patriarchs as role models. Even in the course of an individual AIC leader's lifetime one can discern a gradual change from direct and regular interaction with followers as prophetic healers to greater remoteness as bishops, burdened with administrative and organisational duties. Women, moreover, despite their numeric preponderance in the AICs and despite outlets for their leadership in the healing vocation or in the Mothers' Unions (*Ruwadzano*), are seldom found at the apex of AIC leadership hierarchies. *AAEC eco-spirituality has an impact on AIC patriarchy!* It opens up new opportunities for women and prompts a compassionate ministry of earth-care in which celebratory forms of interaction between the genders, particularly at tree-planting ceremonies, bridge the divide which sometimes characterises leader-follower relations. Here, too, there are signs of the emergence of agape love between earthkeepers as they relate to each other and to nature.

- This breakdown of patriarchal relations and isolating authority patterns is aptly described by the imagery adopted by Matthew Fox in his *A Spirituality Named Compassion* (1992). Fox complains about the exile of compassion in Western Christianity, dominated as it is by the quest for perfection and success. He maintains that the lack of compassion 'has left us with a sexually one-sided spirituality in which the prevailing patriarchal presumptions exclude nurturing, caring, and earthiness' (Fox 1992:37). For an analysis of spiritual experience in such a context he distinguishes between two contrasting symbols: climbing Jacob's ladder and dancing Sarah's circle.

  Christian mystics, says Fox, tended to use the ladder in Jacob's dream as symbol of fleeing the earth in order to experience a transcendent, an 'up-like' God. According to Gregory of Nyssa we climb the ladder away from earthly concerns to the heavenly majesty of God. Augustine insisted that up-ness is divine and down-ness demonic. In such a scheme contemplation is won at the expense of compassion. 'Thus,' says Fox (1992:40), 'compassion is descent; it is also an afterthought, a luxury that one can afford after a very long life-time of contemplative ascending.'

  By contrast, the dancing of Sarah's circle implies a spirituality of laughter and celebration, as Sarah is filled with wonder and surprise at giving birth to Isaac (the name means 'God has smiled') in her old age. Sarah is a symbol of birth-giving, creating, and fruitfulness. She laughed because human wisdom said pregnancy was impossible. But divine wisdom said nothing was impossible. In contrasting the two symbols it appears that the ladder dynamic is restrictive and elitist, whilst the circle motif is welcoming and compassionate.

When the hierarchy becomes normative for spiritual progress the ladder's rungs are divinised and advanced individuals turn into remote 'deities.' In the circle dance, on the other hand, you relate eye to eye: you can see the tears in your neighbour's eyes; you share a built-in equaliser which is lacking when exalted persons operate from on high. Instead of the distance and abstractness of ladder-climbing, the circle dance creates physical nearness, empathy and earthiness. Insisting that the two symbols are irreconcilable, Fox argues for participation in Sarah's circle if a compassionate spirituality is to be developed in our global village—the only kind of spirituality which will turn around the forces of global destruction.

The lives of some outstanding AIC leaders in Zimbabwe did undoubtedly contain an element of Jacob's ladder dynamics. During the period of his call to Christian ministry the late Johane Maranke (AACJM) was considered to have dwelt with Christ in the heavens above, an experience which required isolation, religious contemplation, and fasting up in the mountains. Similar experiences in dreams and visions during periods of seclusion characterise the histories of many AIC male leaders and senior clergy. During his lifetime the late bishop Samuel Mutendi of the ZCC was considered by his followers to be closer to Mwari than they were. He was the one who 'lifted their prayers' to God in heaven. Thus one can speak of a certain elevation of the leader, a mystique of occasional remoteness integral to the kind of iconic leadership which, sometimes, includes black messianic trends.

Both Maranke and Mutendi, however, like the majority of bishops involved in the AAEC, were not meditating mystics in the Western and Eastern sense of the word at all. Their presence in the midst of their followers was real and not an afterthought, as Fox claims for medieval Christian mystics. As indicated above, compassionate interaction between prophetic healer and followers tends to be the norm before the 'dignified distance' of an ageing leader—similar to that of a traditional chief, who delegates considerable responsibility to councillors and elders—sets in.

For men like Maranke and Mutendi, the 'distance' of Jacob's ladder was overcome in their sharing of Christ's great commission with their followers during the paschal celebration. At the point of handing the sacrament to their followers, they drew them into the celebration of dancing Sarah's circle, challenging them as it were to carry the gospel to the wider family of humankind. Distance was overcome and mutuality in compassion became manifest when Christ incarnate, the black icon, handed his black disciples the earth-bound symbols of inner union and boundary-transcending outreach. Compassion became manifest as each ZCC and Apostolic communicant received the bread and wine from the hands and looked into the eyes of either the 'man of God' in Zion City or the African Apostle.

Something similar, but possibly an even more radical departure from AIC patriarchy in its alienating form, is noticeable in the AAEC tree-planting eucharist. First of all, the ecumenical setting is marked by the presence of several bishops. Dignified and revered as they are in their splendid robes, they themselves set an example of servanthood in the earthkeeping ministry. Their sermons reflect compassion for nature and for people as they blend into, rather than stand apart from, the proceedings. It is as if their concern about the plight of nature overrides leadership considerations, at least for the occasion, as action in the struggle unleashes the motivation for unity, equality, and humility.

Second, the bishops and all senior clergy make the same public confession of ecological sins as everybody else. Earth stewardship offers no privileges! Apparently the Spirit is equally relentless in revealing the shortcomings of respected church dignitaries and those of their followers. Mystical sanctification and empowerment erase human pretence and hierarchical privilege in anticipation of earth-care in sacramental union.

Third, the bishops file past the communion table, tree in hand, and later plant their own trees like everybody else. Then they celebrate the good news of new life in the form of trees placed in the earth by dancing the Zionist circle dance—Sarah's circle—together with all the other earthkeepers, and they lay on hands or kneel to receive hands in the closing healing ceremony. *Ndaza* Zionist bishops in fact participate regularly in the circle dances of their churches, but there is a marked difference in the ecumenical *maporesanyika* context. Here they are less in charge of proceedings, deliberately closer to the soil and therefore also more spontaneously included in Sarah's circle, where unity with the earth's family derives from giving comfort to the stricken land.

Apart from the ritual manifestation of patriarchal remoteness being transcended by agape love for nature, female ascendancy and emancipation from male authority are also apparent in the organisation and project implementation of ZIRRCON-AAEC. To the extent that women in their ZIRRCON clubs are contributing to earthkeeping and progress by improving the income and nurture of their families, they are respected and assisted by many of their male partners in the movement. In her public speeches, Raviro Mutonga, coordinator of the Women's Desk, always acknowledges the assistance received from men in preparing their woodlots for tree planting and the willingness of males in leadership positions not to interfere in the income-generating and other projects launched by women. This is a far cry from the resistance, even suspicion, encountered from the side of AIC bishops some twenty years ago when the first attempts were made to launch a Women's Desk in *Fambidzano* (Daneel 1989:476f, 491f). The process of achieving gender equality and overcoming ingrained trends of male domination in church leadership hierarchies is, of course, far from complete. Change, however, is in the air and significantly so when male earthkeeping bishops start discovering and admitting that the lead dancers in Sarah's circle can and should be women, that without the compassion, creativity and leadership of women the entire environmental struggle will flounder.

- Other signs of changing attitudes towards nature prompted by eco-spirituality are the following: the determination of our earthkeepers to devise and implement *an environmental ethic* which clearly distinguishes between earth exploitation and nurturing earth stewardship; the move *from religious exclusiveness to religious inclusiveness* and tolerance as meaningful dialogue in joint ecological action takes shape; and the *breakdown of isolationist church-ism* as the AAEC increasingly takes note and feels part of the Christian fellowship worldwide, involved in the same struggle in the global village and its environs.

Difficult as it is to assess human motives and attitudes, I consider the trends outlined above sufficient evidence of a wide-reaching and profound spiritual phenomenon of inner growth. We observe eco-spirituality spiralling out, stimulating increased and varied responsibility for the environment, and stimulated in its turn by the very action it has generated to gain spiritual depth and enrichment by overcoming the inner enemy of self-seeking eros love and embracing the earth community in agape love.

Environmental Commitment and Vision

Inner eco-spiritual growth, as a condition for and byproduct of environmental endeavour, inevitably includes growing environmental understanding and commitment, resulting in broader horizons. The descriptions in this book of ZIRRCON's involvement in its primary objectives (afforestation, wildlife conservation, the protection of water resources, and the mobilisation not only of religious groups but also of the youth and women) reflect an expansion of programmes and responsibility for nature. This in turn feeds a shared vision among our earthkeepers for outreach, interaction, and joint enterprise beyond the borders of our country. My participation in international eco-theological conferences, the regular visits of sponsors, environmentalists, and other interested parties from abroad, the study of environmental themes by ZIRRCON staff members and the teaching of elementary earth-care in peasant society contribute to this development. To feel part of a global resistance movement, to learn about the green struggle in other countries and to plan ecological action with due regard to both the local religio-cultural context and the more universal perspective—all this helps to mature vision, however slowly, and inspires the day's task in local mission, despite setbacks. It also instils growing realism when soaring idealism comes up against sobering achievements.

Growing, too, is an understanding of the interconnectedness of all that exists in the cosmos. This awareness naturally highlights the limitations of ZIRRCON's threefold ecological goals. The question arises, for instance, how one should evaluate ZIRRCON's apparent afforestation successes in relation to escalating land degradation, caused in part by unjust land distribution and insufficiently controlled population growth. Can one successfully curb deforestation through afforestation projects without dealing with the basic causes more vigorously? It would be easy to argue on behalf of ZIRRCON that available funds and salaried staff set the limits of our endeavour and that too wide a scope of activity could jeopardise the quality of our current ecological work. However, this is the kind of question ZIRRCON will have to face in the future. As its auxiliary forces grow it should be possible for ZIRRCON to extend the scope of its work to match the broader vision and convictions that have emerged.

A few examples of extended responsibility will suffice.

Population Growth

This subject is so important for the future of our planet that no earthkeeper worthy of the name can ignore it. In his informative and challenging book, *Earth in the Balance*, Al Gore (1992:305f) lists the 'stabilizing of world population' as the first of five strategic goals in his proposed Global Marshall Plan, which should direct and inform all attempts to save the global environment. He discusses the population explosion of the past forty-five years (an increase from 2 billion to 5.5 billion) and the expectation that this alarming trend will repeat itself during the next forty-five years. An estimated 94 per cent of the expected increase 'will occur in the developing world, where poverty and environmental degradation are already the most severe' (Gore 1992:308).

Land Distribution

By the very nature of their work, earthkeepers in Zimbabwe's communal lands are confronted with land distribution problems and the nonavailability of land as part of the colonial legacy—no less formidable a dilemma than population pressure on the land. ZIRRCON has essentially adopted the policy of empowering the poor and restricted subsistence farmers in the communal lands (most of whom can barely eke out a living on the land available to them) to tackle with immediate effect the environmental problems they are facing every day. This has always been a realistic ecological option. It does not imply ignoring or acquiescing in pre-Independence land tenure legislation, which historically is largely to blame for the deprivation of African peasant society. But it recognises that nature itself in the communal lands requires urgent remedial attention, irrespective of future land reform measures which will inevitably be preceded by lengthy political and legislative processes. If anything, the difficulty of finding suitable patches of land for woodlots when there is a desperate shortage of arable land has sharpened our earthkeepers' awareness that major land legislation will be required to redress the inequitable situation in our country. Even though ZIRRCON has no official strategy or political agenda in this regard, critical and prophetic voices are regularly heard from both traditionalist and Christian quarters at meetings and in private conversations.

In his attempt to develop a theology of the land which will prophetically remedy the ills of Zimbabwean land apportionment, Bakare (1993:72) uses the apposite metaphor of the 'land as mother' to describe the sacred relationship between African people and the soil. Like a human mother, the land has a very personal relationship with her children and therefore cannot be seen as a saleable commodity. Bakare criticises the mission churches in particular for not opposing the injustice perpetrated on Africans by the land tenure act, and for accepting land 'stolen from Africans' to establish their mission stations. He calls on the church to raise its prophetic voice and help redress the land distribution ills of the past from a position of unwavering identification and involvement with the landless poor and those peripheralised by a system that fosters injustice (Bakare 1993:80, 81).

I fully agree with Bakare's call for the church's ongoing prophetic involvement in land distribution. The AAEC bishops to a large extent represent the landless poor, as do the chiefs and mediums of AZTREC. Hence ZIRRCON is well placed to encourage debate on land issues so as to channel the prophetic voice which is already heard in the ranks of the movement, and then to communicate its message to government and the nation via the media and direct dialogue between delegates of our movement and senior government officials.

Land issues remain complex. There is simply not enough land in the country to accommodate the needs of all people in the traditional sense. Moreover, economic viability cannot be disregarded when it comes to redistributing commercial land. To slice up the commercial lands into agriculturally uneconomic units could have dire economic consequences for the entire nation. There is also the question of the future of the wilderness areas, including the Zambezi valley and the large game parks, Hwange and Gona-re-Zhou. To produce informed policy and prophecy ZIRRCON will have to study and keep abreast of developments in this field.

Education

ZIRRCON has already done much to instil environmental awareness and commitment among the youth. Seed collection, the development of school nurseries and woodlots, ecological competitions, and participation in ZIRRCON's tree-planting rituals have all contributed to this end. This spadework is currently being systematised, consolidated, and expanded by a Youth Desk. In a global perspective, the work of the Youth Desk will become part of what Gore (1992:355f) calls 'Mission to Planet Earth': the gathering of information about what precisely is happening to the global environment and making such information available for public education so that the green revolution worldwide can forge ahead.

Gore's suggestions for the involvement of the youth require urgent attention:

The Mission to Planet Earth should be a Mission by the people of Planet Earth. Specifically, I propose a programme involving as many countries as possible that will use school teachers and their students to monitor the entire earth daily . . . Even relatively simple measurements—surface temperature, wind speed and direction, relative humidity, barometric pressures, and rainfall—could, if routinely available on a more nearly global basis, produce dramatic improvements in our understanding of climate patterns . . . The virtue of involving children from all over the world in a truly global Mission to Planet Earth is, then, threefold: first, the information is greatly needed (and the quality of the data can be assured by regular sampling). Second, the goals of environmental education could hardly be better served than by actually involving students in the process of collecting the data. And, third, the programme might build a commitment to rescue the global environment among the young people involved (Gore 1992:356, 357).

ZIRRCON's inclusion of the youth in earthkeeping has already stimulated awareness and commitment to earth-care among both school teachers and their pupils. Follow-up requires curriculum development to introduce regular environmental education in all schools, drawing students into nature research and monitoring projects of the kind proposed by Al Gore, launching wilderness, game park, and related activities for youth clubs, and extending such work through networking at national, continental, and international levels. All this is easier said than done. One hopes that the spirit of our resistance fighters engaged in the war of the trees will help fire the imagination and concern of today's youth so that the coming generation of earthkeepers will continue building and improvising on what as yet are mere foundations and visions for the future.

The brief discussion of these three subjects—population growth, land distribution, and education—illustrates an uneven process of intensifying awareness, commitment, aspirations, and plans based on growing eco-spirituality and insight born of increasing earthkeeping experience. Despite limited funding, staff, and action, a holistic approach is apparent throughout. The interrelatedness of all beings, ecosystems, countries, and continents and the immense need for local and global change if planet earth is to survive, are a tremendous challenge. Widened horizons also present a chilling scenario of seemingly uncontrollable forces destroying natural resources worldwide in the name of so-called progress—a scenario which could fill any earthkeeper who weighs the significance of local action relative to global ecological needs with a sense of futility and despair. One might well ask whether the environmental point of no return for our planet has not already been reached. Fortunately light overcomes darkness and God-given love for this cosmos can overcome greed. Despite our anguish at the little we achieve, the struggle continues.

GEOGRAPHIC OUTREACH: TOWARDS A UNITED FRONT IN AFRICA

The dynamics of mission to the earth—understood in religious and, more specifically, Christian, terms—implies outreach, crossing frontiers; in this instance, overcoming internal obstacles to personal commitment and crossing the geographical boundaries of countries and continents so as to proclaim, enact and share the good news of liberation or salvation for all creation. As pockets of resistance to earth destruction form all over the world, some of them extend their activities to engage in geographically wide-ranging operations to help liberate the environment. Here the Greenpeace movement comes to mind. Others draw encouragement for their local struggle by sharing information in a growing network of communication and interaction worldwide. Green political parties, environmental departments of governments, and a host of institutions concerned with forestry, natural resources, agriculture, wildlife, and the like seek to awaken the collective conscience of nations, governments, financial and business concerns. In a sense, therefore, a global green revolution has already started.

Much of what is being done for the environment, however, is of purely symbolic significance or for the sake of 'political correctness' in the public eye. Generally earth-care falls woefully short of what is really required for a revolutionary reversal of those trends which seem to be propelling our planet to the precipice of total destruction. The 'first' world still exploits the 'two-thirds' world at the expense of its natural resources. Entire economies still feed military expansion and armaments rather than environmental reform. Rain forests are still being decimated by multinational companies at the expense of healthy conditions for all in the global village, besides extinguishing species of animal and plant life as yet hardly known. Norwegians still continue whaling operations despite international treaties aimed at protecting threatened species of whales, and Japanese fishing fleets continue harvesting certain species of fish illegally despite the irreparable damage already done. In Africa the few remaining black rhino are still being threatened by ruthless profiteers, wilderness areas dwindle as ever growing numbers of people crowd out wildlife, and the processes of deforestation and desertification continue unabated.

In the face of a global environmental malaise which eludes the control of even the most powerful international organisations, how does a small ecological institution with its limited sphere of influence envisage its mission to planet earth? A few simple guidelines were adopted. First, ZIRRCON's resistance fighters refused to be daunted by a global situation which in many respects seemed to be beyond redemption or repair. A growing passion for the earth derived from a spiritual mandate impels it to reach out in mission regardless of the disheartening realities of the global situation.

Second, ZIRRCON decided that the gist of its message elsewhere should initially be restricted to the field in which it had gained local recognition and insight based on experience, namely religiously inspired afforestation. It was confident that the nature of its struggle and the tree-planting model it had developed were relevant not only to Zimbabwe but to other African countries as well. Third, ZIRRCON felt that in the continued development of its religio-ecological ministry, exposed to an extended network of communication and interaction in Africa, it could achieve goals like the following:

- help escalate the green revolution in Africa's grassroots communities;
- contribute to the organisational structure required for continent-wide coordination of the green struggle;
- challenge African religions generally and African Christianity in particular to develop eco-theologies and eco-ministries relevant to their local situations.

Fourth, it envisioned that deepening local earthkeeping commitment, coupled with continental outreach, will eventually send out a noticeable message to the global village—one which will contribute, however modestly, to the kind of change that will draw entire nations into the green revolution.

The South African Connection

Because of my dual position for many years as ZIRRCON director in Masvingo and professor of missiology at the University of South Africa in Pretoria, a natural link was forged between the two institutions. Through regular visits to Masvingo, publications in Unisa's journals on ZIRRCON's activities, lectures to the university's theological faculty at annual seminars (once, rather unconventionally, accompanied by visiting spirit-medium vaZarira Marambatemwa, then president of AZTREC), I managed to keep my colleagues in the south informed about earthkeeping endeavours in Zimbabwe and opened up prospects of establishing a similar project in South Africa. Aware of the importance of Unisa as one of the largest distance-education universities in the world, I proposed the establishment of an endowed chair and a religio-environmental institute with similar objectives to those of ZIRRCON. These proposals were made in a lecture to faculty in 1993 and later published in the journal *Religion and Theology* (1995) under the title 'Contextualising Environmental Theology at Unisa.' The proper locus for such an institute, I suggested, would be the theological faculty, and its objectives would include research, conscientisation, and mobilisation for earthkeeping projects, all based on the ZIRRCON experience yet with sufficient scope for improvisation and adaptation to the Unisa context. Unisa welcomed the proposals, provided the necessary funds could be raised.

Over the next few years I negotiated with representatives of the Gold Fields Foundation and the South African Nature Foundation (now WWF-South Africa). Delegations were sent to Zimbabwe to observe ZIRRCON's earthkeeping programmes, particularly the ecologically inculturated dimension which formed the cornerstone of my grant application. This eventually culminated in the finetuning of proposals, in which the proposed chair was shelved for the time being because of the cost involved. In the course of 1994 it became obvious to me that a research project on African initiatives in Christian mission would keep me out of South Africa for extended periods, rendering my ecological workload unmanageable. As a result I suggested that David Olivier, an eco-theologian and ethicist at Unisa, be appointed to take charge of the envisaged environmental venture. Dr. Olivier drafted the final proposal to the Gold Fields Foundation, participated with me in the final rounds of negotiation, and, once we had been awarded R2. 3 million for the new project at Unisa, was appointed executive director.

Flying under the banner 'Faith and Earthkeeping' (F and E) and operating from within Unisa's Research Institute for Theology and Religion, the project was launched early in 1995. Its original staff was Dr. Olivier (director), whose primary assignment was conscientisation and mobilisation for ecological projects; Michel Clasquin (senior researcher), an authority on oriental religion, who was responsible for creating a resources database, the preparation of new courses, and the publication of a newsletter; and Victor Mohlobi (junior researcher), who was involved in establishing environmentally aware religious organisations, especially among the AICs in Gauteng province. A full-time field operations manager for project implementation still had to be appointed. At the request of our sponsor, Gold Fields, and with a view to continuous interaction between ZIRRCON and F and E, I was appointed F and E consultant for the first few years, as well as chairperson of both its executive and advisory boards.

African Earthkeepers' Union

In Gore's discussion of the need for a world body to coordinate individual nation states' attempts to save the environment he dismisses the notion of a 'world government' as politically impossible and impracticable (Gore 1992:301). Although sceptical about the ability of the United Nations, the world's most important supranational organisation, to do very much, he suggests the formation of a UN Stewardship Council to deal with global environmental issues, as the Security Council deals with matters of war and peace (Gore 1992:302). In addition, he advocates the establishment of a tradition of environmental summit meetings, similar to economic summits, where heads of state can meet annually to consider international agreements, criteria, and action plans for global environmental reform.

Considering the urgent need to tackle environmental issues on a massive scale, these proposals make sense. However, the extent to which a world body will be able to operate effectively will hinge partly on the ability of regional bodies—representing clusters of nation states, such as Southern, Eastern, and West Africa—or continent-wide movements committed to the green revolution to provide the information required, to help mould a vision and strategy for the various regions and to assist with the mobilisation of grassroots endeavour in local religio-cultural contexts. Regional councils will also have to establish a tradition of regular summits to keep abreast of and help direct earthkeeping activities in their own regions or continents. They certainly should facilitate two-way communication between governments and professional environmental organisations on the one hand and grassroots society in their regions on the other, as well as between a world organisation and the societies (earth community) they represent. With a view to this kind of organisational configuration as an essential framework for a global green revolution, I started to canvass for the formation of an African Earthkeeper's Union (AEU) with representation from as many African countries as possible.

Given the ZIRRCON experience, I am inclined to envisage the AEU as a people's movement which, while seeking government support in the countries of operation and enlisting the services of environmental experts and organisations, derives legitimacy and motivation from grassroots society and basic communities in both rural and urban settings. In other words, the fighters in the trenches—the peasants who suffer most from soil degradation and deforestation, the workers in the cities responsible for cleaning up operations and recycling, the key figures among the masses who command religious and political power (church leaders, traditional custodians of the land, chiefs and mediums, etc.) and the communities already engaged in earth-care—should play a leading role in the envisaged union. The voice of the peasants, who 'live with' the barren earth, the plains without firewood, the sparse forests without game, the silted up rivers without fish—in other words the voice of the poor who struggle to survive and who have no option but to engage in earthkeeping—should be heard. These are the people who are not seen or heard at environmental conferences where the professional researchers, field experts, sponsors, and government agencies gather. Not that these professionals are unimportant—their expertise is vitally necessary. But in a people's movement, as is the case with ZIRRCON, it is the key representatives of the masses, the basic communities in the green struggle, who should be empowered to arrange *their* conferences, set the agenda in terms of their needs and experience of environmental care, and invite professionals and government officials whom they consider relevant for the issues *they* face. In this way the green struggle would be expanded and strengthened. While the experts can assist with monitoring, evaluating, and upgrading ecological methods, it is the green fighters at the grassroots—those to whom the struggle is fast becoming a matter of life or death—who can capture the imagination of the masses and thus extend the battle front, expand the numbers of the green forces and instil commitment in the face of inevitable setbacks.

Affiliation to the AEU should be on a regional and institutional basis. A predetermined number of representatives from member states—be they chiefs, headmen, commoners, religious leaders, government officials, environmentalists, etc., or a combination of these—should have voting power in the AEU plenum. Institutions like the following should be granted full membership with voting powers:

- Environmental agencies/movements: ZIRRCON, F and E, the Greenbelt movement (Kenya), WWF-SA, environmental NGOs, and similar organisations known for an emphasis on people's empowerment.
- Traditional authorities: chiefs' councils, traditional healers' associations, spirit-medium guilds, traditionalist environmental organisations, etc.
- Churches and other religious movements: AICs, 'mainline' churches, ecumenical bodies such as national Christian councils, the All Africa Church Conference (AACC), and environmentally active non-Christian religions.

African Christian Theology and Environmental Liberation

Inasmuch as the churches in Africa are bound to play an increasingly significant role in socioeconomic and environmental development and liberationist work, it is important that theologising from within these churches should keep track of developments and provide the necessary guidance. This applies not only to the enacted theology of the AICs, although their innovative liturgical and pastoral response to an abused creation—as indicated in this study—certainly warrants attention, but also to written theology based on academic and spiritual reflection.

In the latter field three basic trends can be distinguished (Ukpong 1984:501):

- *African inculturation theology*, popularly known as African theology, refers to the dialogue between European Christian and African religious thought, aimed at conveying the Christian message in a contextually relevant form and integrating Christianity with African life and culture.
- *South African black theology*, following American black theology, spreads the good news as a message of political and socioeconomic liberation in a situation of oppression and segregation.

- *African liberation theology*, moulded on either the indigenous socioeconomic structure or Latin American liberation theology or both, preaches the gospel as a message of liberation in the African context of poverty, hunger, and political powerlessness.

Ukpong treats African liberation theology as a development of the 1970s, to be found mainly in postcolonial East and West Africa and aimed predominantly at socioeconomic development and upliftment. This theology is significant for its focus on the very dimension which South African exponents of black theology have always found lacking in African theology (cf. Tutu 1975). Ela (1986, chapter 6), one of the most eloquent African liberation theologians, for example, outlines the continuing dependence of African states on Western capital and their enslavement to the manipulation of multinational corporations (e.g., the cocoa dictatorship of Cameroon) despite political independence. He demonstrates very clearly that liberation in postcolonial Africa is an ongoing mandate in view of economically enslaving conditions, declining agrarian economies, misgovernment, and juvenile unemployment. Active concern with socioeconomic development and the fair distribution of the proceeds of production and trade presents the church with an ineluctable challenge to introduce structural reforms. Typical of Ela's realistic approach is the following comment:

> The world is not given to us as a ready made reality, but as a construction project, and this construction project includes political and social tasks. We must therefore move from a religion of nature to faith that lives in history and confrontation (Ela 1986:100).

Ukpong's classification is certainly helpful to distinguish major trends in African Christian theology. However, it tends to obscure the fact that there are liberationist dimensions, admittedly in different applications and varying degrees, in virtually all forms of African theology. Black African theologians' interpretation and translation of the Christian message in and for the African context (Ukpong's first category) are in themselves forms of religio-cultural liberation from the dominance of Western theology. The entire history of AIC growth, moreover, has liberationist features, be it liberation from white missionary tutelage, resistance to oppressive colonial rule, freedom fighting, or liberation from poverty through community development programmes (Daneel 1989, chapter 3). African liberation theology is therefore a much older and richer tradition, as an existential reality of the African church, than the literature on the subject would have us believe.

One dimension which has been hidden or lacking in Africa's liberation theology is that of the environment. A preoccupation with human liberation, human dignity, human progress, human upliftment and so forth is understandable and justifiable, given the erstwhile colonial situation of human oppression, human impoverishment and human suffering. Hence a plea for an ecological focus in African theology should not be interpreted as denigrating its current anthropocentric and humanitarian emphases. These undoubtedly will remain! But the concern for human liberation should be consciously extended to encompass *all* members of the earth community. The former cannot be complete and meaningful if the latter are not included. Our human dignity derives in part from the respect and care we show for the earth. In other words, our claim to dignity and equality in a racial and interpersonal sense rings hollow if we keep living in an abused environment and contribute to its destruction, without any attempt to establish the justice there that we seek for ourselves.

A more comprehensive liberation theology, in the light of Ela's observations, would deal with all impediments to justice and sustainable wellbeing for the entire earth community. The struggle against 'First' World exploitation of the Two-Thirds World will have to be intensified, not only because of its debilitating impact on these economies and therefore on people's living conditions, but also and particularly because of the unaffordable price these countries are paying in loss of natural resources. Ela's view of the world as a 'construction project' will only make real sense if environmental reconstruction is given the same priority as the political and social tasks he refers to. Instead of 'moving away from a religion of nature' we need confrontation, dialogue, and reinterpretation in that very sphere, in our quest for a contextual theology of nature which will meet the current requirements for environmental liberation.

This task requires comprehensive and ongoing interaction between Christian earthkeepers—peasants, villagers, urban workers—and academic theologians. Those who design new eco-theologies because of their dedication to the struggle in the field and those who reach the outside world through their publications should join forces if the green revolution in Africa, in its Christian manifestation, is to escalate to a point where the earth is truly valued, healed, and sustained. Enacted and written eco-theologies have to meet and bond! When this happens, new fellowships in mission, in earthkeeping ministries of compassion, will emerge. It will call for sacrifice. Mention has been made of the price paid by AIC earthkeepers, the grassroots theologians of peasant society. To professional theologians turned eco-prophets, and resistance fighters turned tree planters, the price may be even heavier. Some may well forfeit academic careers at universities or seminaries; others may have to interrupt their traditional teaching and research programmes periodically so as to become 'intermittent earthkeepers' themselves, more than participant observers in the earth community: mouthpieces and authors, who have experienced at first hand what the good news to a ravished earth really signifies and requires.

A number of themes that have emerged in this book will require the attention of African eco-theologians. I mention only a few:

- *Biblical foundations* for ecological stewardship, land use, environmental liberation, and justice for all the earth in African terms.
- *The nature of ecumenical interaction* between earthkeeping churches, as well as between Christian churches, African traditional religions, and other religions. This is a broad theme which includes encounter and dialogue between African Christianity and African traditional religion in earthkeeping praxis, and the implications for an African theology of religions.

- *Ecclesiological perspectives*: What are the implications of an earthkeeping ministry for the liturgies and pastoral programmes of the African church? How does earthkeeping fit into the missionary nature of the church and its propagation of the good news of Christ?
- *Conversion* and *sanctification* of individuals and Christian communities in relation to earth-care.
- *Healing* and *salvation* in holistic African and biblical eschatological perspectives.
- *Sin, evil wizardry, and church discipline* in relation to the earth community and an *environmental ethic* designed both from the 'underside' of the green struggle and from contextual Bible reading.
- *African eco-feminism*: the contribution of African women to community development, environmental reform, and the like.
- *State and church interaction* in earthkeeping; particularly land distribution, land husbandry, and the protection of natural resources.
- *African liberation theology*: the integration and balance between its religio-cultural, political, socioeconomic, and environmental tenets.
- *Earthkeeping at the behest of a trinitarian deity*: a protective creator Father/Mother, a healing/saving Christ, and a life-giving/guiding Holy Spirit.

I am not suggesting that these themes have been entirely neglected by African theologians. I have cited, for instance, Bakare's study of land distribution in Zimbabwe. Nevertheless, full-blown eco-theological studies by African theologians are few and far between. As our experience and insight grow in Africa's escalating green revolution, themes of this nature will require probing scrutiny and committed theologising.

AFRICA AND BEYOND

Zimbabwe's war of the trees is, as we have seen, not an isolated struggle. As a liberation movement which seeks the improvement and wellbeing of the entire earth community it has a ripple effect at the local grassroots, extending and blending with similar movements regionally, throughout Southern Africa, and in the future, it is hoped, across the African continent. In this sense our struggle resembles grassroots endeavours all over the world.

Whether a global groundswell or a global green revolution ensues—one which can help stem the tide of earth destruction and facilitate the historical transition from an industrial epoch to the 'ecozoic age' (Tucker, in Tucker and Grim 1994:13)—also hinges on meaningful communication and enriching interaction between existing green movements, action groups, and institutions worldwide. To reach consensus in the global village on the common good of all members of the earth community the local and global dimensions of earthkeeping will have to be kept in balance. Earthkeepers will have to 'think globally' but 'act locally.' Noel Brown (1994:15), director of the United Nations Environment Programme, endorses this view: 'At a time when the future viability of the planet hangs in the balance, local/global must be seen as a premise for a new kind of responsibility for the earth.' Callicott (1994:38), in his suggestions for the development of a global environmental ethic, adds the following rider: 'Let us by all means think globally and act locally. But let us also think locally as well as globally and try to time our global and local thinking as the several notes of a single, yet common chord.'

The proposed task is too great for individuals operating in isolation. Teamwork—the mobilisation of entire societies, nations—is of the essence. As Gore (1992:277) observes: 'By themselves, well motivated individuals cannot hope to win this struggle [of saving the world's environment], but as soon as enough people agree to make it our central organising principle, success will come within our grasp and we can begin to make rapid progress.' This is not to denigrate the contributions of individuals. Alongside the green fighters in all walks of life, those who have little option but to concentrate primarily on their local earthkeeping responsibilities, we indeed need the individual specialists: academics, visionaries, prophets, bridge-builders between communities, 'intercultural nomads'—in other words, the mobile units of the global battlefront.

These are women and men who identify fully with their local struggle, yet act as link figures between communities, cultures, nations, and continents; those whose task it is to think both locally and globally, to interpret the local struggle and render its contribution fruitful in the family of nations, at the same time feeding information and inspiration from similar struggles in other parts of the world back to the local situation. These are the storytellers who contribute to the myths people need to motivate them for their struggle. These too are the ideologues, philosophers, scientists, and representatives of an amazing variety of faiths, who periodically team up to assess the green struggle and attempt to articulate what is yet to become a global environmental ethic.

The Religio-Philosophical and Scientific Task

Religions, philosophies, and sciences captivate the minds of people and motivate their activities. It is becoming critically significant to examine their underlying assumptions, worldviews, and cosmologies. This provides new insight into the motives, attitudes, and values that have qualified relations between humans, nature, and the supernatural in the past, and suggests possible solutions that could be proposed and implemented in the future. The present study joins up with others in its attempt to probe some of the cosmological roots and belief systems of two religions in Africa and to highlight the significance of religious motivation in the mobilisation of inculturated earthkeeping. The local/global premise is in evidence, albeit modestly, in this attempt to share local African insight and experience from the war of the trees, through the written word, with fellow fighters in the global village.

Anthologies comprising theological and interdisciplinary contributions from all parts of the world reveal acute awareness in academic circles of the task referred to above, as well as a common conviction that there is a need to radically rethink the anthropocentric ethic which has prevailed in many religions and in exploitive industrial societies. I mention a few examples that illustrate this trend. In a collection of eco-theological essays entitled *Liberating Life: Contemporary Approaches to Ecological Theology*, Birch, Eakin, and McDaniel (1990:1) observe a new, emerging consensus among Christian theologians:

> The consensus is that an anthropocentric ethic, understood as an emphasis on human wellbeing at the expense of the earth and other living beings, must be replaced by an ethic of respect for life and environment. We think it quite significant that theologians from different perspectives and backgrounds are moved by this common concern . . . It is as if life itself has cried out for freedom from human exploitation, and they, in different contexts have heard it.

In *Ecotheology: Voices from South and North* David Hallman (1994) observes that the contributors tend to emphasise the interconnectedness of ecological destruction and economic injustice, and the need to address these issues concurrently. As for a new theological agenda, he states:

> We are in the early stages of a profound conceptual shift in theology that will move us far beyond stewardship theology as a response to human exploitation of God's creation . . . Even if we now talk more in terms of responsibility than domination, our approach is still a management model in which we humans think we know best. By breaking open that conceptual prison, feminist theology and insights from the traditions of indigenous peoples are both critically important groundings for the emerging ecotheology, as the articles in those chapters demonstrate (Hallman 1994:6).

By contrast, the collection of essays compiled by Mary Evelyn Tucker and John Grim entitled *Worldviews and Ecology: Religion, Philosophy and the Environment* (1994) presents a wider spectrum of religio-ecological worldviews (Christian, Native North American, Jewish, Muslim, Bahài, Hindu, Buddhist, Jainist, Taoist, and Confucian), as well as contemporary ecological views based on evolutionary cosmology. Characteristic of this book is the recognition of plurality, the premise that 'no one religious tradition or philosophical perspective has the ideal solution to the environmental crisis' (Tucker and Grim 1994:11), and the editors' thesis—endorsed by some of the contributors—that 'a new global environmental ethic will be needed to solve some of the critical issues that face us in the late twentieth century' (Tucker and Grim 1994:12).

Thomas Berry maintains that little progress can be made with global environmental ethics prior to the development of a new science which deals with the integral functioning of the earth itself, a field to which we are as yet newcomers. In anticipation of a creative period which he calls the 'ecozoic era,' Berry (1994:230) outlines a new biological and planetary situation:

> While we generally use the terms 'environmental' and 'ecological,' it might be more appropriate to deal with the situation in terms of a planet which has

become dysfunctional because we do not have an integral sense of the earth or how it functions. We need a new study that might be designated, in the terms of Robert Muller, as a 'Total Earth Science,' a science which has so far never been properly identified as a special field of study.

One of the mechanisms to this end, Berry suggests, could be a new discipline which he calls 'ecological geography,' which will focus less on detached, academic understanding as it relates more purposefully and directly to political decision making, economics, and the dynamics of human culture: 'If economic geography serving the purposes of human exploitation of the planet were to be altered into ecological geography for the purpose of identifying the proper niche of the human within the larger purposes of the earth community, then a great advance may be made toward achieving a viable planetary system' (Berry 1994:235).

The agenda for Christianity appears to be quite complex, as it has to include self-critical confession of complicity in today's rampant exploitation of natural resources by human beings if the biblical impulses for responsible stewardship are to be convincingly extolled and practised. Jay McDaniel arrests attention when he sums up his inspiring 'Christian approach to ecology.' Life in Christ, the new life for ecology, says McDaniel (1994:80), involves '(1) an acceptance of lost innocence; (2) a recognition of the limitless love of God; and (3) an openness to the healing powers of this God as they well up from within the very depths of our existence.' To accept our lost innocence we have to recognise our alienation from fellow human beings and our inclination to evaluate other creatures only or mainly in terms of their usefulness to us. From within our urban-industrial contexts, says McDaniel (1994:81), 'we must confess that we partake of "anthropocentric consciousness." This is part of our sinful existence.' To the extent that we become vessels of God's limitless love and experience the living Christ at the core of our beings 'our own "dominion" will be tempered by a deeper recognition of the sheer goodness, the sheer lovability, of each and every living being whom we influence. As Paul puts it, we will have put on the mind of Christ' (Phil 2:5).

How do we respond to the challenges raised by concerned environmentalists the world over? In terms of my own Southern African earthkeeping context I attempt a few brief suggestions:

First, ZIRRCON could propagate the introduction of earth science courses in Zimbabwean schools. Along with the nature-related practical activities already suggested above, they will help to give the youth an environmental focus and a global view of the ecological crisis at an early stage of their education. The courses should be developed by interdisciplinary teams to combine ecological expertise with the kind of religio-cultural input which ZIRRCON has gained in the field. One could experiment with educational ways of exposing the youth to the elders of AZTREC and the AAEC bishops. Such instruction will put scholars in touch with the roots of their own environmental ethics, both in the traditional, ancestrally informed and in the indigenised Christian sense.

Second, the eco-theological task of developing an African creation or environmental theology, both at the grassroots and at the more sophisticated academic level, should be pursued with vigour. AIC theologians operating in rural and urban societies and African theologians attached to academic institutions should be encouraged to collaborate regularly in such an enterprise. To the same extent that academics would benefit from exposure to the earthkeeping rituals of village or urban communities, AIC earthkeepers could benefit from recognition and participation in events arranged by EATWOT and the WCC's JPIC committees. Empowerment of AIC earthkeepers to relate to Western eco-theological literature and to make their own contribution at the highest level in Western academic institutions will extend North-South dialogue and enrich the local/global dimension in eco-theology.

Third, the ecological contribution of African 'primal traditions' or worldviews needs to be more closely defined and publicised. The earthkeeping activities of AZTREC provide valuable clues to customary conservationist laws and praxis as they relate to an indigenous yet modern earthkeeping movement. In the *mafukidzanyika* ceremonies the interconnectedness of the entire earth community—living, deceased, and unborn humans, soil, water, trees, wildlife, etc.—is ritually enacted over and over again, like the life cycles and seasonal cycles of nature. Caring attitudes towards nature are culturally and spiritually ingrained, and are significantly in evidence and readily available to motivate responsible ecological stewardship in a society where the 'trees of consent' (*mubvumira*) still affirm ancestral approval of human behaviour, the 'trees of exorcism' (*muzeze*) provide symbolic power for demon expulsion, and the 'trees of protection' (*muchakata*) still symbolise the closeness of the apical ancestors and the creator, Mwari.

The future challenge to institutions like ZIRRCON, the F and E project, and the envisaged AEU will be to investigate African cosmologies and the indigenous roots of their environmental ethics, as well as empower basic African communities to become fully active in the green resistance struggle. Then the prophecy of the African earth and the message of the African people will be heard and heeded in the global village, just as modern science and the technology developed to serve creation will inform and assist the struggle in Africa.

Fourth, thematic studies of worldviews, spirituality, traditional knowledge and environmental ethics in primal societies, the perception and functioning of ecologically related community life, the nature and impact of liberation struggles throughout the world, etc., will promote the articulation of a global environmental ethic and the development of global strategies for earthkeeping action.

In the fifth place, the intellectual activity of research and publication underlying much of what is outlined above should be augmented by actual exposure to and participation in African earthkeeping projects. Institutions like ZIRRCON and F and E could be instrumental in such networking. Just as message and prophecy have to be carried from the grassroots to the institutions of academic knowledge and political power, the representatives of academia, capital, and power need to be exposed to earthkeeping experience at the grassroots. Although the mass media help in carrying the earthkeeping story to the furthest corners of global society, it is only when the wealthy, the power brokers, the representatives of multinational interest groups and the intellectuals are wrested from their safe havens and reintegrated with the earth community—where they can feel the scorching sun on denuded plains, the urgent call for justice and healing in dancing feet and the forgiving benediction in the shade of carefully nurtured trees—that the global groundswell of earthkeeping will get underway.

This brings us to the second task: the praxis of the green struggle.

The Task of Mobilising the Struggle

The intellectual task of studying cultures, religions, human values, and behavioural patterns in relation to the environment, and of formulating views and information which could further the quest for a global environmental ethic, is never complete—or at least it shouldn't be. There can never be an abstract or a purely theoretical ecology! Ecology entails passion, action, the struggle for the life of the earth community. The struggle requires reflection, evaluation, publication, and policy making, all activities which require periodic retirement from the battle front. But intellectual endeavour does not mean isolated or elitist academic privilege which entitles one to stay out of the fray. Whether we are actively mobilising political consensus, our own families in recycling ventures, or entire movements in earthkeeping projects; whether we raise or donate funds for earthkeeping; whether we proclaim the good news of earth healing by refraining from using polluting chemicals, fighting for responsible disposal of atomic waste, or risking possible ridicule by publicly identifying with the controversial activities of green movements—the fact remains that private reflection and public action are both integral to earth stewardship if we are genuinely concerned about the future of planet earth. For, as Gore (1992:269) insists, 'we must take bold and unequivocal action: we must make the rescue of the environment the central organising principle for civilisation.'

Gore qualifies our battle for the environment as an extension of the struggles against Nazism and communism, as 'a crucial new phase of the long battle for true freedom and human dignity.' He continues by listing vital issues, threats to the new principle, which need to be faced and corrected: the balance between rights and responsibilities, which is impaired because of the alienation of individuals from community and from the earth; corruption in both the developing and developed worlds, which obstructs our ability to share environmental stewardship on a global scale; mistaken assumptions about development and a mismatch between projects funded by the industrial world and the real needs of the Third World, resulting in ecological destruction and social instability.

Gore also mentions 'a new kind of resistance fighter: men and women who have recognized the brutal nature of the force now grinding away at the forests and oceans, the atmosphere and fresh water, the wind and the rain, and the rich diversity of life itself' (Gore 1992:282). They have been ordinary people, yet uncompromising campaigners in the cause of justice for the earth community. One was Tos Barnett, who narrowly escaped assassination by writing a report exposing the rape of forests in Papua New Guinea by Japanese corporations; another was Chico Mendes, who was martyred for leading rubber trappers in the rain forests of Brazil in their resistance to the landowners and corporations responsible for massive deforestation; a third was Wangari Matthai, who mobilised the women of Kenya in the Greenbelt movement to plant millions of trees (Gore 1992:283–294). All these people in their different ways were and still are engaged in the global war of the trees. These green icons have captured the imagination both of eco-sensitive people in their own cultures and of the emerging earthkeeping community in the global village. Likewise, the Shona icons mentioned in this book—even if their activities seldom reach the news headlines in their own country—appeal to the conscience of large segments of African society. This promotes the steady recruitment of new fighters, the encouragement of the 'pioneers' of the struggle who are already becoming 'veterans,' and the escalation, geographically, of afforestation and related projects.

CONCLUSION

A strategic initiative to plant billions of trees throughout the world, especially on degraded lands, is one of the most easily understandable, potentially popular, and ecologically intelligent efforts on which the Global Marshall Plan should concentrate. The symbolism—and the substantive significance—of planting a tree has universal power in every culture and every society on earth, and it is a way for individual men, women, and children to participate in creating solutions for the environmental crisis (Gore 1992:323).

ZIRRCON's war of the trees endorses this vision for tree-planting. The message, conveyed by the written word and illustrated by the healing hands of African earthkeepers, is so deceptively simple that it is easy to miss but one which we cannot afford to ignore. The world needs billions of trees, not as a one-off achievement of the heroes of the green revolution but as an ongoing greening life style of all inhabitants of the global village: trees for their own sake, trees as a lifeline for living creatures on earth, trees as symbols of hope for a better future, trees as the embodiment of God's salvation, trees in whose rustling leaves and shade we perceive something of the peace of a new heaven and a new earth.

Africa alone needs billions of trees. It seems an unattainable goal considering the funds, time, and effort it took ZIRRCON to plant and nurture only a few million trees—not to mention harsh weather conditions which often frustrate the most valiant attempts to nurture young trees in the soil. Nevertheless, every tree that grows and survives is a symbol of liberation, healing, and achievement for the African poor.

The unfolding story of ZIRRCON provides a key to the mobilisation and empowerment of the peoples of Africa! Will this key be used to unlock the vast potential for human action in the healing of both the land and the people? Will the African Earthkeepers' Union take off and trigger sufficient momentum among African communities to escalate the green revolution like a raging fire across the continent? I believe it is possible for this to happen, provided key figures in every African country and region enact the prophetic message of God's earthbound mission with unflinching commitment. It must happen, whatever obstacles are encountered, particularly the opposition of those who prioritise and isolate human progress, human survival, human development at the expense of the environment and claim that this is where all or the bulk of global development funds should be spent. After all, humans cannot survive without a healthy environment. We really have no alternative but to prioritise for immediate attention the entire earth community, worthy in its entirety of funding for purposes of nurture, healing, and upliftment.

Our widened horizons start at home. Only if we Africans feel the agony of creation in our particular part of the world, and respond with new life styles of sacrificial earth stewardship, will we help to spread the good news of the greening of planet earth in the global village. This is part of God's mission to the world, for in Christ all things hold together.

Seek ye therefore first the kingdom of God . . .

EPILOGUE

Then the Rains Came

Those dry seasons of the late eighties and early nineties drove us to despair. Many peasant families in the communal lands who had lost all their cattle during the drought had to depend on others when they wanted their fields ploughed. Water holes dried up, rural schools closed when pupils became too weak from starvation to attend, and the government had to distribute food regularly to keep entire communities alive. The water level in Lake Kyle (Mtirikwe) dropped to an all-time low. At one point there was only two to three per cent of its water left. The pumps had to be moved nearer the dam wall to keep Masvingo town supplied with water. Even then the water from the taps, despite filtration, was often a muddy brown. The 'better' rainy seasons seldom caused the lake to rise much beyond the 20 per cent mark and came too late for the numerous dried out *muchakata* and other indigenous trees to recover. On Mount Mugabe the squatters started deforesting the steepest slopes in their desperation to increase their crop yields. All they achieved was to strip away the vegetation that protected the mountain against soil erosion. One day as I drove up the pass I was dismayed to see a granite-studded slope, totally unsuitable for cultivation, stripped all the way to the summit. The bare slope just lay there, ugly and defiant, helpless in the afternoon sun. The scene was like an omen, with the seasons holding their breath waiting for something to happen. Waiting, perhaps, for the mountain to be set free.

And happen it did. In the course of 1996 I had noticed some articles in the Masvingo newspapers about the squatter problem on Mount Mugabe. But the chances of the squatters being resettled elsewhere seemed slim, so I paid no further attention and concentrated on my academic duties in South Africa and abroad. Thus, in January 1997, when I took a friend to Morgenster mission late one afternoon, I was unaware of the latest developments. The early rains had fallen, the mountain air smelt fresh and the slopes seemed greener than they had been in a long time.

But it was only when we got out of the car and climbed a granite dome to get a better view of the damage done to the mountain face that the truth dawned on me. The slopes and valleys were already hidden in the long shadows of dusk. There were no voices, no lowing of cattle, no open household fires with mothers preparing food. Just quiet and peace. The shells of abandoned huts were silent reminders of human occupation. Already a green sheen of grass, shrubs, and saplings had taken over, covering the wounded slopes that had been stripped for agricultural produce. In the distance we could hear bulbuls, starlings, and crows prepare for nightfall. The mountain was free. The invader squatters had gone!

We just sat there in the fading light, marvelling at the ability of nature, when left alone, to resuscitate itself. I thought of the lowveld in the south towards Beitbridge where a combination of overgrazing and drought gave the soil a desert-like appearance under shrivelled mopani trees. But in no time at all good rains would turn the lost world into a luscious garden carpeted with sweet grass, grazing for large herds of deer and cattle. I also thought of the ravaging of the Zambezi wilderness on the Zambian side near Feira, where large numbers of refugee families from Mozambique built villages along the river. They had introduced goats and dogs, and planted their banana trees all the way across the banks and into the river bed. There was no big game left in that area. But when I spoke to the villagers they appeared unperturbed by the loss of game in their own territory. They merely vented their frustration at the Zimbabweans who still had large concentrations of big game and mercilessly shot poachers who dared cross the river to hunt on their side. All that was needed to restore the wilderness along the Zambian side of the river was to move the alien villagers out of the area and allow nature to take its course. Within a few years the bush would have recovered and the elephant and buffalo, if left undisturbed, would have returned.

I was aware of the thorny issues involved: politics, land for resettlement in the face of overpopulation, the funding of such an exodus, and the resistance of the villagers. Yet if any of Africa's magnificent wilderness is to be preserved, a price has to be paid. The complexities of restricting human movement and occupation in what is left of Africa's wildlife habitat were dwarfed in my mind by the overpowering assurance that Mwari's creation could recover on its own from virtually any form of human abuse, if only it could be liberated from intrusion and rampant exploitation. Below us the greening valleys and budding new growth from the eroded soil were evidence of this truth. Mount Mugabe had refused to die. Left to itself, it had already covered the afflicted parts of its body with a green garment.

Observing in the twilight the first signs of the mountain's recovery was balm to the earthkeeper's soul. Anguish over the invasion of this very mountain after Independence had been a major motivation for forming our earthkeeping movement and planting millions of trees. It was reassuring to know that our war of the trees was not an isolated venture dependent entirely on the will and action of our own green forces. On the contrary, our limited and at times feeble attempts were anchored in and drew strength from the resilience of Mwari's earth. Through the healing of his mountain Mwari seemed to be telling me not to lose hope as we toiled in his mission. If we could meet only half our responsibility as earth stewards, the healing, growth and restoration we sought would be wrought by the revitalising life force built into creation.

It was as if the liberation of Mount Mugabe was the long-awaited sign for the release of the rains. In the months that followed the skies, heavy with dark clouds, yielded. And the rains came as had last happened in 1974/75; the rivers flooded and Lake Kyle rose to between 70 and 80 per cent. Crops flourished and so did ZIRRCON's newly planted trees.

In the grim context of global ecology our story features, or blurs, like a trivial fairy tale. It is sobering, as I write the last few paragraphs of this epistle, to read the lead article in the *Boston Sunday Globe* (25 May 1997) under the headline, 'A world pact reduced to ashes. Rhetoric of environmental resolve has not translated into action.' I quote from it:

With much smoke but little publicity the Brazilian rain forest is disappearing at a much faster rate than before the 1992 UN Conference on Environment and Development, as the Earth Summit held in Brazil was officially called. Each year an area of rainforest nearly the size of Massachusetts is destroyed . . . By most accounts, the legacy of the Earth Summit and its 70,000 pages of daily press releases has turned out to be mainly hot air . . . Governments that pledged to support environmentally sustainable development by increasing foreign aid contributions have actually decreased them, with the United States leading the slashing . . . On the ground in Paragominas everyday looks like doomsday. It is impossible to tell where the smoke ends and the clouds begin . . . In the charcoal camps (with row upon row of furnaces) the cremation of the rainforest is methodical. Tree trunks are stacked like toothpicks, chopped, burned, raked, and transported to power massive pig iron factories. 'It's hard work and hazardous conditions,' says Sonia Levi of the International Labor Office, a UN agency trying to end child labor. 'They [the children] work directly with fire. Their bodies are impregnated with charcoal dust. They have physical problems, problems with their lungs, they carry heavy loads of wood. They have problems. It must be hell.'

Presented to the world as a means of improving the living conditions of the poor in Brazil, the furnaces of hell are blazing away in Paragominas, destroying both the lives of young people working there and one of the earth's crucial life support systems, the Brazilian rain forest being the largest absorber of carbon dioxide gases in the world. Who benefits from this carnage? Human predators! According to the *Globe* none of the thirty-four logging companies at Paragominas meets the minimum requirements of the regulatory International Tropical Timber Organisation.

Such news fills one with sadness and anger at a world slipping towards an abyss of total environmental bankruptcy. The root of this evil is human greed, of which we are all guilty. In times like these we may have to become like children once more and listen to a few fairy tales of tree planting in Africa. Perhaps they will rekindle our hope and make us strive to give meaning to the good news of justice, peace, and the integrity of creation in what has yet to become a new heaven and a new earth.

Original Constitution of the Association of Zimbabwean Spirit Mediums

1 AFFORESTATION

(a) To protect sacred places and sacred mountains, e.g., Gwindingwi in Bikita; Vinga in Chiwara chiefdom, Gutu; Rasa in Gutu; Murangaranga in Marozva, Bikita; Hozvi in Mukangangwi chiefdom, Bikita; Boromokwa in Ndanga; Mangwandi in Zimuto; Matonjeni in the Matopo hills; Nyuni in Murinye chiefdom, Masvingo; Great Zimbabwe ruins in Masvingo; Chibvumani in Chikuku, Bikita.

(b) To protect all indigenous fruit trees in Zimbabwe e.g., *muchakata* (cork tree), *mushuku* (wild loquat), *mukute* (*syzyguim cordatum*; marshland tree bearing sweet purple fruit), *muonde* (wild fig tree), *mushumba* (*diospyros mespiliformis*), *muchechete* (*minusops zeyhari*; medium to large trees with dense foliage and sweet, aromatic brown berries), *mutamba* (*strychnos* species, bearing orange-sized, hard-skinned fruit with clustered, juicy pips), *nengeni* (sour plum), *mutobge* (*azanza garkeana*; medium-sized tree with edible, dry fruit that requires much chewing; a favourite of the ancestors), *mutunduru* (*garcinia huillensis*; small evergreen tree with dark edible fruit), *musvazva* (*securinega virosa*; small to medium glossy leaved trees found on granite outcrops, bearing red to purple edible fruit).

(c) To protect other indigenous trees such as the acacia species (*muvushe, msasa, mutondo*), *mubvumira* (*kirkia acuminata*), *mupembere* (*combretum molle*), etc. and arrest deforestation by mobilising people in rural areas to start afforestation projects.

(d) To encourage district authorities to form committees in their respective areas which will implement afforestation programmes, and also to elect delegates who will make representations to the government on these issues.

(e) To influence the government to pass laws which make it an offence to fell trees indiscriminately and to prosecute offenders.

(f) To map out new strategies of planting trees in the districts.

2 WATER RESOURCES

(a) To protect all water resources, e.g., springs, marshlands and fountains; particularly pools, dams, and rivers where *njuzu* (water spirits) are found.

(b) To protect dams by preventing people from fishing without permission/licences, and rivers through the prohibition of netting fish.

(c) To discourage people from cultivating river banks and catchment areas, as this will result in the siltation of rivers and dams.

(d) To start special conscientisation programmes on water resources.

3 WILD LIFE CONSERVATION

(a)   To protect wild animals e.g., *shuro* (rabbits), *mhembwe* (duiker), *mhene* (steenbok), and *nyoka* (snakes) at district level.

(b)   To liaise with the Department of National Parks and Wildlife.

(c)   To conscientise rural communities on the conservation of wildlife.

4 PROMOTION OF TRADITIONAL CUSTOMS

(a)   To promote traditional customs and rituals, e.g., to respect the elders, maintain rain ceremonies (*mikwerere*), and observe ancestral rest days (*chisi*).

(b)   To encourage the Ministry of Education to incorporate the teaching of traditional customs into existing school curricula.

(c)   To conscientise people in rural areas to teach their children traditional customs.

APPENDIX 2

Traditional Game Laws

1   Hunting was restricted to the winter season.

2   The killing of young animals of all species was strictly forbidden.

3   Female animals in foal or with young were not to be hunted.

4   Hunting was only allowed for personal or family consumption, not for commercial purposes.

5   Crop-raiding animals and predators which posed a threat to human life could be killed.

6   Limits were set for individual hunters. No hunter was allowed to kill indiscriminately or too frequently.

7   Hunting boundaries for each tribe or clan were clearly delineated.

8   Hunting was subject to community control and misconduct came up for litigation in the chief's court.

9   The killing of sizeable animals had to be reported to the chief, who—as ancestral representative—was always entitled to a specified portion of the meat, for instance the *bandauko* (front leg).

10   Hunting with nets and with the aid of bushfires was subject to permission from chief and council. Young animals and certain species caught in the nets had to be released.

11   Depending on totemic prohibition and the threat of extinction, certain species could not be hunted at all. As eland, for example, became scarce in Gutu area and adjacent districts, it became 'royal game' to all hunters, not just to the Hera people who abstained from hunting this antelope for totemic reasons.

12   Meat of culled game had to be distributed fairly to the benefit of families and/or communities. Individual and commercial exploitation based on the Western conception of human dominion over creation was therefore, at least in principle, proscribed.

13   Certain bird species, particularly the bateleur eagle, and smaller animals and reptiles (e.g., the tortoise, certain ants, and snakes) were protected, as they acted as emissaries from the ancestral world to living descendants.

14   In some areas the culling of wild cats, such as the serval and civet cats and the small spotted genet, was the prerogative of tribal elders, spirit mediums, or *nganga* practitioners, as the skins of these animals form part of their regalia.

15   The spirit mediums are the guardians of such threatened species as ant-bears, pangolins, and bush-babies.

Tree-Planting Sermons in Spirit-Type (Prophetic) Independent Churches

APOSTOLIC SERMONS

TREE-PLANTING CEREMONY AT THE HEADQUARTERS OF THE CHIRATIDZO CHAVAPOSTORI (SIGN OF THE APOSTLES) CHURCH, ZIMUTO DISTRICT, 11 JANUARY 1991

Bishop Kindiam Wapendama: Peace to the believers! Let us pay attention to our book (the Bible). To those of us who want to follow the instructions contained in it, the book is our aunt (*vatete*). The book teaches clearly about good and evil deeds. Pay attention all of you, so that you can fully understand the message it conveys.

Reader: The heading of Hebrews 11 says: What is faith? People can succeed through faith.

Wapendama: It says people can conquer through faith. Peace to you, people of Mwari! There is a kind of faith which does not manifest itself in good works because it is overcome by sin. I often tell you that sin abounds in this world. This is so because there are people who reveal a spirit of evil and cruelty. Wherever they go they need to kill living things. That is truly sinful! You find people without any compassion for others. They scheme against others so as to place them in jeopardy through hatred. That too is sin! Someone thinks: 'Let me chop down as many trees as possible. When they have dried out I shall have plenty of firewood.' Now that is a terrible sin! Peace to you, people of God!

Reader: Hebrews 11:1: Now faith is the assurance of things hoped for, the conviction of things not seen.

Wapendama: People of Mwari, it says that faith concerns the things not seen. Yet faith is strengthened by the signs we observe. We observe many signs in this world. In some areas where we have been we observed good and fertile lands. But now there are gullies which have devastated the land, gullies so deep that you cannot even enter them safely. That is truly a sign, a warning against evil. We have learnt that we have to avoid the sin of destroying the land. Peace to you, people of Mwari.

Reader: Hebrews 11:2: For by it the men of old received divine approval.

Wapendama: The people of old were commended for their good deeds. If they did not protect this land of ours, where do you think we would have been today? We would not have been here at all, because our forebears would have stripped the land completely, so that there would have been no soil for agriculture, no minerals left to mine. But because they thought of the children of tomorrow they protected the land, the environment. They did this so that we can live. So let us follow their example and heed the laws concerning good works. Then our young ones can preach and live according to the word of God. They, too, will avoid being cruel and destructive, for they will recognise that without faith nothing good can be built. The deeds of a person can always be observed. As I have told you, some people only destroy. Even if you have taken the trouble to plant trees you may find that someone has come in the night and chopped down all the trees.

You know that long ago there were not so many illnesses. Illness was prevented from taking hold because this land of ours was fully clad with grass and trees. The vegetation produced clean, healthy air which we could breathe freely and survive. Peace to those who believe! Nowadays the air is polluted. Fresh air no longer abounds. Even the trees are wondering how they can continue breathing. The result of this unhealthy situation is that we are all exposed to many diseases, such as TB, AIDS, and scabies. You find your body suddenly full of sores without knowing the cause. This situation arises because of the lack of trees covering the land. In the past there were many trees producing a perfume which you could smell. This was a sign of fresh air. But nowadays we no longer smell the perfume of those trees, or see them at all. It is a situation which causes us to be fearful. How are we going to succeed in clothing all the barren patches of earth which we have stripped bare?

Increasingly people have difficulty finding firewood. At Chiworese, for instance, I have noticed people burning thorn bushes for lack of proper firewood. Bearing this in mind, we face a great challenge to restore the earth. Our offspring will one day read in history books that we had no trees left, but that we did everything possible in our time to remedy the situation. You see, we shall pass away and others will follow us. They will want to know what works we did, whether we merely destroyed or built something valuable.

Reader: Hebrews 11:3: By faith we understand that the world was created by the word of God, so that what is seen was made out of things that do not appear.

Wapendama: The whole world was created and given order by Mwari through his laws. All people heard the commandments: Don't kill! Don't sin! Avoid evil and follow the righteous way! As I have said: avoid all cruelty! Someone arrives at another's house and out of sheer malice burns it down, together with the trees standing near it. The trees wither away and there is no peace. How can there be peace if such a thing happens?

The things we observe are made out of unseen things (v 3). Look at that large tree over there. Which of you know its age or saw it grow? There it stands. Our forefathers left it to serve as a sign (of the unseen) in this world. So today you still have its shade in which to rest. Peace to you, children of Mwari! Such trees hold a lesson. In some regions people recognise this and declare the trees holy. It is the same as that age-old tree over there on that plain. We call it *muti vehova* (the tree of the river, of water, i.e., a symbol of life). That tree is not to be felled or to be used as fuelwood. It is a sign to the young of something that has endured for ages. [It is a link with the past and represents respect for the history of the forebears.] It is a matter of joy to see these old trees. Likewise our offspring will remember us in the times to come when they observe the trees we have planted.

These old trees also remind us of the forests of the past. Nowadays the land is naked. The lightning strikes all over because there is no protective cover to avert it. The rains no longer fall regularly because the winds bringing the rain clouds have nowhere to come to a standstill. It blows and blows until all the clouds are gone, because there are no trees to hold it. Consequently the clouds yield rain elsewhere.

It is the same with you, a living person in this world. As the world dries up for lack of trees, you will eventually fail to breathe and then drop down . . .

Reader: Hebrews 11:4: By faith Abel offered to God a more acceptable sacrifice than Cain, through which he received approval as righteous, God bearing witness by accepting his gifts; he died but through his faith he is still speaking.

Wapendama: It says that you Christians should do what is pleasing to God, that you should give back to this world what has been destroyed in it. Do not follow those [Cain] who strayed from Jehovah, but bring him a pleasing sacrifice! How pleasing will it be if you could all follow this teaching. We keep considering that our lives greatly depend on trees.

Without trees we cannot breathe. The perfume [oxygen, air] of the trees enters our nostrils, so that we can breathe. We are so concerned with many things in this life which we consider necessary for our survival. But do we really notice the trees, there where they stand breathing in the bush? Is it not so that when the leaves of the indigenous trees start budding some of us feel it in our stomachs? What causes this? It is a matter of us feeling together with the trees and the budding leaves that the seasons are changing. A new kind of breathing, both for the leaves of the trees and for us, has arrived. Those leaves, through which we breathe, tell us through our stomachs of the arrival of another season. When their stomachs are upset, people wrongly think that it is caused by eating *mushamba* [leaf tips of cattle-melon plants, cooked like spinach]. No! The real reason is changed breathing. We of the Spirit, we who work through the [Holy] Spirit, can distinguish this change. Even the cattle undergo this change.

In those areas where there are many trees this change is more pronounced. It is really a sign of good health, for in such areas the perfume of the trees is constantly in people's nostrils. Those who live in barren areas are less healthy; they tend to be thin, as their breathing process is affected.

Keep considering this message of the trees, all of you! First of all, trees provide us with fresh air to breathe. Trees therefore bring life. Second, trees bring rain. Third, trees prevent the formation of gullies, as they check the flow of water. But since the trees have been felled in great numbers and the plains are naked, people nowadays are wondering whether the floodwaters are not the water of Noah of long ago [i.e., the waters of judgment].

In earlier years we did not see all these boreholes. Although the facility is very convenient, it seems as if the earth is being drained of water at the expense of the trees. The water drains away into the earth beyond reach. There is nothing to prevent its passage into the earth, for there are now insufficient tree roots to hold the underground water.

The situation all round will only improve as we restore the land with numerous trees. As the forests become plentiful once again, the people and all of creation will breathe properly. The wind will settle as before and bring enough rain. Sickness will subside in our communities. You will all see the change. Yet this is a formidable task. I *beseech you to place yourselves in the hands of Mwari. He alone can give us the strength to endure in this struggle.* He will strengthen us, together with his messengers [the ZIRRCON-AAEC team].

Mwari saw the devastation of the land. So he called his envoys to shoulder the task of deliverance. Come, you messengers of Mwari, come and deliver us! Together with you [the team of tree planters] we are now *the deliverers of the stricken land. Let us go forth and clothe, heal Mwari's stricken land.* This is not a task through which you can enrich yourselves. No! The deliverers were sent by God on a divine mission. He said: You, go to Africa, for the land is ravaged! Peace to you, people of Mwari. Deliverance, Mwari says, lies in trees, but in the first place the people have to obey. Mwari therefore sends his deliverers to continue here on earth with his own work, with all the work Jesus Christ started here. Jesus said: I leave you, my followers, to complete my work. And that task is the one of healing [all of creation—human beings and the environment]!

We are the followers of Jesus and have to continue his healing ministry. You are the believers who will see his miracles in this afflicted world. *So let us all fight, clothing the earth with trees!* Let us follow the example of the deliverers who were sent by Mwari. God gave this task to a man of his choice. Because this man responded, the task is proceeding as you can see for yourselves today.

It is *our* task to strengthen this *mission* with our numbers of people. You know how numerous we are. Sometimes we count ten thousand people at our church meetings. If we work with enthusiasm we shall clothe the entire land with trees and drive off affliction [evil]. We shall strengthen the hands of the deliverers because they were called to consider the whole of Zimbabwe. As we plant they will visit us and see the growing number of trees. They will bring the visitors from overseas who support this work. When they see the trees they will take heart and persevere.

In doing all this we still praise Mwari, for it is he who inspires and empowers us to accomplish this task. In whom do we do all this? In Mwari! May Jehovah bless you. Amen.

TREE-PLANTING EUCHARIST OF THE CHIRATIDZO CHAVAPOSTORI CHURCH (SIGN OF THE APOSTLES CHURCH), CHIVI DISTRICT, 13 MARCH 1992

Bishop Kindiam Wapendama: Peace to you, people of Mwari! I was not aware of the destruction caused by ground-nesting ants in Chivi. But I know now that if we do not heed the spirit of the adversary in our midst we shall be afflicted by illness. In the first place, we are here to attend tree-planting ceremonies in order to heal the barrenness plaguing our land. The young ones do not really know the different tree species any more. Neither do they know which species are threatened or extinct in their own areas. So we have a great task of promoting *afforestation* and protecting God's creation. I want to make you fully aware of the drastic nature of the environmental situation we are facing. We simply have no right to destroy God's creation, or to neglect that [the trees] which we have taken the trouble to cultivate. Things grow in nature because of God. But we cannot take it for granted. Mwari says: 'I have given trees in your midst. If you fail to plant and take care of the trees, I shall not create new ones any more.' Don't think that if you just fell trees [randomly] Mwari will simply create similar trees in their place. There will be no more trees!

You have no option but to plant trees, as we are doing today. There is no other way. Peace to those who believe in him! Let us heed this message today; each one of us, let us spread the word in our families, namely that uncontrolled tree felling must stop, that trees are sacred.

We have gone to a great deal of trouble over this issue. Since 1985 I have hardly smelt the perfume of flowers, those purple and yellow ones. Which of you have seen any wild flowers around here? There are none! Why? Because we have destroyed them all. Our children do not even know such flowers. They only know the colour green, the colour of trees. But the purple, pink, yellow and red flowers they do not recognise. We have destroyed the colours . . . Now read from our book!

Reader: The heading of Acts 20 says that Paul is instructing the elders of Ephesus.

Wapendama: Likewise I instruct you, the elders of Zimbabwe, and the elders of this district.

Reader: Acts 20:22: And now I commend you to God and to the word of his grace, which is able to build you up and to give you the inheritance among all those who are sanctified.

Wapendama: I thank Jehovah that he sent his Spirit to enter Prof. Muchakata Daneel, causing him to dream and receive power to mobilise the struggle against environmental destruction. You, Prof. Daneel, have received the Holy Spirit who works in you the love for this task. Mwari tells you: 'Proceed! I'll give you strength!' Truly, I have seen that all people will be drawn into this struggle, for Jehovah gives you strength. He has given you and all of us present these hands to work with. So let us work! Our labour will be a sign in this world which will induce our children to follow suit in the years to come. They will praise their parents as wise people and they will not have to travel to other countries to see forests. Right now you cannot afford a red mahogany (*mukamba*) door, even if you wanted one. There are hardly any left in this district. You have felled them all. Besides, you cannot afford one nowadays, for they cost $1,000 each.

Reader: Acts 20:33: I coveted no one's silver or gold or apparel.

Wapendama: Sure, he (Paul) did not covet other people's silver or gold, he only wanted all people to lead good lives. Just look at the dried and lifeless land around you. *I believe that we can change it.* Because we are repairing the damage and are doing penance for our guilt of land destruction, God will heed our wish and give us plentiful rain. Yet we still confront the problem of unchecked winds because of treeless plains. Without cover the winds simply flatten our houses. Read on!

Reader: Acts 20:34: You yourselves know that these hands ministered to my necessities, and to those who were with me.

Wapendama: You all know that these hands of ours have contributed to rectifying a situation of deprivation. Hopefully our work will cause these (*mukamba*, red mahogany) trees to grow to maturity. Let our hands bring about a valuable inheritance for our children, so that they can teach the people of other countries. I am sure some of them will in time become doctors [specialists] of trees. But if we don't plant the trees, with what will they heal? These trees indeed have many purposes. We Christians know that we find the comfort of shade under the trees. The birds find safe places in the branches to build their nests. The hospitals find medicines for all kinds of ailments. Now, with these trees, the hospitals will not fail. We can breathe fresh air because of the trees. In the absence of trees there can only be polluted air, because the trees filter the air. Those tree flowers which cleanse the winds will no longer function if all the trees are felled. Therefore our exercise here today is one of instruction, as well as strengthening our visitors here today, encouraging them to remain steadfast in their striving for a better environment.

In addition I am resolved that in this area with its dams I shall take the responsibility for planting many more trees. I tell you, Mwari will give us plentiful rains because we are paying for that vengeful spirit (*ngozi*) which we have provoked through tree destruction. As we pay to appease the *ngozi*, the damage is repaired. As yet we have merely started the struggle. Let us proceed by creating forests right round all the dams in this area and so protect our water resources and prevent soil erosion. Don't turn a blind eye to this serious problem. God has given us hands to mend the earth. Look for yourselves, use your eyes and then respond to God's command. Let there be obedience from our side, harmony between eyes and hands. Having planted the trees, let us also provide the aftercare lest the trees die. Go and teach your children far and wide that trees must be planted all over: at schools, around dams and in gullies. I myself do not want to see a single patch of barren soil, because the water simply comes and carries it away. Even if you dig for water in barren areas, you will find nothing because all the shade has gone and the soil is dried out. In all this let us recognise the prompting of our eternal saviour! Amen.

ADMINISTERING THE TREE-PLANTING EUCHARIST

Wapendama: Now we thank the son of man who has given us all this through the Holy Spirit, for us to accomplish this task. Let us start by considering his word.

Reader: The heading of Matthew 26 says that the message concerns the *paseka* and eucharist. Matthew 26:17–18: Now on the first day of the unleavened bread the disciples came to Jesus, saying: 'Where will you have us prepare for you to eat the passover?' He said: 'Go into the city to a certain one and say to him, "The teacher says, My time is at hand; I will keep the passover at your house with my disciples."'

Wapendama: It says that we here today have a similar arrangement to the one Jesus had. We arranged that we should come here with the Christian disciples so that in remembrance [of Christ] we can conduct our tree-planting ceremony.

Reader: Matthew 26:19: And the disciples did as Jesus had directed them, and they prepared the passover.

Wapendama: They prepared the *paseka*. Likewise you here have prepared the *paseka* and we have seen it prepared. Our visitors, too, have seen your preparations.

Reader: Matthew 26:20–26 (v 26): Now as they were eating Jesus took bread and blessed and broke it and gave it to the disciples and said, 'Take, eat; this is my body.'

Wapendama: He gave the bread to his followers, reminding them: 'This is my body.'

Reader: Matthew 26:27–28: And he took a cup, and when he had given thanks he gave it to them saying, 'Drink of it all of you; for this is my blood of the covenant, which is poured out for many for the forgiveness of sins.'

Wapendama: This blood of mine was poured for you so that all your sins of felling trees and killing God's living creatures can be forgiven.

Reader: Matthew 26:29: 'I tell you I shall not drink again of this fruit of the vine until that day when I drink it anew with you in my father's kingdom.'

Wapendama: It says that he did not proceed but left matters as they were, having given instructions to his disciples how *they* should proceed until they met him again. Likewise we leave you here today to complete the tasks you are given. If you neglect this responsibility of yours and allow things [the trees planted] to waste away, you will really be in trouble, as you have been given clear instructions what to do. And what are the instructions in this case? To guard over the world and all the created things of God. Peace to those who believe in him!

Reader: The heading of prophet Ezekiel 36:25 says that the Israelites are blessed. The verse reads as follows: 'I will sprinkle clean water upon you and you shall be clean from all your uncleanness, and from all your idols I will cleanse you.'

Wapendama (prays over holy water in a container, then sprinkles the water over the land and seedlings as he moves around): I sprinkle this cleansed water, over which I have prayed, over the soil. You, Jehovah, God of righteousness, I believe that you will bless this water and this entire place. I sprinkle this blessed water so that Jehovah can be seen in this place where he will guide his work. I also sprinkle this holy soil in the knowledge that it will be fed by rain and that the soil will thus receive the trees properly.

Reader: Ezekiel 36:26–29: A new heart I will give you, and a new spirit I will put within you; and I will take out of your flesh the heart of stone and give you a heart of flesh.
    And I will deliver you from all your uncleannesses; and I will summon the grain and make it abundant and lay no famine upon you.

Wapendama: Indeed, I shall summon the maize harvest in your lands and I shall not burden you with drought and famine. [This was a powerful statement of faith in a period of severe drought early in 1992.]

Reader: Ezekiel 36:30: I will make the fruit of the tree and the increase of the field abundant, that you may never again suffer the disgrace of famine among the nations.

Wapendama: I shall give you an abundant harvest of grain from your fields and fruit from your trees, so that you shall not be put to shame among the nations because of your neglect of your land, and that of Jesus. Amen.

Participants take bread and wine, each holding a tree in his/her hands; afterwards the trees are planted in God's acre.

ZIONIST CEREMONIES

Tree-planting eucharist at Bishop Mupure's Zion Christian Church of St. Aaron, Zaka district, 1 February 1992

Bishop Reuben Marinda (combining spontaneous preaching and tree-planting liturgy): Peace to the holy ones of Mwari! We are happy today with our tree-planting eucharist. This ceremony starts off with our confessing our sins of destruction, as we have deforested this entire region. Here at the village of Mazhambe in the ward of headman Murerekwa, the leader of St. Aaron's church has committed himself to a work of restitution: replacing the trees which have been felled by the members of this community. The people here say: 'Indeed, we have no trees left. As a result our water supplies have diminished.'

Now I shall read our tree-planting liturgy which reminds us of the evil of uncontrolled tree felling.

I have been given the duty by the creator to keep the Lord's acre where God planted his trees. The creator said: 'These trees in the Lord's acre will be your brothers, your sisters, your friends. Mwari said: 'Your friends the trees will sustain you and provide all the things you need.'

> They will provide you with shade
> to protect you from the heat of the sun.
> They will give you fruit for you to lead healthy lives.
> These trees will clothe the barren earth.

Before we proceed with our liturgy let us read and consider Genesis 2:15–17.

Reader: It says in our book: 'Then the Lord God took the man and put him in the Garden of Eden to till it and keep it. And the Lord God commanded the man, saying, "You may freely eat of every tree of the garden; but of the tree of the knowledge of good and evil you shall not eat, for in the day that you eat of it you shall die." '

Marinda: Peace to you! It says that God placed man in the garden to work it and take care of it. But man did not obey God's commandment. Instead, he violated God's law. The devil used man to rebel against God and creation. Man became an enemy by cutting down all the trees. As a result the weather patterns of the entire world changed. Man became the destroyer of the rain forests, the killer of the world's ecosystems.

So today we confess to you, our God, our sins of wantonly chopping down trees. We confess our abuse of creation; sins which have caused us to lose good pasture for our cattle and fertile topsoil for our crops. Bad farming methods brought this about. Today the cattle are feeding on soil, oh Lord, because there is no grass. God, you are punishing us with severe drought because we have denuded the land. Look, the rivers are dried up and all the fish have gone, because we cut away all the vegetation on the riverbanks, causing the riverbeds to fill up with sand. People are dying every day because they breathe polluted air. There are no trees to clear the air polluted by smoke from our factories. The trees are our friends who eat the poisoned air and give us fresh air to breathe in return. The clean air gives us life!

Reader: Colossians 1:16–17: For in him (Christ) all things were created, in heaven and on earth, visible and invisible, whether thrones or dominions or principalities or authorities, all things were created through him and for him. He is before all things and in him all things hold together.

Marinda: There are millions of creatures which we cannot even see with our naked eyes. We only observe them with the aid of microscopes. All these beings were created by God. Because we need order everyone must submit to the governing authority, such as those we see here today. Here we have the village headman Mr. Mazhambe, and the headman Mr. Murerekwa. These people were given authority by God, for there is no authority other than that established by God. Those who disobey such authority are rebelling against God and will bring judgment on themselves. We rebel against God by not keeping the environment as God instructed us. The devil is at war with God and the devil is using people to destroy all of creation. This drought which has brought untold suffering to our people, to the animals, the fish in the water, and the birds in the air, is God's judgment on the environmental sins we have committed. Let us all confess our sins, so that our sins through the love of God in Christ may be forgiven.

In Jesus Christ all things hold together, it says in Colossians 1:17. He is the head of the body, the church. He is the beginning of all creation and he reigns supreme. God reconciled all things in heaven and on earth with himself through Christ. Christ is Lord over all creation. He works salvation for humankind because humans are the crown of creation. *Humans in turn have the duty to extend salvation to all of creation* [as Christ's co-workers].

If we look at the history of sin offerings in the Old Testament, we are told that each person had to bring an animal or bird to be offered at the Tent of Meeting before the Lord. The priest had to burn these sacrificial animals on a wood fire on the altar of burnt offerings. This was in fact a cruel practice, because many animals and birds had to die for the iniquities of humankind. Trees were felled in great numbers to provide firewood for the burnt offerings. Christ came as the last offering, to forgive the sins of the entire world. Through his death on the cross he saved the animals, the birds, and the trees. So he saves his entire creation! The plan of God's salvation of humankind through Jesus Christ included the salvation of all creation.

Liturgy

The holy communion of which we partake today introduces us to the new eucharist of tree planting.

On the night Jesus was betrayed he took bread, broke it, and said:
'This is my body, which is for you. Eat it in remembrance of me.'
Then he took the cup of wine, saying:
'This is the new covenant in my blood; whenever you drink it, remember me.' For whenever you eat this bread and drink this cup, you proclaim the Lord's death until he comes.

Jesus one day went down to Capernaum with his mother, brothers, and disciples.
It was about time for the Jewish passover.
In the temple he found people selling cattle, sheep, and doves. These were to be used as sin offerings.
When Jesus heard the lowing and bleating he knew the poor creatures were crying to be saved from the cruel merchants—they who had turned God's holy dwelling into a marketplace of debauchery.

So Jesus made a whip out of cords and lashed the corrupt merchants until they fled.
He saved the animals and birds from the cruel fate that awaited them.
Christ came to save all creation.
Through his blood, the animals, the birds, the trees were saved.
Since then, in the new covenant, people no longer bring live sin offerings to have their sins forgiven.

Our eucharist of tree planting symbolises Christ's salvation of all creation, for in him all things hold together.
Let us celebrate this eucharist with humble hearts,
confessing our wanton tree felling without replacing any in return.

There was war in heaven, says the Bible.
Michael and his angels fought the devil and his angels.
The devil lost his position in heaven.
He was hurled down,
that ancient serpent called Satan,

he who leads the whole world astray.

Rejoice, you who dwell in heaven,
but woe to the earth and the sea
for the devil has gone down to you.
He is filled with fury
for his time is short.

So the devil is deceiving the whole world
causing man to fight creation.
Possessed by the demon
man is destroying nature's beauty.
All living things suffer—
the trees, the animals, water.
It shall continue until man erases all life on earth.
If we continue to kill the trees we hurt ourselves.

At the end of the world,
when the world is ultimately destroyed
it will be the doing of man.

You all know our African custom.
If a person kills another the deceased rises as *ngozi* against the murderer and his family to
     settle the matter.
Restitution is needed.
Mutumbu (literally 'body') of cattle must be paid for the body of the deceased.
Relatives of the one turned *ngozi* receive the *mutumbu* cattle.
Their sacrifice causes the spirit to rest
and the two families to be united in peace.

So today we have brought these trees
as *mutumbu* payment for the trees we have destroyed.
This is the only way we can seek forgiveness for having caused the nakedness of the land

(Then follows the blessing of the Lord's acre with holy water and soil.)

TREE-PLANTING CEREMONY AT BISHOP MACHOKOTO'S ZION APOSTOLIC CHURCH IN MASVINGO DISTRICT, 15 MARCH 1992

Bishop Machokoto (AAEC president): Peace to all of you! All things that you see here today were created by God. He knows why he created them. We have no right to kill anything created by God, not even an ant. Let me give you an example, that of a dung beetle. It is a very good creature. God placed it in a world where there were no toilets. This beetle is not lazy at all. It collects the faeces of human beings and the droppings of animals, then buries them in the soil. So God created it for a specific purpose, that of clearing the filth and making the soil fertile.

Today we have gathered to fight the war of the trees. We are confessing to God, saying: 'We have cut down your trees in ignorance. Today we are replacing that which we have destroyed.' When we consider a tree, we know that first of all it represents fuelwood. Trees are of the first order. They are the whip [that cracks to draw instant attention]. They are medicine. Do you understand what I say? It means: *the tree is life!* If we build a house with poles we know that the entire family has shelter, has life. Without trees there is no life, for the air we breathe comes from trees. We in this area are fortunate to enjoy good health. That is because trees abound and we breathe clean air. People who live in the territories of chiefs Murinye, Chikwanda, and Nyakunuwa do not suffer many illnesses. They breathe the clean air of forests which are still plentiful.

Both God and the government encourage us to plant trees. We are prohibited from felling trees, unless there is a justifiable purpose for doing so. We, the churches, are now united in action in this war of the trees—ourselves preventing tree felling. We operate together under the name of the AAEC, which means that we are the protectors of all created things. Prof. Daneel started this organisation. Under the name of Muchakata (wild cork tree) he worked out a battle strategy, based on the unity of our black churches. See for yourselves the unity we share. Here we have Mr. Chinovuriri of the Dutch Reformed Church. There is a representative of the Roman Catholic Church, and over there a minister of the African Methodist Church. Add to that all our Zionist churches congregated here today. We are bound in battle to plant and not to fell trees. Peace to you all!

In the Bible we are told to *love* one another. It says that love manifests itself in deeds. It originates in God. If you love a person created by God you know God. Love means to respond positively when your help is requested. Love requires *holiness* if we are to really care for each other. Peace to you! Without holiness no love will last. We have to heed Colossians 3:1, where it says that if we have been raised with Christ we should seek the things that are above where Christ is . . .

When the Apostle Paul arrived at Corinth he found conflict among the believers. It is the same with us. We bicker saying: I am not of Bishop Machokoto, not of Bishop Makamba, neither Madekwana nor Mageza. Today Paul says: 'Was Mageza crucified on the cross for you, was Machokoto?' In 1 Corinthians 1:10 Paul appeals to the believers to stop their squabbling and become fully united. Was Machokoto crucified for you? No. The Bible talks of only one saviour who died on the cross, so that there can be salvation for all creation, freedom in the world. The Bible tells us that the council of heaven assembled to decide who was going to die for the sins of the world. First the council thought of Abraham. They said: 'It is good for Abraham's son to die for the sins of the world. After all we gave him the promised son Isaac, who could be sacrificed at Mount Sinai.' But then they thought better of it, realising that flesh cannot die for flesh [an ordinary human being cannot atone for others]. I, Machokoto, cannot die for the people. The heavenly council therefore decided that spirit should die for flesh. They decided to send their son, Jesus Christ, to come and die for our sins.

Because of this decision we are new people. The old things have passed. In 2 Corinthians 5:17 we read that if we are in Christ we are made new. Once we have passed through Jordan [been baptised] the old things are left behind. We used to hate, bewitch and be jealous of each other. But all these things are no longer known among true believers.

Gone, too, is the attitude which says: 'I cannot worship with so-and-so, because I belong to so-and-so.' For Christ who was crucified for us, was one person. In him we are united. All of you who are here did not come to worship Machokoto or Mageza. Together we worship one Christ, he who forgave the sins of the Jews, the Greeks, the black people and the white people. He is the king of kings, the one who reconciles all people and nations. Blessed therefore are the conciliators, the peacemakers for they shall be called the sons of God (Mt 5:9). Peace to you!

Reader: Colossians 3:1: Set your hearts on things above.

Machokoto: If you have been raised with Christ, do not set your hearts on the things of this world. Set your hearts on the things of heaven. The son of God is sitting on the right hand of God. It is this attitude which finds expression in our meeting today.

Where do you think we would have found food for all our guests? [SATV crew was present; hence more whites than at other AAEC gatherings.] But they don't mind, because they were drawn here by the love of God. These white people mix with us without constraint, as if we are their own people. I thank all of you congregated here that you received our white guests like your own family; like *vazukuru* [sister's sons], fathers and grandmothers.

In the Bible it says we are all one, because we are now new creatures. There is no more Jew, Greek, black, or white. We are all one house, one family! I am happy that they [the whites] came and ate with us in our houses. Peace be with you!

BISHOP CHIMHANGWA'S SERMON AT TREE-PLANTING EUCHARIST AT MACHOKOTO'S ZAC HEADQUARTERS, MASVINGO DISTRICT, 15 MARCH 1992

Bishop Chimhangwa: Peace to you all! We are all very happy to be united here today with fellow believers and townspeople. I fully endorse what Bishop Machokoto has said: if you say that you love God but hate your brother, you are a liar. How can you know God if you still hate others? Your pride and conceit will not save you from the wrath of God. Keep watch, because you do not know the time when the son of man comes. He may be coming at night.

Fathers and mothers, we should all consider the reason for our presence here. We are here because of Christ. If a person does not know that he or she is in Christ, the full reason for that person's presence here is not understood. Hatred and gossip must go!

Reader: Colossians 3:1: Since, then, you were raised with Christ . . .

Chimhangwa: Peace to you all! Because we were buried and raised with Christ, we seek to do the will of God. It means that we unite in love, because Bishop Machokoto is father to all of us! Bishop Mageza is our father—to all of us! Bishop Andreas Shoko [a pioneer of Zionism in Zimbabwe] is our father—to all of us! Peace to all of you!

Let us together consider our task of tree planting. I am talking about the trees we plant here today. Two days ago we conducted a tree-planting eucharist in Chivi district [near Bishop Chimhangwa's headquarters]. We are indeed faced with a very serious situation [both drought and deforestation]. Rev. Marinda told us that we are planting trees to appease the avenging *ngozi* spirit, the evil spirit which has risen against us [causing drought] because of our mindless felling of trees. We are planting these trees to remedy the situation, to compensate for our wrongdoing. We committed a crime before God, one which requires confession. We all know that each of us has a special axe at our homesteads, sharpened and kept for tree felling only. So all of us are guilty of the crime of deforestation. Many of us simply fell trees without considering the consequences.

So, today we plant trees as an *act of reconciliation* between us and all creation, in Jesus Christ. We thank him for his atonement, which makes this act of reconciliation possible.

You heard that there is conflict and hatred among the churches, which caused our hearts not to meet. But Jesus said: 'No! There is no Jew or Greek. There is no bondage or slavery left. All people are free.' Because of this we are free to call on all people to be involved in tree planting. We of the churches must cooperate with the VIDCOs, the WADCOs [local government structures], the chiefs and the headmen. As God is the source of the chiefs' authority, they must be informed of all our [earthkeeping] activities.

I address you on the subject of trees as the Old Testament prophet Jeremiah did.

Reader: Jeremiah 14:1–2: The word of the Lord which came to Jeremiah during the drought: Judah mourns and her gates languish; her people lament on the ground, and the cry of Jerusalem goes up.

Chimhangwa: In this country of ours the president and all the MPs are desperate for rain. They say: 'What shall we do?'

Reader: Jeremiah 14:3: Her nobles send their servants for water; they come to the cisterns, they find no water, they return with their vessels empty; they are ashamed and confounded and cover their heads.

Chimhangwa: Last night I woke up and asked my wife, 'Why are you making such a noise?' She said, 'I want to go to the cistern to see if there is any water. Perhaps I shall find a little.'

In some places people rise at four o'clock in the morning, sometimes without finding a drop of water. So wherever and whoever we are, we have to pray for rain. Do not say: 'Oh well, I am too young' or 'I am a woman.' No! We never know which prayer God is going to answer. Let us kneel down and pray for rain, for the people go to the cisterns and return with empty containers.

Reader: Jeremiah 14:4: Because the land is cracked because of lack of rain the farmers are ashamed; they cover their heads.

Chimhangwa: My wife asked me whether we could grind the fifty kilograms of mealies which we had bought for planting into meal. She did this because we could not find mealie meal anywhere. That same day minister Musika was at our village to assess the drought situation. The famine is now so bad that the tortoises have started climbing the trees [idiomatic expression, a desperate situation].

I want to advise you who have planted trees here today to save some water for the trees, our friends. In times gone by people also had to face droughts. Others also went to the cisterns to find them empty. We ploughed our lands and planted our maize and groundnuts. But there are no crops. Is that not a painful experience? If God was a person, don't you think I was going to question him about this? Ah! It is impossible to question God! Peace to you, people of the Lord.

I believe the trees planted today will be well cared for. When we come here again in the future we shall be given fruit to eat. [Several fruit trees were planted in Bishop Machokoto's orchard.]

Reader: Romans 1:9: I mention you always in my prayers, asking that somehow by God's will I may now at least succeed in coming to you . . .

Chimhangwa: There you are, my friends. The AAEC president, Bishop Machokoto, and the general secretary, Bishop Marinda, visited us in Chivi and asked us to come. Now I respond as the apostle did to the Romans. We shall keep visiting you and pray for you so that you can have courage to persevere in the war of the trees. Let us continue planting more and more trees, also taking care of them through regular watering. I thank you all.

REV. SAURO MASORO'S SERMON AT BISHOP MACHOKOTO'S TREE-PLANTING EUCHARIST, 15 MARCH 1993

Rev. Masoro: Peace to all of you! The gospel we preach here today belongs to Mwari because he is the creator of all things. First he created the earth, then he created the trees and animals. Thereafter he created human beings, placing them amongst the trees. Human beings had the task of looking after all the vegetation. Peace to you all! We shall first of all consider the message of Genesis 2:8. We have to be quite clear on the issue of trees. Without them we cannot survive. Here, while we worship under this *muchakata* tree, it provides air for us to breathe. The same tree absorbs the polluted air that we breathe out. It means that we and the *muchakata* tree are one! This we did not heed before. We took the creation story for granted without realising the interdependence of humans and plant growth. Yet if we ponder creation, it is significant that God made a garden before he created humankind.

Reader: Genesis 2:8: And the Lord God planted a garden in Eden, in the east; and there he put the man whom he had formed.

Masoro: Peace to all of you! Listen carefully to God's word. Mwari planted trees in a garden in the east, then placed the humans he had created in the garden so that they could breathe fresh air deriving from the trees. They in turn had to look after the garden. It is God who made man from the soil, forming him in his own image, then breathing *mweya* (life-giving spirit) into him. Today it is still like that. When I die people can still see my body, but they say the person, *munhu*, has gone. It is the spirit placed in the body by Mwari which departs when death sets in.

Reader: Genesis 2:9: And out of the ground the Lord God made to grow every tree that is pleasant to the sight and good for food, the tree of life also in the midst of the garden.

Masoro: Peace to you. The *muchakata* fruit that we eat from this tree you see here is medicine which heals us. The *mutamba* fruit we eat is medicine to us which heals us. Even if we eat a mango, guava, or orange, it is still healing medicine to us. In the distant past when we did not yet have all these [exotic] species of fruit the illness of scabies abounded. There was no proper cure. But nowadays we are healed by mangoes, pawpaws, oranges, and bananas.

Reader: Ezekiel 31:8: The heading says that God likens Egypt to a cedar tree. Verse 8 reads: 'The cedars in the garden of God could not rival it, nor the fir trees equal its boughs . . . no tree in the garden of God was like it in beauty.'

Masoro: It says that the splendour of Egypt is compared to cedar trees. A country with many trees prospers. If it is treeless it becomes a barren landscape of little value. Progress is seen in forests or in marshlands with many copses of trees *(matenhere)*.

The Israelites complained to Moses that he alone was conversing with Mwari. They, too, wanted to communicate directly with God. So God said: 'Let them wash and prepare themselves before we converse.' But God did not speak out on the open plains. Whenever he spoke he was hidden in a copse of trees *(denhere)*. And the people had to lie prostrate in his presence. This shows that the tree and the human being are one!

The tree of God [Egypt] described in Ezekiel 31:8 was not an ordinary tree. Likewise, we here today are the trees of God. We are not really trees but we are likened to trees.

Reader: Ezekiel 31:9: I made it beautiful in the mass of its branches; and all the trees of Eden envied it, that were in the garden of God.

Masoro: Yes, the human being is like a wonderful tree with huge branches. It reminds us that we are the branches in Christ, as described in John 15.

Reader: John 15:1: Jesus says: I am the true vine.

Masoro: Yes, Jesus says I am the true vine and my Father is the gardener who has made the garden of Eden. He made the tree of life, meaning Jesus, so that we, too, can have life by being in Jesus.

Reader: John 15:2: Every branch of mine that bears no fruit, he takes away, and every branch that bears fruit he prunes, that it may bear more fruit.

Masoro: Are these green branches of the *muchakata* tree not bearing fruit? Are we not like these green branches right here where we are congregated? Through Jesus we are green branches bearing fruit, not dead wood to be removed.

Reader: John 15:3: You are already made clean by the word I have spoken to you.

Masoro: We cannot bear fruit if we are not in Christ, the true vine. If we do not go and ask for tree seedlings to plant we shall not have the trees which heal and clean us. For our well-being as believers and for our physical health, let us fetch the trees and plant them at our homesteads, ridding ourselves in the process of scabies.

God help us. Amen.

APPENDIX 4

Tree-Planting Sermons in Ethiopian-Type (Non-Prophetic) Independent Churches

SHONGANISO MISSION (AFRICAN REFORMED CHURCH) SERMON

TREE-PLANTING CEREMONY AT REV. ZVOBGO'S SHONGANISO MISSION IN MASVINGO DISTRICT, 13 DECEMBER 1990

Rev. Mandondo (senior minister of the ARC) directed the proceedings:

Prayer: Our Father, we thank you today that we can appear here in your presence. We are thankful that you have given us the strength on this good day to come and perform this wonderful task, the task which you yourself performed with your own hands. Now, our Father, please place your hands on these trees of yours which we are about to plant. Guide us so that it will be as if our hands are your hands, the hands [signs] that you left us here on earth. You left us the mountains, the trees, the rivers, the fountains from which to drink water. Up to this day they are all still there. We, too, are encouraged to plant trees today which we hope will grow and last forever, and that under your guidance. You are the one who will water these trees [with rain] and who will make them grow. Strengthen those who teach us about tree planting and teach us all to do your work. Forever, amen.

Sermon: Let us start by considering how trees came into existence. If we look at Genesis I we learn that Mwari created all things. And among the things he created were the trees. According to Genesis 1:11 God said, 'Let the earth put forth vegetation, plants yielding seed, and fruit trees bearing fruit in which is their seed, each according to its own kind upon the earth.' So, it is clear that at the beginning God produced the trees, grass, and all kinds of vegetation. Subsequently human beings became involved in planting trees in many different ways. Even the government nowadays is planting trees, sending out its ministers and members of parliament to encourage people to direct such activity.

The trees contain [produce] fresh air, which we require for breathing. Of this the government is aware. Hence its attempt to restore the land, so that it can be as good and healthy as it was originally. Over the past ten years the government has made some attempts. Today we have Prof. Daneel and his supporters here on a similar mission. Once I attended a ZINHATA meeting where the importance of trees—mainly for the medicines of *nganga* practitioners—was emphasised. Long ago, they said, it was possible for some *nganga* to cure barrenness with medicines from plants. Many diseases were in fact effectively treated, witchcraft attacks were properly counteracted and the people survived. It was Mwari who created all plants with a purpose, namely to aid human beings to overcome their tribulations.

According to our Christian faith Mwari created and ordered all creation. He told the waters to move aside, thus causing dry land and the oceans to come into existence. To cover the barren land God created vegetation and trees. So he is the one who first planted trees. He is the one who gave the trees life and strength to grow. He made the trees his children. We human beings, in our turn, are the inheritors of this garden, this *kingdom of God* consisting of trees and animals. Inheriting this kingdom means that we are responsible for the continuation of the work God started. We say that as Christians we are the inheritors, belonging to God. If we are serious about this claim, it means that we, too, are children of God and as such have to proceed with the task of planting trees and taking care of living things. Genuine inheritors are stewards of the land.

If you look at Luke 23:43 you find that Jesus told the one man next to him on the cross: 'Today you will be with me in paradise.' This tells us something about Jesus's power over us children of God. As a messenger from heaven he came to empower us. Whatever we do as believers depends on this power from on high, the power of heaven. No work that we do can be complete without God's *approval* and his *empowerment*. About this we can be sure: God planted trees. If we, too, plant trees God's power from heaven will strengthen us and our efforts will succeed. Without his power our labours will be futile. No trees will be planted.

How can we determine whether we are doing all this as the will of God and that we can count on his supportive strength? We read in Exodus 2:3 that God wanted to speak to Moses. So he sent an angel who addressed Moses from a bush. That means the angel was in a tree while communicating with Moses. After God had made an agreement with Moses, he broke a branch off the tree and carved Moses a staff. This staff was the sign of the agreement God had made with Moses. It represents God's power. In the wars that were to come Moses always held this staff—which God had prepared from a tree—in his hands. There were actually two staffs. One was for Aaron. With these staffs all the wars were won.

The first war Moses faced was the crossing of the Red Sea, when the Israelites were desperate to escape from the Egyptians. The trumpets of the Egyptian army could be heard and the Israelites were trapped. They were caught on the banks of the Red Sea. But Moses held out his staff over the waters, and the waters feared the staff made of a tree and separated this way and that, leaving a dry road in between. That is where Moses and the Israelites entered and passed through. God saw that Moses needed something [concrete, visible] to work with—a sign of their agreement. So God chose a tree. First he spoke to Moses from a tree, then he gave Moses a staff from a tree. This indeed emphasises the significance of trees.

There was also the time when Zacchaeus (Lk 19), out of sheer eagerness to see Jesus, climbed a wild fig tree. In that way he succeeded. If there had been no fig tree, Zacchaeus would not have seen Jesus and their meeting would not have taken place. Once again we notice the significance of trees in the relationship between God and human beings. Thus, as God is the creator of trees, you children of God [as inheritors of God's kingdom] should also take on the task of planting trees. Do this in order to restore the damage done by the enemies of creation!

If we really think about Scripture, the importance of trees is only too apparent. It is on the wood of a tree that Jesus was crucified. He had two convicts on crosses next to him, one on each side. The one rebuked the other when he was scoffing at Jesus and said, 'Jesus, remember me when you come into your kingdom' (Lk 23:42). And Jesus said to him, 'Today you will be with me in paradise.' We know that paradise is a garden of fruit trees, a place of many trees. It says in the Bible that when God created man, he did not build him a house.

Does it say there that houses were built in the garden of Eden? No, the Bible says only that the first human beings were placed in the garden. God said: 'Live there among the trees. Eat the fruit of trees.' What did they eat to survive? The fruit of trees, of course! Were they worried about the rising prices of fruit? No! They simply picked fruit from the trees and ate. Then they went to the river and drank water until they had their fill. Mwari saw that people could stay alive because of trees.

When Jesus conducted holy communion for his disciples he used wine made from grapes. We know that in the kingdom of heaven we shall partake of wine made of grapes. Where does the food of heaven come from? It is picked off the grapevine! And what will you do if you hear that the *mupfura* [marula tree] also stands in the new garden? You will not fell it or allow anybody else to do so. So what do we do about people chopping down mango trees and *mishuku* [wild loquat]? What does the Bible say? Jesus said, we eat the fruit of trees. Yet we fell the fruit trees. Ultimately, however, we will not be able to escape our responsibility for the trees. It is simply that we are not used to this stewardship. When confronted with the responsibility our consciences will accuse us and we will have to obey. It is a matter of adapting to the things done and ordered by the Lord. We must simply get used to tree stewardship.

The correct thing for us to do, therefore, is to go out and plant different species of trees: fruit trees and trees for the forests. When we want to plant fruit trees, we don't plant teak. How can you expect to pick mangoes or guavas off teak trees? So we have to be clear about our objectives whenever we plant trees.

If we want to be the children of Mwari, let us shoulder the task we have been given. God wanted to build a good relationship with Adam. So he said: 'This man must live without undue suffering. Let him live in peace. If he suffers hunger he will be in trouble.' So God placed him in a garden of fruit trees where he could find fruit at all times and rejoice in abundance. Those were God's plans. Eventually man also ate the meat of animals, but the fruit came first. Therefore, people of God, let us plant trees!

Let us consider the situation we are now facing. Whenever someone is given a site for a homestead and new gardens he starts sharpening his axe, saying: 'Let me chop out all those trees.' As a result the entire countryside has become barren. The trees are all gone. There is no shelter left for poultry. The hawks simply swoop down and take them as if there were no people around. Among the homesteads there are no shade trees any longer. This situation is not acceptable at all. There is no protection against strong winds. How can you hold back the force of the wind if there are no trees to restrain it? But meanwhile those with new sites where there are still forests do not heed the threat of deforestation. They simply sharpen their axes and commence felling trees.

We have to remedy the situation ourselves. From today on each adult should consider making every one of their children plant two, three, or more trees annually. They will soon be proud, saying to each other: 'Look, I have a wonderful plantation of trees. I had no trouble finding poles for my cattle kraal.' You Christians, we are confronted with this serious task of God. Let us be united in our efforts, not shirking our responsibility. For if we don't heed God's command we shall be judged. He will say: 'You have destroyed the earth. You have refused to consider my wishes. Consequently my land is now barren and ashamed.'

So the task is ahead of us. We accept it. If we dedicate ourselves we shall succeed and accomplish this task, just as Mwari did himself. You will see the miracles of Mwari if you persevere. Up in the mountains I can see Mwari. In the rocks and the trees I see Mwari. There his strength and his works are revealed. If you go to Mount Selinda you will be shown trees called *miti mikuru* [tall trees]. Whose strength do those massive trees reveal? Mwari's, of course. There you will witness God's work. His work is clearly seen in the things he has created. Follow the rivers and observe the running waters. Whose work do you think it is? Mwari's! But the works of God are now destroyed. We do not see them any longer. We ourselves are responsible for the destruction of creation. So let us restore God's works, accepting that the task is ours. Let us replace the trees we have felled. God will rejoice when he observes this.

Who makes the trees grow? It is God himself, according to his own wishes. Those trees we have planted, we do not actually control or see their growth. God is the one who does all that. You will see eventually: some trees mature, others don't. And the explanation for this variation? The control behind it? It is the power of Mwari. But somehow Mwari's work is no longer seen on these barren, treeless plains. You only see the many tracks of human beings in the sand. What are they? Shoe prints in the sand of those who exploit the earth, leaving it barren. It seems as if the works of God are replaced by the fruitless works of humankind.

But today we have done God's work. You will see, in a short space of time the trees will grow tall. And we shall say: 'God surprises us. God exists. God does what pleases him.' Today we have done his bidding. Today we have learnt that if we want to be God's children, we must do *his* work. We are the inheritors, existing by virtue of the inheritance—in this instance the fruit of trees. Today we did what God sent us and commanded us to do. It is not so much a matter of success or failure, but in the first place, complying with God's will, giving him joy through our obedience.

I wish to thank Prof. Daneel for giving us the trees and Mr. Dhewa for helping us and instructing us about tree planting. Let them not tire of this work, or become dispirited. Let them continue providing us with trees, so that we can do God's work and please God.

That work of felling trees, what does it imply? Rebellion against Mwari! What are you, brothers and sisters, going to do? Continue felling trees at random, even up in the mountains, on the pretext that you need timber for roofing? And are you going to complain about the scarcity of trees by suggesting that the wrath of God is upon you? That would be the behaviour of a fool! What does God do to you for just taking from creation, just felling trees? Does he swallow you? No! He loves you and he reveals his love to you through trees, because he spoke to Moses from a tree and he gave Moses a staff from a tree. Likewise he placed Adam in a garden so that he could be a friend of the trees. God has great love for us human beings. If we realise this we will spread this message wherever we go. All of you, persevere in this task. Don't forget the God-given importance of trees! Amen.

FIRST ETHIOPIAN CHURCH (TOPIA) CEREMONY

HOLY COMMUNION CONFERENCE, FOLLOWED BY TREE-PLANTING CEREMONY AT THE TOPIA HEADQUARTERS OF BISHOP ISHMAEL GAVHURE, NORUMEDZO, BIKITA DISTRICT, 12–13 JANUARY 1991

Prof. Muchakata Daneel: Thank you, Bishop Gavhure, for your kind words of introduction. It is a great pleasure to be here with you this afternoon. Peace to all of you! In addition I say: Forward with the war of the trees! Down with the ones who oppose tree planting!

I know that there are many confusing rumours in the villages about our work, so I shall use this opportunity to explain to you what we are doing . . .

Years ago I visited Bishop Nheya Gavhure here at the *Topia* headquarters. It was in the period 1965 to 1967, when I was doing research and preparing to write the history of the Zimbabwean Independent Churches. I was given that task by Mwari. Having completed part of the task, I returned in 1972 to start an ecumenical body to unite the African churches. So *Fambidzano* came into being, a very significant development in the existence of the black churches in which I was privileged to participate. So the research we all did together to start with resulted in a great work of unifying black churches in our country. Part of the ecumenical programme was development. And the tree planting I shall be talking about this afternoon is part of that development already started some years ago.

In recent years I started another research project on the history of the liberation struggle. You all are only too familiar with that history. It was hot out here at Norumedzo. You were caught between two fires, the guerrilla fighters and the army. While writing this history it was clear to me that the old religion of your forefathers played an important role for many people. The spirit-mediums in particular were at the forefront, representing the wishes of the guardian ancestors of the land and national ancestors such as Chaminuka, Nehanda, and Kaguwi. Here in this region the senior guardian ancestors of the Duma people are Pfupajena, Dumbukunyuka, and others.

Currently it appears, however, that the spirit-mediums are pushed aside (by the government) and told to go to rest. Yet they wanted to continue playing a meaningful role in the country and needed assistance. So I decided to help them, despite the fact that their religion differs from mine. I myself am a Christian and I was born at Morgenster mission. My clan name is Gumbo Madyirapazhe, as you know. Peace to you all!

So the *masvikiro* started coming to my house where we arranged funding and drafted a constitution. At our meetings I prayed Christian prayers. Thereafter they poured snuff on the floor in honour of their ancestors—doing their old religion. We did not question each other's religious identity. Together we have decided to plant trees, conserve wildlife and protect water resources. Hence the *masviro*, together with the chiefs and a number of ex-combatants, are mobilising many people in the communal lands to plant trees and look after the woodlots.

This activity has confused the people, who have become used to my working mainly among the Independent Churches. Some of them asked: 'Has Daneel become a backslider, rejoining the world?' I told them, 'No, it is simply that everybody must be involved in tree planting. The traditionalists should do so and the churches should do so.' Therefore we formed three departments. The top one is ZIRRCON. It takes care of research, funding, and organisation. Then on the one side you have the traditionalists, working in terms of their convictions, and on the other side the churches, arranging their own tree-planting ceremonies. I have been hoping that *Fambidzano* will take up the challenge.

So I implore all of you not to be disturbed by all those rumours, as if traditional religion is going to be forced on the churches, or as if religions are to be mixed without respect for each other. This rumour that the *masvikiro* and the churches are to be placed in one basket is totally unfounded. ZIRRCON arranges for the churches to make their own contribution on their own terms. Remember this message! Counter the false rumours by telling the people: 'The churches are not imposed upon; we plant trees in accordance with our own church regulations.' It is up to you church people whether you allow spirit-mediums to attend your ceremonies as observers. But they cannot interfere with your arrangements. Neither will you interfere with theirs if you should be invited to attend traditionalist tree-planting ceremonies.

The churches, therefore, are in a position to have their own nurseries and woodlots. This is a great challenge. It is the work of God. It should be done by the churches; it can also be done by others.

In Isaiah 41:17 and 18 we read: 'When the poor and the needy seek water, and there is none . . . I, the Lord will answer them . . . I will open rivers on the bare heights and fountains in the midst of the valleys; I will make the wilderness a pool of water, and the dry land springs of water.'

We see here at Norumedzo that what was promised by Mwari was done right here. Is it not so that you have pools and springs of water in greater abundance than at Masvingo? It seems as if the sinners abound in Masvingo, for it is not raining there at all. Perhaps the people do not want to repent and confess their sins. So Mwari is disciplining them ('giving them *shamhu*,' literally 'whipping them'). There is no water. Out here you are blessed by Mwari who has given you rain. Peace to you!

In Isaiah 41:19 we read: 'I will put in the wilderness the cedar, the acacia, the myrtle and the olive; I will set in the desert the cypress, the plane and the pine together.' Here in our land it means that Mwari will put in our acacia trees: the *mutondo, msasa, and muvuzhe*. Instead of olives, he will put in *nhengeni* (sour plum), *mutunduru* (*garcinia huillensis*) and *musvazva* (*securinega virosa*) trees. In addition he will give us *howa and mafirifiti* [popular mushroom species]. And in the place of pines and cypress trees, he shall give us *mukurumbira* (teak) and *makamba* (red mahogany). All this Mwari will do, as he says in verse 20, 'so that man may see and know . . . that the hand of the Lord has done this, the holy one of Israel has created it.'

We from our side plant the trees because the entire land has become barren and eroded. We want the land to be clothed with vegetation. But in doing so we realise that it is the hand of the Lord doing this, so that the world can observe and give praise to God. There is no way that we can boast and be vain about our tree-planting accomplishments, because Jehovah is telling us right here that it is all *his* doing. See the hand of God moving in our work and give praise to him! To me, the one claiming to have been inspired to do this work, the temptation is to claim that all the ideas and plans derived from my research work. No! How else did my research start but through the moving of the Holy Spirit? Even this Bible here is a book of research, for the authors arranged the contents according to their observations and insight. But in reality the book was inspired [*rakafemerwa*, 'breathed into,' ensouled] by the Holy Spirit. Likewise I have been shown by Mwari to do this work of the trees. That leaves no room for boasting. Because of Mwari's hand moving we are, nevertheless, faced with a huge task of earthkeeping.

You have congregated here to participate in holy communion. This is the occasion when you take bread and wine in remembrance of the death of Christ on the cross. In this commemoration the body of Christ is central. 1 Corinthians 11:29 emphasises the importance of recognising this truth. It says there that 'anyone who eats and drinks without discerning Christ's body, eats and drinks judgment upon him or herself.' Hang on to this idea that we should *know* the body of Christ. In Colossians 1:15–17 the body of Christ is explained in a special way. He is the image of the unseen God, the firstborn of all creation. All things were created in him and for him, the seen and the unseen. Because of this *all things hang together in Christ*. Through Christ's death and resurrection all power in heaven and earth has, moreover, been given to him (Mt 28:18). From all this we conclude that Christ is not only Lord of creation, but that his body *is* all of creation. All created things are part of his body. The implication for us as stewards of creation is that if we fell trees indiscriminately, we are actually killing the body of Christ.

In Colossians 1:18 we read that 'he [Christ] is the head of the body, the church.' Two main points emerge in these texts from Colossians: first, the body of Christ is the entire created world; second, his body is the church, the body of believers. In the past when we celebrated holy communion we tended to remember the one aspect of this twofold truth, namely that we celebrate our unity in Christ's body as the church. We neglected the other aspect of Christ's body. So I wish to remind you here today that whenever you celebrate holy communion, be mindful that in devastating the earth we ourselves are party to destroying the body of Christ. We are *all* guilty in this respect. Both the whites and the blacks are exploiters of the environment.

We will have to start afresh, confessing our sins. You know yourselves how we come to the 'gates' and confess publicly our sins of adultery, jealousy, and hatred to the prophets. You prophets, you know what I am talking about. People seldom confess that they are wizards [*varoyi*]. But when they say that they have brought their owls and *zvidoma* [witch familiars] to be burnt, we know they are confessing to wizardry.

Today I am telling you of a form of *uroyi* that is even worse than hereditary [*kamutsa mapfiwa*, 'lifting the cooking stones'] or deliberately acquired [*kutemerwa*, to join the profession by rubbing medicine into incisions so that the bloodstream absorbs it] wizardry. Peace to you! But there is no peace in a matter of this nature. I am referring to the third type of *uroyi*: that of killing the earth. It is more serious even than the old *uroyi* where a destroyer targets only one or a few individuals. For in destroying our environment we are endangering all of life! Remember when you confess your sins before the eucharist that you have sinned against the body of Christ, Christ himself, the earth. Say: 'I have killed the earth; I have felled twenty trees this year without planting any in return; I have caused soil erosion by neglecting the contour ridges; I have destroyed the vegetation on riverbanks.' The prophet listening to your confession will only be convinced if your willingness to rectify the situation is evident. That is why, after confession and taking the sacrament, we take seedlings and plant them straight away. Can you see that in this way tree planting becomes part of the eucharist? What we have done in the eucharist in the past is still there. It is good, and not wrong. It is just that we are reminded these days of something we have neglected. We are healing and restoring that part of Christ's body which we have unwittingly abused. That is the message I leave with you today: *Clothe the barren earth! Heal the earth! It is fully part of our lives as Christians . . .*

[Then followed an exposition of tree species: the need to focus less on blue gum trees than on indigenous trees, as well as the use of chimurenga *tree names to show identification with the environmental liberation struggle. Having referred to spirit-medium vaZarira's use of the name Marambatemwa and my own Muchakata, I concluded as follows:]*

Possibly your own bishop here will eventually have a special name for his involvement in the green struggle. He may choose *Mushuku* [wild loquat] because it is a popular fruit tree. But I would choose him another: *Murwiti* [black ebony], because the ebony's wood is exceedingly tough. We need tough fighters. So let your bishop be strong and tough in the struggle. When you see him appear at a tree-planting ceremony, greet him, saying: 'Oh, Murwiti, you have come!' Forward the war of the trees! Peace to you! Amen.

BISHOP ISHMAEL GAVHURE, PRINCIPAL LEADER OF THE FIRST ETHIOPIAN CHURCH (ELDEST SON AND SUCCESSOR OF THE LATE BISHOP NHEYA GAVHURE)

Bishop Gavhure: Peace be to you all! We thank you for the teaching on environmental conservation this afternoon. We still have to digest this message.

We were disturbed and confused about Prof. Daneel working with the *masvikiro*, thinking that maybe he is introducing them into the churches. I told him: 'You were a friend of my father and many *Topia* members know you. They all remember how you came to help bury my late father.' But I told him: 'We do not want you to bring spirit-mediums here to mix with the church people.' [Note: no request of this kind had actually been made, neither had Bishop Ghavure and I discussed the *Topia* tree-planting ceremony beforehand. The bishop was therefore reacting to rumours about the alleged mixing of religions to allay the fears which may at that time, when the AAEC was only starting to come into its own, have troubled some *Topia* members.] So, if you people of the church see *masvikiro* coming here, know that they do not have the permission of the church elders to do so. We don't allow them to be among us! Peace to you all!

What we are really interested in and need to know more about is this new approach to environmental conservation. You know, each person has a gift from God. Prof. Daneel's gift for writing and teaching is from God. You cannot imagine the books he has written. Long ago he did work with the chiefs (traditional religion). But then he worked for many years with our black churches, until he became the founder of *Fambidzano*, which taught us to understand the kingdom of God. Peace to you all!

Trees are of the greatest importance. Even in the Bible we are told about their significance. When God created the earth he produced vegetation and ordained that it be respected. A married woman is respected when she is well dressed. The same applies to boys and girls. Those addressing you here this afternoon are all well dressed. But what if we appeared here before you, naked? What then? No! It is impossible for such a thing to happen. But that is exactly the state of the land these days. It is naked. That is why the government is no longer allowing people to fell trees whenever they wish. The land will die. So the land must be clothed.

Do you know why we no longer have regular rainfall? It is because of the lack of trees. Where do the rain clouds come from? They are drawn by the trees. God's way to improve the situation is to send us wise people so that we can rebuild our country. Therefore I do not see any problem in our receiving these trees from ZIRRCON to plant. We do not really mind what rumours people will be spreading about us, as long as we are building the country. Peace to you!

Prof. Daneel has been studying our indigenous trees. When the trees arrived here, you could hear people gossiping, asking among themselves: 'Are these trees going to be used for the medicines of traditional doctors [*nganga*]?' As if there is something the matter with that . . . After all, we have the medicines of African people. We have white cultures and black cultures. In our black culture we obtain medicines from a *nganga*. Are we all *ngangas*? Some practise *unganga*; others are Christians. Likewise, among the whites some are spirit-mediums and others are Christians.

That is why I say, God does as he pleases. If people are encouraged to plant trees, is it not a good thing that they are clothing the barren earth? Why should anyone be negative about it?

Peace be with you! We thank Jesus Christ this afternoon, for he does good things to us.

Our scripture reading is from Genesis 1:11. God created all things before he created humans. He saw that the earth should not remain a mass of water.

Reader: Genesis 1:11: Let the land produce vegetation . . .

Gavhure: Peace to you all! God created all the plants and trees, in great variety. He commanded it to happen, as he has power over everything. Why should it surprise you then if someone comes along to teach us about the different tree species? Do you think that because he (Daneel) talks about *matunduru* and *nengeni* trees—species which I myself have not even heard of before—he is some alien being, created differently from the way we are created as human beings? Is it I who taught him all those tree names, so that he can come and teach you? Ah! God creates different kinds of people. The same applies the other way around. There are blacks with gifts who go and do missionary work in white cultures. There, in their turn, the whites will be surprised at what the blacks are doing among them. God indeed uses people as he wills . . .

Reader: Genesis 1:12: The earth brought forth vegetation, plants yielding seed according to their own kinds, and trees bearing fruit . . .

Gavhure: If people want to make ropes they use the bark of trees. If we want to build huts we get poles from trees. But these days, where can you find poles for hut building? I don't know; because to destroy trees has become a sin. You, Prof. Daneel, have today convinced me that to chop down trees without purpose is a sin. Ah, what is sin? Who knows the full depth of it? But this afternoon Jehovah shakes us out of complacency with the question: Have you confessed your sins of tree felling? Do you openly confess how many trees you have felled? Do you all confess?

Nobody here has ever thought of confessing the sins of tree felling and environmental destruction. But today God has revealed to us a new way: that of confessing those [ecological] sins. God shows us that to fell trees indiscriminately is the same as a *muroyi* killing a human being. From today on we shall consider all people who do not confess in this way and who do not repent through planting trees themselves, to be *varoyi* [wizards].

We are all inclined to ask: does the government then place a ban on house building? No! The government is correctly restricting tree felling because of the nakedness of the land. Peace to you all.

Today we all thank you, Prof. Daneel. I think we all understand what you have taught us today. Tree planting is not really a novelty. Our chiefs and headmen have tried to introduce it in the past. But we responded by saying, 'These troublesome people.' Today, however, God is addressing us about tree planting in a different way and through other people.

Today, ah, I have been converted to the new gospel of tree planting. My only objection is to plant trees together with *masvikiro*. That I oppose! Traditional religion does not go together with Christianity. Although we are all God's people, these religions are different and they oppose each other. Nevertheless we can encourage each other to fight deforestation. If the *masvikiro* plant trees we shall encourage them. But they don't interfere with our work, as we don't interfere with theirs.

Once the trees we have planted mature, we shall allow people to cut poles from these plantations for their buildings. In that way we shall prevent them from denuding the surrounding mountain slopes by chopping down indigenous trees.

Once again we say thank you for providing trees. If you can help us, Prof. Daneel, to start a nursery here at church headquarters, we shall be in a position to provide all our congregations in outlying districts with seedlings. Now, let us go out to plant some trees before the sun goes down. Amen.

NOTES

PREFACE TO THE 'AFRICAN INITIATIVES IN CHRISTIAN MISSION EDITION'

1. Nomenclature varies on the two groups of African churches. 'Mission Churches' have also been called 'Historical' or 'Established Churches.' The acronym 'AICs' originally stood for 'African Independent Churches,' a term which is still preferred by many scholars. In recent years, the World Council of Churches has tended to use the term 'African Initiated Churches.' In this series, authors are free to use any of the three they choose. But in the introduction to the series the editors generally refer to 'African Initiated Churches' because the term resonates with the title 'African Initiatives in Christian Mission.'

2. LIBERATION OF THE LOST LANDS

1. This study does not deal with foreign missions and mission-related 'younger churches.' The omission does not imply that these churches have been inactive in the ecological field. They have undoubtedly dealt with sociopolitical and ecological issues in various ways. But this is subject matter for another study.

2. Beach (1980:222f) contests the cult's link with the Rozvi dynasty and argues in favour of a recent Venda origin in the south. Huizer (1991:18) apparently holds a similar view. He refers to an interview with the cult priest at the Njelele shrine which suggests that 'the main centre of the Mwari cult was moved after long residence in Venda country [in present-day Northern Province, RSA], from whence the name Njelele, meaning "sacred mountain," was taken' (see Ranger 1967:19–20). As often happens with oral traditions, conclusive proof cannot be provided and the speculative element in the arguments outweighs the alleged evidence. When Beach (1980:249) claims, for instance, that 'the traditions of the shrine priests themselves give Venda origins, except when they choose to claim a Karanga origin to a Karanga clientele,' he seems to forget that many of the priests in fact belong to the Mbire Shoko tribe, and as Karanga they claim to have interacted closely with the Rozvi in administering the Mwari cult in the distant past. Such claims suggest a Rozvi-Mbire rather than a Venda origin. Considering, in addition, the minor function of Venda cultists in the Matopos shrine complex where they act as keepers (*vachengeti*) of the shrines, the Venda connection in Northern Province, RSA, may well indicate a Zimbabwean origin through Rozvi-Venda contact, rather than a recent introduction of the cult from the south. This argument, of course, does not rule out ethnic interaction and Venda influence on the cult.

3. A complex of shrines kept functioning in the Matonjeni area at Njelele, Dula, Wirirani, Dzilo, Vembe (in more recent years), and other places. Through a network of cult messengers (*vanyai*), supportive chiefs throughout central and southern Mashonaland, Matabeleland, and even as far afield as Botswana and the Venda areas in Northern Province, RSA, the cult maintained a geographically wide sphere of influence.

4. Barrett (1968:116,156f), for example, posited the theory that African 'reaction to missions' is the root cause of the emergence and growth of these churches (cf Daneel 1987:97–101).

5. This information is based largely on my discussions with senior priest Jonas Chokoto at Dzilo during the late 1980s and early 1990s prior to his death, and with his brothers, the late Simon and Adamu Chokoto, who were operating the Wirirani shrine when I first visited Matonjeni in the 1960s and 1970s.

6. My impression from many interviews with ex-combatants is that Lan's sharp distinction (1985:166–170), in respect of the Dande district, between chiefs compromised by their financial dependence on the white administration and their—to the liberation forces—more trustworthy counterparts, the spirit mediums, who proved more loyal in the struggle, does not apply in equal measure to Masvingo Province. Ex-combatants indicated that they were aware at the time of the difficulties facing the chiefs and the inevitability of their playing virtually double roles in the war situation. They were satisfied that the majority of chiefs in the province supported the struggle. In a few cases detachment and section commanders even considered accompanying certain chiefs from the Bikita district to the relative safety of Mozambican camps because their overt support of the struggle was placing them in jeopardy.

7. This case study was compiled from several interviews with Bishop Musariri and some of his clergy, as well as from *chimurenga* sermons preached in postwar Zimbabwe in an attempt to recapture the Patmos message of liberation.

3. EARTHKEEPERS' DECLARATION OF WAR

1. An outstanding Zionist intellectual, Rev. Zvanaka holds diplomas in bookkeeping, theology (Lutheran Theological Seminary, Mapumulo, RSA), and social work (University of Zimbabwe) and is studying for a bachelor's degree in theology at Unisa. Having held the positions of assistant principal of the Bible school and senior development officer in *Fambidzano*, he is admirably qualified for his present work in ZIRRCON. One also hopes that he will find time to write on the rich theology of the AICs. Bishop Marinda has a Diploma in Theology (United Theological College, Harare) and has done courses in development and project writing with the Zimbabwean Council of Churches. Having occupied the posts of principal of *Fambidzano* TEE programmes and assistant development officer of this movement, his experience ideally suits his role as mobiliser of earthkeeping churches, teacher at AAEC workshops, and developer of courses in a praxis-oriented theology of the environment.

2. Makamba himself spearheaded the opposition to my proposals. He claimed that Daneel was attempting to 'place spirit mediums and AICs in one basket'—an unfounded allegation in view of my repeated explanations that ZIRRCON intended to host two ecological organisations, the one operating along traditionalist and the other along Christian lines, without any constitutionally built-in confrontation over religious leadership and identity. Unfortunately Makamba had already committed himself publicly to an anti-ZIRRCON stance, prior to any discussions with me and prior to my address to the administrative board. It took the form of letters to *Fambidzano*'s overseas sponsors, in which he dissociated himself from my latest ecological venture and expressed *Ndaza* Zionist opposition to an AZSM tree-planting ceremony in December 1988. This left little room for any modification of viewpoints by the time I was given an opportunity to address the *Fambidzano* executive.

6. ENVIRONMENTAL CUSTODIANSHIP AND EARTH COMMUNITY

1. If the Zimbabwe bird was indeed originally intended as an image of Mwari, my guess is that the bird of prey, which it appears to be, is a *njerere* (brown hawk or kite) and not the *hungwe* (fish eagle), as is often claimed by Zimbabweans. My reasons for this deduction are threefold: first, although the brown kite does not have the majestic appearance of a fish eagle or bateleur, it is more closely associated with rain. At the onset of the rainy season these hawks fly together, often in large numbers, and feed on flying ants. Their presence to many peasants connotes the benevolence of Mwari as rain-giving God. Second, Mwari's main shrine in the Matonjeni region is called Njelele. If the term derives from the Shona *njerere*, it could imply recognition of the symbolic link between the divin-

ity as rain-giver and rain-messenger bird. Third, the connection between Mwari and *njerere* has not escaped AZTREC's earthkeepers. Spirit medium vaZarira Marambatemwa, for instance, considers *njerere* 'messengers of Mwari.' Their presence in the skies, she says, is a reminder of Mwari's care, through rain, of his/her people.

The crocodile below the Zimbabwe bird, in turn, could well symbolise Dzivaguru, the God of mystery beneath the water, giver of fertility. Since female witches often have crocodiles as familiars, it is possible that the dangerous, capricious or judgmental side of the divinity is implied by this symbol.

Considering oral tradition, which specifically refers to centralised religious rituals at Great Zimbabwe in the distant past similar to those still practised at Matonjeni, the symbolic link between African notions of a supreme being and the Zimbabwe bird may not be far-fetched. My observations in this connection are admittedly speculative. Yet they raise significant questions: Are the similarities between symbolic images of divinities in 'primal' or 'indigenous' religions in various parts of the world indicative of a religious heritage common to all humanity—in Jungian terms, a 'collective unconscious,' which could explain such similarity? Or, in Christian terms, is it possible that general revelation in nature, alluded to in Romans 1:19f, gives rise to similar perceptions of God, regardless of the relative isolation of emergent religions from each other in their historic development and of the distorted interpretation caused by human limitations? I do not pretend to know the answers to such questions. But by asking them I come a step closer to understanding my own fascination and identification with the Mwari cult and other aspects of African religion. At a deeper, inexplicable level of self lurks an understanding of the Creator written in the soaring flight of an eagle or hawk, and in the mysterious depths of pools, rivers, and oceans.

2. For a detailed description of Bavinck's exegesis of these texts in terms of general revelation see Visser (1997:118f). This excellent dissertation on the life and mission theology of Bavinck provides a concise yet comprehensive tool for interpreting one of the most inspiring and wide-ranging missiologists of our time.

3. See Bavinck (1949:123, 124, 127, 163, 167; 1966:118, 120); as in Visser (1949:120).

4. Bavinck (1949:126, 174).

5. In his missiological classic *The Christian Message in a Non-Christian World*, (1969:126) Kraemer says of Romans 1: 'God works in man and shines through nature. The religious and moral life of man is man's achievement, but also God's wrestling with him; it manifests a receptivity to God, but at the same time an inexcusable disobedience and blindness to God.'

6. See, for instance, his *Christus en de mystiek van het Oosten* (Kampen, 1934); *Christusprediking in de volkerenwereld* (Kampen, 1939); *The Impact of Christianity on the Non-Christian World* (Grand Rapids, 1945); and *The Church Between Temple and Mosque* (Grand Rapids, 1966).

7. Bavinck develops 'elenctics' as a subdiscipline of missiology. The name in itself connotes his appraisal of the confrontational nature of Christian/non-Christian encounter. (See Bavinck 1954:234, 245.) Throughout his elenctic approach the revelation of God in Christ remains focal (Visser 1997:243).

8. For a brief analysis of Bavinck's use of the term *possessio*, see Visser (1997:248–259).

9. I was the last student to complete my doctoral examination in missiology under his tuition, prior to his death in Amsterdam in 1964.

10. A few days before Bavinck's death he requested my presence in his hospital room. There he blessed me with laying-on of hands and prayer, as an Old Testament patriarch would bless a son. His prayer for my envisaged ministry in Africa has carried me through many spells of questioning, even despair, in a mission which at times appeared 'impossible.'

11. See my *Old and New in Southern Shona Independent Churches*, vols. 1–3 (1971, 1974, 1988).

12. CURRENT DEVELOPMENTS AND CHALLENGES FOR ZIRRCON

1. Ms. Irma Aarsman, for instance, made several documentary films and produced an extensive report on 'The Role of Shona Traditional Religion in Ecology' in part fulfilment of a doctorate in anthropology at the University of Utrecht, The Netherlands. Ms. Marcelle Manley has completed an outstanding master's dissertation at Unisa, South Africa, entitled 'Blood and Soil: Shona Traditional Religion in Twentieth-Century Zimbabwe'—a study which focuses largely on the changing religio-political roles of chiefs in recent years. Dr. Tinus Benade is scheduled to do research on the TEE (theological education by extension) programmes for Zimbabwean AICs, with ZIRRCON's assistance, for his doctoral thesis at Unisa.

GLOSSARY OF SHONA TERMS AND PHRASES

babamukuru	father's elder brother; great father
bato remasvikiro	association of spirit mediums
bute	ancestral snuff
chapungu	bateleur eagle
chidoma	witch's familiar; animal of psychic nature, conceived of as smaller than apolecat
chimurenga	Zimbabwe's liberation struggle
chipanda	lit. "forked stick"; the sister to whom a man is linked for the provision of his marriage cattle
chisi	ancestral rest day
dare	council
dare rechimurenga	ancestral war council
denhere	cluster of trees
dombo	rock; granite shrine of oracular deity
dunhu	tribal ward; subdivision of chiefdom
Dzivaguru	Great Pool; praise name of the Shona high-God, Mwari, which connotes female attributes
evangheri yemiti	gospel of the trees
Fambidzano	cooperation or union; popular designation of ecumenical association of Shona Independent Churches, founded in 1972
gono guru	big bull; the bull dedicated to the family's senior ancestral (or more distant guardian) spirit for ritual purposes
goronga	eroded gully; pl. *makoronga*
hama	kin
ivhu yataura	the soil has spoken
Jesu Krestu	Jesus Christ
jukwa	*shavi* spirit, closely associated with the traditional high-God and his/her rainmaking powers
kubatana	united action
kuchengetedza zvisikwa zva Mwari	to care for or protect God's creation; popular descrption of the AAEC's basic objective
kufukidza nyika	to clothe the earth (by planting trees); (see *mafukidzanyika*)
kugadzira	to settle the spirit of a deceased person; this term connotes the induction rite through which the spirit of a deceased relative is 'brought back home' and simultaneously elevated to the status of ancestorhood
kugara nhaka	to inherit a deceased person's estate, and/or to succeed to his/her position in the kin-group and society; *kugova nhaka*, to distribute a deceased's estate
kukwidza	to lift, uplift
kumira pamukova	to stand at the door; description of the protective function of the home ancestors; by 'standing at the door' the *midzimu* prevent evil forces from entering the dwelling places of their living descendants

kuperekedza	to escort, accompany
Mabweadziva	literally 'rocks of the pool'; Mwari's shrine in the Matopo hills
madambakurimwa	traditional sanctuary or holy grove where plant and animal life were protected; see *marambatemwa*
madzibaba	fathers, pl. for *baba*, father
mafirifiti	small orange mushrooms, mostly found among the dead leaves of wild loquat trees
mafukidzanyika	'clothing the land' tree-planting ceremony; the term is mainly used to indicate AZTREC's traditionalist tree-planting ceremonies
Mafuranhunzi	literally 'the one who shoots the fly,' that is, sharp-shooter; Shona nickname for a hunter of repute
maporesanyika	land-healing ceremony; term used by member churches of the AAEC to emphasize the healing nature of tree-planting eucharists
marambatemwa	literally 'refusal to have the trees felled'; popular designation of traditional holy groves, the implication being that the ancestors buried there sanction the prohibition of tree-felling and related customary, conservationist laws
mambo	king, chief; in the past this term was used for the Rozvi rulers
Matangakugara	You, who sat (existed) first—one of the names of the Shona high-God
Matonjeni	the hills; *Mwari waMatonjeni*, 'God of the Matopo hills'; popular name of the Shona oracular deity and rain giver
mazambiringa	grapevine
mbira	dassie, rock rabbit
mbonga	woman dedicated (usually as a young girl) to the service of the Shona high-God *Mwari*; sometimes referred to as the 'wife of *Mwari*'
mhandara	virgin, girl of marriageable age
mhondoro	literally 'lion'; tribal spirit of repute, considered to be involved in land issues and tribal politics
midzimu enyika	ancestors of the land
Midzimu yappumusha	home ancestors:patri- and matrilineal ancestors directly concerned with the welfare of a family group
miti echivanhu	literally 'trees of the people'; indigenous trees
miti mikuru	tall trees
msasa or musasa	indigenous hardwood tree; *brachestygia spiciformis*
mubvamaropa	literally 'that from which blood flows'; blood-wood or kiaat tree; see *mukurumbira*
mubvumira	literally 'to approve'; wild syringa tree; *kirkia akuminata*
muchakata	wild cork tree; *parinari curatellifolia*
muchecheni	wait-a-bit thorn tree; *ziziphus makoronata*
muchechete	red milkwood tree
muchengeti	keeper; keeper of cult shrine
mudziavashe	literally 'heat of the chief'; fuelwood tree reserved for tribal dignitaries; *combretum molle*; also called *mupembere*

mudzimu	pl. *mi* or *vadzimu*; ancestral spirit
Mudzimu Mukuru	Great Ancestor, God
Mudzimu Unoyera	literally 'Holy Ancestral Spirit', referring to biblical Holy Spirit
mukamba	red mahogany tree; *afzelia quanzensis*
mukoma	elder brother
mukombe	calabash, gourd
mukonde	tree which is considered to provide protection against lightning; *euphorbia ingens*
mukuru	elder; senior person
mukute	water berry tree
mukurumbira	kiaat, *mukwa* tree; *pterocarpus angolensis*
mukwerere	rain ritual during which senior tribal spirits are propitiated at their graves and/or at a pole enclosure (*rushanga*) under a *muchakata* tree; these rituals are conducted at the commencement of each rainy season or if rains have failed; it is also called *mutoro*
munhengeni	sour plum
munhunguru	batoka plum
munjii	bird plum
munyai	messenger, go-between; a *munyai* in the Mwari cult is the person who maintains contact between the local district he represents and the priest colony at the cult centre; he annually visits the cult centre in the Matopo hills to request rain for his district and to discuss local (often political) matters of general significance
munyamharadze	tree which symbolises social discord; *lonchocarpus capassa*
muonde	wild fig tree (with latex); *ficus capensis*
mupani	indigenous hardwood tree; *colophospermum mupane*
mupembere	see *mudziavashe*
mupfura	indigenous fruit tree bearing edible fruit; *sclerocarya caffra*
mupi vemazano	literally 'giver of advice'; advisor
muponesi	saviour
muPostori	pl. *vaPostori*; Apostle, popular Shona term for Johane Maranke's African Apostolic Church followers
murapi	healer
Murapi Venyika	'Healer of the Land'; function attributed to the Holy Spirit
muridzi	pl. *varidzi*; *venyika*; guardian of the land
muroyi	pl. *varoyi*; wizard; witch or sorcerer
murungu	white person from Europe
murwiti	black ebony tree; *dalbergia melanoxylon*
musasa yevaroyi	wind-break or encampment of the wizards
mushavhi	wild fig tree; *ficus burkei*
mushonga	medicine
Musiki	Creator
mushuku	wild loquat tree; *uapaca kirkiana*
mutamba	monkey orange tree
mutezvo	believer, church member
mutobge	indigenous fruit tree with edible fruit, which in the holy

	groves are reserved for ancestors; *ficus sonderi*
mutondo	indigenous hardwood tree; *julbernardia globiflora*
mutongi	pl. *vatongi*; judge
mutorwa	alien
mutumbu	literally 'corpse'; sacrificial offering of cattle to appease the vengeful *ngozi* spirit
mutunduru	yellow sour plum
muuyu	boabab tree; *adansonia digitata*
muvuzhe	mountain acacia; *brachystegia glauscens*
muzambiringa	grape vine
muzeze	indigenous tree with yellow flowers; branches used for purification after burial rites; *peltoforum africanum*
muzhuzhu	indigenous tree which symbolises ancestral protection against wizardry attacks; *maytenus sezegalensis*
muzukuru	'grandchild'; nephew, niece
Mwari	God; most common name for the Shona high-God
mweya	spirit
Mweya Mutsvene	Holy Spirit
Ndaza Zionist	Zionist of the holy cord; popular classificatory term to distinguish the robed Zionists from the uniformed members of Mutendi's Zion Christian Church
nganga	traditional doctor; diviner-herbalist
Ngatifukidze nyika!	Let us clothe the earth! (earthkeepers' slogan)
ngombe youmai	motherhood cow or heifer; gift of husband to wife's mother in honor of the procreative powers of the matriline
ngombe yovutete	'cow or heifer of the aunt'; payable by a deceased male's namebearer or other descendant to the deceased's sister, who acts as ritual officiant during the 'home bringing' (*kugadzira*) ceremony on behalf of the deceased
ngozi	avenging spirit; harmful or dangerous influence which threatens life
nhumbi	possession(s)
njuzu	*shavi* spirit, associated with water and healing activities
nyusa	*Mwari* cult messenger; this term is sometimes used for a deceased cult messenger (*munyai*) who is considered to continue with his former duties in the ancestral world
Pamberi nechimurenga!	Forward the liberation struggle! (guerrillas' slogan)
Pamberi nehondo yemiti!	Forward the war of the trees! (earthkeepers' slogan)
Paseka	Paschal ('Passover') celebrations; popular name of annual festivals, which include the celebration of the holy communion, and are conducted at the main or regional headquarters of the Spirit-type Churches
poshito	guerrilla hideout
povo	the civilian masses (this term was popularised by the guerrrillas during the liberation struggle for mobilisation purposes)
pungwe	guerrilla-organized night-vigil during the liberation struggle, for political instruction and/or disciplinary measures
roora	bridewealth
rudo	love

rudzi	tribe
runyaradzo	consolation ceremony conducted on behalf of the relatives of the recently deceased
ruponeso	salvation
rushanga	pole enclosure, frequently built aroung the trunk of a *muchakata* tree for ritual purposes
Ruwadzano	Mothers' Union
sadunhu	headman of a tribal ward
sadza	stiff porridge
samarombo	tree-dwelling ancestors
sekuru	grandfather or mother's brother
shamhu	whip or cane; to be given *shamhu* means to be disciplined by the church and/or by God
shavi	alien spirit which does not belong to the lineage of the host whom it possesses; various types of *shavi* spirits bestow a variety of skills, for example healing, hunting, dancing or blacksmithing to their hosts
Shinga Postora	'Courageous Apostles'; schismatic group with its roots in Johane Masowe's Apostolic movement; Shinga derived from *kushinga*; to be diligent or brave
shumba	lion; *shumba dzavadzimu*, lions of the ancestors
svikiro	pl. *masvikiro*; spirit medium
tateguru	paternal grandfather or great grandfather
tonhodzo	coolness
Topia	popular designation of First Ethiopian Church
tsvimbo	knobkierie, club
ungano yembeu	seed conference, during which the seed to be sown by peasant families is blessed and prayed over by church leader to ensure good crops
upenyu	life
uroyi	wizardry; *uroyi venyika*; land wizardry, that is, wanton destruction of the environment
vakomana vesango	literally 'boys of the bush'; that is, bush fighters, guerrillas
vamwene	husband's sister who is the 'owner' of his wife
vanhu venyika	people of the world; non-believers
vanonamata mumabhuku	those who worship according to the books; Christians
vanonamata muvhu nezvibako	those who worship according to the soil (ancestors) and the snuff containers
vanyai	see *munyai*
vatete	paternal aunt
vatongi	see *mutongi*
Watangakugara	the One who sat (existed) first; that is, God
Wokudenga	the One in heaven, God
Wokumusoro	the One above, God
zvidoma	see *chidoma*
zvirombo	destitute, capricious spirits

BIBLIOGRAPHY

Abraham, D. P. 1959. 'The Monomotapa Dynasty,' in *Native Affairs Department Annual*, No. 36, Salisbury.

Abraham, D. P. 1966. 'The roles of Chaminuka and the Mhondoro Cults in Shona Political History,' in Stokes and Brown (eds.), *The Zambesian Past Studies in Central African History*, Manchester.

Bakare, S. 1993. *My Right to Land—in the Bible and in Zimbabwe: A Theology of Land in Zimbabwe*. Harare, Zimbabwe Council of Churches.

Barrett, D. B. 1968. *Schism and Renewal in Africa: An Analysis of Six Thousand Contemporary Religious Movements*. Nairobi, Oxford University Press.

Bavinck, J. H. 1934. *Christus en de mystiek van het Oosten*, Kampen, Kok.

Bavinck, J. H. 1939. *Christusprediking in de volkerenwereld*, Kampen, Kok.

Bavinck, J. H. 1948. *The Impact of Christianity on the Non-Christian World*, Grand Rapids, Eerdmans.

Bavinck, J. H. 1949. *Religieus besef en Christelijk geloof*, Kampen, Kok.

Bavinck, J. H. 1954. *Inleiding in de Zendingswetenschap*, Kampen, Kok.

Bavinck, J. H. 1966. *The Church Between Temple and Mosque*, Grand Rapids, Eerdmans.

Beach, D. N. 1979. '"Chimurenga": The Shona Rising of 1996–97,' *Journal of African History*, Vol. 20, No. 3.

Beach, D. N. 1980. *The Shona and Zimbabwe 900–1850*, Gweru, Mambo Press.

Beach, D. N. 1986. *War and Politics in Zimbabwe 1840–1900*, Gweru, Mambo Press.

Berkouwer, G. C. 1953. *Het werk van Christus*, Kampen, Kok.

Berry, T. 1994. 'Ecological Geography.' In Tucker, M. E. and Grim J. A. (eds.) *Worldviews and Ecology—Religion, Philosophy and the Environment*, Maryknoll, Orbis Books.

Beyerhaus, P. 1969. 'An Approach to the African Independent Church Movement,' *Ministry*, 9.

Birch, C., Eakin, W. and McDaniel, J. (eds.) 1990. *Liberating Life: Contemporary Approaches to Ecological Theology*, Maryknoll, Orbis Books.

Bonhoeffer, D. 1963. *The Cost of Discipleship*, New York, Macmillan.

Bosch, D. B. 1974. *Het evangelie in Afrikaans gewaad*, Kampen, Kok.

Bosch, D. B. 1987. 'The Problem of Evil in Africa: A Survey of African Views on Witchcraft and of the Response of the Christian Church.' In De Villiers, P. G. R. (ed.) *Like a Roaring Lion; Essays on the Bible, the Church and Demonic Powers*, Pretoria, University of South Africa.

Bourdillon, M. F. C. 1982. *The Shona Peoples*, Gweru, Mambo Press.

Bratton, S. P. 1992. 'Loving Nature: Eros or Agape?' *Environmental Ethics*, Journal of the Center for Environmental Philosophy, University of North Texas, 14(1).

Brown, N. J. 1994. 'Foreword.' In Tucker, M. E. and Grim, J. A. (eds.) *Worldviews and Ecology*, Maryknoll, Orbis Books.

Burrows, W. R. 1995. 'Need and Opportunities in Studies of Mission and World Christianity,' *International Bulletin of Missionary Research*, 19(4).

Buthelezi, M. 1976. 'Daring to Live for Christ.' In Anderson, G. H. and Stransky, T. F. (eds.) *Mission Trends No. 3, Third World Theologies*, Grand Rapids, Eerdmans.

Callicott, J. B. 1994. 'Toward a Global Environmental Ethic.' In Tucker and Grim (eds.) *Worldviews and Ecology*, Maryknoll, Orbis Books.

Carmody, J. 1983. *Ecology and Religion: Toward a New Christian Theology of Nature*. New York, Paulist.

Cobbing, J. R. D. 1977. 'The Absent Priesthood: Another Look at the Rhodesian Risings of 1896–1897,' in *Journal of African History*, Vol. 18, No. 1.

Daneel, M. L. 1970. *The God of the Matopo Hills: An Essay on the Mwari Cult in Rhodesia*, The Hague, Mouton.

Daneel, M. L. 1971. *Old and New in Southern Shona Independent Churches*, Vol. 1: *Background and Rise of the Major Movements*, The Hague, Mouton.

Daneel, M. L. 1973. 'The Christian Gospel and the Ancestor Cult,' in *Missionalia*, Vol. 1, No. 2.

Daneel, M. L. 1974. *Old and New in Southern Shona Independent Churches*, Vol. 2: *Church Growth: Causative Factors and Recruitment Techniques*, The Hague, Mouton.

Daneel, M. L. 1980. 'Missionary Outreach in African Independent Churches,' *Missionalia*, 8(3).

Daneel, M. L. 1982. 'Black Messianism: Corruption or Contextualization?' Inaugural lecture, Unisa.

Daneel, M. L. 1987. *Quest for Belonging—Introduction to a Study of African Independent Churches*, Gweru, Mambo Press.

Daneel, M. L. 1988. *Old and New in Southern Shona Independent Churches*, Vol. 3: *Church Leadership and Fission Dynamics*, Gweru, Mambo Press.

Daneel, M. L. 1989(a). *Fambidzano—Ecumenical Movement of Zimbabwean Independent Churches*, Gweru, Mambo Press.

Daneel, M. L. 1989(b). 'The Encounter Between Christianity and Traditional African Culture: Accommodation or Transformation?' in *Theologia Evangelica*, Vol. 22, No. 3.

Daneel, M. L. 1990. 'Exorcism as a Means of Combating Wizardry: Liberation or Enslavement?' *Missionalia* 18(1).

Daneel, M. L. 1991. 'The Liberation of Creation: African Traditional Religious and Independent Church Perspectives,' in *Missionalia*, 10:2, 1991.

Daneel, M. L. 1993. 'African Independent Church Pneumatology and the Salvation of all Creation,' in *International Review of Mission*, Vol. 82, No. 326, Geneva.

Daneel, M. L. 1995. *Guerrilla Snuff* (see: Gumbo, Mafuranhunzi).

De Witt, C. B. 1991. *The Environment and the Christian—What Can We Learn From the New Testament?* Grand Rapids, Baker Book House.

Dickson, K. 1984. *Theology in Africa*, Maryknoll, Orbis Books.

Dorm-Adzobu, C. O. (and Ampadu Agyel and Peter Veit) 1991. *Religious Beliefs and Environmental Protection: The Malshegu Sacred Grove in Northern Ghana*, Nairobi, WRI, Acts Press.

Dregne, H. E. 1983. *Evaluation of the Implementation of the Plan of Action to Combat Desertification*, Nairobi, UNEP.

Duchrow, U. and Liedke, G. 1987. *Shalom—Biblical Perspectives on Creation, Justice and Peace*. Geneva, WCC Publications.

Ela, J. M. 1986. *African Cry*, Maryknoll, Orbis Books.

Fashole-Luke, E. W. 1976. 'The Quest for African Christian Theologies.' In Anderson, G. H. and Stransky, T. F. (eds.) *Mission Trends No 3: Third World Theologies*, Grand Rapids, Eerdmans.

Fox, M. 1992. *A Spirituality Named Compassion*, San Francisco, Harper Collins.

Goba, B. 1980. 'Doing Theology in South Africa: A Black Christian Perspective, *Journal of Theology for Southern Africa*, 31, June.

Gore, A. 1992. *Earth in the Balance*, New York, Penguin.

Granberg-Michaelson, W. 1994. 'Creation in Ecumenical Theology.' In Hallman, D. G. (ed.) *Ecotheology*, Maryknoll, Orbis Books.

Grim, J. A. 1994. 'Native North American Worldviews and Ecology,' in Tucker, M. E. and Grim J. A. (eds.) *Worldviews and Ecology: Religion, Philosophy and the Environment*, Maryknoll, NY, Orbis Books.

Gumbo, Mafuranhunzi. 1995. *Guerrilla Snuff*, Harare, Baobab Books.

Hallman, D. G. 1994. *Ecotheology—Voices from South and North*, Geneva, WCC; and Maryknoll, NY, Orbis Books.

Hoekendijk, J. C. 1950. 'The Call to Evangelism; *International Review of Missions*, Vol. 32.

Huizer, G. 1991. *Folk Spirituality and Liberation in Southern Africa*, Bordeaux, Centre d'Étude d'Afrique Noire.

Idowu, E. B. 1962. *Olodumare: God in Yoruba Belief*, London/New York.

Ingenoza, A. O. 1985. 'African Weltanschaung and Exorcism: The Quest for the Contextualization of the Kerygma,' *African Theological Journal*, 14.

Kibicho, S. G. 1968. 'The Interaction of the Traditional Kikuyu Concept of God with the Biblical Concept,' *Cahiers des religions Africaines*, 4(2).

Kibongi, R. B. 1969. 'Priesthood.' In Dickson, K. A. and Ellingworth, P. (eds.) *Biblical Revelation and African Beliefs*, London, Lutterworth.

Kolié, C. 1991. 'Jesus as Healer?' In Schreiter, R. J. (ed,) *Faces of Jesus in Africa*, Maryknoll, Orbis Books.

Kraemer, H. 1969. *The Christian Message in a Non-Christian World*, Michigan.

Kyung, C. H. 1994. 'Ecology, Feminism and African and Asian Spirituality of Eco-Feminism.' In Hallman, D. G. (ed.) *Ecotheology*, Maryknoll, Orbis Books.

Lagerwerf, L. 1987. *Witchcraft, Sorcery and Spirit-Possession: Pastoral Responses in Africa*, Gweru, Mambo Press.

Lan, D. 1985. *Guns and Rain: Guerrillas and Spirit Mediums in Zimbabwe*, Harare, Zimbabwe Publishing House.

Makamuri, B. B. 1991. 'Ecological Religion,' in Virtanen, P. (ed.) *Management of Natural Resources in Zimbabwe: Report on the Research and Training Programme on Energy, Environment and Development*, Tampere, University of Tampere.

Martin, D. and Johnson, P. 1981. *The Struggle for Zimbabwe*, London, Monthly Review Press.

Martin, M. L. 1964. *The Biblical Concept of Messianism and Messianism in Southern Africa*, Morija, Mission Press.

Mbiti, J. S. 1969. *African Religions and Philosophy*, London, Heineman.

Mbiti, J. S. 1970. *Concepts of God in Africa*, London, SPCK.

Mbiti, J. S. 1971. *New Testament Eschatology in an African Background*, London, Oxford University Press.

Mbiti, J. S. 1980. 'The Encounter of Christian Faith and African Religion,' *The Christian Encounter* (August).

Mbiti, J. S. 1986. *Bible and Theology in African Christianity*, Nairobi, Oxford University Press.

McDaniel, J. 1994. 'The Garden of Eden, the Fall, and Life in Christ.' In Tucker, M. E. and Grim, J. A. (eds.) *Worldviews and Ecology*, Maryknoll, Orbis.

McDaniel, J. B. 1995. *With Roots and Wings: Christianity in an Age of Ecology and Dialogue*, Maryknoll, NY, Orbis Books.

McDonagh, S. 1985. *To Care for the Earth—A Call to a New Theology*, Santa Fe, Bear and Co.

McDonagh, S. 1994. *Passion for the Earth—The Christian Vocation to Promote Justice, Peace, and the Integrity of Creation*, Maryknoll, Orbis Books.

Messer, D. E. 1992. *A Conspiracy of Goodness—Contemporary Images of Christian Mission*, Nashville, Abingdon Press.

Milingo, E. 1984. *The World in Between—Christian Healing and the Struggle for Spiritual Survival*, Maryknoll, Orbis Books.

Moltmann, J. 1985. *God in Creation—An Ecological Doctrine of Creation*, London, SCM Press.

Moorcraft, P. L. and McLaughlin, P. 1983. *Chimurenga! The War in Rhodesia 1965–1980*, Marshalltown, Sygma Books.

Mosothoane, E. K. 1973. 'Communio Sanctorum in Africa,' *Missionalia*, 1(2).

Neill, S. C. 1991. *God's Apprentice* (autobiography, edited by Jackson, E. M.), London, Hodder and Stoughton.

Nthamburi, Z. 1991. 'Christ As Seen By an African: A Christological Quest.' In Schreiter, R. J. (ed.) *Faces of Jesus in Africa*, Maryknoll, Orbis Books.

Nyamiti, C. 1984. *Christ As Our Ancestor*, Gweru, Mambo Press.

Nyamiti, C. 1991. 'African Christologies Today.' In Schreiter, R. J. (ed.) *Faces of Jesus in Africa*, Maryknoll, Orbis Books.

Oosthuizen, G. C. 1968. *Post Christianity in Africa—A Theological and Anthropological Study*, London.

Pauw, B. A. 1960. *Religion in Tswana Chiefdom*, Oxford, Oxford University Press.

Pobee, J. S. 1979. *Towards an African Theology*, Nashville, Abingdon Press.

Ranger, T. O. 1966. 'The Role of Ndebele and Shona Religious Authorities in the Rebellions of 1896 and 1897,' in Stokes and Brown (eds.), *The Zambesian Past*, Manchester.

Ranger, T. O. 1967. *Revolt in Southern Rhodesia (1896–97)*, London, Heineman.

Ranger, T. O. 1968. 'Connections Between "Primary Resistance" and Modern Mass Nationalism in East and Central Africa: II.' *Journal of African History*, IX (4).

Ruether, R. R. 1992. *Gaia and God—an Ecofeminist Theology of Earth Healing*, San Francisco, Harper Collins.

Schreiter, R. J. 1985. *Constructing Local Theologies*, London, SCM Press.

Schreiter, R. J. (ed.) 1991. *Faces of Jesus in Africa*, Maryknoll, Orbis Books.

Setiloane, G. M. 1975. 'Confessing Christ Today.' *Journal of Theology of Southern Africa*, 12 (September).

Setiloane, G. M. 1976. 'I Am an African.' In Anderson and Stransky (eds.) *Mission Trends, No. 3, Third World Theologies*, Grand Rapids, Eerdmans.

Setiloane, G. M. 1976. *The Image of God Among the Sotho-Tswana*, Rotterdam, Balkema.

Setiloane, G. M. 1979. 'Where Are We in African Theology?' In Appiah-Kubi, K. and Torres, S. (eds.) *African Theology En Route*, Maryknoll, Orbis Books.

Shorter, A. 1985. *Jesus and the Witchdoctor—An Approach to Healing and Wholeness*, Maryknoll, Orbis Books.

Singleton, M. 1980. 'Who's Who in African Witchcraft?' In *Pro Mundi Vita: Dossiers, African Dossier* 12: 1–41.

Sundkler, B. G. M. 1960. *The Christian Ministry in Africa*, London, SCM Press.

Sundkler, B. G. M.1961. *Bantu Prophets of South Africa*, London, Oxford University Press.

Sundkler, B. G. M. 1976. *Zulu Zion and Some Swazi Zionists*, London, Oxford University Press.

Taylor, J. V. 1963. *The Primal Vision—Christian Presence Amid African Religion*, London, SCM Press.

Timberlake, L. 1985. *Africa in Crisis: The Causes, the Cures of Environmental Bankruptcy*, London, Earthscan Series.

Timberlake, L. 1995. *Africa in Crisis: The Causes, The Cures of Environmental Bankruptcy*, London, Earthscan Series.

Torres, S. and Fabella, V. (eds.) 1978. *The Emergent Gospel*, Maryknoll, Orbis Books.

Tucker, M. E. and Grim, J. A. (eds.) 1994. *Worldviews and Ecology—Religion, Philosophy and the Environment*, Maryknoll, NY, Orbis Books.

Tu Wei-ming 1994. 'Beyond the Enlightenment Mentality,' in Tucker, M. E. and Grim, J. A., *Worldviews . . .*

Tutu, D. 1975. 'Black Theology—African Theology: Soulmates or Antagonists?' *Journal of Religious Thoughts*, 32(2).

Ukpong, J. S. 1984. 'Current Theology: The Emergence of African Theologies,' *Theological Studies*, 45.

Van der Merwe, W. J. 1957. *Shona Idea of God*, Masvingo, Morgenster Mission Press.

Verkuyl, J. 1975. *Inleiding in de nieuwere Zendingswetenschap*, Kampen, Kok.

Virtanen, P. (ed.) 1991. *Management of Natural Resources in Zimbabwe*—Report on the Research and Training Programme on Energy, Environment and Development, Tampere, University of Tampere.

Visser, P. J. 1997. *Bemoeienis en getuigenis—het leven en de missionaire theologie van Johan H. Bavinck*, Zoetermeer Uitgeverij Boekencentrum.

Von Sicard, H. 1994. *Mwari der Hochgott der Karanga*, in the series: *Wiener Beiträge zur Kulturgeschichte und Linguistik*—Jahrgang 6.

Walls, A. F. 1982. 'The Gospel as the Prisoner and Liberator of Culture,' *Missionalia*, 10.

Wilkinson, L. 1991. *Earthkeeping in the '90s—Stewardship of Creation*, Grand Rapids, Eerdmans.

Witvliet, T. 1984. *Een plaats onder de zon: bevrijdingstheologie in de Derde Wereld*, Baarn, Ten Have.

Zerbe, G. 1991. 'The Kingdom of God and Stewardship of Creation.' In De Witt, C. B. (ed.) *The Environment and the Christian*, Grand Rapids, Baker Book House.

INDEX

acacia (*mitondo*) tree, 46-47, 97-98, 108, 256

acculturation, enforced, 178-79

Adam, 158-59, 219-20

adaptation model, 140

Africa in Crisis: The Causes, the Cures of Environmental Bankruptcy (Timberlake), 10

African Initiated Churches (AIC): and AAEC, 145-46, 261-65; Christology of, 34-35, 203-204, 218-19; in ecological crisis, 40-43; emerging attributes, 153-59; healing practices, 17, 22-24, 130, 146-47; and Holy Spirit, 232-47; liberationist activities, 17, 21-24, 30-35, 147-49, 281; liturgies of, 164-74; and mission, 123-27; and Mwari cult, 80-81; theology of, 138-47, 152-53, 157-59, 167, 175-80, 264-65, 268-70; and war of trees, 14-15, 51-52, 149-53, 229

African Earthkeepers Union (AEU), 279-80

African Initiatives in Christian Mission program, Pew Charitable Trusts, 250

African religious culture: God in, 176, 179-80, 182; holism of, 10, 46; magical belief system in, 233, 236; management of sociological problems, 16-35; significance for world ecology movement, 104-22; theology in, 175-80, 203-205

agape vs. eros, 266-68

Agritex, 43, 101

Akan tribe, 217

ancestral spirits, 27-30, 56, 62-72, 92-93, 111-17, 177, 213, 219-22

'animism,' 95, 247

Apostles of Maranke, 23-24

Apostolic churches, 23-24, 30-31, 52, 53, 154, 181

Association of African Earthkeeping Churches (AAEC): and AICs, 145-46, 149-50, 261-65; and ancestors, 111; Christology of, 205-12, 214-16, 218-20, 223-24; composition of, 1; disciplinary measures by, 105, 156-57, 159, 166; ecumenism of, 153-55, 261-65, 282; and *Fambidzano*, 148-50, 153-54; iconic leaders in, 207-11, 270-72; and mission, 123-27, 155-56; and Mwari, 184, 186-91, 197-98; founding of, 51; growth of, 57-60; theology of, 141-47, 196-200, 263; and traditionalists, 193-94; and tree-planting, 126-27, 150-53, 157-59, 165, 167-74, 185-88, 195, 207, 212, 215, 225-30, 235-36, 260, 269; and wizardry, 239-47; and ZIRRCON, 42-43, 51-56, 143, 168, 248-55, 261-73

Association of Zimbabwean Spirit Mediums (AZSM), 42, 45-47, 76-85

Association of Zimbabwean Traditional Ecologists (AZTREC): and AAEC, 55-56, 126-27, 154-55, 210, 262; as community, 113-17; composition of, 1; dream directives to, 15; and ecology, 91-102; and liberation struggle, 61-85; as mission, 122-24; and oracle of Mwari, 73-83, 117-22; origin of, 42-48; and rain, 193-94; significance for world ecology movement, 104-22; and tree-planting ceremonies, 63-65, 69-72, 287; and ZIRRCON, 42-43, 50-51, 61-63, 248-49, 251-57, 260-62, 267-68, 287

AZTREC Trust, 61-62

335